THE SUKKOT AND SIMHAT TORAH ANTHOLOGY

THE
JEWISH
PUBLICATION
SOCIETY
OF
❧ AMERICA ❧

PHILADELPHIA · 5733/1973

THE SUKKOT AND SIMHAT TORAH ANTHOLOGY

PHILIP GOODMAN

※ ※ ※

The editor herewith expresses his sincere appreciation to the following publishers and authors who have kindly granted permission to use the material indicated from their published works.

※ ※ ※

ACUM Ltd. Societe d'Auteurs, Compositeurs et Editeurs de Musique en Israel, Tel Aviv: Hebrew lyrics of *"Sisu ve-Simhu be-Simhat Hag"* by B. Caspi. Copyright © B. Caspi, Israel.

American Jewish Archives, Cincinnati: excerpt from *American Jewry: Documents: Eighteenth Century* by Jacob R. Marcus, Hebrew Union College Press, Cincinnati.

American Jewish Historical Society, Waltham: excerpt from *Publications of the American Jewish Historical Society*, vol. 21 (1913), pp. 110-11.

American Zionist Youth Foundation, New York: "Sukkot in a North African Mellah" by Moshe Dluznowsky from *The Jews of Morocco*, Zionist Youth Council, 1956.

Dr. Gersion Appel, New York: "The Historic Assembly on Sukkot" by Aaron Halevi, from "The *Mitzvah* of *Hakhel*: A Historic Assembly in Jerusalem," by Gersion Appel, *Tradition: A Journal of Orthodox Jewish Thought*, vol. 20, no. 1 (Fall, 1959).

Ben Aronin, Chicago: "All the World Is Dancing," translation of *"Yom Tov Lanu."*

Barton's Candy Corporation, Brooklyn, N.Y.: "The Beautiful Willow," reprinted by permission of Barton's Candy Corporation.

Behrman House Inc., New York: "The Welcome to Guests in the *Sukkah*," "Meditation on Entering the *Sukkah*," "Save Us Now," and "Summons to the Bridegroom of the Law" from *The Traditional Prayer Book for Sabbath and Festivals*, ed. and trans. by David de Sola Pool, 1960; "The Unbroken Torah Cycle" from *Sabbath Queen* by Alexander Alan Steinbach, 1936; "Dance Hasidic" from *Hath Not a Jew . . .* , by A. M. Klein, 1940; "The Etrog" from *Poems for Young Israel* by Philip M. Raskin, 1925; *"Yom Tov Lanu"* and *"Sisu ve-Simhu"* from *Jewish Holiday Dances* by Corinne Chochem, 1948; *"Berakhot Shel Sukkot"* and "Harvest" from *Gateway to Jewish Song* by Judith Kaplan Eisenstein, 1939.

Belwin-Mills Publishing Corp., New York: *"U-Sheavtem Mayim"* ("Mayim, Mayim"), copyright © 1952 by Israel Composers League Publications Ltd. Used with permission of Belwin-Mills Publishing Corp.

Dr. Joseph L. Blau, New York: "Say It with Flowers" from *The Wonder of Life* by Joel Blau, Macmillan Co., 1926.

Bloch Publishing Co., New York: selections from *Rejoice in Thy Festival: A Treasury of Wisdom, Wit and Humor for the Sabbath and Jewish Holidays* by Philip Goodman; "Shemini Atzeret—The Concluding Day," "Building the *Sukkah*," and "The Willow of the Brook" from *Jewish Feasts and Fasts* by Julius H. Green-

Yale University Press, New Haven: excerpts from *Pesikta Rabbati: Discourses for Feasts, Fasts and Special Sabbaths*, trans. by William G. Braude, 1968; excerpts from *The Midrash on Psalms*, trans. by William G. Braude, 1959; excerpts from *The Code of Maimonides: Book Three: The Book of Seasons*, trans. by Solomon Gandz and Hyman Klein, 1961; "The Tabernacle Feast of the Falashas" from *Falasha Anthology*, trans. by Wolf Leslau, 1951; illustration of the tympanum of the niche in the Dura-Europos synagogue.

Yeda-Am, Tel Aviv: "Sukkot in My Native Salonica" by Baruch Uziel, *Yeda-Am*, vol. 5, nos. 1–2 (Autumn, 1958).

The Zionist Federation, London, England: "Simhat Torah in Jerusalem" by Harold Fenton, *The Gates of Zion*, vol. 22, no. 2 (Winter, 1967).

Credits for the illustrations are included in the list of illustrations that follows the Contents.

꙲ ꙳ ꙲

מוקדש
לנכדתי
דבורה סימונה
בת הרב יצחק ויהודית רובין

❦ PREFACE ❦

❦ ❦ ❦

The Sukkot and Simhat Torah Anthology intends to present the
varied aspects of the festival's background, its historical development
through the ages, and the spiritual verities it proclaims for Jews
and for mankind. This volume, like those previously published in
the Jewish holidays series of The Jewish Publication Society of
America, attempts to elucidate the traditions, customs, and practices
of the Feast of Booths and the Festival of the Rejoicing in the Law
through source materials selected from the wealth of Jewish literature
of all generations. While only a portion of the extensive literature
on the festival could be included in this volume, it represents the

most comprehensive treatment of Sukkot and Simhat Torah in the English language. The Bibliography indicates additional sources of interest to all members of the family.

Sukkot, Passover, and Shavuot constitute the three pilgrimage festivals; Sukkot is the last, the longest, and the most joyous of these sacred occasions. It is the culmination of the High Holy Days, following shortly after the solemn Days of Awe—Rosh Hashanah and Yom Kippur. The Jew is enjoined to begin the erection of a *sukkah* immediately upon the termination of the Day of Atonement, in fulfillment of the biblical injunction "that future generations may know that I made the Israelite people live in booths when I brought them out of the land of Egypt" (Leviticus 23.43). The booth was the temporary dwelling of vintners and harvesters in the biblical period.

In ancient days Sukkot was an agricultural festival, called the Feast of Ingathering. It was celebrated by multitudes of pilgrims who, at the harvest season, thronged to Jerusalem, where elaborate ceremonies were performed within the precincts of the Temple and ecstatic festivity reigned in the streets of the Holy City. Celebrated throughout the long existence span of the Jewish people with thanksgiving and rejoicing for the bounties of the Almighty, Sukkot is distinguished to this day by colorful and impressive pageantry—the booths bedecked with greenery, the processions waving the festival bouquets of the Four Species, the beating of the willows, and the circuits with the Scrolls of the Law on Simhat Torah.

The Sukkot cycle, including Shemini Atzeret (the Eighth Day of Solemn Assembly or the Concluding Festival), termed in the liturgy the "Season of Our Rejoicing," is climaxed with Simhat Torah, the Festival of the Rejoicing in the Law. The most exuberant of all festival days, Simhat Torah has its source neither in the Bible nor in the Talmud. It was created in Babylonia in the medieval period, to affirm the Jew's deep and abiding dedication to the Torah. Its observance was subsequently universally accepted, although the customs associated with it have varied from land to land.

While Shemini Atzeret is considered to be "a festival unto itself" (Sukkah 48a) and Simhat Torah to be the second day of Shemini Atzeret (both are observed on the same day in Israel), the title *The Sukkot and Simhat Torah Anthology* utilizes the more popular names to convey the gaiety of this festival season.

Today Sukkot and Simhat Torah are acutely relevant to two major concerns of world Jewry—Israel and Soviet Jewry. Observance of this Festival of Ingathering, celebrating the harvest in the land of our forefathers—the residence in temporary booths, the waving of the Four Species typical of Israel's flora, the recital of the prayer for rain to enable the earth to produce a bountiful yield—binds the Jews in the Diaspora to the destiny of their brethren in the land of Israel. The Simhat Torah demonstrations in the Soviet Union in recent years have sparked a resurgence of Jewish identity and consciousness among Russian Jews. Their gallant example has inspired Jewish communities in other countries to support actively their just demands for religious freedom, for the prerogative to study Torah, and for the right to immigrate to Israel.

Jews pray for the fulfillment of the prophecy of Zechariah (14:16): "And it shall come to pass, that every one that is left of all the nations that came against Jerusalem shall go up from year to year to worship the King, the Lord of hosts, and to keep the Feast of Tabernacles."

The publication of this book was initiated by Dr. Chaim Potok, editor, and facilitated by Lesser Zussman and David Gross, past and present executive vice-president, respectively, of The Jewish Publication Society of America. The Society's copy editor, Mrs. Kay Powell, examined the manuscript with great care. I am pleased to extend to them my warm appreciation.

The preparation of the anthology as a labor of love could not have been accomplished without the generous assistance of many people to whom I am deeply indebted. I have enjoyed the cooperation of several librarians and their staffs who have generously made their valuable resources available, notably, Dr. I. Edward Kiev, Hebrew Union College–Jewish Institute of Religion in New York; Harry J. Alderman, American Jewish Committee; and Sylvia Landress, Zionist Archives and Library. I have also utilized the growing library of my son-in-law, Rabbi Irving Rubin, Congregation Kesher Israel, West Chester, Pennsylvania.

I am particularly grateful to the following for providing me with illustrations: Dr. Abram Kanof, for some of the photographs that appeared in his *Jewish Ceremonial Art and Religious Observance*; and Professor Herbert C. Zafren, director of libraries, Hebrew Union College–Jewish Institute of Religion, Cincinnati. Further acknowledgments will be found in the List of Illustrations.

While in certain literary areas there is an abundance of excellent material in English from which selections were made for inclusion in this anthology, in others there are lacunae. To fill these gaps, I invited several persons to write original articles and others to make translations. Dr. Joseph Gutmann, professor of art history, Wayne State University, Detroit, Michigan, contributed the article on "Sukkot and Simhat Torah in Art." Cantor Paul Kavon, director, Department of Music, United Synagogue of America, compiled and edited the music. Solomon Feffer, associate professor of Hebraic studies, Rutgers University, Newark, New Jersey, wrote on "Unusual Booths in Israel." "Second *Hakkafot* in Israel" was penned by Moshe Kohn, literary editor, *The Jerusalem Post*. New translations were prepared by Solomon Feffer, Rabbi Leonard B. Gewirtz, Dr. Herbert Parzen, and Simon Raskin. All unsigned articles and translations for which no English source is cited are my work.

My thanks to Fred Berk, director, Israel Folk Dance Institute, for his kind advice. I am most grateful for the benefit of the wide erudition of Dr. Sidney B. Hoenig, dean of the Bernard Revel Graduate School of Yeshiva University, who read the entire manuscript and offered numerous constructive criticisms and helpful suggestions. Dr. Alexander Alan Steinbach, distinguished poet, author, and editor of the *Jewish Book Annual* and *Jewish Bookland*, meticulously examined the manuscript with critical acumen and contributed considerably to the enhancement of the literary style. His invaluable guidance and sound judgment have been a great boon to me in this and other literary undertakings.

My devoted partner in life, Hanna, patiently typed and retyped the manuscript as well as hundreds of pages that were not included in the final draft. Her understanding and tolerance during all the days and nights I spent on this book are beyond recompense.

Philip Goodman

New York City
Av 12, 5732

❧ CONTENTS ❧

❧ ❧ ❧

5 ❧ *Sukkot and Simhat Torah in Jewish Law* 58

6 ❧ *Sukkot and Simhat Torah Liturgy* 72

❧ ILLUSTRATIONS ❧

❧ ❧ ❧

THE SUKKOT AND SIMHAT TORAH ANTHOLOGY

❦ 1 ❦

SUKKOT IN THE BIBLE

❧ ❧ ❧

The festival of Sukkot is rooted in the Bible, which delineates its basic laws and recounts the historical events related to it. According to the Pentateuch, *Hag ha-Sukkot* (Feast of Booths) or *Hag ha-Asif* (Feast of Ingathering), as the holiday is alternately termed, is one of the three festivals on which the Israelites were enjoined to make a pilgrimage to the chosen place in Jerusalem. It prescribes the manner of observance—dwelling in booths, prohibition of work on the first and eighth days, offering sacrifices, use of the Four Species, and rejoicing over the harvest.

The people were commanded to assemble and hear the reading of the Law of Moses every seventh year, on the Feast of Booths.

The dedication of the Temple in Jerusalem during the reign of King Solomon took place on Sukkot, and this historic event is described in detail in 1 Kings and 2 Chronicles. First Kings also describes the rebellion of Jeroboam against Rehoboam, King Solomon's successor. To show his independence, Jeroboam, among other changes, moved the date for the commemoration of the feast.

The biblical books of Ezra and Nehemiah contain accounts of the reinstitution of the celebration of Sukkot in Jerusalem after the Babylonian exile.

The prophet Zechariah foresaw a period when all nations will worship one God and will observe the Feast of Booths. The idea of a universal religious brotherhood is confirmed in the rabbinic dictum: "On the Feast of Tabernacles, the Israelites offered seventy bullocks for the seventy nations of the world" (*Midrash Tanhuma* on *Pinhas*).

❦ ❦ ❦

THE FEAST OF INGATHERING

Three times a year you shall hold a festival for Me: You shall observe the Feast of Unleavened Bread—eating unleavened bread for seven days as I have commanded you—at the set time in the month of Abib, for in it you went forth from Egypt; and none shall appear before Me empty-handed; and the Feast of the Harvest, of the first fruits of your work, of what you sow in the field; and the Feast of Ingathering at the end of the year, when you gather in the results of your work from the field.

Exodus 23.14–16[1]

After the ingathering from your threshing floor and your vat, you shall hold the Feast of Booths for seven days. You shall rejoice in your festival, with your son and daughter, your male and female slave, the Levite, the stranger, the fatherless, and the widow in your communities. You shall hold festival for the Lord your God seven days, in the place that the Lord will choose; for the Lord your God will bless all your crops and all your undertakings, and you shall have nothing but joy.

Three times a year—on the Feast of Unleavened Bread, on the Feast of Weeks, and on the Feast of Booths—all your males shall appear before the LORD your God in the place that He will choose. They shall not appear before the LORD empty-handed, but each with his own gift, according to the blessing that the LORD your God has bestowed upon you.

Deuteronomy 16.13–17

❧ ❧ ❧

THE FEAST OF BOOTHS

The Lord spoke to Moses, saying: Say to the Israelite people:

On the fifteenth day of this seventh month, there shall be the Feast of Booths to the LORD, [to last] seven days. The first day shall be a sacred occasion: you shall not work at your occupations; seven days you shall bring offerings by fire to the LORD. On the eighth day you shall observe a sacred occasion and bring an offering by fire to the LORD; it is a solemn gathering: you shall not work at your occupations. . . .

Mark, on the fifteenth day of the seventh month, when you have gathered in the yield of your land, you shall observe the festival of the LORD [to last] seven days: a complete rest on the first day, and a complete rest on the eighth day. On the first day you shall take the product of goodly trees, branches of palm trees, boughs of leafy trees, and willows of the brook, and you shall rejoice before the LORD your God seven days. You shall observe it as a festival of the LORD for seven days in the year; you shall observe it in the seventh month as a law for all time, throughout the generations. You shall live in booths seven days; all citizens in Israel shall live in booths, in order that future generations may know that I made the Israelite people live in booths when I brought them out of the land of Egypt, I the LORD your God.

So Moses declared to the Israelites the set times of the LORD.

Leviticus 23.33–36, 39–44

☙ ☙ ☙

THE PUBLIC ASSEMBLY

Moses wrote down this Teaching and gave it to the priests, sons of Levi, who carried the Ark of the Lord's Covenant, and to the elders of Israel.

And Moses instructed them as follows: Every seventh year, the year set for remission, at the Feast of Booths, when all Israel comes to appear before the LORD your God in the place which He will choose, you shall read this Teaching aloud in the presence of all Israel. Gather the people—men, women, children, and the strangers in your communities—that they may hear and so learn to revere the LORD your God and to observe faithfully every word of this Teaching. Their children, too, who have not had the experience, shall hear and learn to revere the LORD your God as long as they live in the land which you are about to cross the Jordan to occupy.

Deuteronomy 31.9–13

☙ ☙ ☙

THE TEMPLE DEDICATION ON SUKKOT

Then Solomon assembled the elders of Israel, and all the heads of the tribes, the princes of the fathers' houses of the children of Israel, unto king Solomon in Jerusalem, to bring up the ark of the covenant of the LORD out of the city of David, which is Zion. And all the men of Israel assembled themselves unto king Solomon at the Feast [of Booths] in the month Ethanim, which is the seventh month. And all the elders of Israel came, and the priests took up the ark. And they brought up the ark of the LORD, and the tent of meeting, and all the holy vessels that were in the Tent; even these did the priests and the Levites bring up. And king Solomon and all the congregation of Israel, that were assembled unto him, were with him before the ark, sacrificing sheep and oxen, that could not be told nor numbered for multitude.

1 Kings 8.1–5

So Solomon held the feast at that time seven days, and all Israel with him, a very great congregation, from the entrance of Hamath unto the Brook of Egypt. And on the eighth day they held a solemn assembly; for they kept the dedication of the altar seven days, and the feast seven days. And on the three and twentieth day of the seventh month he sent the people away unto their tents, joyful and glad of heart for the goodness that the LORD had shown unto David, and to Solomon, and to Israel His people.

2 Chronicles 7.8–10

❊ ❊ ❊

THE REBELLION OF JEROBOAM

Then Jeroboam built Shechem in the hill-country of Ephraim, and dwelt therein; and he went out from thence, and built Penuel. And Jeroboam said in his heart: "Now will the kingdom return to the house of David. If this people go up to offer sacrifices in the house of the LORD at Jerusalem, then will the heart of this people turn back unto their lord, even unto Rehoboam king of Judah; and they will kill me, and return to Rehoboam king of Judah." . . .

And Jeroboam ordained a feast in the eighth month, on the fifteenth day of the month, like unto the feast that is in Judah, and he went up unto the altar; so did he in Beth-El, to sacrifice unto the calves that he had made; and he placed in Beth-El the priests of the high places that he had made. And he went up unto the altar which he had made in Beth-El on the fifteenth day in the eighth month, even in the month which he had devised of his own heart; and he ordained a feast for the children of Israel, and went up unto the altar, to offer.

1 Kings 12.25–27, 32–33

❦ ❦ ❦

SUKKOT IN THE SIXTH CENTURY B.C.E.

And when the seventh month was come, and the children of Israel were in the cities, the people gathered themselves together as one man to Jerusalem. Then stood up Jeshua the son of Jozadak, and his brethren the priests, and Zerubbabel the son of Shealtiel, and his brethren, and builded the altar of the God of Israel, to offer burnt-offerings thereon, as it is written in the Law of Moses the man of God. And they set the altar upon its bases; for fear was upon them because of the people of the countries, and they offered burnt-offerings thereon unto the LORD, even burnt-offerings morning and evening. And they kept the feast of tabernacles, as it is written, and offered the daily burnt-offerings by number, according to the ordinance, as the duty of every day required.

Ezra 3.1–5

❦ ❦ ❦

IN THE DAYS OF EZRA

And when the seventh month was come, and the children of Israel were in their cities, all the people gathered themselves together as one man into the broad place that was before the water gate; and they spoke unto Ezra the scribe to bring the book of the Law of Moses, which the LORD had commanded to Israel. And Ezra the priest brought the Law before the congregation, both men and women, and all that could hear with understanding, upon the first day of the seventh month. And he read therein before the broad place that was before the water gate from early morning until midday, in the presence of the men and the women, and of those that could understand; and the ears of all the people were attentive unto the book of the Law. . . .

And on the second day were gathered together the heads of fathers' houses of all the people, the priests, and the Levites, unto Ezra the scribe, even to give attention to the words of the Law. And they found written in the Law, how that the LORD had commanded by Moses, that the children of Israel should dwell in booths in the feast of the seventh month; and that they should publish and proclaim in all their cities, and in Jerusalem, saying: "Go forth unto the mount, and fetch olive branches, and branches of wild olive, and myrtle branches, and palm branches, and branches of thick trees, to make booths, as it is written." So the people went forth, and brought them, and made themselves booths, every one upon the roof of his house, and in their courts, and in the courts of the house of God, and in the broad place of the water gate, and in the broad place of the gate of Ephraim. And all the congregation of them that were come back out of the captivity made booths, and dwelt in the booths; for since the days of Joshua the son of Nun unto that day had not the children of Israel done so. And there was very great gladness. Also day by day, from the first day unto the last day, he read in the book of the Law of God. And they kept the feast seven days; and on the eighth day was a solemn assembly, according unto the ordinance.

Nehemiah 7.73–8.3, 13–18

❦ ❦ ❦

ALL NATIONS TO OBSERVE SUKKOT

And it shall come to pass, that every one that is left of all the nations that came against Jerusalem shall go up from year to year to worship the King, the LORD of hosts, and to keep the feast of tabernacles. And it shall be, that whoso of the families of the earth goeth not up unto Jerusalem to worship the King, the LORD of hosts, upon them there shall be no rain. And if the family of Egypt go not up, and come not, they shall have no overflow; there shall be the plague, wherewith the LORD will smite the nations that go not up to keep the feast of tabernacles. This shall be the punishment of Egypt, and the punishment of all the nations that go not up to keep the feast of tabernacles.

Zechariah 14.16–19

❦ 2 ❦

SUKKOT IN POSTBIBLICAL
WRITINGS

※ ※ ※

The postbiblical period has bequeathed to us a number of major
Jewish works. Among them are *The Second Book of Maccabees* and
The Book of Jubilees included in the Apocrypha and Pseudepigrapha. Written during the period of the Second Commonwealth,
these works, known as "outside" or "hidden" books, were excluded
from the canon of the Hebrew Bible.

The dominant themes in *II Maccabees*, ascribed to Jason of
Cyrene, a Hellenistic Jew, are the Jewish struggle for religious
freedom and the sundering of despotic Syrian rule. Its allusions to
the observance of Sukkot as coinciding with that of Hanukkah are
emended by scholars to indicate that Hanukkah was celebrated in a

manner similar to that of Sukkot. However, *II Maccabees* 10.6–7 may also imply that the Jews' inability to celebrate Sukkot in its proper season in 165 B.C.E., because of the war, necessitated its observance jointly with Hanukkah.

The pseudepigraphical *Book of Jubilees*, an old narrative similar to Genesis and the early chapters of Exodus, is recognized as a source for the study of ancient Jewish law. Its author ascribes the origin of Sukkot to the patriarch Abraham, and the addition of the eighth day, Shemini Atzeret, to Jacob.

Philo of Alexandria (c. 20 B.C.E.–c. 50 C.E.) attempted to interfuse Judaism and Hellenism in his philosophical writings. He explained the Scriptures through the use of allegory, deriving exalted spiritual and ethical meanings from the texts. In interpreting the Feast of Tabernacles, Philo deduced moral imperatives that may be drawn from it.

Flavius Josephus (c. 38 C.E.–c. 100 C.E.), who apparently was conversant with the books of the Maccabees, made use of them and added his own embellishments for his classical history, *The Antiquities of the Jews*. Although he was branded by many as a traitor for having deserted to the Roman camp, his historical writings are recognized as a major source for the Second Temple period. Included in this chapter are a number of selections from Josephus's *Antiquities* and a passage from another of his works, *The Jewish War*.

Among the recently discovered documents in the Judean Desert is an Aramaic letter on papyrus sent by Simeon Bar Kokhba, probably prior to Sukkot in the year 134 C.E. In this communication the leader of the Jewish revolt against the Roman emperor Hadrian orders a supply of the Four Species for his army, testifying to his personal piety.

❧ ❧ ❧

HANUKKAH OBSERVED IN THE MANNER OF SUKKOT

Now Maccabaeus and his followers, under the leadership of the Lord, recaptured the Temple and the city, and pulled down the altars erected by the aliens in the marketplace. . . . Now it so happened that the cleansing of the sanctuary took place on the very day on which it had been profaned by aliens, on the twenty-fifth day of the same month, which is Kislev. And they celebrated it for eight days with gladness like a Feast of Tabernacles, remembering how, not long before, during the Feast of Tabernacles they had been wandering like wild beasts in the mountains and the caves [and were unable to celebrate it]. So bearing wands wreathed with leaves and fair boughs and palms, they offered hymns of praise to Him who had prospered the cleansing of His own place. . . .

To the brethren, the Jews in Egypt, greeting. The brethren, the Jews in Jerusalem and throughout the land of Judea, wish you perfect peace; yea, may God do good unto you, and remember his covenant with Abraham and Isaac and Jacob, his faithful servants. . . . See that ye keep the days of the Feast of [instead of *of*, substitute *like*] Tabernacles in the month Kislev. . . . Whereas we are now about to celebrate the purification of the Temple in the month Kislev, on the five and twentieth day, we deem it our duty to inform you, that you too may keep the Feast of [instead of *of*, substitute *like*] Tabernacles.

II Maccabees 10.1–2, 5–7; 1.1–2, 10, 18[1]

1. *Lulav* and *etrog.*
Silver coin of the
second revolt of Bar Kochba,
133 C.E. See Chapter 9.

⚘ ⚘ ⚘

ABRAHAM INAUGURATES THE FEAST OF TABERNACLES

We [the angels] announced to him [Abraham] all the things which had been decreed concerning him . . . and we announced to Sarah all that we had told him, and they both rejoiced with exceeding great joy. And he built there an altar to the Lord who had delivered him, and who was making him rejoice in the land of his sojourning, and he celebrated a festival of joy in this month seven days, near the altar he had built at the Well of the Oath. And he built booths for himself and for his servants on this festival, and he was the first to celebrate the Feast of Tabernacles on the earth. . . . And he celebrated this feast during seven days, rejoicing with all his heart and with all his soul, he and all those who were in his house, and there was no stranger with him nor any that was uncircumcised. . . . And he blessed and rejoiced, and he called the name of this festival of the Lord, a joy acceptable to the Most High God. . . . For this reason it is ordained on the heavenly tablets concerning Israel, that they shall celebrate the Feast of Tabernacles seven days with joy, in the seventh month, acceptable before the Lord—a statute forever throughout their generations every year. And to this there is no limit of days; for it is ordained forever regarding Israel that they should celebrate it and dwell in booths and set wreaths upon their heads, and take leafy boughs and willows from the brook. And Abraham took branches of palm trees, and the fruit of goodly trees, and every day going round the altar with the branches seven times [a day] in the morning, he praised and gave thanks to his God for all things in joy.

Book of Jubilees 16.16, 19–21, 25, 27, 29–31[2]

⚘ ⚘ ⚘

JACOB ADDS AN EIGHTH DAY TO THE FEAST

And on the fifteenth of this month, he [Jacob] brought to the altar fourteen oxen from amongst the cattle, and twenty-eight rams, and forty-nine sheep, and seven lambs, and twenty-one kids of the goats as a burnt-offering on the altar of sacrifice, well-pleasing for a sweet savor before God. This was his offering, in consequence of the vow which he had vowed that he would give a tenth . . . and thus he did daily for seven days. And he and all his sons and his men were eating [this] with joy there seven days and blessing and thanking the Lord who had delivered him out of all his tribulation and had given him his vow. . . .

And he celebrated there yet another day, and he sacrificed thereon according to all that he sacrificed on the former days, and called its name "Addition" [Shemini Atzeret], for this day was added and the former days he called "The Feast." And thus it was manifested that it should be, and it is written on the heavenly tablets: wherefore it was revealed to him that he should celebrate it, and add it to the seven days of the feast. And its name was called "Addition," because it was recorded amongst the days of the feast days, according to the number of the days of the year.

Book of Jubilees 32.4–7, 27–29[3]

✺ ✺ ✺

THE LAST OF THE ANNUAL FEASTS
PHILO OF ALEXANDRIA

The last of the annual feasts, called Tabernacles, recurs at the autumn equinox. From this we may draw two morals. The first is that we should honor equality and hate inequality, for the former is the source and fountain of justice, the latter of injustice. The former is akin to open sunlight, the latter to darkness. The second moral is, that after all the fruits are made perfect, it is our duty to thank God who brought them to perfection and is the source of all good things. . . . Further, the people are commanded, during the time of the feast, to dwell in tents. The reason of this may be that the labor of the husbandmen no longer requires that they should live in the open air, as nothing is now left unprotected but all the fruits are stored in silos or similar places to escape the damage which often ensues through the blazing sunshine or storms of rain. . . . But when all the fruits are being gathered in, come in yourself also to seek a more weatherproof mode of life and hope for rest in place of the toils which you endured when laboring on the land.

Another reason may be that it should remind us of the long journeyings of our forefathers in the depths of the desert, when at every halting place they spent many a year in tents. And indeed it is well in wealth to remember your poverty, in distinction your insignificance, in high offices your position as a commoner, in peace your dangers in war, on land the storms on seas, in cities the life of loneliness. For there is no pleasure greater than in high prosperity to call to mind old misfortunes. But besides giving pleasure, it is considerable help in the practice of virtue. . . . Again, the beginning of this feast comes on the fifteenth day of the month for the same reason as was given when we were speaking of the season of spring, namely, that the glorious light which nature gives should fill the universe not only by day but also by night, because on that day the sun and moon rise in succession to each other with no interval between their shining, which is not divided by any borderland of darkness. As a crown to the seven days he adds an eighth, which he calls the "closing," not meaning apparently that it is the closing of that feast only, but also of all the yearly feasts which I have enumerated and described. For it is the last in the year and forms its conclusion.

Special Laws 2.204, 206–211[4]

❦ ❦ ❦

THE TURNING POINT TO THE WINTER SEASON

FLAVIUS JOSEPHUS

On the fifteenth of this same month [Sukkot], at which the turning point to the winter season is now reached, Moses bids each family to fix up tents, apprehensive of the cold and as a protection against the year's inclemency. Moreover, when they should have won their fatherland, they were to repair to that city which they would in honor of the Temple regard as their metropolis, and there for eight days keep festival: they were to offer burnt-offerings and sacrifices of thanksgiving to God in those days, bearing in their hands a bouquet composed of myrtle and willow with a branch of palm, along with fruit of the persea [*etrog*]. On the first of those days their burnt sacrifice should consist of thirteen oxen, as many lambs and one over, two rams, and a kid to boot in propitiation for sins. On the following days the same number of lambs and of rams is sacrificed, together with the kid, but they reduce that of the oxen by one daily until they reach seven. They abstain from all work on the eighth day and, as we have said, sacrifice to God a calf, a ram, seven lambs, and a kid in propitiation for sins. Such are the rites, handed down from their forefathers, which the Hebrews observe when they erect their tabernacles.

Antiquities of the Jews 3.10.4[5]

✼ ✼ ✼

THE SEPTENNIAL READING
OF THE LAW
FLAVIUS JOSEPHUS

When the forty years had, save for thirty days, now run their course, Moses called together an assembly nigh to the Jordan, where today stands the city of Abila in a region thickly planted with palm trees, and addressed to a congregation of the whole people the following words: . . .

"When the multitude hath assembled in the Holy City for the sacrifice, every seven years at the season of the Feast of Tabernacles, let the high priest, standing upon a raised platform from which he may be heard, recite the laws to the whole assembly; and let neither woman nor child be excluded from this audience, nay nor yet the slaves. For it is good that these laws should be so graven on their hearts and stored in the memory that they can never be effaced."

Antiquities of the Jews 4.8.1, 12[6]

⅍ ⅍ ⅍

EZRA EXHORTS THE PEOPLE TO REJOICE
FLAVIUS JOSEPHUS

In the seventh month they celebrated the Festival of Tabernacles and, when almost all the people had gathered for it, they went up to the open court of the Temple near the gate which faced the east, and asked Ezra to read to them the laws of Moses. So he stood up in the midst of the multitude and read them, taking from early morning until noon. And, as they listened to the laws being read, they learned how to be righteous for the present and the future, but they were troubled about the past and were moved to tears as they bethought themselves that they would not have suffered any of the evils which they had experienced if they had observed the law. But, when Ezra saw them so affected, he bade them return to their homes and shed no tears, for, he said, it was a festival, on which it was not right to weep nor was it lawful. He exhorted them rather to turn to feasting and do what was in keeping with the festival and was pleasant, for in their repentance and sorrow over the sins which they had formerly committed, they would have a security and safeguard that the like would not happen again. Accordingly, at this reassurance from Ezra, they began to celebrate the festival and kept it in their tabernacles for eight days, after which they returned to their homes, singing hymns to God and expressing thanks to Ezra for rectifying the offenses against the laws of the state.

Antiquities of the Jews 11.5.5[7]

⅍ ⅍ ⅍

A TRUCE DECLARED FOR SUKKOT
FLAVIUS JOSEPHUS

When Hyrcanus observed that his great numbers were a disadvantage because of the rapid consumption of provisions by them, and that the work which was being accomplished in no way corresponded to the number of hands, he separated from the rest those who were useless, and drove them out, and retained only those who were in the prime of life and able to fight. But Antiochus, on his side, prevented those who had been rejected from going out, and so, wandering about the walls between the lines, they were the first to be exhausted by their cruel sufferings and were on the point of perishing miserably. Just then, however, the Festival of Tabernacles came round, and those within the city took pity on them and admitted them again. And Hyrcanus sent to Antiochus, requesting a truce of seven days on account of the festival, which Antiochus, deferring to his piety toward the Deity, granted and moreover sent a magnificent sacrifice, consisting of bulls with gilded horns and cups of gold and silver filled with all kinds of spices. And those who were at the gates received the sacrifice from the men who brought it, and took it to the sanctuary, while Antiochus feasted his army, being very different from Antiochus Epiphanes who, when he captured the city, sacrificed swine upon the altars and bespattered the Temple with their grease, thus perverting the rites of the Jews and the piety of their fathers, by which acts the nation was driven to war and became his implacable enemy. This Antiochus, on the other hand, because of his exaggerated devoutness was by all men called Eusebes (the Pious).

Antiquities of the Jews 13.8.2[8]

❧ ❧ ❧

ALEXANDER PELTED WITH CITRONS
FLAVIUS JOSEPHUS

As for Alexander, his own people revolted against him—for the nation was aroused against him—at the celebration of the festival, and as he stood beside the altar and was about to sacrifice, they pelted him with citrons, it being a custom among the Jews that at the Festival of Tabernacles everyone holds wands made of palm branches and citrons—these we have described elsewhere; and they added insult to injury by saying that he was descended from captives and was unfit to hold office and to sacrifice; and being enraged at this, he killed some six thousand of them, and also placed a wooden barrier about the altar and the Temple as far as the coping (of the court) which the priests alone were permitted to enter, and by this means blocked the people's way to him.

Antiquities of the Jews 13.13.5[9]

⚜ ⚜ ⚜

A BATTLE ON THE SABBATH OF SUKKOT
FLAVIUS JOSEPHUS

From Antipatris Cestius advanced to Lydda and found the city deserted, for the whole population had gone up to Jerusalem for the Feast of Tabernacles. Fifty persons who showed themselves he put to the sword, and after burning down the town resumed his march; and, ascending through Bet-horon pitched his camp at a place called Gabao, fifty furlongs distant from Jerusalem.

The Jews, seeing the war now approaching the capital, abandoned the feast and rushed to arms; and, with great confidence in their numbers, sprang in disorder and with loud cries into the fray, with no thought for the seventh day of rest, for it was the very Sabbath which they regarded with special reverence. But the same passion which shook them out of their piety brought them victory in the battle; for with such fury did they fall upon the Romans that they broke and penetrated their ranks, slaughtering the enemy.

The Jewish War 2.19.1[10]

⚜ ⚜ ⚜

AN ORDER FOR THE FOUR SPECIES
SIMEON BAR KOKHBA

Simeon to Yehudah Bar Menashe to Kiryat Aravaya: I have sent to you two donkeys that you shall send with them two men to Yehonatan Bar Be'ayan and to Masabala in order that they shall pack and send to the camp, toward you, palm branches and citrons. And you, from your place, send others who will bring you myrtles and willows. See that they are tithed [literally, set in order] and send them to the camp. (The request is made) since the army is big. Be well.[11]

3

SUKKOT IN TALMUD AND MIDRASH

The Talmud is an inexhaustible mine from which the Jewish people have extracted enduring spiritual and educational ores that have served as their guide and inspiration for more than a millennium and a half. Embodying a corpus of law and legend, legal disputations, maxims, parables, ethical homilies, and moral teachings, this monumental work has been a vital source that nourished the Jews in their long insecure sojourn in the Diaspora. Indeed, it became an indispensable link in the "Chain of Tradition" that began with Moses at Mount Sinai.

For many generations the sages and students at the academies of Sura, Pumpedita, and Nehardea in Babylon pursued their studies and carried on their erudite discussions orally. Some students may have taken notes, but the bulk of the studying was based completely on memory. This accounts for the appellation "Oral Law" as distinguished from the Bible, the "Written Law." It became increasingly difficult to commit this vast material to memory. Therefore, about the year 200 C.E., Rabbi Judah the Prince, a revered and prestigious scholar, compiled the laws taught by the *tannaim* (teachers) into the Hebrew work called the Mishnah. It was arranged systematically according to subject matter into six sections. The Gemara, which was finally redacted in the fifth century, is the product of the *amoraim* (interpreters) who expounded and amplified the teachings of the Mishnah. The Mishnah and the Gemara combined constitute the Talmud.

There are two versions of the Talmud: the Jerusalem Talmud, which is the product of the study of the Mishnah by scholars within Palestine, and the Babylonian Talmud, by far the more popular of the two. Both constitute a prodigious encyclopedia of Jewish learning and Jewish spiritual striving. They are legacies that continue to fuel the torch of Jewish learning even in our contemporary era.

While references to the Feast of Tabernacles are scattered throughout the Talmud, an entire tractate is devoted to it. Tractate Sukkah deals primarily with an exposition of the laws relating to Sukkot. The construction of the festive booth, its function and use, the persons required to dwell in it and those exempt are all detailed. The tractate also expounds the laws governing the ceremonial Four Species and the festival prayers. The Sukkot observance in the Temple and other joyous and picturesque ceremonies associated with the festival are graphically delineated. The Mishnah selections in this chapter are indicated by chapter and paragraph numbers (i.e., 1.2) while the Gemara passages are cited by page numbers (i.e., 12a).

The extensive midrashic literature, also created over a long time span, attempts to adduce ethical and spiritual meanings from the Scriptures. Midrash (study, investigation, commentary) generally implies homiletic interpretations of biblical texts, presenting insights that may not be readily discernible. By the use of commentaries, legends, homilies, and legal prescriptions, midrash deepens and expands the Bible's literal meaning while adhering closely to its spirit.

2. Torah niche of Dura-Europos synagogue,
Syria, showing *etrog* and *lulav* (upper left). Circa 245 C.E. See Chapter 9.

The earliest midrashim appeared in the tannaitic period. *Mekilta de-Rabbi Ishmael* (literally, "Rule of Rabbi Ishmael") dates from this time. It is a commentary on a portion of Exodus and contains material of legal import as well as narrative exposition.

Pesikta Rabbati, probably compiled in the seventh century, is a collection of discourses for the feasts, fast days, and special Sabbaths of the Jewish year, delivered in the Palestinian synagogues and houses of learning during the first five centuries of the Common Era. One chapter (*piska*) is devoted to Sukkot and another to Shemini Atzeret. According to Rabbi William G. Braude, translator of *Pesikta Rabbati* into English, this title might be translated "The Long Anthology of Discourses on the Lessons Designated to be Read Annually" or "The Long Anthology of Discourses on the Brief Lessons of the Year."

Midrash Rabbah ("Great Midrash") on the Pentateuch and the Five Scrolls is the most important of these collections. It is the product of many hands over a period of many centuries up to the twelfth.

Yalkut Shimoni ("Anthology of Simon"), evidently compiled in the thirteenth century by Simon, called *Ha-Darshan* (the preacher), is actually a thesaurus of midrashim. It was collected by the author from numerous books, and its quotations are arranged according to the biblical sequence. It is one of the most popular in the genre of these literary works and has been printed in many editions.

Midrash Tehillim ("Midrash on Psalms") dates from the talmudic period and was redacted by the thirteenth century. It presents homilies on verses and passages in the Book of Psalms, interspersed with allusions to biblical and postbiblical history and legends.

⚹ ⚹ ⚹

THE NEW RECKONING BEGINS ON SUKKOT

A comment on the verse *On the first day you shall take* (Leviticus 23.40). Can the words *the first day* mean the first day of the month? No, for scripture has fixed the day as *the fifteenth day of the seventh month* (Leviticus 23.39). But why should Scripture have shifted over from counting by days in the month to counting by days in the festival? R. Mani of Shaab and R. Joshua of Siknin citing R. Levi replied as follows: The matter may be explained by a parable—the parable of a city which owed the king its tax. The king sent collectors to take up the money, but the people of the city would not pay what they owed the king. Thereupon the king said, "I will go myself and collect it." When the people of the city heard that the king was on his way to collect the tax, the notables of the city went out to meet him a distance of ten parasangs and said to him, "O king, our lord, we acknowledge that we owe you money. But right now we have not the means to pay the entire amount. We entreat you, have pity on us." The king, seeing that they were seeking a peaceful settlement with him, remitted a third of the sum the citizens owed. When the king came to within five miles of the city, the city councilors came out, prostrated themselves before him and said, "O king, our lord, we have not the means to pay." So the king remitted another third of the sum the citizens owed. Then when he entered the city, the very moment he entered it, the entire city, everyone in it, men and women, grownups and little ones, came out, prostrated themselves at his feet, and pleaded with him. The king said, "Suppose I ask no more than one part in four of what you owe." They replied, "Our lord, we have not the means." What did the king do? He remitted the entire amount and wrote off their debt in full. What did all the people of the city do then? They went, the grownups and the little ones, and brought myrtles and palm branches and sang praise to the king. The king said, "Let bygones be bygones; from this moment on we shall commence a new reckoning." The application of the parable is as follows: Throughout the days of the year, Israel sins. Then on New Year's Day the Holy One [goes up on His throne and] sits in judgment. What do the people of Israel do then? They gather and pray in synagogues, and after reciting the ten verses asserting God's sovereignty, the ten verses asserting God's remembrance of His creatures, and the ten verses alluding to the *shofar* [of revelation], they blow the *shofar*. Thereupon the Holy One remits one third of the punishment for Israel's iniquities. Between New Year's Day and the Day of Atonement those men who are notable for their piety fast as they avow penitence. Thereupon the Holy One remits another third of the punishment for Israel's iniquities. Then when the Day of Atonement comes, all Israel fast as they avow penitence, men, women, and children. Indeed they avow complete penitence, for they put on white garments, even though they are bare of foot like the dead. They say to Him: Master of the universe, we are two things at once: in our white garments we are like the angels who are eternal, but bare of foot we are like the dead.

When the Holy One sees Israel resolved upon complete penitence, He forgives all sins and writes off Israel's debt to Him, as is written *For on this day atonement shall be made for you to cleanse you of all your sins* (Leviticus 16.30). When Israel see that the Holy One has made atonement for them and has written off their debt, what do they do? During the four days between the Day of Atonement and the Feast of Tabernacles they go and fetch myrtle and willows and palm branches and build booths and sing praises to the Holy One. The Holy One says to them: Let bygones be bygones. From this moment on commences a new reckoning. Today is to be the first day in the new reckoning of iniquities. As Scripture says, *On the first day* (Leviticus 23.40).

Pesikta Rabbati 51.8[1]

❦ ❦ ❦

BOOTHS TO THE LORD

I [the Lord] have an easy commandment which is called *sukkah*; go and carry it out.

Avodah Zarah 3a[2]

This is my God and I will glorify Him (Exodus 15.2). R. Ishmael says: And is it possible for a man of flesh and blood to add glory to his Creator? It simply means: I shall be beautiful before Him in observing the commandments. I shall prepare before Him a beautiful *lulav*, a beautiful *sukkah*, beautiful fringes and beautiful phylacteries.

Mekilta de-Rabbi Ishmael, Shirata 3[3]

He who makes a *sukkah* for himself recites: "Blessed art Thou O Lord, our God, King of the universe, who has kept us in life and has preserved us and has enabled us to reach this season." When he enters to sit therein he recites: "Blessed . . . who has sanctified us with His commandments and has commanded us to dwell in a *sukkah*."

Pesahim 7b

What is Bet Shammai's reason [for declaring an old *sukkah* invalid]?—Scripture says, *there shall be the Feast of Booths to the Lord, [to last]seven days* (Leviticus 23.34), [implying therefore] a *sukkah* made expressly for the sake of the Festival. And Bet Hillel [who pronounced an old *sukkah* valid]?—They need that [verse] for the same deduction as that of R. Sheshet, R. Sheshet having said in the name of R. Akiba, Whence do we know that the wood of the *sukkah* is forbidden [to be used for secular purposes] all the seven [days of the festival]? From Scripture which states, *The Feast of Booths to the Lord, [to last] seven days,* and it was taught, R. Judah b. Bathyra says: Just as the Name of Heaven rests upon the festival offering, so does it rest upon the *sukkah*, since it is said, *the Feast of Booths to the Lord, [to last] seven days*: just as the Festival [offering] is *to the Lord,* so is the *sukkah* also *to the Lord.* And Bet Shammai also, do not they need the verse for this deduction?—Yes, indeed. What then is Bet Shammai's reason?—There is another Scriptural verse: *You shall make the Feast of Booths for seven days* (Deuteronomy 16.13). This implies a *sukkah* made expressly for the sake of the festival. And Bet Hillel?—They need this [verse for the deduction] that a *sukkah* may be made in the intermediate days of the festival [if one did not make it prior to the festival]. And Bet Shammai?—They hold the same opinion as R. Eliezer, who laid down that no *sukkah* may be made in the intermediate days of the Festival.

Sukkah 9a

The Israelites journeyed from Raamses to Succoth (Exodus 12.37), to the place where they actually put up booths, as it is said: *But Jacob journeyed on to Succoth, and built a house for himself and made booths for his cattle* (Genesis 33.17)—these are the words of R. Eliezer. But the other sages say: Succoth is merely the name of a place, for it is said: *They set out from Succoth and encamped at Etham* (Numbers 33.6). Just as Etham is the name of a place, so also is Succoth. R. Akiba says: Succoth here means only clouds of glory, as it is said: *And the Lord will create over the whole habitation* of Mount Zion, and over her assemblies, a cloud and smoke by day, and the shining of a flaming fire by night; for over all the glory shall be a canopy. And there shall be a pavilion for a shadow in the daytime (Isaiah 4.5–6).

Mekilta de-Rabbi Ishmael, Pisha 14[4]

❧ ❧ ❧

THE *SUKKAH* CONSTRUCTION

A *sukkah* that is more than twenty cubits high is not valid; R. Judah, however, declares it valid. One that is not ten handbreadths high, or that has not three walls, or that has more sun than shade, is not valid.

If one made his *sukkah* under a tree, it is as if he made it within the house [as though there are two roofs, and it is, therefore, invalid]. If one *sukkah* is erected above another, the upper one is valid but the lower is invalid. R. Judah said, If there are no occupants in the upper one, the lower one is valid.

Sukkah 1.1–2

If one erects his *sukkah* on the top of a wagon [though it is on the move] or on the deck of a ship [where it is exposed to gales], it is valid and they may go up into it on the festival. If he made it on the top of a tree, or on the back of a camel, it is valid, but they may not go up into it on the festival. . . . This is the general rule: whatever can stand by itself if the tree were taken away is valid, and they may go up into it on the festival.

Sukkah 2.3

He who erects his *sukkah* on the deck of a ship, R. Gamaliel declares it invalid and R. Akiba valid. It happened with R. Gamaliel and R. Akiba when they were journeying on a ship [in the week of the festival] that R. Akiba arose and erected a *sukkah* on the deck of the ship. On the morrow the wind blew and tore it away. R. Gamaliel said to him, Akiba, where is thy *sukkah*?

Abaye said, All are in accord that where it [a *sukkah*] is unable to withstand a normal land breeze it is nothing; if it can withstand an unusually [strong] land breeze, all are in accord that it is valid. Where do they dispute? Where it can withstand a normal land breeze, but not a normal sea breeze; R. Gamaliel is of the opinion that the *sukkah* must be a permanent abode, and since it cannot withstand a normal sea breeze, it is nothing, while R. Akiba is of the opinion that the *sukkah* must be a temporary abode, and since it can withstand a normal land breeze, it is valid.

Sukkah 23a

R. Judah, holding in accordance with his own principle, that the *sukkah* must have the character of a permanent residence, considers [the *sukkah*] is liable to a *mezuzah*, while the Rabbis, following their own principle, hold that the *sukkah* must have the character of an incidental residence, and hence requires no *mezuzah*.

Yoma 10b

If one covered it [the *sukkah*] according to law and decorated it with hand-made carpets and tapestries, and hung therein nuts, almonds, peaches, pomegranates and bunches of grapes, vines, [decanters of] oils and fine meal, and wreaths of ears of corn, it is forbidden to make use of them [to eat, for instance, any of the fruits] until the termination of the last day of the festival.

Betzah 30b

❦ ❦ ❦

DWELLING IN BOOTHS

R. Eliezer said, A man is obliged to eat fourteen meals in the *sukkah* [during the seven days of the festival]. One on each day and one on each night. The sages however say, there is no fixed number except on the first night of the festival alone [when one must eat a meal in the *sukkah*]. R. Eliezer said in addition, If a man did not eat in the *sukkah* on the first night of the festival, he may make up for it on the last night of the festival.

Sukkah 2.6

What is the reason of R. Eliezer?—*You shall live in booths* (Leviticus 23.42) implies just as you normally dwell. As in a [normal] abode [a man has] one [meal] by day and one by night, so in the *sukkah* [he must have] one meal by day and one by night. And the Rabbis?—[They say that the implication is] like an abode. Just as in an abode a man eats if he desires and if he does not so desire he does not eat, so also with the *sukkah*; if he desires he eats, and if he does not so desire he does not eat.

Sukkah 27a

Our Rabbis taught, If he was eating in the *sukkah*, and rain fell, and he left [the *sukkah* in order to finish his meal in the house], he need not trouble to return there until he has finished his meal. If he was sleeping in the *sukkah* and rain fell and he left, he need not trouble to return until it is dawn.

Sukkah 29a

R. Eliezer said, Just as a man cannot fulfill his obligation on the first day of the festival with the palm branch of his fellow since it is written, *On the first day you shall take the product of goodly trees, branches of palm trees* (Leviticus 23.40), i.e., from your own, so a man cannot fulfill his obligation with a *sukkah* of his fellow, since it is written, *you shall hold the Feast of Booths for seven days* (Deuteronomy 16.13), i.e., of your own. The sages, however, say, Although the Rabbis said that a man cannot fulfill his obligation on the first day of the festival with the palm branch of his fellow, he may nevertheless fulfill his obligation with the *sukkah* of his fellow, since it is written, *all citizens in Israel shall live in booths* (Leviticus 23.42) which teaches that all Israel are able to sit in one *sukkah*.

Sukkah 27b

Raba said, He who is in discomfort is exempt from the obligation of *sukkah*. But have we not learnt: *Invalids and their attendants are free from the obligation of sukkah,* [from which it follows] only an invalid but not one who is merely in discomfort?—I will explain: An invalid is free together with his attendants, whereas he who is in discomfort is himself free, but not his attendants. . . .

Our Rabbis taught, Day travellers are free from the obligation of *sukkah* by day [since one is to live in the *sukkah* as in a house. As a day traveller does not use his house during the day so he need not

3. *Mahzor.* Southern Germany. Circa 1320. See Chapter 9.

use his *sukkah*] but are bound to it at night. Night travellers are free from the obligation of *sukkah* at night, but are bound to it by day. Travellers by day and night are free from the obligation both day and night. Those who are on a religious errand [though they travel in the daytime only] are free both by day and by night, as in the case of R. Hisda and Rabbah son of R. Huna who, when visiting on the Sabbath of the festival the house of the Exilarch, slept on the river bank of Sura, saying, "We are engaged on a religious errand and are [therefore] free [from the obligation of *sukkah*]."

Sukkah 26a

Women, slaves and minors are free from the obligation of *sukkah* but a minor who is not dependent on his mother is bound by the law of *sukkah*.

Sukkah 2.8

❧ ❧ ❧

THE FOUR SPECIES

Just as a man cannot fulfill his obligation on the Feast of Tabernacles unless all Four Species are bound together, so Israel can only be redeemed when all Israelites hold together.

Yalkut Shimoni 188a

Of the four kinds [of plants] used for the *lulav* . . . the [absence of] one invalidates the others for it is written, *you shall take* (Leviticus 23.40), signifying the taking of them all. . . . It was taught: Of the four kinds used for the *lulav* two are fruit-bearing [the citron and the palm branch] and two are not [the myrtle and the willow]; those which bear fruits must be joined to those which bear no fruits and those which bear no fruits must be joined to those which bear fruits. And a man does not fulfill his obligations unless they are all bound in one band. And so it is with Israel's conciliation with God, [it is achieved] only when they are all in one band.

Menahot 27a

You shall take . . . branches of palm trees (Leviticus 23.40):
Like the palm tree which has a single heart that keeps reaching
upwards, so Israel has a single heart reaching upwards—up to their
Father in heaven.

Of the four plants that make up the *lulav* cluster, two bear fruit
and two do not. Those that bear fruit must be bound closely to the
ones that do not bear fruit. The former represent disciples of the
wise whose prayers, in keeping with the admonition from Palestine,
are meant to bear fruits of mercy for ordinary householders. . . . On
the other hand, the plants that do not bear fruit must be bound close
to those that bear fruit, since the former represent those persons who
are meant to provide a shelter of physical comfort for the Sages and
their disciples.

In another comment the verse is read *Take for your own sake . . .
[a cluster including] the product of goodly trees, etc.* (Leviticus
23.40), *the product of goodly trees* [the *etrog*] standing for [some
men in] Israel: even as the *etrog* has aroma and has edible fruit, so
Israel have in their midst men who have knowledge of Torah and
also have good deeds. *Branches of palm trees* (ibid.) also stands for
[some men in] Israel: as the palm tree has edible fruit but no
aroma, so Israel have in their midst men who have knowledge of
Torah but have not good deeds. *Boughs of leafy trees* (ibid.) also
stands for [some men in] Israel: as the myrtle tree has aroma but
has not edible fruit, so Israel have in their midst men who have good
deeds but have not Torah. *And willows of the brook* (ibid.) also
stands for [some men in] Israel: even as the willow has neither edible
fruit nor aroma, so Israel have in their midst men in whom there is
neither knowledge of Torah nor good deeds. The Holy One says:
In order to make it impossible for Israel to be destroyed, let all of
them be bound together as plants are bound into a cluster, so that
the righteous among them will atone for the others. Hence Moses
charged Israel: *Take for your own sake on the first day* [a cluster],
etc. (Leviticus 23.40).

Pesikta Rabbati 51.2[5]

All my bones shall say: "Lord, who is like unto Thee" (Psalms
35.10). This verse was said in allusion to nought else than the *lulav*.
The rib of the *lulav* resembles the spine of a man; the myrtle resembles the eye; the willow resembles the mouth, and the *etrog*
resembles the heart. David said: There are none among all the limbs

greater than these, for they outweigh in importance the whole body. Therefore [when the four species are held it is as David said in Psalms], *All my bones shall say.*

Leviticus Rabbah 30.14⁶

A dry *lulav* is not permissible. R. Abun in the name of R. Yudah Bar Pazzi said: Because it is written, *The dead praise not the Lord* (Psalms 115.17).

Yerushalmi Sukkah 53c

R. Ammi said, A withered [palm branch] is invalid because it is not *goodly* (Leviticus 23.40); a stolen one is invalid because it constitutes a precept fulfilled through a transgression.

Sukkah 30a

If the larger part of the *etrog* is covered with scars, or if its nipple is removed, if it is peeled, split, perforated, so that any part is missing, it is invalid. If its lesser part only is covered with scars, if its stalk is missing, or if it is perforated but naught of it is missing, it is valid. An Ethiopian [black] *etrog* is invalid. If it is green as a leek, R. Meir declares it valid and R. Judah declares it invalid.

The minimum size of an *etrog*, R. Meir says, is that of a nut. R. Judah says that of an egg. The maximum [size] is such that two can be held in one hand. These are the words of R. Judah. R. Jose said, Even one [that he can hold only] in both his hands.

Sukkah 3.6–7

The *lulav* [the festive wreath consisting of the palm, myrtle and willow branches] may be bound only with [strands of] its own species; so R. Judah. R. Meir says it may be bound even with a cord. R. Meir observed, It actually occurred that the men of Jerusalem used to bind their *lulavim* with strands of gold. The Rabbis answered him, but they bound it with [strands of] its own species underneath [the strands of gold, the former serving as binders and the latter as mere ornaments].

Sukkah 3.8

Rabbah stated, The *lulav* [must be held] in the right hand and the *etrog* in the left. What is the reason? The former constitutes three commandments [those of the palm, the myrtle and the willow which are bound together] and the latter only one [as the right hand is regarded as the more important, and in it, therefore, one must hold the more important part of the species].

R. Jeremiah enquired of R. Zerika, Why in the blessing do we say only "to take the palm branch"?—Because it towers above the others.

Sukkah 37b

And where [in the course of the recital of the *Hallel* psalms on Sukkhot] is [the *lulav*] waved? At the commencement and the conclusion of the psalm, *O give thanks unto the Lord* and at *Save now, we beseech Thee, O Lord.* These are the words of Bet Hillel. Bet Shammai say, Also at *O Lord we beseech Thee, send now prosperity.* R. Akiba stated, I watched R. Gamaliel and R. Joshua, and while all the people were waving their *lulavim* [at other verses], they waved them only at *Save now, we beseech Thee, O Lord.*

Sukkah 3.9

R. Johanan explained, [One waves them] to and fro [in honor of] Him to whom the four directions belong, and up and down [in acknowledgment of] Him to whom are heaven and earth.

Sukkah 37b

Formerly the *lulav* was taken for seven days in the Temple, and in the provinces for one day only. When the Temple was destroyed, R. Johanan b. Zakkai instituted that the *lulav* should be taken in the provinces for seven days in memory of the Temple.

Sukkah 3.12

R. Eleazar b. Zadok stated, This was the custom of the men of Jerusalem. When a man left his house he carried his *lulav* in his hand; when he went to the synagogue his *lulav* was in his hand, when he read the *Shema* and his prayers his *lulav* was still in his hand, but when he read in the Law or recited the priestly benediction he would lay it on the ground. If he went to visit the sick or to comfort mourners he could go with his *lulav* in his hand. . . . What does this teach us?—It serves to inform you how zealous they were in the performance of religious duties.

Sukkah 41b

A story is told that a certain man had two sons, one of whom practiced charity while the other did no charitable deed at all. The one who practiced charity sold his house and all that he had and spent the proceeds on charity. Once, on Hoshana Rabbah, his wife gave him ten *pulsin* and said to him, "Go and buy something for your children in the market." No sooner had he gone out than the charity collectors met him. They said, "Here comes the lord of charity! Give your share," they begged, "to this charity, for we are buying a wedding dress for a certain orphan girl." He took the ten *pulsin* and gave them to the men. Being ashamed to go home, he went to the synagogue. There he saw some of the citrons that the children throw about on Hoshana Rabbah. Now we have learned elsewhere that it is permitted to take away the palm branches from the children, as well as to eat their citrons [since they are merely playing with them]. So he took the citrons from them, filled a sack with them and set out on a voyage upon the Great Sea, in order to reach the king's province. When he arrived there, it so happened that the king felt a pain in his bowels and was told in a dream, "This is your cure: Eat of those citrons which the Jews use in their prayers on Hoshana Rabbah and you will be healed." Thereupon they searched all ships and all the province but could find none. They went and found that man sitting on his sack. "Have you anything with you?" they asked him. "I am a poor man," he replied, "and I have nothing to sell." They rummaged in his sack and found some of those citrons. "Where are these from?" they inquired. He told them that they were of those which the Jews used in their prayers on Hoshana Rabbah. They lifted the sack and brought it to the king, who ate the citrons and was cured. They emptied the sack and filled it with *denarii*. . . . This confirms the text, *For the work of a man will He requite unto him* (Job 34.11).

Leviticus Rabbah 37.2

❧ ❧ ❧

THE WATER-DRAWING CEREMONY IN JERUSALEM

He who has not seen the Rejoicing at the Place of the Water-Drawing has never seen rejoicing in his life. At the conclusion of the first festival day of Tabernacles they [the priests and Levites] descended to the court of the women where they had made a great enactment.

There were there golden candlesticks with four golden bowls on top of each of them and four ladders to each, and four youths drawn from the priestly stock in whose hands were held jars of oil containing one hundred and twenty *log* which they poured into the bowls.

From the worn-out drawers and girdles of the priests they made wicks and with them they kindled the lamps; and there was not a courtyard in Jerusalem that was not illumined by the light of the place of the water-drawing.

Men of piety and good deeds used to dance before them with lighted torches in their hands and sing songs and praises. And Levites without number with harps, lyres, cymbals and trumpets and other musical instruments were there upon the fifteen steps leading down from the court of the Israelites to the court of the women, corresponding to the fifteen songs of ascent in Psalms [chapters 120–135]. It was upon these that the Levites stood with their instruments of music and sang their songs. Two priests stood by the upper gate which leads down from the court of the Israelites to the court of the women, with two trumpets in their hands. When the cock crowed they sounded a *tekiah* [long drawn-out blast], a *teruah* [tremulous note] and again a *tekiah*. . . . When they reached the gate which leads out to the east, they turned their faces from east to west [thus facing the Temple] and proclaimed "Our fathers who were in this place [stood] with their backs toward the Temple of the Lord, and their faces toward the east, and they worshiped the sun toward the east, but as for us, our eyes are turned to the Lord."

Sukkah 5.1–4

Of Hillel the Elder, it was said that when he used to rejoice at the Rejoicing at the Place of the Water-Drawing, he used to recite thus, "If I [referring to God (Rashi)] am here, everyone is here, but if I am not here, who is here?" . . .

They said of R. Simeon b. Gamaliel that, when he rejoiced at the Rejoicing at the Place of the Water-Drawing, he used to take eight lighted torches [and throw them in the air] and catch one and throw one and they did not touch one another. . . .

Levi used to juggle in the presence of Rabbi [Judah I] with eight knives, Samuel before King Shapur with eight glasses of wine, and Abaye before Rabbah with eight eggs or, as some say, with four eggs.

It was taught: R. Joshua b. Hanania stated, When we used to rejoice at the place of the water-drawing, our eyes saw no sleep. How was this? The first hour [was occupied with] the daily morning

דיר תהלה

לצורא עלילה בבי זאת עלה"

אדררנינם אעלסה כנתרנינם ז

בגעלסה לבילך רם ונשא"

רתי ארבע בבי מספר רובע

להן על ארבע"

אסלד בשבחי ותדיה לפני קהל ועלה

פלוקחי לילב ואגדיה קדוש"

רוש בבי צדק לשפטם ליצדק

דינם להוינא ליצדק"

ללכם אפינה ומליצי ירצה

וכיהב איגא"

רוכבן בפתח יבוש וחטם בצולתן

תבבוש קדאתיך אל אבוש"

sacrifice; from there [we proceeded] to prayers; from there [we proceeded] to the additional sacrifice, then to the house of study, then the eating and drinking, then the afternoon prayer, then the daily evening sacrifice, and after that the Rejoicing at the Place of the Water-Drawing [all night].

Sukkah 53a

⚘ ⚘ ⚘

THE OBSERVANCE OF HOSHANA RABBAH

R. Johanan b. Beroka said, They used to bring palm twigs and beat them on the ground at the sides of the altar, and that day was called "[the day of] the beating of the palm twigs."

Sukkah 4.6

What kind of victory is meant in the clause *In Thy right hand there are pleasures of victory* (Psalms 16.11)? That kind in which the victor receives a wreath. For according to the custom of the world, when two charioteers race in the hippodrome, which of them receives a wreath? The victor. Thus on New Year's Day all the people of the world come forth like contestants on parade and pass before God, and the children of Israel among all the people of the world also pass before Him. Then the guardian angels of the nations of the world declare: We were victorious, and in the judgment shall be found righteous. But actually no one knows who was victorious, whether the children of Israel or the nations of the world were victorious. After New Year's Day is gone, all the children of Israel come forth on the Day of Atonement and fast thereon, clothed in white and comely garments. But even after the Day of Atonement is gone, still no one knows who was victorious, the children of Israel, or the nations of the world. When the first day of Tabernacles comes, however, all the children of Israel, they that are grown as well as the little ones, take up their festive wreaths in their right hands and their citrons in their left, and then all people of the world know that in the judgment the children of Israel were proclaimed victorious. Moreover, when Hoshana Rabbah comes, the children of Israel, taking willows of the brook, circle seven times therewith, while the reader of the synagogue, like an angel of God, stands up with the Scroll of Torah in his arm, the people circling about him, as though he were the altar. Of this circling our Masters taught: Every day of the first six days of Tabernacles they circled about the altar once, saying, *We beseech Thee, O Lord, save now! We beseech Thee, O Lord, make us now to prosper* (Psalms 118.25). But on the seventh day, they circled about the altar seven times. This circling of the altar is clearly referred to by David, king of Israel, in the verse *I will wash my hands in innocency; so will I compass Thine altar, O Lord* (Psalms 26.6). Thereupon, the ministering angels rejoice, and say: "The children of Israel are victorious; the children of Israel are victorious," and they also say, *The Victory of Israel will not lie nor repent* (1 Samuel 15.29). Therefore, David meant to say this: If you perform the rite of the festive wreath known as "a pleasure" and take up the wreath "in the right hand" to praise therewith the Holy One, blessed be He, behold! He has made known to you the paths of life. Hence David said: *Thou makest me to know the path of life; in Thy presence is fullness of joy, in Thy right hand there are pleasures of victory* (Psalms 16.11). By *the path of life* David meant New Year's Day and the Day of Atonement; by *fullness of joy* he meant the Feast of Tabernacles; by *in Thy presence* he meant Israel's appearance in Jerusalem as ordained in the verse *Three times a year . . . all your males shall appear before the Lord your God* (Deuteronomy 16.16); by *in Thy right hand there are pleasures* he meant the festive wreath of *lulav* called "a pleasure," which is held in the right hand; and by *of victory* he meant: I bring thee the glad tidings, that at the judgment thou art proclaimed victorious over the nations of the world, as is said *The Victory of Israel will not lie nor repent.*

Another comment on *in Thy presence is fullness* (sova) *of joy*: Do not read *sova*, "fullness," but *sheva*, "seven," for the seven things mentioned in the verse *you shall take the product of goodly trees, branches of palm trees, and boughs of leafy trees and willows of the brook, and you shall rejoice before the Lord your God seven days* (Leviticus 23.40). The seven are the booth, the branch of the palm tree, the willow, the myrtle, the citron, the libation of water, and the joyous procession to and from the well. If the children of Israel thus observe the Feast of Tabernacles, the Lord will give them pleasure, and with His right hand will declare them victorious at the judgment.

Midrash on Psalms 17.5[7]

❦ ❦ ❦

SHEMINI ATZERET—THE EIGHTH DAY OF SOLEMN GATHERING

The Eighth Day is a separate festival, for, just as the seven days of the Festival must have [their own] sacrifices, psalms, benediction and staying overnight, so the Eighth Day must have its own sacrifice, psalm, benediction and staying overnight.

Sukkah 47a

The Hallel [was recited] and the [peace-offerings of] rejoicing [were offered] on all the eight days—how is that? This teaches that one is bound to recite the Hallel, [offer peace-offerings of] rejoicing and show honor to the festival, on the last day, as on all the other days of the festival.

Sukkah 4.8

R. Joshua b. Levi said: By rights, the Eighth Day of Assembly should have followed Tabernacles after an interval of fifty days, as Pentecost follows Passover. But since at the Eighth Day of Assembly summer passes into autumn, the time is not suitable for traveling. [God was like] a king who had several married daughters, some living nearby, while others were a long way away. One day they all came to visit their father the king. Said the king, "Those who are living nearby are able to travel at any time. But those who live at a distance are not able to travel at any time. So while they are all here with me, let us make one feast for all of them and rejoice with them."

Song of Songs Rabbah 7.2

R. Levi said: What God intended was this—to give to Israel a festival for every month during the summer: Passover in Nisan, the minor Passover in Iyar, Pentecost in Sivan. But on account of the transgressions and evil deeds that blackened Israel's hands when they made the golden calf, God took away the festivals He had intended for the months of Tammuz, Av, and Elul. He had the following month, Tishri, make up, however, for Israel's being deprived of the festivals He had intended them to celebrate during the three previous months by celebrating the three festivals within Tishri's span: New Year's Day to make up for the missing festival in Tammuz; the Great Fast to make up for the missing festival in Av; the seven days of the Feast of Tabernacles to make up for the missing festival in Elul. Then said the Holy One, blessed be He: Since Tishri makes up for the other months and has not been given a festival that is his own, let him be given his own day. Hence Israel is charged: *On the eighth day, you shall hold [an additional] solemn gathering* (Numbers 29.35).

Pesikta Rabbati 52.2[8]

It is the way of Israel that when Thou givest them holidays, they eat and drink and rejoice and go into synagogues and schools, and increase the number of prayers, and increase the number of additional offerings, and increase the number of regular offerings. Therefore Scripture says, *On the eighth day, you shall hold [an additional] solemn gathering* (Numbers 29.35).

Pesikta Rabbati 52.1[9]

A comment: *On the eighth day* (Numbers 29.35). The Holy One, blessed be He, said to Israel, "My children, I know that during all seven days of the Feast of Tabernacles you have been occupied with offerings in behalf of the nations of the earth. But let this day be a day of rejoicing solely for you and Me. I shall not ask you for too burdensome an offering—only one bullock and one ram." When Israel heard this, they began praising the Holy One, blessed be He, saying, *This is the day which the Lord hath made; we will rejoice and be glad in it* (Psalms 118.24).

Pesikta Rabbati 52.7[10]

❧ ❧ ❧

THE PRAYER FOR RAIN

On Tabernacles judgment is passed in respect of rain.

Rosh Hashanah 1.2

Why did the Torah enjoin us to perform the water-pouring on Tabernacles? The Holy One, blessed be He, said, Pour out water before Me on Tabernacles, so that your rains this year may be blessed.

Rosh Hashanah 16a

When do we [begin to] mention the "Power of Rain" [in the *Amidah*]? R. Eliezer says: On the first day of the Feast [of Tabernacles]. R. Joshua says: On the last day of the Feast. . . .

We pray for rain only close to the rainy season. R. Judah says: The last to step before the ark [to recite the *Amidah* of the Additional Service] on the last day of the Feast [of Tabernacles] makes mention, the first does not.

Taanit 1.1–2

❧ ❧ ❧

ISRAEL PRAYS FOR THE NATIONS OF THE WORLD

The people of Israel said to the nations of the earth: Because of us, the Holy One, blessed be He, does all these [good] things for you, and yet you hate us, as is said *In return for my love they are my adversaries* (Psalms 109.4). At the Festival of Tabernacles we offer up seventy bullocks [as an atonement] for the seventy nations, and we pray that rain will come down for them. Yet *In return for my love they are my adversaries: but I am all prayer* (Psalms 109.4). "*Shall evil be recompensed for good?*" (Jeremiah 18.20). Even though *they have laid upon me evil for good* (Psalms 109.5), I am all prayer.

Midrash on Psalms 109.4[11]

❧ ❧ ❧

REJOICING ON THE FESTIVAL

You find three expressions for rejoicing written regarding the festival [of Sukkot]: *you shall rejoice in your festival* (Deuteronomy 16.14); *you shall have nothing but joy* (Deuteronomy 16.15); and *you shall rejoice before the Lord your God seven days* (Leviticus 23.40). However, you do not find even one expression of rejoicing concerning Passover. Why? Because on Passover man does not yet know the result of his harvest. Similarly, you find that there is only one expression of rejoicing related to Shavuot: *Then you shall observe the Feast of Weeks . . . you shall rejoice* (Deuteronomy 16.10–11). Why? Because the crop has been [harvested and] gathered indoors. . . . But about Sukkot when the crop and the fruit of the tree are already stored [and man has atoned for his sins on Yom Kippur], three expressions of rejoicing are written.

Yalkut Shimoni Leviticus 23

Rejoicing on a festival is a religious duty. For it was taught, R. Eliezer said: A man has nought else [to do] on a festival save either to eat and drink or to sit and study. R. Joshua said: Divide it—[devote] half of it to eating and drinking, and half of it to the house of study.

Pesahim 68b

4

SUKKOT IN MEDIEVAL JEWISH LITERATURE

❧ ❧ ❧

This chapter presents a sampling from the copious Jewish literature of the Middle Ages. During this creative period, many scholars were engaged in writing in numerous fields, including philosophy, poetry, biblical exegesis, law, and mysticism.

Moses ben Maimon (1135–1204), known as Maimonides and Rambam, was a physician, philosopher, and codifier of law whose impact on Jewish life is potent even today. A prolific author, he wrote *Moreh Nevukhim* ("Guide for the Perplexed"), an exposition of Judaism that is still a dominant factor in Jewish thought and has evoked considerable interest on the part of non-Jewish philosophers.

The portion excerpted from the "Guide" for this chapter deals with the meaning of dwelling in booths and of the Four Species.

Although the *Zohar* ("Splendor" or "Light"), written in Aramaic, first appeared in the thirteenth century through the cabalist Moses de Leon, it was traditionally attributed to Rabbi Simeon ben Yohai and his second-century school. Considered the most sacred book in Jewish mysticism, the *Zohar* interprets the Bible symbolically by means of homilies, parables, and esoteric discourses. Among the passages presented here is one that discusses the tradition of extending a symbolic invitation, on entering the *sukkah*, to "holy guests" (*ushpizin*)—Abraham, Isaac, Jacob, Joseph, Moses, Aaron, and David. This is interpreted by the *Zohar* as an obligation to invite needy persons as guests who will represent these seven patriarchs while partaking of the meals served in the *sukkah*.

Sefer ha-Hinukh ("The Book of Training"), written at the end of the thirteenth century by Aaron Halevi of Spain, is an elucidation of the 613 commandments in the Bible. Among books on this subject, it ranks next to Maimonides' *Sefer ha-Mitzvot* ("The Book of Commandments"). It is concerned with ethical and philosophical explications of the laws. This work includes two interpretations of the significance of the Four Species and an explanation of the *Hakhel*, the assembly convened in Jerusalem on Sukkot every seventh year.

Menorat ha-Maor ("Candelabrum of Light") by Isaac Aboab (about the fifteenth century) is a collection of homilies and teachings emphasizing Jewish ethics. This treatise achieved widespread popularity both in the original and in the Yiddish translation.

Selections from the works of three classical commentators on the Torah are also excerpted in this chapter. Emulating his grandfather Rashi, Rabbi Samuel ben Meir (c. 1080–c. 1158), a French scholar known as Rashbam, wrote commentaries on the Bible and the Talmud, as well as a literal exposition of the Pentateuch. Moses ben Nahman (1194–c. 1270), called Nachmanides or Ramban, was a foremost biblical commentator, talmudic scholar, and the leader of Spanish Jewry in his day. He wrote a sophisticated critique on the Torah, interweaving legal and ethical explanations with mystical and literal interpretations. Scion of an illustrious Sephardic Jewish family, Don Isaac Abravanel (1437–1508) was treasurer to Portugal's King Alfonso V and financial advisor to King Ferdinand and Queen Isabella of Spain. His literary contributions are embodied in various philosophical and expository writings, notably *Perush ha-Torah* ("Commentary on the Torah").

❦ ❦ ❦

THE FEAST OF REJOICING AND GLADNESS

MOSES MAIMONIDES

The Feast of Tabernacles, which is a feast of rejoicing and gladness, is kept seven days, in order that the idea of the festival may be more noticeable. The reason why it is kept in the autumn is stated in the Law: "When you gather in the results of your work from the field" (Exodus 23.16); that is to say, when you rest and are free from pressing labors. Aristotle, in the ninth book of his *Ethics*, mentions this as a general custom among the nations. He says: "In ancient times the sacrifices and assemblies of the people took place after the ingathering of the corn and the fruit, as if the sacrifices were offered on account of the harvest." Another reason is that in this season it is possible to dwell in tabernacles, as there is neither great heat nor troublesome rain.

The two festivals, Passover and the Feast of Tabernacles, imply also the teaching of certain truths and certain moral lessons. Passover teaches us to remember the miracles which God wrought in Egypt, and to perpetuate their memory; the Feast of Tabernacles reminds us of the miracles wrought in the wilderness. The moral lessons derived from these feasts is this: man ought to remember his evil days in his day of prosperity. He will thereby be induced to thank God repeatedly, to lead a modest and humble life. We eat, therefore, unleavened bread and bitter herbs on Passover in memory of what has happened unto us, and leave [on Sukkot] our houses in order to dwell in tabernacles, as inhabitants of deserts do that are in want of comfort. We shall thereby remember that this has been our condition. . . .

We join to the Feast of Tabernacles the Feast of the Eighth Day, in order to complete our rejoicing, which cannot be perfect in booths, but in comfortable and well-built houses.

As regards the Four Species [the branches of the palm tree, the citron, the myrtle, and the willows of the brook] our sages gave a reason for their use by way of Aggadic interpretation, the method of which is well known to those who are acquainted with the style of our sages. . . . I believe that the Four Species are a symbolical expression of our rejoicing that the Israelites changed the wilderness,

5. *Mahzor* in Miscellany. Ferrara [?], Italy. Circa 1470. See Chapter 9.

"A place with no grain or figs or vines, or pomegranates; there was not even water to drink" (Numbers 20.5), to a country full of fruit trees and rivers. In order to remember this we take the fruit which is the most pleasant of the fruit of the land, branches which smell best, most beautiful leaves, and also the best of herbs, i.e., the willows of the brook. These four kinds have also these three purposes: first, they were plentiful in those days in Palestine, so that everyone could easily get them. Secondly, they have a good appearance, they are green; some of them, viz., the citron and the myrtle, are also excellent as regards their smell, the branches of the palm tree and the willow having neither good nor bad smell. Thirdly, they keep fresh and green for seven days, which is not the case with peaches, pomegranates, asparagus, nuts, and the like.

Guide for the Perplexed 3.43[1]

⚘ ⚘ ⚘

THE WORLD IS BLESSED THROUGH ISRAEL

When the community of Israel is blessed all worlds are blessed. For this reason it was customary to go in procession round the altar on this festival [Tabernacles]. We have learnt in the book of Rab Hamnuna the Elder that the powers which are in charge of these plants receive each one their blessings of joy above only at this time, and the gladness of those above and of these trees below is all at this season, and so when Israel lift up these branches, all is roused to activity at this time and the community of Israel is blessed, so as to pour down blessings on the world. . . .

On the seventh day of Tabernacles the judgment of the world is finally sealed and the edicts are sent forth from the King, and God's might is aroused, and the "willows of the brook" depend on it, and we require to awaken the might which sends the rain and to go round the altar seven times and sate it with the water of Isaac, because the well of Isaac is filled with water, and then all the world is blessed with water. We therefore pray that the rain-giving power may be manifested, and afterwards destroy willow twigs, since judgment is closed on this day.

Zohar 31b–32a[2]

❦ ❦ ❦

HOLY GUESTS IN THE *SUKKAH*

When a man sits in this abode of the shadow of faith, the Divine Presence spreads her wings over him from above and Abraham and five other righteous ones make their abode with him. R. Abba said, "Abraham and five righteous ones [Isaac, Jacob, Joseph, Moses, and Aaron] and David with them. Hence it is written: 'You [plural] shall live in booths seven days' (Leviticus 23.42) . . . and a man should rejoice each day of the festival with these guests who abide with him." R. Abba further pointed out that first it says "you shall live" and then "all citizens in Israel [they] shall live in booths" (Leviticus 23.42). The first refers to the guests, and therefore Rab Hamnuna the Elder, when he entered the booth used to stand at the door inside and say, "Let us invite the holy guests and prepare a table," and he used to stand up and greet them, saying, "You shall live in booths seven days. Sit, most exalted guests, sit; sit, guests of faith, sit." He would then raise his hands in joy and say, "Happy is our portion, happy is the portion of Israel, as it is written: 'the Lord's portion is His people' (Deuteronomy 32.9)" and then he took his seat. The second "live" refers to "all citizens in Israel"; for he who has a portion in the Holy Land and holy people sits in the shadow of faith to receive the guests so as to rejoice in this world and the next. He must also gladden the poor, because the portion of those guests whom he invites must go to the poor. . . . R. Eleazar said, "The Torah does not demand of a man more than he can perform, as it says: 'Each with his own gift, according to the blessing that the Lord your God has bestowed upon you' (Deuteronomy 16.17). A man should not say, I will first satisfy myself with food and drink, and what is left I shall give to the poor, but the first of everything must be for the guests. And if he gladdens the guests and satisfies them, God rejoices with him."

Zohar 103b–104a[3]

❧ ❧ ❧

JOY IN THE SERVICE OF GOD
AARON HALEVI

Man is governed by the deeds that he does habitually, and all his thoughts and ideas are influenced by the work of his hands whether good or bad. Since God wished to bestow merit on His chosen people Israel, He gave them many *mitzvot* to perform, so that their souls would be occupied with meritorious actions all the day. One of these *mitzvot* that He commanded us which is designed to mold our thoughts is that of *tefillin.* . . .

Similarly, the *lulav* and its three accompanying species are inspired by the same concept. The days of the festival [of Sukkot] mark a time of great joy for Israel, being the season of the ingathering of the corn and the fruits of the tree. . . . God therefore ordained a festival at this time [of natural rejoicing] in order to direct their principal joy to Him. Since such rejoicing has a tendency to lead men after material desires and to divert him from spiritual thoughts at that time, the Almighty commanded us to take in our hands things that would remind us that all joy should be turned towards Him, to pay Him homage. It was His will that the objects reminding us of our spiritual obligations should also evoke joy in keeping with the joyous time. . . . and it is well known that the Four Species by their nature make the hearts of all who gaze on them to rejoice.

Moreover, these Four Species are symbolic of something else. They are likened to the principal human limbs: the *etrog* resembles the heart, the seat of the mind, alluding to the service of the Creator with the mind; the *lulav* to the backbone, intimating that the entire body should be engaged in His service, may He be blessed; the myrtle is like the eyes to warn that one should not let his eyes stray on the day of the rejoicing of his heart; and the willow resembles the lips, signifying that one should control his speech and fear God even in the time of joy.

Sefer ha-Hinukh 285[4]

❧ ❧ ❧

THE HISTORIC ASSEMBLY ON SUKKOT
AARON HALEVI

We have been commanded that all the people of Israel, men, women, and children, shall assemble on the second day of the festival of Sukkot at the close of the sabbatical year, and that portions of the Book of Deuteronomy shall be read to them.

Of this assembly the Torah states: "Every seventh year, the year set for remission [*shemitah*], at the Feast of Booths, when all Israel comes to appear before the Lord your God in the place which He will choose, you shall read this Teaching aloud in the presence of all Israel. Gather the people—men, women, children, and the strangers in your communities—that they may hear and so learn to revere the Lord your God and to observe faithfully every word of this Teaching. Their children, too, who have not had the experience, shall hear and learn to revere the Lord your God as long as they live in the land which you are about to cross the Jordan to occupy" (Deuteronomy 31.10–13).

This is the commandment of *Hakhel*, which is mentioned in the Talmud, as in tractate Kiddushin wherein it is stated that, although *Hakhel* is a mandatory commandment dependent upon a prescribed time, its fulfillment is nonetheless incumbent also upon women, this being one exception to the general rule that women are exempt from mandatory commandments that are limited as to time.

The reason for this commandment is as follows: Since the whole essence of the people of Israel is the Torah, whereby they are distinguished from all other peoples meriting therewith life eternal and an everlasting delight which is unsurpassed by anything of this world, it is fitting that they should all assemble at an appointed time to hear its words, so that everyone, men, women and children, may enquire, "For what purpose have we all gathered together in this great assembly?"; whereupon the answer will be, "To hear the words of the Torah, which is our whole being, our splendor and our glory." . . .

The specific laws pertaining to this commandment, as expounded by our Sages, of blessed memory, are the following: It is the duty of the king to read before the people, the reading to take place in the

Women's Court of the Temple. He can read while sitting, but it is deemed praiseworthy if he reads while standing. He reads from the beginning of the Book of Deuteronomy. . . .

In what manner is the reading done? They blow the trumpets throughout Jerusalem and erect a large, wooden platform in the center of the Women's Court. The king seats himself upon it so that his reading could be heard, and all Israelites who have made the pilgrimage for the festival gather about him. The minister of the synagogue takes a Scroll of the Torah and gives it to the chief of the synagogue, and the chief of the synagogue gives it to the prefect, and the prefect gives it to the high priest, and the high priest gives it to the king. This procedure is followed in order to honor the Torah in the presence of the multitude of people. The king receives the Scroll while standing, and, if he wishes, seats himself, and opens the Scroll and pronounces the benediction customarily recited by all who read from the Torah in the synagogue. He then reads the chapters indicated above and pronounces the closing benediction as it is customarily recited in the synagogue. Following that he adds seven benedictions. . . .

This commandment is to be observed at the time that Israel is upon its land.

Sefer ha-Hinukh 612[5]

✻ ✻ ✻

THE LESSON OF THE *SUKKAH*
ISAAC ABOAB

The commandment to dwell in the *sukkah* is intended to teach us that a man must not put his trust in the size or strength or salutary conveniences of his house, even though it be filled with the best of everything; nor should he rely upon the help of any man, even though he be the lord of the land. But let him put his trust in Him whose word called the universe into being, for He alone is mighty and faithful, and He does not retract what He promises.

Menorat ha-Maor 3.6.1

❧ ❧ ❧

BOOTHS TEACH HUMILITY
SAMUEL BEN MEIR

Do not say in your heart, "My own power and the might of my own hand have won this wealth for me" (Deuteronomy 8.17); you should remember the Lord your God, as it is He who gives you strength to make progress. Therefore, the people leave [their] houses, which are full of everything good at the season of the ingathering, and dwell in booths, as a reminder of those who had no possessions in the wilderness and no houses in which to live. For this reason, the Holy One established the Feast of Tabernacles at the time of the ingathering from the threshing floor and the wine press, that the people should not be proud of their well-furnished houses.

Rashbam, *Leviticus* 23.43

❧ ❧ ❧

THE *SUKKAH* AS A MEMORIAL
MOSES BEN NAHMAN

" . . . that future generations may know that I made the Israelite people live in booths" (Leviticus 23.43). Rashi's explanation is [that the booths are] clouds of glory. In my opinion this is correct as it is the literal meaning. He ordered that the generations should know the great deed of God that He wondrously performed for them by causing them to dwell in clouds of glory. . . . As it has already been clarified that the cloud of glory was over them during the day and the pillar of fire at night (Exodus 13.21–22), it is merely said: "I made the Israelite people live in booths," that is to say: "I made for them clouds of My glory as booths to protect them."

At the beginning of the summer He commanded them about the memorial of the exodus from Egypt in its month and season; and He commanded about the memorial of the effective miracle which was performed for them during all the days of their stay in the desert,

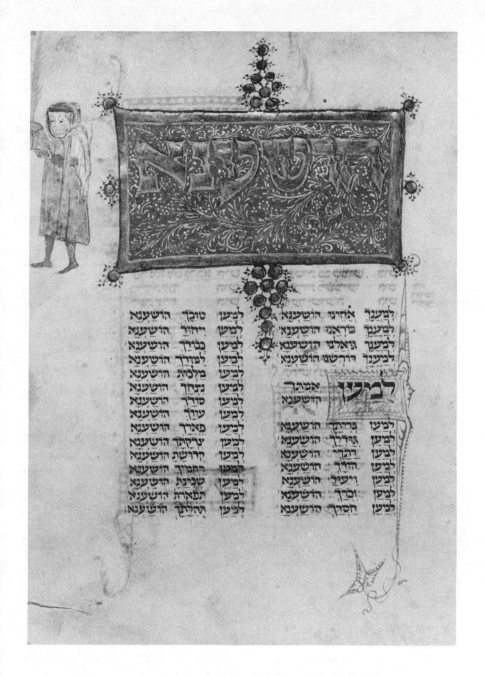

6. *Siddur* in Miscellany. Southern Germany. 14th century. See Chapter 9.

at the beginning of the rainy season. He who holds that they made actual booths for themselves, [it can be explained that] they began making them at the onset of winter due to the cold, in accordance with the custom of [nomad] camps; therefore, He commanded them at that time. The memorial is that they will know and remember that they were in the desert for forty years where they did not enter any house nor did they find any city for residing; and God was with them and they lacked for nothing.

Ramban, *Leviticus* 23.43

※ ※ ※

SEVEN DAYS OF JOY
DON ISAAC ABRAVANEL

"After the ingathering from your threshing floor and your vat, you shall hold the Feast of Booths for seven days . . . in the place that the Lord will choose . . . and you shall have nothing but joy" (Deuteronomy 16.13–15). The reason one remains in Jerusalem for the Feast of Booths for seven days, while only one day for Passover and Shavuot, because it is said [with respect to Sukkot], "and you shall have nothing but joy." This implies that on the festivals of Passover and Shavuot when you make the pilgrimage [to Jerusalem] your mind is preoccupied with the crops in your field, but now, when you have gathered them in and the Lord your God has blessed all your crops and all your undertakings, you can surely rejoice without any other thought. . . .

Regarding Passover it is said that after the first day "in the morning you may start back on your journey home" (Deuteronomy 16.7), as one was then concerned about his crops; for the same reason Shavuot is observed only one day so that one need not tarry in Jerusalem and can return to gather his crops. Surely now [on Sukkot] that you have gathered in [the produce] from your threshing floor and your vat, it is proper that you remain in Jerusalem all seven days as your mind will not be anxious at all, "and you shall have nothing but joy."

Furthermore, the statement "and you shall have nothing but joy" is an assurance that if one is joyous and glad on the Feast of Booths, he will be happy and kindhearted throughout the year. If you will be sad at the beginning of the year, "in anguish shall you eat" (Genesis 3.17). This is the nature of reality: he who is satisfied with his portion will gain joy and happiness.

Perush ha-Torah, Deuteronomy 16

❧ 5 ❧

SUKKOT AND SIMHAT TORAH
IN JEWISH LAW

❧ ❧ ❧

The continuous development of Jewish law based on the Torah, the Talmud, and the later writings of Jewish sages created a large and diffuse corpus of literature by the twelfth century, when it was codified by Moses Maimonides (1135–1204), renowned philosopher and legalist, in his *Mishneh Torah* ("Second Torah"). This monumental work presented Jewish laws, collected from numerous sources, in an organized and logical sequence, thus facilitating their observance. The *Mishneh Torah*, although not completely acceptable to all rabbis, had to be taken into consideration in practically every discussion of Jewish law.

Halakhic literature continued to grow at a rapid pace. By the sixteenth century, there were a number of compendiums of laws that guided Jews in the Diaspora. The systematic compilation of a code of Jewish law, entitled *Shulhan Arukh* ("Prepared Table"), by Joseph Karo (1488–1575), together with the additions of Moses Isserles (c. 1515–1572), is the authoritative basis for traditional practices to this day. *Orah Hayyim* ("Way of Life"), the first part of this massive work, deals with the obligations of daily life, including the laws pertaining to the festivals. Solomon Ganzfried (c. 1800–1886) adapted the *Shulhan Arukh* for everyday usage in his *Kitzur Shulhan Arukh* ("Abridged Prepared Table").

The selections from the *Mishneh Torah* and the *Kitzur Shulhan Arukh* in this chapter point up both the variety and the complexity of the laws of Sukkot. There are detailed instructions concerning the construction and use of the *sukkah*, and the selection and usage of the Four Species. The selected examples of the Sukkot laws that follow should be read for edification; they are not necessarily intended as rules for practical guidance.

⚹ ⚹ ⚹

LAWS CONCERNING THE BOOTH
MOSES MAIMONIDES

The standard dimensions of a booth for the Feast of Tabernacles are as follows: its height must be not less than ten handbreadths* nor more than twenty cubits,† and its area must be not less than seven handbreadths square. One may, however, add to this minimum area. . . .

If a booth has many doors and windows in its walls, it is nevertheless valid—provided that none of the doorways is more than ten cubits wide—even if the total of open space exceeds the total of boarded space. If, however, one of the openings, be it even an opening with "the shape of a doorway," is more than ten cubits wide, the total of open space may not exceed the total of boarded space.

If the inside height is more than twenty cubits, but the palm leaves

---

* handbreadth = the width of four fingers joined, about 2½ to 4 inches.
† cubit = the distance from the elbow to the tip of the middle finger, approximately 18 inches.

in the covering hang down to within twenty cubits of the floor and the shade cast by them exceeds the sunlight which they let through, they are regarded as part of a thick roof, and the booth is valid.

Anything whatsoever is fit to serve as the wall of a booth, for all that is required is a partition of some kind. . . .

If a booth is covered with something which did not grow from the soil, or has not been detached from the soil, or is susceptible to ritual impurity, the booth is invalid. If, however, the covering, though still in violation of the law, consists of something that merely withers or sheds its leaves, or has an evil odor, the booth is valid, for the sages forbade the use of this kind of covering only as a safeguard, lest a person should be tempted to leave the booth and go elsewhere. One should also take care that the twigs and leaves in the covering do not hang down to within ten handbreadths of the ground, as this would make the booth uncomfortable to sit in.

If the booth is covered with green vegetables which shrivel up as they wither and are reduced to almost nothing, the space they occupy is regarded as empty air space and they themselves as nonexistent, even though at the moment they are still fresh.

Planks less than four handbreadths wide may be used to cover a booth, even if they have been planed smooth. If they are four or more handbreadths wide, they may not be used, even if they have not been planed smooth—this being a precaution, lest one should sit under an ordinary house ceiling and imagine that he is sitting in a booth.

Any kind of booth made in conformity with the law, even if not made specifically for the purpose of fulfilling the commandment, is valid, as long as it was made to provide shade.

If a garment is spread over the booth covering—or underneath it, for protection against falling leaves—the booth becomes invalid. If the garment is spread to beautify the booth, the booth remains valid. Similarly, if a booth has a valid covering, and this is subsequently decorated with various kinds of fruits, delicacies, and utensils in order to beautify it, the booth remains valid, whether these decorations are suspended from the covering itself or from the walls.

How is the commandment to dwell in a booth to be observed? One should eat, drink, and reside in the booth day and night throughout the whole of the seven days of the festival, exactly as one resides in his house during the rest of the year. During these seven days one should regard his house as a temporary home and the booth as his permanent home, in accordance with the verse "You shall live in booths seven days" (Leviticus 23.42). Thus one's finest utensils and bedspreads should be kept in the booth, as well as one's festive drinking vessels, like goblets and cups. Eating vessels, like pots and dishes, however, should be kept outside the booth. One's candelabrum should normally be kept in the booth, but if the booth is small, it may be left outside.

Both by day and by night, one should eat, drink, and sleep in the booth throughout the whole of the seven days. No meal may be eaten outside the booth on any of the seven days, unless it is merely a casual snack—an egg's bulk, or a little less, or a little more—and not even a casual nap may be taken outside the booth. It is permissible, however, to drink water or eat fruit outside the booth, but one who is strict with himself and does not drink even water outside the booth is to be commended.

It is obligatory to eat in the booth on the first night of the festival. Even if one eats as little as an olive's bulk of bread, he has fulfilled his duty. Therefore the matter is optional: if one wishes to eat a regular meal, he must eat it in the booth, but if he prefers to eat only fruit or parched ears outside the booth during the remainder of the seven days, he may do so. This is thus analogous to the law concerning the eating of unleavened bread during Passover.

Throughout the seven days, one should do his reading inside the booth, but if he wishes to cogitate and examine the implications of what he has read, he should do it outside the booth, in order that his mind should be more at ease. Prayers may be recited both in the booth and outside. . . .

Whenever one enters a booth during the seven days in order to sit in it, he should recite the following benediction before sitting down: "Blessed art Thou, O Lord our God, King of the universe, who has sanctified us with Thy commandments and commanded us to dwell in a booth." On the first night of the festival, one should recite first the benediction for the booth and then the seasonal benediction. All the benedictions should be recited over a cup of wine. Hence first the sanctification benediction is recited standing, then the benediction ending with "to dwell in a booth," whereupon one sits down, and then the seasonal benediction. This procedure, with the sanctification benediction recited standing as just explained, was the one customarily observed on the first night of the Feast of Tabernacles by my teachers and the other rabbis of Spain.

Nowadays, when festivals are celebrated for two days instead of one, one should dwell in a booth for eight days instead of seven. On the eighth day, which is also the first day of the Concluding Festival of Solemn Assembly, one must dwell in the booth but need not recite the benediction concluding with "to live in a booth."

Mishneh Torah, Book of Seasons 6.4–6[1]

❧ ❧ ❧

LAWS CONCERNING THE PALM BRANCH
MOSES MAIMONIDES

The "branches of palm trees" (Leviticus 23.40) mentioned in Scripture are newly sprouted shoots of a palm tree, before their leaves spread out on both sides. Such a shoot resembles a scepter and is termed *lulav*.

The "product of goodly trees" (ibid.) mentioned in Scripture is the citron. The "boughs of leafy trees" (ibid.) mentioned in Scripture refer to the myrtle whose leaves cover its twigs—i.e., it has three or more leaves growing from each bud. If, however, there are two leaves opposite each other at one level and a third leaf above them, the myrtle is not regarded as "leafy" but is termed wild myrtle.

The "willows of the brook" (ibid.) mentioned in Scripture do not signify every tree growing near a brook, but only a definite species known by this name. Its leaf is elongated like a brook and has a smooth edge, and its twig is red. It is known as *aravah* (willow). Most trees of this species grow beside brooks, and that is why Scripture speaks of "willows of the brook"; but such a tree is valid even if it grows in the desert or in the mountains.

The Four Species enumerated above constitute a single commandment, and the absence of any one of them renders the others invalid. The four together are termed "the commandment concerning the *lulav*." The number of species may be neither diminished nor increased, and if one species is unobtainable, another similar species may not be substituted for it.

The commandment is best performed by binding together the *lulav*, the myrtle, and the willow, so that the three of them form a single bunch.

How many units of each kind should be taken? One *lulav*, one citron, two twigs of willow, and three twigs of myrtle. If one wishes to increase the number of myrtle twigs in order to make the bunch larger, he may do so, this being regarded as an embellishment of the commandment. The number of units of the other species, however, may be neither increased nor diminished.

What is the minimum length of each of the several species? The *lulav* must be not less than four handbreadths long, and remains valid however much longer it may be. It is measured from the tip of its spine, not from the tip of its leaves. The myrtle and the willow must be not less than three handbreadths long, and remain valid however much longer they may be. Even if each twig has only three fresh leaves on it, it is valid, provided that these are at the tip of the twig. If the *lulav* is bound in a bunch, the spine of the *lulav* must protrude a handbreadth or more above the myrtle and the willow.

The minimum size of a citron is that of an egg, and it remains valid however much larger it may be.

The normative method of fulfilling the commandment is to lift up the bunch of three species in the right hand and the citron in the left, and to move them to and fro and up and down, shaking the *lulav* three times in each direction.

Thus one should move the *lulav* forward and vibrate its tip three times, then move it back and vibrate its tip three times, and then repeat the process during the upward and downward motion.

One who is obligated to hear the ram's horn and to dwell in a booth is also obligated to take up the *lulav*; one who is exempt from hearing the ram's horn and dwelling in a booth is likewise exempt from taking up the *lulav*. A minor who knows how to shake the *lulav* is obligated, on the authority of the Scribes, to take up the *lulav*, as part of his training in the observance of commandments.

A law transmitted by Moses from Sinai states that another willow used to be brought into the Temple, in addition to the willow contained in the *lulav*, and that one did not fulfill his duty by bringing in only the willow in the *lulav*. Even a single leaf on a single twig was sufficient for this purpose. . . . Since this willow is not explicitly mentioned in Scripture, it is not taken up nowadays on each of the seven days—as a memorial of the Temple usage—but only on the seventh day. What is the procedure? One or more twigs of willow, apart from the willow in the *lulav*, are taken up and struck against the ground or against an article of furniture two or three times. No benediction need be recited, because the procedure is merely a custom introduced by the Prophets.

If any part of it is missing, the citron is ineligible for use, however small the missing part may be. If its nipple—that is, the smaller tip where the knob is located—has been removed, the citron is ineligible for use. If the stalk by which the citron was attached to the tree is removed from the base of the citron, leaving a depression, the citron is again ineligible for use.

Although a commandment prescribes rejoicing on all festivals, there was a day of special rejoicing in the Temple during the festival of Tabernacles, in accordance with the verse, "You shall rejoice before the Lord your God seven days" (Leviticus 23.40). What was the procedure? On the eve of the first day of the festival, a raised section for women and a lower section for men were set up in the Temple—to insure that the sexes did not mix. Rejoicing began at the termination of the first day of the festival; on each of the intermediate days it began after the regular afternoon sacrifice had been offered, and went on for the rest of the day and the whole of the following night.

What form did this rejoicing take? Fifes sounded, and harps, lyres, and cymbals were played. Whoever could play a musical instrument did so, and whoever could sing, sang. Others stamped their feet, slapped their thighs, clapped their hands, leaped, or danced, each one to the best of his ability, while songs and hymns of praise were being recited. However, this rejoicing did not take place on the Sabbath or on the first day of the festival.

Rejoicing in the fulfillment of a commandment and in love for God who had prescribed the commandment is a supreme act of divine worship. One who refrains from participation in such rejoicing deserves to be punished, as it is said: "Because you would not serve the Lord thy God, in joy and gladness over the abundance of everything" (Deuteronomy 28.47). If one is arrogant and stands on his own dignity, and thinks only of self-aggrandizement on such occasions, he is both a sinner and a fool. It was this that Solomon had in mind when he uttered the warning: "Glorify not thyself in the presence of the King" (Proverbs 25.6). Contrariwise, one who humbles and makes light of himself on such occasions, achieves greatness and honor, for he serves the Lord out of sheer love. . . . True greatness and honor are achieved only by rejoicing before the Lord, as it is said: "King David leaping and dancing before the Lord" (II Samuel 6.16).

Mishneh Torah, Book of Seasons 6.7–8[2]

❦ ❦ ❦

LAWS CONCERNING THE *SUKKAH*
SOLOMON GANZFRIED

It is a duty to build the *sukkah* on the day immediately following the Day of Atonement, even if it is the eve of the Sabbath, for when one has an opportunity to fulfill a commandment he should not delay it. He should select a clean site on which to erect it. Every man is obligated to participate in the building of the booth and in the laying of its roof covering, even if he be an eminent personage, since it is an honor for one personally to fulfill a precept. One should be zealous to beautify the booth and to adorn it with attractive vessels and fine dining couches, according to his means.

Since not everyone is well versed in the many diversified laws concerning the walls of the booth, it is obligatory to make complete, strong walls so that the wind will not shake them nor extinguish the candles; if one does not have sufficient [boards or other materials] for the walls, it is preferable that he make three complete rather than four incomplete walls.

If one possesses the means, it is incumbent upon him to have a booth with a roof that can open and close on hinges, so that he may close it when it rains and open it when the rains cease; thus the thatching will remain dry for the proper observance of the precept.

There are also many laws concerning the roof covering. We observe the custom of covering [the booth] with branches of trees or with canes that grow in the soil and are detached from it.

It is necessary to place [sufficient] covering so that there will be more shade than sunlight [entering the booth]; if there is more sunlight than shade, it is unfit for use according to the Torah. Therefore, it is necessary to be careful to place an amount enabling the shade to predominate even after the covering dries up. It is also essential that there be no open space of three handbreadths in any one place. At the beginning, there should be a little open space in the thatching sufficient to render the stars visible; nevertheless, even if it is so opaque that the stars are not seen, it is fit for use. However, if the booth is so densely covered that heavy rains cannot penetrate inside, it is considered like a house and unfit for use.

Concerning a booth with a [solid] roof that can be opened, the roof must be raised before the laying of the covering. If subsequently one closes the roof and then opens it again, no harm is done; it is tantamount to spreading a sheet on top [as a protection during a rainfall, for example] and then removing it. In every circumstance, one should strictly observe [the precept] that the roof is open at the commencement of the festival. Furthermore, it is essential that the roof be wide so that it is perpendicular with the wall of the booth; if it is not perpendicular but inclines slightly over the booth covering —even though this may not be enough to invalidate the booth— one should avoid sitting in the place over which the roof slopes.

It is not permitted to use the wood of the booth, both of the walls and of the covering, until after Simhat Torah, as they were set aside for [the fulfillment of] a religious duty; it is even forbidden to take a splinter for a toothpick. The decorations of a booth, even if they fall down, are also prohibited from being used.

On the afternoon before Sukkot one should not partake of food in order that he may dine in the booth with a [hearty] appetite. On the day prior to Sukkot one should increase [his deeds of] charity.

One should maintain the booth respectfully, as precepts are not to be regarded with irreverence. Therefore, one should not bring into it unbefitting vessels, such as pots, water pails, receptacles in which flour is held, kneading troughs, cooking kettles, frying pans, mortars, and the like. After the meal, the plates should be removed, but drinking cups may remain in the booth.

Dining in the *sukkah* on the first night [of Sukkot] is an obligation requiring the eating of bread, at least an amount equal to the size of an olive. Even if one is distraught, he is obligated to eat in the booth. If it rains and it appears that the rain will stop in an hour or two, he should wait [until it ceases], then pronounce the Sanctification and eat in the booth in the proper manner. If he sees that the rain is not stopping, or if he waited and it did not cease, he pronounces the Sanctification and the blessing "who has granted us life" (*sheheheyanu*); he must be aware that this blessing applies also to the *sukkah*, but he need not recite the blessing "to dwell in a booth." He then washes his hands, blesses the bread, eats a piece of bread about the size of an olive, and proceeds into the house to finish his meal.

Concerning sleeping in a booth during a light rain that disturbs one's sleep, one is permitted to leave. If he went into his house and lay down to sleep, and later the rain ceased, he is not duty bound to return to the booth the entire night; he should sleep in his house until morning.

One who is exempted from the *sukkah* and does not leave it is called a simpleton. He neither receives merit for it, nor is he permitted to pronounce the blessing ["to live in a booth"], since it would constitute a benediction said in vain.

Kitzur Shulhan Arukh 134–135

❦ ❦ ❦

LAWS CONCERNING THE PALM BRANCH AND THE OTHER SPECIES
SOLOMON GANZFRIED

It is a custom in Israel that a purchaser of a citron and palm branch who is not knowledgeable [about them] should show them to a rabbi to ascertain whether or not they are ritually fit, since there are many diversified laws applying to them.

One should be scrupulous to purchase a new [fresh] *lulav*, inasmuch as a dry one is unfit for use except in an emergency.

If one does not have Four Species of choice quality, it is preferable that he fulfill his obligation with those of a friend. However, he is duty bound to possess his own Four Species, according to his means, with which to perform the waving ceremony during *Hallel* and for the circuits [around the synagogue].

One should hold the *lulav* wreath in his right hand with the palm branch spine facing him and the *etrog* in his left hand. The citron must be held in its growing position, that is, the stalk cut from the tree should be on the bottom and the pestlelike protuberance on top. Since a benediction must be recited for all commandments before performing them, when taking the citron before reciting the blessing, one should hold it in the reverse position—the stalk on top and the protuberance on bottom—thereby he will not yet be performing the commandment. He pronounces the blessing "on

7. *Mahzor.* Ulm, Germany. 1459/1460. See Chapter 9.

taking the palm branch" while standing. (Since the *lulav* is the tallest [of the Four Species] and is considered the most important, the composite wreath is called by its name.) On the first day he also recites the benediction "Who has granted us life." If the first day [of Sukkot] occurs on the Sabbath, when the *lulav* is not held, then "Who has granted us life" is said on the second day. After the blessings are recited, the position of the citron is reversed; it is drawn close to the palm branch so that there is no space between them. They are then waved in four directions: east, south, west and north, [also] upwards and downwards.

During the entire festival, after the additional service a Scroll of the Law is brought customarily to the reader's desk; the holy ark is left open until after the *Hoshanot* [prayers for deliverance] are said and the Scroll is then returned [to the ark]. Everyone with a citron and palm branch circles the reader's desk, where the Scroll of the Law is held during the recital of the *Hoshanot*. Daily one circuit is made; on the seventh day, Hoshana Rabbah, all the Scrolls of the Law are brought to the reader's desk and seven circuits are made, in commemoration of [the service in] the Temple, where daily they would encircle the altar once and on the seventh day seven times.

Kitzur Shulhan Arukh 136–137

✹ ✹ ✹

LAWS OF HOSHANA RABBAH, SHEMINI ATZERET AND SIMHAT TORAH
SOLOMON GANZFRIED

It is customary to remain awake the entire night before Hoshana Rabbah, the fifth of the intermediary days [of Sukkot], to study the Torah according to the [special] printed text; for on Hoshana Rabbah judgment is passed on water, and man's whole life depends on water. This is also the last day of the festival, and everything depends upon the conclusion. In the morning more [than the usual number of] candles are lit in the synagogue as on the Day of Atonement, and the cantor wears a white robe.

It is a custom [instituted] by the prophets that on this day everyone takes a willow in addition to the willow in the *lulav* wreath. The strict fulfillment of the precept requires many leaves and long stalks. It is a beautiful custom to take five willow stems and bind them together with palm branch leaves.

At the conclusion of the reading of the *Hoshanot*, it [the willow wreath] is waved and stroked against the floor five times; this number is adequate even if the leaves are not thereby lessened. After the striking it should not be thrown on the floor, so as to avoid profaning the precept. It is best to save it and then cast it into a fire on which *matzot* are baked; since it was used for one precept, let it be utilized for another.

On the night of Shemini Atzeret one should wait until nightfall before pronouncing the Sanctification; the blessing "who has granted us life" is added since it is a festival in its own right. The benediction "to live in a booth" is not said, because in the prayers and in the sanctification "the Eighth Day, this Festival of Solemn Assembly" is recited; if the blessing "to live in a booth" were recited, it would be a contradiction in terms. On the night of Shemini Atzeret and during the entire day one eats in the booth.

The last day of the festival, which is also Shemini Atzeret, is called Simhat Torah. The reading of the Pentateuch is completed on it, and we rejoice therewith. Following the *Amidah* in the evening service, circuits [with the Scrolls of the Law] are made; the Scrolls are then returned to the ark, except one from which three men read the scriptural portion "This is the blessing . . ." (Deuteronomy 33.1–17). After the circuits in the daytime, three Scrolls of the Law are left out [of the ark]; in one Scroll the scriptural portion "This is the blessing . . ." up to "The ancient God is a refuge" (Deuteronomy 33.27) is read several times; at the end, all the children are called up [to the Torah reading], and it is appropriate that the eldest recites the blessing and the others listen; then the portion "The angel who has redeemed me from all harm—bless the lads . . ." (Genesis 48.16) is read for them. Next, the "bridegroom of the Law" is called up, and he reads from "The ancient God is a refuge" to the conclusion (Deuteronomy 34.12). The "bridegroom of Genesis" reads in the second Scroll, and then half-*Kaddish* is said. The *maftir* [reads the portion of the Prophets after he] reads in the third Scroll. It is customary in many places to be meticulous in calling up a highly esteemed person as the "bridegroom of the Law."

It is customary for the "bridegroom of the Law" and the "bridegroom of Genesis" to pledge contributions [to charity] and to invite their friends to a feast for rejoicing to mark the completion of the reading of the Torah and its commencement anew.

Kitzur Shulhan Arukh 138

6

SUKKOT AND SIMHAT TORAH
LITURGY

The liturgy of the three pilgrimage festivals—Pesah, Shavuot, and Sukkot—is basically similar, although each has its own distinctive elements. Likewise, each of these holidays has special readings from the Torah.

Since the Festival of Tabernacles, also called *Zeman Simhatenu,* Season of Our Rejoicing, is a period of joyous thanksgiving and reverent exuberance, these motifs predominate in the additional prayers and *piyyutim* (poetical hymns) for those days. *Hallel* (a selection of psalms of rejoicing) is recited as on all festivals.

The rich Sukkot symbolism gave rise to meditations or introductory prayers when one is entering the *sukkah* and on holding the *etrog* and *lulav.*

Hoshanot, supplications for divine deliverance, mostly composed by the great ninth-century liturgical poet Eleazar Kalir, are unique to Sukkot and an integral part of the service. On Hoshana Rabbah, the Great Hosanna, many *Hoshanot* are chanted during the seven processions encircling the synagogue while the Four Species are held aloft by the congregants.

Yizkor, the memorial prayer, which is recited also on the other two festivals and on the Day of Atonement, and *Geshem*, the prayer for rain, are features of Shemini Atzeret.

Over eight hundred *piyyutim* in Hebrew, Aramaic, Ladino, Yiddish, and Judeo-Arabic were written for recital on Simhat Torah, much more than for any other festival. Of the above number, 250 hymns were composed for chanting during the circuits with the Scrolls of the Law.

The *hatan Torah* (bridegroom of the Law), and the *hatan Bereshit* (bridegroom of Genesis) are called to the Torah reading with elaborate introductions befitting those whom the congregation honors with these titles.

The entire Sukkot festival is marked by cheerful worship voicing gratitude for the Lord's bounty, and reaffirming love of His sacred Law.

⚜ ⚜ ⚜

THE WELCOME TO GUESTS
IN THE *SUKKAH*

The cabalist Isaac Luria (1534–1572) established the custom, based on the Zohar, *of extending an invitation to "holy guests" to enter the sukkah. The elaborate invitation is concluded with a special mention of one of the "holy guests," as on each of the seven festival days a different one is invited.*

Enter, holy guests from on high, enter, hallowed fathers, to take your place under the protecting cover of exalted faith in the Holy One, blessed be He. Enter Abraham, and with you also Isaac, Jacob, Moses, Aaron, Joseph, and David.

I am spiritually ready and prepared to fulfill the command of dwelling in a booth as the Creator, blessed be His Name, commanded me to do in the words "You shall dwell in booths seven days, all that are Israelite born shall dwell in the booths, in order that your generations may know that I made the children of Israel dwell in booths when I brought them out of the land of Egypt."

Take your place, take your place, guests from on high. Take your place, take your place, hallowed guests. Take your place, take your place, guests of exalted faith under the protection of the Holy One, blessed be He. A holy privilege is this our lot and the lot of Israel, for it is written that "the portion of the Lord is His people, Jacob the lot of His inheritance." It is our precious privilege in carrying out this command to glorify the sacred name of Thy hallowed unity and Thy indwelling presence among us and among all Israel.

"Let the beauty of the Lord our God be upon us; establish for us the work of our hands, the work of our hands establish Thou it."

I invite to my meal exalted spiritual guests, Abraham, Isaac, Jacob, Joseph, Moses, Aaron, and David.

Translated by David de Sola Pool[1]

❦ ❦ ❦

MEDITATION ON ENTERING
THE *SUKKAH*

This meditation or introductory prayer is recited, as one enters the sukkah, *to invoke God's acceptance of the performance of this commandment.*

Lord God, and God of our fathers, this command of dwelling in the tabernacle we are fulfilling with reverence and love for the divine unity of Thy holy name, blessed be Thou. May it be Thy will that in Thy recognition of this Thou wilt set Thy Divine Presence among us and spread over us Thy Tabernacle of Peace. As the eagle stirs its nest, so mayest Thou in the empyrean o'er our heads strengthen us from the sublimity of Thy pure and hallowed glory.

For those who know hunger and thirst mayest Thou give food and drink that shall not fail. Implant in me, Thy servant, the desire to follow the tenor toward life. "Wash me thoroughly from guilt and cleanse me from sin." I have gone forth from my home to this taber-nacle because I would walk firmly in the way of Thy commandments wherever they may take me.

Lord, pour out on me Thy great blessings and give me life, and when the time must come that I shall leave this world, may mine be the merit of dwelling in the cover of Thy protecting wings. Yet may it be my lot to be sealed in the Book of Life on earth for many days to come, and living in the Holy Land in reverent service of Thee. Blessed evermore be the Lord. Amen. Amen.

Translated by David de Sola Pool[2]

❧ ❧ ❧

PRAYER FOR SUKKOT

In the Reform ritual, the reader offers this prayer at the evening service of Sukkot.

Creator of the universe, we come before Thee on this harvest festival to extol Thy greatness and goodness. Thou art revealed to us in the glorious promise of spring, in the mysterious power of summer's growth, and in the rich fulfillment of autumn's harvest.

In this season of the year, when our fathers had gathered the fruits of the field, they made joyous pilgrimage to Thy sanctuary to voice their gratitude for Thy loving care. To us today, as to our fathers of old, Thou art the fountain from which all blessings flow. In all the experiences of life, we recognize that Thy guiding hand establishes our work and that Thy love lifts our lives to nobler effort.

May the inspiration of this day strengthen our faith in Thee. Purify our spirits that in our daily tasks we may be conscious of Thy presence. As when we plant so when we reap, may we turn our thoughts to Thee and to Thy plan for the children of men. Help us to see that no work truly prospers unless it bring blessing to other lives, and no gain truly enriches if it add not to the happiness of others. Grant that we may never seek to dispossess others of what they have planted, nor build our joy on the misfortune of our fellow-men. Help us so to live that when we shall have gathered our final harvest, many shall rise up and call us blessed.

Union Prayer Book[3]

⚘ ⚘ ⚘

PALMS AND MYRTLES
אאמיר אותך סלה
ELEAZAR KALIR

This beautiful piyyut (liturgical hymn) *is chanted in some congregations in the morning service of the first day of Sukkot.*

Thy praise, O Lord, will I proclaim
In hymns unto Thy glorious Name.
O Thou Redeemer, Lord and King,
Redemption to Thy faithful bring!
Before Thine altar they rejoice
With branch of palm, and myrtle-stem,
To Thee they raise the prayerful voice—
Have mercy, save and prosper them.

May'st Thou in mercy manifold,
Dear unto Thee Thy people hold,
When at Thy gate they bend the knee,
And worship and acknowledge Thee.
Do Thou their heart's desire fulfill,
Rejoice with them in love this day,
Forgive their sins, and thoughts of ill,
And their transgressions cast away.

They overflow with prayer and praise
To Him, who knows the future days.
Have mercy Thou, and hear the prayer
Of those who palms and myrtles bear.
Thee day and night they sanctify
And in perpetual song adore,
Like to the heavenly host, they cry
"Blessed art Thou for evermore."

Translated by Alice Lucas[4]

℀ ℀ ℀

GOD'S TABERNACLE
אז היתה חנית סכו
ELEAZAR KALIR

*In this poem, which is included in the morning ritual of the first day
of Sukkot, there is a comparison between God's tabernacle—the
Temple in Jerusalem—and the festival booth. The original Hebrew
verses consist of six stanzas of six lines each; the following is a partial
and free translation.*

Where flaming angels walk in pride,
Where ministers of light abide,
Where cavalries of heaven ride,
Where souls have rest at eventide,
     There, 'mid the sapphire and the gold,
     God's tabernacle rose of old.

Yet here, as in a mead aflower,
Here, as in a bridal bower,
Here, where songs of praise and power,
Wreathe Him, every day and hour,
     Here, in an earthly booth as well
     His glory did not spurn to dwell.
              Translated by Theodor H. Gaster[5]

℀ ℀ ℀

THY CLOUD ENFOLDED THEM
יפי עניניך סככת
JEHIEL BEN ISAAC

*This poem reflects the tradition which compares the sukkah to the
"clouds of glory" that protected the Israelites when they departed
from Egypt and wandered in the desert. Composed by Jehiel ben
Isaac of Zulpich (thirteenth century), it is recited on the second
evening of Sukkot.*

Thy cloud enfolded them, as if that they
Were shelter'd in a booth; redeem'd and free,
They saw Thy glory as a canopy
Spread o'er them as they marched upon their way.

And when dryshod they through the sea had gone,
They praised Thee and proclaimed Thy unity;
And all the angels sang the antiphon,
And lifted up their voices unto Thee.
      "Our Rock, our Savior He"—thus did they sing—
      "World without end the Lord shall reign as King!"
                 Translated by Theodor H. Gaster[6]

❧ ❧ ❧

SAVE THOU US
כהושעת אדם
MENAHEM BEN MACHIR

On each day of Sukkot during the period of the Temple, the priests and the people encircled the altar, carrying the Four Species and reciting, "We beseech Thee, O Lord, save now! We beseech Thee, O Lord, make us now to prosper!" (Psalms 118.25). On the seventh day, Hoshana Rabbah, seven circuits were made. This practice is now continued in synagogues while Hoshanot *(derived from* hosha na, *"please save") are chanted. These litanies of deliverance are in the form of alphabetical acrostics. Although this one was written by an eleventh-century poet, most of these prayers in the Ashkenazic ritual are attributed to Eleazar Kalir. This and the following two selections are included in the* Hoshanot.

As Thou hast saved and shielded the first man, the work of Thy hands, and on the holy Sabbath let him find atonement and grace, so save Thou us. . . .

As Thou hast saved in Thine eternal shrine Solomon and his people who sought Thy favor with their festival of twice seven days, so save Thou us.

As Thou hast saved those who returned redeemed from exile in Babylon when they read from Thy Torah each day of this festival, so save Thou us.

As Thou hast saved those who rejoiced Thee in rebuilding the Temple renewed, in the holiness of which they carried the palm branch all seven days of this festival, so save Thou us.

As Thou hast saved those who even on the Sabbath beat the willow branch and laid boughs from Motsa at the altar's base, so save Thou us.

As Thou hast saved those who praised Thee with slender, long, lofty willow branches, and on leaving acclaimed the altar saying, "Beauty is thine, O altar," so save Thou us.

As Thou hast saved those who thanked Thee and steadfastly hoped in Thee, antiphonally chanting, "We are all His and our eyes are toward Him," so save Thou us.

As Thou hast saved those who with green shoots encircled Thy hewn-out altar, singing, "We beseech Thee, O Lord, to save us," so save Thou us.

Translated by David de Sola Pool[7]

8. Eating in a *sukkah*. From *Cérémonies et coutumes religieuses,* by Bernard Picart, Amsterdam, 1723. See Chapter 9.

❊ ❊ ❊

SAVE! O SAVE!
אל נא תעינו
ELEAZAR KALIR

O God! like sheep we all have gone astray;
From out Thy book wipe not our name away.
　　　Save! O save!

O God! sustain the sheep for slaughter; see
These dealt with wrathfully and slain for Thee.
　　　Save! O save!

O God! Thy sheep! the sheep whom Thou didst tend
In pasture; Thy creation and Thy friend.
　　　Save! O save!

O God! the poor among the sheep! Give heed:
Answer in time of favor to their need.
　　　Save! O save!

O God! they lift eyes to Thee, long sought
Let those who rise against Thee count as naught.
　　　Save! O save!

O God! they pour out water, worshiping—
Let them be drawing from salvation's spring.
　　　Save! O save!

O God! to Zion saviors send at length,
Endowed of Thee, and saved by Thy Name's strength.
　　　Save! O save!

O God! in garb of vengeance clad about,
In mighty wrath cast all deceivers out.
　　　Save! O save!

O God! and Thou wilt surely not forget
Her, by love-tokens bought, that hopeth yet.
　　　Save! O save!

O God! they seeking Thee with willow bough,
Regard their crying from Thine heaven now.
      Save! O save!

O God! as with a crown bless Thou the year;
Yea, Lord, my singing, I beseech Thee, hear.
      Save! O save!

Translated by Nina Salaman[8]

❧ ❧ ❧

A VOICE HERALDS

אומץ ישעך

ELEAZAR KALIR

O hark to the herald of sure salvation, I hear my beloved,
    his voice is high,
He comes with his myriads of hovering angels, on the
    Mount of Olives to stand and cry.

The herald comes—be the trumpet sounded, beneath his
    tread be the mountain cleft.
He knocks—at his radiant glance the hillside shall half
    from the eastward be rent and reft.

Fulfilled is his ancient prophetic saying, the herald is come
    with his saints around;
By all upon earth shall a still small voice to the uttermost
    islands be heard resound.

The seed he begot and the seed he reared hath been born
    as a child from its mother's womb.
But who then hath travailed and who brought forth, and
    a similar thing hath been told to whom?

The perfectly Pure hath achieved this marvel, what mortal
    hath seen such a wondrous way?
Salvation, redemption in one united, the earth bringing
    forth in a single day!

Though He in the heights and the depths be potent, yet
　　how can a nation at once be born?
The radiant One shall redeem His people, and then at the
　　evening it shall be morn!

And up to Mount Zion shall march her saviors, for Zion
　　hath travailed and bringeth forth,
A voice is proclaiming in all her borders, thy tent-place
　　enlarge both to south and north,

Thy dwelling extend unto far Damascus, thy sons and thy
　　daughters again to take,
Exult and be joyful, O rose of Sharon, beholding the sleepers
　　of Hebron wake.

Return unto me and be saved, O Israel, if only today ye
　　would hear my voice!
A man hath sprung forth, and the Branch his name is—
　　yea David himself, 'tis King David, rejoice!

Up, up! in the dust lie no longer buried! ye dwellers in
　　ashes awake and sing!
The desolate city shall rise imperial to hail as aforetime her
　　ransomed king.

The name of the wicked shall God extinguish—He grants
　　His anointed celestial grace.
Then make of our seed an eternal people, preserving forever
　　King David's race.

　　　　　　　　　　　　　　Translated by Israel Zangwill[9]

❧ ❧ ❧

PRAYER FOR RAIN
תפלת גשם
ELEAZAR KALIR

This supplication for rain, intoned on Shemini Atzeret, is an alpha-
betical acrostic in the original Hebrew. The six stanzas recount
righteous acts related to water by Abraham, Isaac, Jacob, Moses,

Aaron, and the twelve tribes; God is implored to send rain, a source
of blessing for the land, for their sake. By offering this prayer at
the beginning of the rainy season in Israel, Jews everywhere reaffirm
their eternal bond with the Holy Land.

Our God and God of our fathers,
Remember Abraham
Who yearned for Thy Presence,
Who was blessed by Thee
As a tree planted by streams of water,
Who was shielded by Thee
When in his faith
He braved fire and water.
> For his sake,
> O refuse not the gift of water.

Remember Isaac
Whose father was ready
To offer him as a sacrifice to Thee,
To shed his blood like water.
His own faith soared high,
Trusting in Thee
He dug to find wells of water.
> For his sake,
> O refuse not the gift of water.

Remember Jacob
Who trusted in Thee
When staff in hand
He crossed Jordan's water.
His heart was whole in faith
When he removed the stone
From the well of water,
When he wrestled with the angel,
The prince of fire and water.
Thou didst promise to be with him
Through fire and water.
> For his sake
> O refuse not the gift of water.

Remember Moses
Who was drawn in an ark

From the reeds by the edge of water.
He found for his flock
An ample store of water.
And when Thy chosen seed thirsted,
He struck the rock
And there came gushing water.
> For his sake,
> O refuse not the gift of water.

Remember the Temple priest;
In the holy rites of Atonement Day
He performed five ablutions.
In prayer he raised hands
Cleansed, sanctified in water.
He read the Law
And again poured on his flesh
The cleansing water.
He served in a lonely vigil
Remote from the people
Unstable as water.
> For his sake,
> O refuse not the gift of water.

Remember the twelve tribes of Israel
For whom Thou didst part water;
For whom Thou didst sweeten bitter water.
For Thee their sons were ever set
To shed their blood like water.
Turn to us for we are encircled
By many foes like water.
> For their sake,
> O grant Thy gift of water.

For Thou art the Lord our God who caused the wind to blow and the rain to descend:

For a blessing and not for a curse.   Amen.
For life and not for death.   Amen.
For abundance and not for famine.   Amen.

Translated by Ben Zion Bokser[10]

❦ ❦ ❦

THE SOUL OF SAGES
נשמת מלומדי מורשה
MENAHEM BEN MACHIR

*On Simhat Torah morning, this poem by the liturgist Menahem
ben Machir of Ratisbon (eleventh century) is chanted; it is a prayer
for those who study Torah. The six italicized lines are from Psalms
19.8–10.*

The soul of sages, learned in the Scroll,
    Their heritage, called children of the free—
    Lord, plant their soul a deathless plant to be:
His Law is perfect; it restores the soul.

Soul that art guarding treasures, now arise,
    Mighty and sinless, wise in words revealed;
    Ah, Lord, may this soul rule—and I be healed:
His word is true; it makes the simple wise.

The soul of sons of knowledge—with a voice
    Glad from the heart's well-being—shall impart
    The hidden secrets dwelling in the heart:
His laws are right; they make the heart rejoice.

Lord, let the soul of sons that hold aright
    The scales of justice—let their soul make clear
    Thy beauty, let it help the ears to hear;
Pure His command; unto the eyes a light.

Honor the soul of them that have for stay
    The knowledge of Thy Law within their heart;
    Support their footsteps lest they fall apart;
Unsullied is His fear; it stands for aye.

Those loved of Thee, the singing of their soul
    Exalting Thee, their hand a two-edged sword—
    For ever shall their soul extol Thy word:
True are His judgments; they are justice whole.

The soul of those assembled in their throng
   In lands of exile; all those left of Thine,
     Scattered—their soul shall praise Thee when they shine
Enthroned again where glory and grace belong,
Saying "Would, like the sea, our mouth were full of song!"
                Translated by Nina Salaman[11]

❧ ❧ ❧

WE BESEECH THEE, O LORD, SAVE US
אנא יי הושיעה נא

*This hymn by an unknown medieval poet is sung on Simhat Torah
during the seven circuits (hakkafot) with the Scrolls of the Law. The
first two stanzas are chanted during the first procession, one each
during the next five, and the last two stanzas are for the seventh
circuit.*

We beseech Thee, O Lord, save us.
We beseech Thee, O Lord, do Thou cause us to prosper.
O Lord, answer us in the day that we call.

God of all souls save us.
Thou who searchest hearts, do Thou cause us to prosper.
Though mighty Redeemer, answer us in the day that we call.

Thou who utterest righteousness, save us.
Thou who art clad in glory, do Thou cause us to prosper.
Everlasting and gracious God, answer us in the day that we call.

Thou who art pure and upright, save us.
Thou who pitiest the needy, do Thou cause us to prosper.
A good and bountiful Lord, answer us in the day that we call.

Thou who knowest our thoughts, save us.
Mighty and resplendent God, do Thou cause us to prosper.
Thou who art clothed in righteousness, answer us in the day that
   we call.

King of the universe, save us.
Source of light and majesty, do Thou cause us to prosper.
Thou who supportest the falling, answer us in the day that we call.

Thou who helpest the poor, save us.
O Redeemer and Deliverer, do Thou cause us to prosper.
Thou Rock of Ages, answer us in the day that we call.

Holy and revered God, save us.
Merciful and Compassionate One, do Thou cause us to prosper.
Thou who keepest the covenant, answer us in the day that we call.

Thou who upholdest the innocent, save us.
Sovereign of eternity, do Thou cause us to prosper,
Thou who art perfect in Thy ways, answer us in the day that we call.

Translated by Morris Silverman[12]

❧ ❧ ❧

SUMMONS TO THE
BRIDEGROOM OF THE LAW

מרשות האל

Before the reading of the last portion of the Pentateuch at the Simhat Torah morning service, the reader calls the one who is honored by being designated hatan Torah *with the chanting of the following summons, consisting of praise for the Torah and blessings for the bridegroom. A similar summons is included in the liturgy for the bridegroom of Genesis, who is called when the Torah cycle is commenced anew.*

With the permission of God, the great, powerful and awe-inspiring, and with the permission of the precious Torah, which is richer than fine gold and precious pearls, and with the permission of the holy and pure Sanhedrin, and with the permission of the learned heads and leaders of academies of the Torah, and with the permission of the elders and the young there assembled, I would open my lips in lauding hymn to sing the praise of God who dwells in light. He has given us life and sustained us in purifying reverence of Him, and has brought us to the happiness of this rejoicing in His Torah which gladdens the heart and enlightens the eyes. The Torah gives life with riches, honor, and glory. It makes happy those who walk in its ways of goodness and right. By adding to their strength it lengthens the days of those who love it and keep it with all its guiding commands, who, occupying themselves with it, cling to it with reverence and love.

May it be Thy will, Almighty God, to give life with Thy lovingkindness and crowning glory to ——, who has been chosen to complete the reading of the Torah. May he be singled out for a life with honor and happy companionship. Guide him in purity as he follows Thy light. Mayest Thou direct him and crown him by teaching him with Thy instruction of right. Keep him from all harm as Thou wilt give him Thy support, clearly sustaining him and bearing him ever forward. Give him delight and maintain him in that which is right among the people Thou has created. Draw him near to Thee in Thy love and keep him from all trouble and distress. Strengthen him, uphold him and be his support in his humility of spirit.

Arise, arise, ——, *Hatan Torah*, and give glory to God the great and awesome. From the God of awe may there come to you the reward of seeing children and children's children occupied with the Torah and carrying out its commandments among their cleansed and purified people. May you be privileged to share in the joy of rebuilding the Holy Temple, and may your countenance reflecting glory shine with righteousness. May we see the realization of the prophecy of Isaiah, who was filled with the spirit of counsel and insight and who said: "Rejoice with Jerusalem and be glad in her. Rejoice with her in joy all who are mourning for her" in grief and sorrow.

Arise, arise, ——, *Hatan Torah*, with the permission of all this holy congregation, and complete the reading of the Torah. Arise ——, *Hatan Torah*.

Translated by David de Sola Pool[13]

❦ ❦ ❦

THIS FEAST OF THE LAW
שישו ושמחו

Both this and the following selection are by unknown authors of the early Middle Ages and are sung after the Torah reading on Simhat Torah. Zangwill's lilting poetic translations have been set to music.

9. Booths. From *Jüdisches Ceremoniel*, by Paul C. Kirchner,
Nuremberg, 1726. See Chapter 9.

This Feast of the Law all your gladness display.
    Today all your homages render.
What profit can lead one so pleasant a way,
    What jewels can vie with its splendor?
Then exult in the Law on its festival day,
    The Law is our Light and Defender.

My God I will praise in a jubilant lay,
    My hope in Him never surrender,
His glory proclaim where His chosen sons pray,
    My Rock all my trust shall engender.
Then exult in the Law in its festival day,
    The Law is our Light and Defender.

My heart of Thy goodness shall carol alway.
    Thy praises I ever will render;
While breath is, my lips all Thy wonders shall say,
    Thy truth and Thy kindness so tender.
Then exult in the Law on its festival day,
    The Law is our Light and Defender.

            Translated by Israel Zangwill[14]

❧ ❧ ❧

THE ANGELS CAME A-MUSTERING
התקבצו מלאכים

The angels came a-mustering,
    A-mustering, a-mustering,
The angels came a-clustering
    Around the sapphire throne.

A-questioning of one another,
    Of one another, of one another,
A-questioning each one his brother
    Around the sapphire throne.

Pray who is he, and where is he,
    And where is he, and where is he,
Whose shining casts—so fair is he—
    A shadow on the throne?

Pray, who has up to heaven come,
    To heaven come, to heaven come,
Through all the circles seven come,
    To fetch the Torah down?

'Tis Moses up to heaven come,
    To heaven come, to heaven come,
Through all the circles seven come,
    To fetch the Torah down!

            Translated by Israel Zangwill[15]

7

HASIDIC TALES AND TEACHINGS

✣ ✣ ✣

Stories of the *Hasidim* are legion; they number in the thousands and fill many volumes. The accounts of the wisdom of Hasidic rabbis and tales of their subtle and penetrating wit reveal charm, simplicity, and an exemplary depth of piety. The innumerable anecdotes told about the leaders of Hasidic dynasties reflect their implicit faith in God and their unalloyed devotion to Torah. Love for the people of Israel and compassion for the underprivileged are among the dominant themes in Hasidic lore, as is evident in the tales that follow.

The Hasidic movement infused in its adherents a profound religious spirit that emphasized mystical and joyful communion with

God throughout the year. On the festivals it bursts into ecstatic celebration amid jubilation, dancing, and singing. A predecessor of the Lubavitcher Rabbi once said, "On the first day of each festival, God extends us an invitation to observe a day of rejoicing with Him; on the second day, we invite Him to rejoice with us. God commanded us to observe the first day of the festival; the second day we instituted ourselves."

It was only natural that Sukkot, the Season of Our Rejoicing, with its culmination on Simhat Torah, should be invested with an added dimension by the *Hasidim*. Their spiritual mystique found full expression on this festival, which they observe with an awesome fervor.

※ ※ ※

SERVING GOD WITH ONE'S WHOLE BEING

The Medizbozer Rabbi said, "During the High Holy Days in the month of Tishri a Jew serves God with his whole being: on Rosh Hashanah, the Day of Remembrance, with his brain, since memory enwreathes the mind; on Yom Kippur with his heart, since fasting strains the heart; on Sukkot with his hands, as he grasps the *etrog* and *lulav*; and on Simhat Torah with his feet, when he parades in the circuits and dances with the Torah."[1]

※ ※ ※

JOYFULNESS FOLLOWS HOLINESS

The Kotzker Rabbi maintained that joyfulness follows as a by-product of holiness. It is therefore natural that after Yom Kippur, when we are cleansed of sin and sanctified, we celebrate Sukkot, which is called "Season of Our Rejoicing."

❧ ❧ ❧

A PROMISE REDEEMED

The Jews of Berditchev were sorely distressed because no *etrog* was available for Sukkot. To solve the problem, Rabbi Levi Isaac dispatched a messenger to purchase at least one *etrog*, regardless of cost. On the outskirts of Berditchev, the messenger encountered a Jew from another town carrying a beautiful *etrog* and escorted him to Rabbi Levi Isaac. The rabbi tried in every way to persuade the stranger to remain in Berditchev over the festival so that the entire community could pronounce the benediction over his *etrog*, but the man was adamant. He had to be on his way to spend the festival with his family.

Finally, Rabbi Levi Isaac offered this proposal: "If you will remain in Berditchev for Sukkot, I promise you will share with me my portion in the future world."

Upon hearing this promise by the righteous rabbi, the Jew acquiesced and brought joy to the Jews of Berditchev.

Later, the rabbi told his sexton to advise the Berditchever Jews not to let the stranger enter any *sukkah* in the town.

On the first night of Sukkot the Jew wished to enter the *sukkah* of the inn where he was lodging, but to his amazement he was refused admittance. He tried several other nearby booths, with the same result.

Realizing that there was undoubtedly a plot against him, he ran in desperation to the rabbi and bitterly cried, "Have I sinned? Haven't I allowed you to use my *etrog*? Why don't you permit me to fulfill the commandment of dwelling in a *sukkah*?"

Rabbi Levi Isaac replied, "If you will release me from my promise concerning the future world, I will arrange for you to be permitted to enter any *sukkah* in Berditchev."

The stranger reflected on the choices confronting him. On one hand, it was no light matter to renounce the privilege of sharing the future world with so pious and learned a man as Rabbi Levi Isaac; on the other hand, it was inconceivable that he should disregard the urgent commandment of dwelling in the *sukkah*. The latter consideration weighed heavily on his mind, and he accepted the rabbi's ultimatum.

At the conclusion of the festival, Rabbi Levi Isaac summoned the stranger and said to him, "I herewith restore my promise to you. I was reluctant for you to earn a share of my portion in eternal life by means of bartering. However, having been tempted to violate God's commandment and having courageously overcome the temptation, you truly merit my original promise."

❦ ❦ ❦

REQUISITES FOR SUKKOT

The Dzikover Rabbi was besought by one of his *Hasidim* for a special benediction to insure his obtaining a stately palm branch, a perfect *etrog*, and beautiful twigs of myrtle and willows of the brook for the observance of Sukkot.

The rabbi answered, "What you require for Sukkot is an honest mind, a generous heart, and a meek spirit. When you have acquired these attributes, you may obtain an exceptionally fine *etrog* and *lulav*."

❦ ❦ ❦

A NEGLIGIBLE DUTY

On the eve of Sukkot, it was a custom of the famous Rabbi Hayyim Halberstam of Sandz to spend the day dispensing charity. To meet the needs of the many indigent persons who sought his assistance, he would borrow money from the citron merchants, who had available cash at that time.

Once his son said to him, "Father, you could not afford to buy a beautiful *etrog* and *lulav* and our *sukkah* is smaller than usual, yet you are giving away borrowed money. I know that charity is an important duty, but nowhere is it written that a person is obligated to borrow money to be charitable."

The father angrily chided his son. "How can you say such a thing? What would you have me do? You know that I have neither knowledge of the Torah nor fear of God. I can only dispense charity —and you would want me to relinquish even that duty."

✣ ✣ ✣

HOSPITALITY IN THE *SUKKAH*

Every year Rabbi Zusya of Hanipol invited many simpletons and ignoramuses to his *sukkah*. When asked why he extended hospitality to such people, the sage replied, "In the future world, where the righteous will dwell in the Tabernacle of Eternal Peace, I will also want to be among them. I fear that I may not be permitted to enter the Tabernacle, because it is unseemly that a lowly person like me can be on the same level as the righteous; therefore, I am establishing a just claim for myself. If the angels ask me, 'How can you, an ignorant man, expect to be admitted into the *Sukkat Shalom*?' I will be able to reply, 'I welcomed simple people into my *sukkah*.'"

✣ ✣ ✣

"COME INTO MY *SUKKAH!*"

On the eve of Sukkot, a carpenter, attired in work clothes and carrying his tools slung over his back, was wending his way homeward through a forest to observe the festival. To his great distress, he lost his way and wandered aimlessly. When darkness fell, he saw lights in a small dwelling not far ahead. Approaching cautiously, he opened the door slightly and peeked in.

In the room he saw Rabbi Israel of Rizin and a group of *Hasidim* in festive garments seated in a beautifully decorated *sukkah*, partaking of a sumptuous meal. Ashamed because of his appearance, the carpenter was on the verge of leaving when Rabbi Israel, in a cordial tone, called to him. "What are you staring at? Is it beneath your dignity to sit in my *sukkah*? Come into my *sukkah* and join us!"

❦ ❦ ❦

A *SUKKAH* WITHOUT GUESTS

Rabbi Pinhas of Koretz, widely renowned for his wisdom, was besieged by *Hasidim* who flocked to present their sundry problems to him. As a result, he found little time to devote to the study of Torah and to worship. Consequently, he refused to see any *Hasidim*, separated himself from the community, and spent his days and nights in prayer and study. The only time he joined with others was for public worship.

With the advent of Sukkot, Rabbi Pinhas invited several townsmen to be his guests in the *sukkah*, but they declined; he had become unpopular since isolating himself.

On the first night of Sukkot, Rabbi Pinhas entered his booth and in accordance with custom recited the *Ushpizin*, inviting the holy guests—our patriarchal ancestors—to join him. He saw a vision of Father Abraham standing outside and refusing to enter. When the rabbi inquired of Abraham why he did not come into the *sukkah*, the latter replied, "I will not enter a place where there are no guests."

Since then Rabbi Pinhas again opened his heart and his home to the *Hasidim*.

❦ ❦ ❦

ZEALOUSNESS TO BUILD A BOOTH

It was a practice of Rabbi Mordecai of Lechovitz to purchase lumber before Sukkot and distribute it among the poor people of his town so that they could build booths for the festival.

One year on the eve of Sukkot, during a heavy rainstorm, an indigent shoemaker who was lame in one leg came to Rabbi Mordecai and asked for some lumber to erect his *sukkah*. By that time the rabbi no longer had any boards left. The poor man, dejected and tearful, went from house to house in the pouring rain seeking materials to build a *sukkah*. When Rabbi Mordecai saw through his window the shoemaker's intense effort, he cried out, "Lord of the universe, look down from heaven and see how Your people Israel love Your commandments. A simple, poor Jew, hardly able to walk, is plodding through the mud in this downpour and his spirit is suffering. Why? Because he cannot fulfill the precept of dwelling in a *sukkah*!"

Immediately Rabbi Mordecai summoned his servant and bade him, "Hurry and gather up the boards I have put aside for my *sukkah*, and we will take them to the hapless shoemaker. We will both help him build his booth."

That year Rabbi Mordecai ate all his meals in the *sukkah* of the poor shoemaker.

❧ ❧ ❧

THE FITNESS OF A BOOTH

Rabbi Nahman of Bratzlav was invited by a humble Jew to visit his *sukkah*, on which he had spent more than he could afford. He had purchased the finest lumber, expensive decorations, and beautiful pines for the roof covering.

Rabbi Nahman accepted the invitation and paid a visit during the festival, accompanied by a disciple. When they entered the booth, the disciple whispered to Rabbi Nahman that the *sukkah* was not constructed according to all the laws; but the latter remained silent.

After they left the *sukkah*, Rabbi Nahman observed to his disciple, "This Jew went to so much trouble and spent so much money for the booth, and you raise questions as to its validity because of legal stringencies!"

❦ ❦ ❦

THE RESULT OF DWELLING
IN A *SUKKAH*

On the festival of Sukkot, a *Hasid* was not feeling well. Despite his wife's warning that he might catch a cold if he slept in the *sukkah*, he spent most of the holiday there in accordance with Jewish tradition. As his wife foresaw, he caught a cold that developed into pneumonia.

The wife chided her husband. "See what happened to you because you slept in the *sukkah*."

"You don't understand," the pious Jew retorted. "It's true that I'm ill because I fulfilled the commandment of dwelling in a *sukkah*. However, can you imagine how severe my illness would have been if I had not done my duty?"

❦ ❦ ❦

THE HUNGRY RABBI

Before Rabbi Ber of Radishitz obtained a rabbinical post, he lived in dire poverty and often went hungry. One year he was reluctant to leave the synagogue on the first night of Sukkot, as he had been unable to prepare any provisions for the festival. He was too depressed to enter his *sukkah*, which was not set up for the festival meal. When he finally went there, he opened the door of his *sukkah* and saw, to his amazement, that the table was set with lit candles, *hallah*, fish, and potatoes. Questioning his wife, he learned that she sold her last piece of jewelry and was thereby able to purchase food so that they could celebrate the festival properly.

Rabbi Ber recited the *Kiddush*, washed his hands, said the appropriate blessings, and then, not having eaten a full meal for some time, fell on the food. Suddenly, in the midst of gorging himself, a thought struck him and he said to himself, "Berel, you are not sitting

10. Sukkot scenes. From *Kirchliche Verfassung der heutigen Juden,*
by Johann C.G. Bodenschatz, Erlangen, 1748.

in the *sukkah* to fulfill the commandment, but only to satisfy your stomach."

Immediately he stopped eating.

❧ ❧ ❧

THE WAY OF THE JEWS

The Duke of Mannheim once asked Rabbi Tzvi of Berlin, "What is the reason that children ask the 'Four Questions' on Passover and not on Sukkot? After all, on Sukkot you have more customs than on Passover, especially since you leave your permanent homes and live in temporary booths."

"Let me explain it to you," replied Rabbi Tzvi. "On Passover a child sees the family seated around a table with many tempting dishes, and they are freely relaxed in a way we Jews are not always permitted to enjoy. Therefore the child is surprised and asks the questions. But what does the little one see on Sukkot? The people of Israel leave their homes and sit outside without a roof over their heads. This is no surprise, for even a child knows that is the way for Jews in the Diaspora."

❧ ❧ ❧

CHOOSING *ETROGIM*

It was a custom in Slonim that before a Jew bought an *etrog* he would bring it to Rabbi Eizel Harif for an opinion as to its suitability for use. One year the rabbi was dissatisfied with the entire crop of *etrogim* being sold. As each Jew came with the citron he had selected to purchase, the rabbi refused to give his stamp of approval.

When the *etrogim* dealer became aware of what was happening, he hastened to the rabbi and complained bitterly. "What are you doing to me, Rabbi? No one is buying the citrons, and I'll suffer great financial loss. I depend for a livelihood on the sale of *etrogim*, and, because of your advice, I'll not have the means to support my family during the coming year."

The rabbi, sincerely distraught that he might be the cause of a human's suffering, told the dealer, "It's a fact that your *etrogim* are unsuitable and, when my judgment is asked, I must tell the truth. God forbid, however, that I should cause a Jew to suffer. I'll tell you what to do. Give every prospective buyer two citrons instead of one. When he asks me which one of the two *etrogim* is better, I'll be able to answer truthfully that one is better than the other, and your sales will be assured."

❧ ❧ ❧

A RARE PRIVILEGE

Before Rabbi Mordecai of Neschiz entered the rabbinate he engaged in a small business that was not lucrative. Nevertheless, by stinting he saved a few coins regularly so that he would have enough to purchase an *etrog*. The week before the holiday he went to Brody with his frugally hoarded money to obtain an *etrog*. Entering the town, he encountered a coachman weeping copiously alongside a dead horse.

Rabbi Mordecai inquired sympathetically, "Why are you so dejected?"

"My horse was just killed in an accident. Without a horse I can't earn a living."

The rabbi was not slow in responding. Handing his *etrog* money to the coachman, he told him to buy another horse. He thought to himself, "The *etrog* is a precept of the Lord, and charity is a precept of the Lord."

When Rabbi Mordecai returned to Neschiz, in a mood of exhilaration, many of his townsmen gathered about him and asked to see the *etrog*. "All Jews will pronounce the benediction over the *etrog* during Sukkot," Rabbi Mordecai jestingly informed the curiosity seekers. "Only I have been granted the rare privilege of reciting the blessing over a horse."

❧ ❧ ❧

NO BLESSING REQUIRED

Reb Leibele, son of Rabbi Ber of Wilna, a rich and pious house-holder, was meticulous in fulfilling all the Torah commandments. He was especially particular about an *etrog* suitable for Sukkot, and no price was too high for him to procure the best available.

On the first day of the festival, he rose early to perform the duty of reciting the blessing over the *etrog*. Reb Leibele's servant, who had the same idea, rose even earlier. Taking the *etrog* from its silver case, the servant began to recite the preliminary prayer *Yehi Ratzon*. Suddenly, he was surprised and shocked to hear the approaching footsteps of Reb Leibele. His hands trembled, and the *etrog* fell to the floor. Looking down, he was further distressed to see that the *pitma* was broken off. At that moment, Reb Leibele entered the room and observed the pale, frightened face of his servant staring at the now unfit *etrog*.

Reb Leibele, his face wreathed in kindness, gently said, "If the *etrog* is unsuitable for use, the blessing need not be said."

❧ ❧ ❧

THE LOT OF A BEAUTIFUL *ETROG*

Reluctant to function in the active rabbinate, Rabbi Jacob Koslover declined an invitation to serve as the rabbi of Brezshan. His wife, however, anxious to be the *rebbetzin* of such an important Jewish community, kept urging him to reconsider.

During the week preceding Sukkot, the *rebbetzin* was nagging him more than usual. Finally, Rabbi Jacob said to her, "If you will buy a beautiful *etrog* for me, I will reconsider the offer."

The wife hastened to the marketplace and selected the choicest *etrog* available, for which she gladly paid an exorbitant price.

Learning of his exceptional *etrog*, many Jews flocked to Rabbi Jacob's home on the first day of Sukkot to pronounce the blessing over it. Before the day was over, the *etrog* became black and spotted and lost its beautiful appearance.

Pointing to the now unseemly *etrog*, Rabbi Jacob said to his wife, "You can now see that even the most exquisite *etrog* becomes spoiled when it falls into communal hands."

❦ ❦ ❦

A SIMHAT TORAH CELEBRATION

Hasidim of the Baal Shem Tov were at his home celebrating Simhat Torah with song, dance, and wine. Fearing they might exhaust the supply of wine, the host's wife complained to her husband. "Tell your disciples to cease dancing and drinking, for soon no wine will be left for *Kiddush* and *Havdalah*."

With a smile on his lips, the Baal Shem Tov replied, "You are undoubtedly correct. Tell them to stop and to go home."

The dutiful wife opened the door of the room where the *Hasidim* were rejoicing. When she witnessed their pervasive spiritual ecstasy, she brought them more wine.

Later the Baal Shem Tov asked his spouse if she told them to go home. She rejoined, "You should have told them yourself!"

❦ ❦ ❦

REJOICING WITH HIS BROTHER

Rabbi Naftali of Ropshitz recounted how an ordinary workingman triumphed over him. One Simhat Torah he saw an ignorant wagon-driver singing in a loud voice and dancing exuberantly with the Torah during the processional circuits. The rabbi chided the wagon-driver, "Why are you so joyful? Have you studied the Torah during the past year that you should demonstrate such excessive happiness with it?"

Without interrupting his dancing the wagon-driver retorted, "So what? When my brother has a joyous occasion, should I not rejoice with him? Isn't his joy also my joy?"

❦ ❦ ❦

MIXTURE OF JOYS IS FORBIDDEN

The daughter of Rabbi Meir of Premislan was critically ill during the festival of Sukkot, and by Simhat Torah she was closer to death than to life.

When the pious rabbi was participating in the processional circuits with the Torah, his followers besought him to seek a means of saving his daughter. When Rabbi Meir entered her room and saw that she was near death, he prayed, "Lord of the universe! You commanded us to blow the *shofar* on Rosh Hashanah, and Meir blew; You commanded us to fast on Yom Kippur, and Meir fasted; You commanded us to dwell in the *sukkah* on the festival, and Meir dwelt therein; You commanded us to rejoice on Simhat Torah, and Meir is rejoicing. And now You caused Meir's daughter to be sick and Meir must accept everything with joy, because a man is obliged to pronounce a blessing on the evil as well as on the good, to accept both with joy. Yet, Lord of the universe, You know the law is explicit that 'one does not commingle one joy with another joy!'"

Immediately the sick daughter took a turn for the better and was restored to good health.

8

SUKKOT AND SIMHAT TORAH
IN MODERN PROSE

THE AUTUMN FEAST
HERMAN WOUK

author of best-selling novels including The Caine Mutiny, The
Winds of War, Marjorie Morningstar, *and* This Is My God, *an
exposition of traditional Judaism*

We are back in the light of the full moon, the moon of the
autumnal equinox, the fifteenth of Tishri. Everything that the earth
will yield this year lies heaped in the storehouses: the fruit, the
grain, the wine, the oil: piles of yellow and green and red, vats
brimming purple and gold. The farmers of ancient Israel, like
farmers in all lands and times, gather for the autumn thanksgiving.

The full moon sheds its light on every man, woman, and child in Palestine. Nobody is indoors. The law of Moses requires that for seven days and nights all Jews live in huts partially roofed by green boughs, palm branches, or piles of reeds. In these frail structures the families feast, and sing, and visit, and sleep. At the mercy of the weather, they live as their ancestors did in the desert, in the first forty years of independence, before they conquered Canaan.

Sukkot is so preeminently a gay and rollicking time that its talmudic name is simply *The Festival.* For a folk settled in a rich farm country, contemplating their heaping harvests, the *sukkah* custom may have helped to limit the smugness of prosperity. In the *sukkah* under the night sky, wind and rain could at any moment make life dismal. The moon shone through the loose ceiling of boughs, the old warning of the way fortune changes. The stars—the law suggests that the stars be visible through the roof—may have been reminders that life at its richest is a brief spark in a black mystery. Or so you can interpret the ordinance, if you will. Moses wrote that by dwelling in huts once a year Israel would remember that they had once lived in *sukkot* in the desert, and he went no further.

With the dispersion of the Jews to colder climates, the customs surrounding the *sukkah* have changed. There are pious Jews who still sleep in the hut when the weather permits it, but most of them today confine their observance to eating meals and praying there.

In American Jewish life, especially with the rise of suburban communities, Sukkot is recovering much of its old charm and excitement. For the harvest-time hut (the archaic word is "tabernacle") is a perfect instrument for delighting and instructing the children. Those who mourn the absence of something like a Christmas tree in our customs have never given the *sukkah* a thought, or more likely have not heard of it.

You can construct the hut in your own yard. There are portable ready-made *sukkot* which take most of the work out of the job. What is wanted is nothing more than three or four walls, some slats of wood at the top, and the covering for the roof—branches, boughs, grass, reeds. There has to be room in the *sukkah* for a table and chairs. Decorating the *sukkah* becomes a pleasant game of improvising patterns with fruits, vegetables, flowers, and anything else that adds color and gaiety. The small children dart in and out of the booth, playing some version of cops-and-robbers, as the children doubtless did in the hills of Judah thirty centuries ago when the *sukkah* was going up. Older children help in decorating the *sukkah* or they take over the job entirely, and find enormous fun in doing it. The heaps of fruit, flowers, corn, squash dwindle on the table. The bare walls of the *sukkah* disappear under loving patterns of yellow, scarlet, and green.

Night falls. The family dines by candlelight and moonlight in the open air, in the curious hut filled with harvest fragrance. The old holiday melodies and chants sound strangely new outdoors. Maybe it is so cool that they dine in coats. Maybe the weather holds, and they have an idyllic dinner alfresco, in the scented gloom of the *sukkah*. Sometimes it rains, and a half-annoyed half-hilarious scramble indoors ensues. The charm of broken routine, of a new colorful way of doing familiar things, makes Sukkot a seven-day picnic—one that is dedicated and charged with symbol, as well as delightful.[1]

❧ ❧ ❧

GOD'S PROTECTING COVERING
SAMSON RAPHAEL HIRSCH

rabbi, statesman, philosopher, and leader of Orthodox Jewry in Germany (1808–1888); his influence is still evident today

The building of the tabernacle teaches you trust in God. Whatever may be your station in life, whether you are richly or poorly endowed with the goods of this world, you are neither dazzled by abundance nor frightened by want. The goods of the earth are not your goods. It is with that which others reject and despise that you build this tabernacle of your life. You know that whether men live in huts or in palaces, it is only as pilgrims that they dwell; both huts and palaces form only our transitory home. You know that in this pilgrimage only God is our protection, and it is His grace which shields us. You would not be daunted even if you had to wander through deserts with wife and child. You know that the God who for forty years led our ancestors through the wilderness with their wives and children, sheltered them in huts and fed them with manna, you know that this same God is your God, and accompanies you also in your wanderings through deserts, knows every soul in your tabernacle and can distribute the manna of His grace to each one.

We may in the quantity of our possessions be divided into a thousand grades. One may build his walls of hewn stones and the other of modest planks, while a third is able to make only two partitions and merely to indicate a third. But in respect of our actual protection, of that which covers and shields us—the *sekhakh* [roofing foliage]—we are all equal. This is not anything which bespeaks human craftsmanship, not anything which has to fear the breath of transitoriness. In the walls we may differ, but in the *sekhakh* we are all equal. For it is not human wealth or strength or skill, but the grace and blessing of God which protects us and covers palaces and huts with the same love.

Not troubled and careworn, not sad and gloomy is the life which we lead in the tabernacle built by the trust in God and covered by the love of God. Why should it worry you that it is only a transitory hutment, that one day it will leave you or you will leave it? The walls may fall, the covering may wither in the storm, God may call you outside; but the sheltering love of God is everywhere and constantly with you, and where it bids you dwell, where it protects you, there you dwell, were it only for a moment, in the most fleeting and transitory dwelling, as calmly and securely as if it were your house forever.

Translated by Isidor Grunfeld[2]

✻ ✻ ✻

THE FESTIVAL OF WANDERING
AND REST
FRANZ ROSENZWEIG

born into an assimilated German Jewish family, he was on the brink of conversion to Christianity, but reverted to Judaism and became its devoted protagonist; an existentialist thinker and author of The Star of Redemption, *a major Jewish theological work; translator of the Hebrew Bible into German in collaboration with Martin Buber; head of the Free House of Jewish Study in Frankfort on the Main (1886–1929)*

The Feast of Booths is the feast of both wanderings and rest. In memory of those long wanderings of the past which finally led to rest, the members of the family do not have their merry meal in the familiar rooms of the house but under a roof which is quickly constructed, a makeshift roof with heaven shining through the gaps. This serves to remind the people that no matter how solid the house of today may seem, no matter how temptingly it beckons to rest and unimperiled living, it is but a tent which permits only a pause in the long wanderings through the wilderness of centuries. For rest, the rest of which the builder of the first Temple spoke, does not come until all these wanderings are at an end, and his words are read at this feast: "Blessed be He that has given rest unto His people."

The passages from the Prophets read on the occasion of this festival again prove—if there is still need of such proof—that this double meaning is the meaning of the feast, that it is a feast of redemption only within the circle of the three festivals of revelation. Because of this, redemption is celebrated here only as the hope and certainty of future redemption; and while this feast is celebrated in the same month as the Days of Awe, which are the feasts of a redemption present and eternal, and borders on these Days in neighborly fashion, it does not coincide with them. On the first day of the Feast of Booths the majestic closing chapter from Zechariah is read, the chapter concerning the day of the Lord with the prediction that concludes the daily service: "And the Lord shall be King over all the earth; in that day shall the Lord be One, and His name: One."

This ultimate word of hope concludes the daily service of the assembled congregation and also comes at the conclusion of the spiritual year. On the other days of the festival, these words are paralleled by the ones Solomon spoke at the dedication of the Temple, when the wandering ark at last found the rest the people had already found under Joshua. Solomon's concluding words wonderfully connect the hope for future recognition "that all the peoples of the earth may know that the Lord, He is God; there is none else," with a warning to the one people: "Let your heart, therefore, be whole with the Lord." And in the chapter from Ezekiel read at this festival, classical expression is given to this merging into each other of unity of the heart, unity of God, and unity of peoples which, in the concept of the sanctification of God's Name through the people for all the peoples, forms the inmost basis of Judaism. . . .

Thus the Feast of Booths is not only a festival of rest for the people, but also the festival of the ultimate hope. It is a festival of rest only in that it breathes hope. In this festival of redemption there is no present redemption. Redemption is only a hope, only something expected in the source of wanderings. And so this feast cannot be the last word, since it does not include redemption in its own domains but only glimpses it and lets it be glimpsed from the mountain of revelation. As the Sabbath flows back into the weekday, so this close of the spiritual year is not permitted to be an actual close but must flow back into the beginning. On the festival of Rejoicing in the Law, the last word in the Torah gives rise to the first. And the old man

11. The circuits on Hoshana Rabbah. Copper engraving.
By Joseph Herz. From *Mahzor le-Sukkot*. Sulzbach, Germany, 1826.

who, in the name of the congregation, is in charge of this transition, is not called "husband of the Torah," but goes by the name of "bridegroom of the Torah." It is not without good cause that the book full of corroding doubt, Ecclesiastes, is assigned to be read at the Feast of Booths. The disenchantment which follows upon the Sabbath the moment its fragrance has been breathed for the last time and the weekday asserts itself in all its old unbroken strength is, as it were, included in the festival itself through the reading of Ecclesiastes. Although the Feast of Booths celebrates redemption and rest, it is nevertheless the festival of wandering through the wilderness. Neither in the feasts that unite people at a common meal, nor in those that unite them in common listening, does man have the experience of community begot by ultimate silence. Beyond the mere founding of the community in the common world, beyond the expression of the community in a common life, there must be something higher, even if this something lies at the farthest border of community life and constitutes community beyond common life.

Translated by William W. Hallo[8]

♵ ♵ ♵

SAY IT WITH FLOWERS
JOEL BLAU

rabbi, essayist, and instructor of midrashic literature and homiletics at the Jewish Institute of Religion (1878–1927)

Say it with flowers and all the festal beauty of the green things that adorn the tabernacle. Wave your palm branch toward the four winds, to bind the influences that sway the world. Let the citron be uplifted in your hand, a gracious offering to the spirit of beauty that dwells everywhere. Let the myrtle sprig timidly hug the strength of the palm, even as man's weakness is confidently nestled against God's might. Let the downhanging willow leaves still tremble in your grasp, as they did while shaking in the winds that swept over the brook and wept—wept with the tears of things, wept over the fate that lies in wait for all. Say it with flowers and green things! You have much to say, if you but knew it. . . .

Nature lives beautifully, and dies beautifully. Moreover, just as the spirit of beauty is the permanent element in the midst of a world constantly destroyed, so the soul of goodness is the stable element in the life of a humanity constantly dying. This soul of goodness, at all events, abides through all the fearful accidents of the changing individual existence, as through all the heave and havoc of human history. This alone is the source of our strength: to know that all the vicissitudes of our life on earth tend inevitably to the betterment and ultimate perfection of the race. Say it with flowers, and say it with the green boughs in your festal wreath, that, although the whole world is wet with the tears of things, there is a heroic spirit within man denying death and defying destruction.

Not the weeping willow, therefore, holds the real secret of life, but the other component parts of the ceremonial wreath: the goodly fruit with its noble beauty, the bride-adorning myrtle with its maternal promise of ever-renewing life; and, above all, the upright palm branch with its hint of unconquerable strength, with its aura of eternity brought straight from the edge of the desert.

Say it with flowers, and with green festal boughs that Israel, desert-born as the palm, walks among men enhaloed with this eternal aura. To Israel, weakest of people, belongs the strength that laughs at death. And though all the world be banded against the eternal people, the enemy cannot prevail. For, more than any other people, God's chosen drew into itself the permanent elements of life. What do these festal flowers we wind around our booth, what does this festal wreath we carry in solemn procession, say but this: Israel has never given up its hope of returning to the land of the fathers, and therefore return it will, for return it must! These goodly fruits, these green sprigs, these palm branches, that are still redolent with the fragrance of Palestine, are a prophecy. Who was it said that a nation that cannot forget its fields and flowers, must one day return to its native soil, the cradle place of its being? Let us add, that a nation that still builds booths reminiscent of the open-air life in the warm East will yet build cities and people the waste places with men. Say it with flowers, and say it with green things, that the Hope of Israel still lives in the breast of every faithful Jew; and that, although storms may come and storms may go, and our poor little hut may be tossed about by every tempest, Israel will abide forever.

Say all this with flowers, and not with poor human words, for there is something in the deep life of this world, which can best be expressed in the dumb speech of growing and dying things.[4]

☙ ☙ ☙

THE ROLE OF THE MESSIAH
ISRAEL HERBERT LEVINTHAL

*rabbi and author; visiting professor of homiletics at The Jewish,
Theological Seminary of America*

Now, all peoples, all creeds, emphasize the importance of charity,
of helping one's fellowman in distress. But the special importance
and the uniqueness of Sukkot lie in this: that it extends this philosophy beyond the relationship of individuals and makes it the guiding
principle of nations as well. On this festival of Sukkot, there was a
unique system of sacrificial offerings, wholly unlike the sacrifices offered on all other holy days. Seventy offerings were brought to the
altar on the seven days of Sukkot, while on the eighth day—as on
all other festivals—only one offering was sacrificed. The rabbis explain this procedure and interpret for us the distinctive character
of this festival in this fashion: "These seventy offerings are for the
seventy nations that inhabit the earth! On Sukkot, the Jews offered
these sacrifices to invoke God's favor upon all the peoples of the
earth, even before they prayed for themselves; only on the concluding
day was the offering brought to seek God's favor upon Israel!" Here
is the great contribution which this festival makes in the field of
human relations. Not only individuals, but nations and peoples, too,
must learn this lesson of sharing their joys and their happiness.
Peoples must learn to sacrifice for each other's interests and welfare
—that is the clarion note sounded by this festival day. . . .

And the important symbols of the festival emphasize the same
truth. The walls of the *sukkah*, or hut, wherein the Jew dwells these
eight days, may be strong and firm, in order to give its resident the
feeling of personal security. But according to Jewish Law, there
must be an opening in the *sekhakh*—the covering above—to enable
the one who enters the *sukkah* to look out and see the stars in the
heavens. The *sukkah* is essentially the home of the Jew. The *sukkah*
speaks to him in terms of his own history, his own sufferings, his
own problems, his own hopes. But though it is the abode of the Jew,
it must possess enough of an opening to make him see the universe,
to make him realize that there are peoples and nations outside his

own, so that he must think of them and concern himself with them and their interests as well as with those of his own.

And the palm branch—the *lulav*—that is used at the Sukkot service is a further symbol emphasizing the same lesson. When the benediction over the palm branch is recited, the branch is waved to the north, to the south, to the east, and to the west, above and below, to signify again that God's sovereignty is over all mankind and that when we pray for salvation and help we must think of these blessings not only for ourselves but for all humanity as well— for those living in every corner of the earth, for the lowliest as well as the greatest amongst them.

No wonder that the wise R. Haninah felt that this would be the important task of the Messiah—to teach all the nations of the world these lessons of the *sukkah* and the *lulav*: that the world's salvation can and will come only when nations will accept this fundamental truth that no nation can enjoy happiness unless that happiness is shared by all other nations, that national selfishness is as grievous a sin as is individual selfishness, that isolationism among nations is a policy that is the greatest obstacle to world harmony.[5]

✹ ✹ ✹

THE *SUKKAH*—FORTRESS OF DEFENSE
ABRAHAM ISAAC KOOK

chief rabbi of the Ashkenazic community of Palestine and mystical religious thinker; he emphasized, both in word and in deed, the centrality of the Land of Israel in Jewish life (1865–1935)

The *sukkah* is for us a fortress of defense: "Thou concealest them in a booth from the strife of tongues" (Psalms 31.21). It is written of the Men of the Great Synagogue, who extinguished the fervor for idolatry among Israel, that they made *sukkot* the likes of which were not made since the days of Joshua son of Nun. "And all the congregation of them that were come back out of the captivity made booths, and dwelt in the booths; for since the days of Joshua the son of Nun unto that day had not the children of Israel done so. And there was very great gladness" (Nehemiah 8.17). And what were these beautiful *sukkot*? The Talmud explains: "Ezra [considered by tradition to be among the first of the Men of the Great Synagogue] had prayed for mercy because of the predilection for idolatry [among the people] and in quenching it, his merit [prayer] shielded them like a booth" (Arakin 32b). Thus we see that the *sukkah* is an instrumentality for defense.

Is it not extraordinary that a temporary abode like the *sukkah* can so protect us, that we can unhesitatingly adopt the booth as our model for defense and security? How can such a structure, which is required by Halakhah to have "two full walls and a third needing only a handbreadth in width," be transformed into a fortress and a buckler against an adversary? It devolves upon us to reveal this abiding truth to all: precisely because the *sukkah* is so flimsily built that its external appearance seems unfit to be called an "abode," for this very reason it merits being our strong tower and citadel before every foe and antagonist. In what way can the fragile booth, open on all sides, be transformed into a dwelling place? Obviously, not by virtue of its physical strength, which is frail and weak.

Only through the Law,* which is the word of God, who decreed that on the days of this holy festival, the Feast of Ingathering, it shall become our [spiritual] home. This should be our lesson for generations. For the effort required to construct our house, the building of our national home, we need particularly the spiritual potency, the vigor of this festival, the might of God's eternal word. Man's most modern weapons of destruction may breach the strongest fortresses with gaping holes and destroy thick metal walls. But neither they nor any other manufactured object can demolish the strong invincible wall of the Law. This makes us aware that the Law is our eternal fortress and our security.

Even in our own day and age, as we venture to build our national home on the land of our fathers, let us recognize the ineluctable truth that the spiritual Law is God's word that enjoined the House of Israel to be rebuilt. Verily, that is our fortified tower, even though man's myopic vision cannot recognize its immunity and hardiness.

When we come to build our own *sukkah*, which protects us with elimination of all forms of idolatry, ancient and modern, may the Law be our law, and may the commandments of our holy Torah endure forever!

---

* *Hok*, usually translated as "statute," is the term in the original Hebrew; however, it is here used in a transrational sense to convey the idea of living commandments.

Naturally, we must beautify the *sukkah*. Adorning the *sukkah* was always our wont from generation to generation. It was customary "to adorn it with embroidered hangings and sheets, and hung therein nuts, almonds, peaches, pomegranates, bunches of grapes, wreaths of ears of corn, phials of wine, oil or fine flower" (Sukkah 10a). This describes the typical Israeli *sukkah*. Likewise we are called upon to beautify the Law, for it is our strength. As the Talmud declares: "Jerusalem was destroyed only because they gave judgment therein literally in accordance with biblical law" (Baba Metzia 30b). They were not prepared to go beyond the letter of the law. We, however, are ready to adhere to the highest and holiest compass of God's word, to relate to our brothers not only according to the literal interpretation of the law, but also to transcend its requirements. Let this dimension of beauty, extending beyond the law's literal demands, become our *sukkah*, a mighty tower against every enemy. May the House of Israel be rebuilt in all its strength and beauty on its own land, and may the "fallen *sukkah* of David" be restored for us, speedily in our time. Amen.

Translated by Leonard B. Gewirtz

❧ ❧ ❧

THE UNIVERSAL NATURE OF SUKKOT
ANDRÉ NEHER

professor of Hebrew language and literature at the University of Strasbourg, France; author of biblical studies

It is interesting to note that the prophets not only interpreted the idea of the desert in the sense Moses attached to it, but also the rite expressing this idea in the Pentateuch. If the Passover actually restores the moment of the Exodus from Egypt in a ritual manner, the march across the desert is repeated in the feast of Sukkot (Leviticus 23.33–44). Each year for seven days the Jews symbolically leave their solid man-made houses and shelter under leaves and branches in the open air, thus restoring the fullness of nomad life.

Nomad, or rather human. For though it is not to be denied that from ancient times the feast of Sukkot was celebrated in the definite desire not to renounce the value of nomad life for good, it is no less characteristic that the historical significance of the desert was very early associated with it. If there is a prophet for whom the central position of Israel and Jerusalem is one of the fundamental realities of history, it is certainly Zechariah. "Yea, many people and mighty nations shall come to seek the Lord of hosts in Jerusalem. . . . In those days it shall come to pass, that ten men shall take hold, out of all the languages of the nations, shall even take hold of the skirt of him that is a Jew, saying, We will go with you, for we have heard that God is with you" (Zechariah 8.22–23). In the fourteenth chapter of his prophecy Zechariah expands this gravitation round the Jew to the measure of a cosmic eschatology, and he localizes its internal principles in the rites of the feast of Sukkot. It is this feast, the final resurrection of the march across the desert of Egypt, that will receive not only individuals, but nations; not only those who wish to pray, but those who hunger after life. And the Talmud also knows that the seventy bulls, the sacrifice of which at the feast of Sukkot is prescribed by Leviticus, symbolize the presence of the seventy nations of the earth in the very center of all religion, in the Temple of Jerusalem. Rabbi Johanan says: "Had the nations understood the significance of the Temple, they would not have destroyed it, but built it with their own hands, for the sacrifice, offered there, was for them."

There is no rite which shows the sacramental insertion of the chosen people into a framework of universal scope more forcibly than the Feast of Tabernacles. If the consciousness Israel possesses of her special election may be described as *Paschal,* it may be said that the universal nature of this election is *Sukkothic.*

Translated by Irene Marinoff[6]

⚘ ⚘ ⚘

THE UNBROKEN TORAH CYCLE
ALEXANDER ALAN STEINBACH

poet, author, and editor of the Jewish Book Annual *and of* Jewish Bookland; *recipient of National Jewish Welfare Board Frank L. Weil Award for distinguished contributions to American Jewish culture*

One of the most beautiful festivals in the Jewish calendar is Simhat Torah, Rejoicing in the Law. It is the crowning celebration of a religious cycle that begins with Rosh Hashanah on the first day of Tishri, includes Yom Kippur on the tenth, Sukkot on the fifteenth, Shemini Atzeret on the twenty-second, and finally ends with Simhat Torah on the twenty-third. The first part of this cycle is solemn and serious. It centers around the austere days of Rosh Hashanah, the Ten Days of Penitence, and the Day of Atonement. But the second part is more joyful, for it brings us the merry Feast of Tabernacles with its beauty and rich ceremonials. Most gladsome of all is Simhat Torah, not only because it is the feast on which children parade with the procession of the Torah Scrolls, but also because it symbolizes the deathlessness of the Jewish people.

At this time of the year we finish the last *sidrah* in Deuteronomy, but we immediately turn the Scroll back to Genesis and begin anew the reading of the Torah. . . .

What is the meaning of this custom? It is the symbol of our loyalty to the Torah and of our unconquerable spirit as a people. It is our answer to the command God gave to Joshua: "This Book of the Law shall not depart out of thy mouth, but thou shalt meditate therein day and night, that thou mayest observe to do according to all that is written therein." No matter what circumstances our people were required to face, we remained faithful to the contents of that Book. No amount of persecution could take it from us, no suffering could make us surrender it. For it has been "our life and the length of our days," our comfort in sorrow and our stronghold in every crisis. From Genesis to Deuteronomy and then back again to Genesis—this has been our practice throughout the years. In some countries where laws prohibited our fathers from studying the Torah, many were thrown into the fire together with the Torah Scrolls. But always they cried out, "The Scrolls burn but the words ascend to heaven." Neither fire nor water, neither rack nor dungeon, hate nor cruelty, ever succeeded in shaking our fidelity to our Torah Bride. And that is why we live today. . . .

When a Jewish child is born, the blessing pronounced over him is that he might grow "in the study of the Torah, enjoy the bliss of marriage, and perform good deeds in life." The important question in Judaism is not how tall or how broad the child will grow, but how true he will be to the Torah to which his people is forever wedded. How willing will he be to dedicate his life to the performance of acts of charity and kindness and benevolence? The Romans used to pray that their children might become rugged and muscular so that they would become good soldiers. But we Jews pray that our children might grow big in heart and noble in spirit, so that they will become worthy followers of the Torah. This distinction is accentuated again on Simhat Torah, and our greatest rejoicing lies in the fact that we are able to turn the Scroll back from the last line of Deuteronomy to the first verse of Genesis: "In the beginning God created the heaven and the earth."[7]

❦ ❦ ❦

THE JOY OF THE LAW
SOLOMON SCHECHTER

lecturer in rabbinics at Cambridge University; discoverer of important manuscripts in the Cairo Genizah; president of The Jewish Theological Seminary of America and molder of the institutions of Conservative Judaism (c. 1849–1915)

The joy experienced by the rabbinic Jew in being commanded to fulfill the Law, and the enthusiasm which he felt at accomplishing that which he considered to be the will of God, is a point hardly touched upon by most theological writers, and if touched upon at all, is hardly ever understood. Yet this "joy of the Law" is so essential an element in the understanding of the Law, that it "forms that originality of sentiment more or less delicate" which can never be conceived by those who have experienced it neither from life nor from literature. . . .

This principle of joy in connection with the *mitzvah* is maintained both in the Talmud and in the devotional literature of the Middle Ages. The general rule is: Tremble with joy when thou art about to fulfill a commandment. God, His salvation, and His Law, are the three things in which Israel rejoices. Indeed, as R. Bahya ibn Pakudah declares, to mention one of the later moralists, it is this joy experienced by the sweetness of the service of God which forms a part of the reward of the religionist, even as the prophet said: "Thy words were found, and I did eat them; and Thy words were unto me the joy and the rejoicing of my heart" (Jeremiah 15.16). R.

Bahya ben Halawa, again, declares that the joy accompanying the carrying out of a religious performance is even more acceptable to God than the *mitzvah* itself. The righteous, he points out, feel this ineffable delight in performing God's will in the same way as the spheres and planets (whose various revolutions are a perpetual song to God) rejoice in their going forth and are glad in their returning; whilst R. Joseph Askari of Safed (sixteenth century) makes joy one of the necessary conditions without which a law cannot be perfectly carrried out. And I may perhaps remark that this joy of the *mitzvah* was a living reality even in modern times. I myself had once the good fortune to observe one of those old type Jews, who, as the first morning of the Feast of Tabernacles drew near, used to wake and rise soon after the middle of the night. There he sat, with trembling joy, awaiting impatiently the break of dawn, when he would be able to fulfill the law of the palm branch and the willows![8]

12. *Sukkah* interior. Painted on wood. Fischach, Germany. 1823. See Chapter 9.

❧ ❧ ❧

JOY IN THE HOLY DAYS
HERMANN COHEN

professor of philosophy at the University of Marburg and a founder of the Society for the Advancement of Jewish Studies in Berlin (1842–1918)

It was great meaning that those Jewish holidays which are not directly dedicated to the idea of atonement are dedicated to joy. "You shall rejoice in your festival, with your son and daughter, your male and female slave, the Levite, the stranger, the fatherless, and the widow in your communities" (Deuteronomy 16.14). Joy is the very purpose and goal of a holiday: not the joy around Dionysus or Bacchus, but one defined by its being shared with strangers and the poor. Such joy is to bring the poor closer to yourself; you are to be happy with them and they are to be happy with you. Such joy is to raise man above social affliction; though this affliction cannot be ignored, it is, on the day of festival, at least to be overcome. The holidays would indeed lose all meaning and value if they were unable to implant for a short time joy in the heart of celebrating man.

And therefore joy in the festival—which joy is its very meaning and foundation—is also a symbol of peace. If it is true that holidays make joy a reality among men, the road to peace becomes a road to life. It is no illusion that the holidays are festivals of joy. The joy that is realized in the holiday of freedom, of deliverance from slavery, and of the divine call to become a kingdom of priests, is no deceptive joy. It is a truly historical joy that celebrates the revelation on Mount Sinai, the legislation of a moral world. And it is also a true joy which links the Festival of Harvest with the wanderings through the wilderness, concluding with the Rejoicing in the Law as a whole.

Joy is a well-established rubric for these holidays. Joy in the holidays proves peace a fundamental force of the soul and an important road to virtue. . . .

Peace in the joy of the festival is a characteristic of Jewish life. It is a miracle that, in spite of all the sufferings which have marked his history, the Jew has been able to preserve such equanimity, even humor, without which he could not have managed to rise out of the deepest humiliation to such proud heights. This miracle is due to the festivals! On the Sabbath as on the holidays, there was joy in the ghetto, no matter what sufferings the week had brought. Joy in the festival was a religious duty, and became an unshakable and vital force in Jewish consciousness.

Translated by William Wolf[9]

❦ 9 ❦

SUKKOT AND SIMHAT TORAH
IN ART

❧ ❧ ❧

JOSEPH GUTMANN

No contemporary illustrations of the colorful rites, dances, and processions that took place in the Jerusalem Temple during the *Simhat Bet
ha-Shoevah* have come down to us; nor have the ritual implements
—the golden flagons and the golden lampstands—used during the
fire and water libation ceremonies survived (Mishnah Sukkah 4–5).
The Talmud specifically commands the making of a "beautiful *sukkah*" (Shabbat 133b) and its adornment (Shabbat 22a and Sukkah
28b), but again we have no visual records.

Only the coins of the first (66–70 C.E.) and second (132–135 C.E.)
revolt against Rome feature the *lulav* and *etrog* very prominently in

several issues (fig. 1). The Sukkot symbols of *lulav* and *etrog* are also found in a painting of the third-century synagogue of Dura-Europos in Syria (fig. 2) and in the many synagogue mosaic floors excavated in Israel dating from the late Roman and Byzantine periods (fourth to sixth centuries c.e.).[1]

Medieval prayer codices (*mahzorim* and *siddurim*) from fourteenth- and fifteenth-century southern Germany and northern Italy have splendid illuminated pages of the Sukkot liturgy. A south German *mahzor* of the early fourteenth century has a decorated frame around the opening word of the *piyyut, Akhtir* ("I will crown with a wreath of praise"), recited during the *Yotzer* of the morning service on the first day of Sukkot (fig. 3). Next to the word panel we see a Jew wearing the pointed medieval Jew's hat and holding a *lulav* and *etrog*. In the lower margin are Leviathan and Behemoth, for according to tradition God will command these mythical beasts to engage in mortal combat: "Behemoth will with its horns pull Leviathan down and rend it, and Leviathan will, with its fins, pull Behemoth down and pierce it through" (*Leviticus Rabbah* 13.3). The struggle of Leviathan and Behemoth are depicted because the Sukkot liturgy expressed the fervent hope that God would use Leviathan's skin to construct a *sukkah* for the banquet of the righteous in messianic times.[2] Another *mahzor* from southern Germany, c. 1320, has a decorated word panel of the same *piyyut* (fig. 4). A Jew with the head of a bird displays the *etrog* and *lulav*.

A page from a richly illuminated north Italian manuscript, dating around 1470, has *Hoshana* ("save, I pray"), the opening word of the poetical prayer of the *musaf* service recited during the *hakkafot*, the seven ceremonial processions made around the *bimah* on Hoshana Rabbah (fig. 5). Next to the word *Hoshana* is a man in prayer shawl holding the prescribed *etrog* and *lulav*. Enclosed in a wattled fence underneath the word are two young children mounted on young deer playfully jousting like knights. Next to the *Hoshana* word panel in a fourteenth-century German *siddur*, in the margin, appears a Jew with prayer shawl, *etrog*, and *lulav* who marches in the *hakkafot* (fig. 6).

Fascinating and totally unexpected is the humor displayed in the marginal illustration of a *mahzor* written in Ulm, Germany, in 1459/1460. Next to the word panel *Af* ("Af Bri is the name of the prince of rain"), the opening word in the *piyyut* read during the *musaf* service on Shemini Atzeret, we see an ape who is ladling something from a bowl (fig. 7). The streamer above him carries the words of the *piyyut*: *Af bri utas*; the illustration is simply a wordplay on the Hebrew, which literally transposed into German is "Aff der Brüh ausass" ("ape who ate the broth").

Central to the celebration of Sukkot is, of course, the *sukkah*. One of the earliest illustrations of the building of a *sukkah* is found in a north Italian *mahzor* of the late fifteenth century (Collection Georges Weill, Strasbourg). In the lower margin we see on the left four wooden poles upholding a latticed roof, which is being covered by branches. On the right the family is seated around the table in the garden *sukkah,* while the head of the house raises the cup to recite *Kiddush*.[3]

Bernard Picart gives us an eyewitness account of an intimate family *sukkah* scene in eighteenth-century Holland. The family is being served the festive meal; Picart has depicted himself as an observer behind the mother breast-feeding her child (fig. 8). A wooden framework forms a dome above the walls of the *sukkah*. In the center of the dome hangs a silver festival lamp surrounded by a crown of garlands. Oriental lanterns hang from the roof. Contrasted with this elaborate *sukkah* is a more humble one erected next to it. Paul C. Kirchner in the eighteenth-century illustrations to his *Jüdisches Ceremoniel* depicts various types of *sukkot* set up in attics of German homes. One attic *sukkah* has two specially hinged wooden sides on the roof, which can be opened to expose the sky (fig. 9).

In 1938 the Israel Museum was able to rescue from Germany a *sukkah* made in 1823 for the Deller family, in the little village of Fischach, near Augsburg, Germany. The collapsible wooden dwelling has naive and charming paintings done by local folk artists (fig. 12). Most of the scenes were borrowed from illustrations of Jewish holidays in printed books. The paintings relate to the Jewish past by showing such biblical scenes as the giving of the Law to Moses and the sacrifice of Isaac, alluding thereby to the celebration of Shavuot and Rosh Hashanah. They also point to the present by depicting the Judengasse (Jew Alley) with its buildings and surroundings. Finally the paintings reveal a view of the messianic future—the visionary Holy City of Jerusalem crowned by the Mount of Olives.[4]

Moritz Oppenheim (1800–1882) in a sentimental painting renders a temporary outdoor *sukkah* similar to the one from Fischach. Curious schoolchildren peer through the open door of the *sukkah* on the right; the maid, on the left, brings the steaming hot soup to the family gathered within (fig. 13). The *sukkah* itself is garlanded and has a tablet hanging from the wall. A *sukkah* tablet from eighteenth-century Germany shows at the top left Samson rending the lion and below, King Solomon. On the right is David slaying Goliath and playing his lyre. The roundel contains the inscription from Leviticus 23.42: "You shall live in booths seven days." The prayer in the panel below the roundel refers to the *ushpizin*—the seven biblical guests: Abraham, Isaac, Jacob, Joseph, Moses, Aaron, and King David—who, according to mystical tradition, visit the *sukkah* on successive days of the holiday (fig. 14.) Another *sukkah* decoration, made by Israel David Luzzatto of eighteenth-century Italy, has the entire book of Ecclesiastes, recited during the Sukkot holiday, written out in micrography in the shape of a globe (fig. 17). The engraver Griselini made a *sukkah* decoration that dates from late eighteenth-century Italy. Within its frame stand Aaron and Moses, two of the *ushpizin,* on either side of the cartouche, which carries the opening verse from Psalms 76.1. The roundels and panels around the margin contain imaginary scenes of the impressive Sukkot rites performed in the Jerusalem Temple (fig. 18).[5]

A rare and unusual white tablecloth with gold brocade appliqué from Oberzell, Germany, dated 1781, may have been intended for the *sukkah* table on Hoshana Rabbah. In the center of the tablecloth are the *hoshanot*, the special willow branches beaten in the synagogue. Around the sides are inscriptions taken from Psalms 136.26, Isaiah 44.4: "like willows by flowing streams," Jeremiah 11.20, and Psalms 68.5 (fig. 19).

Not all ceremonies and art connected with the festival were restricted to the *sukkah*. A curious, superstitious folk belief, which arose in the Middle Ages and is now discarded, is illustrated in the *Sefer Minhagim* (fig. 22). On Hoshana Rabbah night it was customary to look at one's shadow cast by the light of the moon. If the shadow was headless, as in this woodcut, it was an omen that the person would die during the ensuing year. Tradition had proclaimed that even though the fate of every Jew was sealed on Yom Kippur, the verdict was not finally decreed until Hoshana Rabbah.

Within the synagogue, Hoshana Rabbah, the last day of Sukkot, was joyously celebrated by the seven ceremonial processions around the *bimah* with *lulav* and *etrog,* in memory of the circuits made by the priests around the altar in the Jerusalem Temple. Bernard Picart captures this moment by showing us the venerable members of the eighteenth-century Sephardic congregation in Amsterdam. Wearing the fashionable wigs and three-cornered hats of the day, they are circling around the *tevah* (*bimah*) of the Amsterdam synagogue carrying their *lulavim* and *etrogim* (fig. 23). The Torah Scrolls in our engraving have been taken from the ark. For this occasion, as well as for the entire Sukkot holiday, specially made Torah mantles and curtains were often used, primarily in Ashkenazic synagogues. The *tas* (Torah shield), placed over the Torah mantle, contained interchangeable identifying plates for various holidays, as in the *tas* shown, made in 1708 in Prague (fig. 24). A *menorah* is in the center of our silver shield, flanked by twisted columns. Judith with the head of Holofernes is on the left, and Aaron with his priestly vestments on the right. Both figures are crowned, while a double-headed eagle surmounts the entire shield. The *etrogim* carried by the congregants in the Picart engraving had to be protected, for a broken *pitum* would render the *etrog* unfit for use. Hence, sugar bowls, candy dishes, soap dishes made of silver, wood, and glass were frequently adapted as *etrog* holders in the eighteenth and nineteenth centuries. One of the earliest surviving *etrog* containers comes from Augsburg, Germany, c. 1670, and was fashioned in the shape of the fruit itself (fig. 25). Made of silver gilt, it gracefully rests on a high foot. From late nineteenth-century Austria comes another *etrog* container in the form of the citron (fig. 26). Around the lid is the inscription from Leviticus 23.40: "You shall take the product of *hadar* trees" (for tradition interpreted the enigmatic "*hadar*" to mean *etrog*); in the center another *etrog* is displayed.[6] The contemporary artist Ludwig Wolpert has fashioned a handsome and functional container that is enhanced by the delicate Hebrew lettering quoting the words from Leviticus 23.40 (fig. 29). A more fanciful creation to hold the *etrog* by the late Ilya Schor (1904–1961) illustrates the whole story of Sukkot. The *ushpizin*, the invited biblical guests of the *sukkah*, encircle the silver container. The lid has a decorative band containing the signs of the zodiac, and is topped with a family within a *sukkah* (fig. 30).

While the sacred Scrolls are paraded in procession around the *bimah* of the synagogue on Simhat Torah evening, the children join in the gay festivities by marching along with their elders. In their hands, they carry flags made by folk artists. One example from nineteenth-century Poland has a rampant lion whose banner carries the words "Flag of the camp of Judah" and a stately stag on the left. Below is the inscription "Be swift as a stag and strong as a lion" (fig. 31). Another flag includes a portrayal of the sacrifice of Isaac and the legend "Exult and be merry on Simhat Torah" (fig. 32).

The mood of rejoicing on Simhat Torah has been recorded by the Israeli artist Jossi Stern in a lithograph. Like musical notes, his figures respond to an inner rhythm; even the buildings in the background seem to be dancing (fig. 33). Marc Chagall, in his gay drawing of Simhat Torah for his wife Bella's book, *Burning Lights,* renders visually the description of the text: "Shoulder to shoulder, each hangs on the other. They do not let go, as though they feared that if they were left alone they would fall in pieces" (fig. 36). "The Rejoicing of the Law" by the English artist Solomon Alexander Hart (1806–1881) is in a more somber and dignified mood. The detailed painting done in the academic tradition represents the procession of the Scrolls in the Leghorn synagogue (fig. 37).

In the synagogue on Simhat Torah morning, honorary titles—*hatan Torah* and *hatan Bereshit*—are bestowed on two distinguished members of the congregation. The *hatan Torah,* the bridegroom of the Torah, reads the last verses of the Torah; the *hatan Bereshit,* the bridegroom of Genesis, begins reading the first verses of the Torah. Both are given places of honor next to the Torah ark, as in the Picart engraving showing the interior of the famous Sephardic Amsterdam synagogue (fig. 38). They are feted like bridegrooms, since symbolically they represent Israel about to be wedded to bride Torah. Frequently special couches or chairs were set aside for them on this occasion, as in the pair of carved and gilded chairs made in 1775 for the Mantua synagogue (fig. 39).[7] When leaving the synagogue, the bridegrooms are regally escorted home by prominent members of the community with lit torches and music, as recorded for us in Bernard Picart's engraving from eighteenth-century Holland (fig. 40).[8]

The illustrations of customs and ceremonial objects of the Sukkot and Simhat Torah holidays permit us to experience and relive, even if only fleetingly, the beauty and piety of this joyous celebration in ages gone by.

10

THE DEVELOPMENT
OF THE FESTIVAL

THE ORIGIN OF SUKKOT

ISAAC N. FABRICANT

The Book of Jubilees, which was composed about 130 B.C.E., claims that Sukkot was celebrated long before the granting of the Law. It declares that Abraham was the founder of the custom of the festival of Sukkot. When he came to live in Beersheba he set up his tents and instituted a ceremony which centered round these tents. He erected an altar and made circuits around it accompanied by prayer—"And Abraham built booths for himself and his servants in the seventh month, and he was the first to celebrate the festival of Sukkot in the Holy Land" (Book of Jubilees 16.21). This book declares that this celebration which Abraham inaugurated was the inspiration for the law of Sukkot found in our Torah.

There is an ancient legend based on Genesis 33.16–17, "So Esau started back that day on his way to Seir. But Jacob journeyed on to Sukkot. . . ." In this legend Esau represents sin and temptation and Seir stands for the Day of Atonement. (Leviticus 16 gives the law of Seir or goat on the Day of Atonement.) When Seir departed, i.e., the Day of Atonement, Jacob came to the *sukkah*. Here is to be found the origin of the custom of beginning the building of the *sukkah* soon after the termination of Kippur. There is a midrash which tells us that Jacob not only observed Sukkot but also added Shemini Atzeret.

In the days of the First Temple, Sukkot was considered the culminating festival and because of its importance became known as "The Festival." King Solomon chose this festival as the occasion for the celebration of the dedication of the Temple (1 Kings 8.2).

Ezra and Nehemiah instructed those who had returned to Zion to build booths. Apart from the *mitzvah* of the *sukkah* which was taught in the Torah, they were also anxious to recapture some of the splendor of former times, and Sukkot with its rich ceremonials could provide the atmosphere they sought. The Bible tells us that those who returned cooperated with enthusiasm in the observance of the festival and celebrated it so that the glory of former days returned.

In the days of the Second Temple the sacrifices were more lavish than at any other festival, requiring seventy animals. Those sacrifices were made on behalf of the seventy heathen nations. The rabbis declared: "When the heathen destroyed the Temple, they destroyed the atonement that was made for them" (Sukkah 55b).

In addition to the colorful procession in the Temple in which the *lulav* and the *etrog* were carried by the worshipers whilst the *Hallel* (Psalms 113–118) was recited, there was the libation of water in the Temple on each of the seven days at the morning service. According to the Mishnah a golden flask holding about three pints was filled with water from the fountain of Siloam, carried up to the Water Gate, where the procession was greeted by three calls on the ram's horn by the priests. The officiating priest ascended the ramp on the south side of the great altar, and turned to the left (west), where there were two silver basins, one for the pouring of the wine, and into the other the water was poured. At the moment when the priest was about to pour the water into the basin, the people shouted to him, "Raise your hand!" because once a certain priest spilled it on his feet. On one occasion Alexander Jannaeus (103–76 B.C.E.), king and high priest, was pelted with citrons by the worshipers standing around because he showed contempt for the rite by spilling the water at his feet.

The pouring out of water had no biblical support. According to R. Nehunya it was a law given by God to Moses at Sinai, but was not recorded in the Scriptures. Scholars maintain that there was a belief current amongst many nations that the pouring out of water at the time the first autumnal rains were due would magically induce rain to fall. Judaism would not tolerate this superstition and so it took an ancient custom of the nations and incorporated it in the Temple service, and the libation of water became a symbol of rain. R. Akiba explains the custom thus: "Why does the Law say, Make a libation of water at the Feast? The Holy One, blessed is He, says, Make a libation of water before Me at the Feast in order that the rains of the year may be blessed to you."[1]

❧ ❧ ❧

HOSHANA RABBAH
HIRSCHEL REVEL

Hoshana Rabbah, the twenty-first day of Tishri, which is the seventh day of the Sukkot festival and the last of its intermediate days (Hol ha-Moed), has been of special significance since biblical times. Talmudic sources relate that on every day of the Sukkot festival there was a procession around the altar in the Temple, each person holding in his hands the four plants, *lulav, etrog,* myrtle, and willow, bound together. While circling the altar they would chant in unison, "We beseech Thee, O Lord, save now! We beseech Thee, O Lord, make us now to prosper" (Psalms 118.25), and "I and He, save now." On Hoshana Rabbah, however, the people would first march joyfully to Motza (about thirty minutes' distance from Jerusalem), where they would cut many willow branches, and then return to the Temple, where they decorated the altar with them. After making seven circuits around the altar they would beat a small bunch of willow sprigs against the ground. According to some, this custom of beating the willow sprigs is of Sinaitic origin, while according to others, it originated in the time of the prophets, either as a general practice, or as a practice of the few.

13. "The *Sukkah*." By Moritz Oppenheim (1800–1882). See Chapter 9.

In the gaonic period these circuits were repeated at the afternoon service. The seven circuits recall God's mercies at the time when the wall of Jericho collapsed after it had been circled seven times. The willow was the symbol of the fruitfulness of rain, for tradition held that on the next day (Shemini Atzeret) the amount of rain to be sent to the earth for the ensuing year was determined.

In later and in modern times the custom is to take the Scrolls out of the ark, and make seven circuits, singing short liturgical litanies, which are called *Hoshanot*. This is why the day is referred to as Hoshana Rabbah, or "the day of many *Hoshanot*," although originally the day was known as "the day of willow sprigs." The word "Hoshana," which is found six times in the New Testament, where it is used to denote a cry of admiration and jubilation, is based upon this usage. After the seven circuits are completed, the bundle of the four plants is put aside, and while the verse, "The messenger announces good tidings" is repeated three times, a bundle of the willow sprigs is beaten a few times against the floor or against a bench. . . .

The *Zohar* has popularized the conception of Hoshana Rabbah as a "day of judgment," when the decrees decided by God on Yom Kippur for every individual commence to take effect. According to a midrash cited by Isaac Tyrnau in his *Minhagim* (under Hoshana Rabbah), God promised Abraham that if his children had not been forgiven on Yom Kippur, they would have an opportunity until Hoshana Rabbah to repent and be forgiven. However, from the *Midrash ha-Gadol* which reads, "on this day [Hoshana Rabbah] . . . Israel . . . enters into their blessings," it would seem that Hoshana Rabbah has a significance independent of that of Yom Kippur. For while on Yom Kippur one's fate for the ensuing year is sealed insofar as punishments for past misdeeds are concerned, the extent of the blessings which will fall to one's lot is not determined until Hoshana Rabbah, after God has had an opportunity to observe how wholeheartedly one has carried out the commandments relative to the Sukkot festival, and to what extent he deserves to be rewarded. . . .

Since the time of Abudraham (fourteenth century), many Jews have observed the custom of remaining awake the night of Hoshana Rabbah, spending the time in study and in reciting the *Tikkun*, which contains selections from the Bible, Talmud, and *Zohar*, as well as special prayers. Unpaid pledges to charity are usually paid on this day. Although some were accustomed to fast on Hoshana Rabbah, this practice was forbidden by Simon ben Zemah Duran, because fasting is not permitted on the intermediate holidays. In honor of the sanctity of the day, candles are often lit and ritual baths are taken as on Yom Kippur, and the *kittel* is worn over the Sabbath clothes. Some congregations include sections from the Yom Kippur liturgy, as the general plan of the prayers is somewhat changed in order to conform to the sanctity of the day.

Many interesting superstitions and customs have arisen in connection with Hoshana Rabbah. The oldest and most famous of these is that if one looks at his reflection on the night of Hoshana Rabbah and if one's head is missing from the reflected shadow, one will not live out the year, unless he repents and is then visited by a severe illness. The root of this superstition is found in the *Zohar*. A variation of this superstition is that if one looks at his reflection in a dish of well-water and if the eyes and the mouth of the reflection are closed, one will not live out the year. These superstitions were already decried by Moses Isserles (sixteenth century) and they were ridiculed by Rabbi Jacob Ettlinger. Since the thirteenth century it has been customary for pious Jews to save the willow sprigs after they are beaten and use them as fuel to heat the oven in which the Passover *matzot* are baked. These used willow sprigs, when placed in a secluded spot in the home, were supposed to banish fear and make for a sense of security.[2]

❧ ❧ ❧

SHEMINI ATZERET— THE CONCLUDING DAY

JULIUS H. GREENSTONE

The concluding day of the Sukkot festival is designated in the Bible and in the liturgy as Shemini Atzeret, usually rendered "the Eighth Day of Solemn Assembly." In a homiletic way, the rabbis explained the nature of the day by means of the following parable: "A king once gave a feast to which the diplomatic representatives of many nations were invited. The feast lasted for seven days. When they were all ready to depart, the king called aside his son who was also among the guests and said to him, 'While all these strangers were around we hardly had an opportunity to have an intimate conversation. Tarry thou one day longer, when we shall hold a simple feast all by ourselves.' Thus, God arranged for the feast of Sukkot when seventy offerings are made in behalf of the seventy nations of the world. On the conclusion of the feast, He begs of Israel to tarry (*atzar,* hold, keep back) one day longer when only one bullock and one ram are offered in behalf of Israel." In its literal sense, however, this day is called thus because it serves as the conclusion to the holiday, as is also the name given to the last day of Passover. Shavuot is likewise called Atzeret, and is regarded as the concluding day of the Passover holiday. This again is explained by the rabbis in the following manner. Atzeret of Sukkot should really be observed on the fiftieth day after the holiday, as is Shavuot on the fiftieth day after Passover, but because the rainy season begins just about this time, the people were excused from the trouble of traveling to Jerusalem then, and the feast was set for the day immediately following the conclusion of the Sukkot holiday.

The most distinctive feature of the festival as observed in the synagogue has been the chanting of a special prayer for rain, recited during the *musaf* service. This is known as *Geshem* (rain) and the prayers compiled in this connection are chanted with a peculiar intonation, while the *hazzan* is clothed in a white gown similar to that worn on the High Holy Days. The rainy season in Palestine begins about this time and the farmer waits for it with hope and faith. During the holiday, the thousands of pilgrims who would come to Jerusalem from all over Palestine, most of them farmers, would watch anxiously the drift of the smoke from the altar in the Temple. If it drifted toward the north, they looked forward to plenty of rain, while if it turned toward the south they were apprehensive that the rain may be scarce. After Shemini Atzeret, a phrase expressive of the power of God in causing the rain to come down in its proper season is inserted in the *Shemoneh Esreh* and recited until the first day of Passover. The actual prayer for rain, however, inserted in the ninth benediction, is not said until much later, at the autumnal equinox, about December 5th, out of consideration for the pilgrims, who were given time to return to their homes before the rain started. Prayers and fasting for rain to come down were also said and practiced during other periods of the year, and the Mishnah has a special treatise set aside for the consideration of the various laws regulating these customs. Already in Temple times, we are told that the high priest, while performing his arduous duties on the Day of Atonement, invoked God to send rain in due season. Drought was regarded as a punishment for sins, and in the *Shema* the rewards and punishments enumerated for the obedience or disobedience of the commandments of the Lord were mainly the coming of rain in the proper season or the withholding of the rain when it was most needed. The prayer for rain proved efficacious when offered by pious and virtuous men. Teachers of children were selected for that office because of their exalted calling. The rabbis mention a personality, Honi ha-Maagal, who appeared to be most successful in having his prayers for rain answered.

The special prayer for rain said on Shemini Atzeret takes into consideration the climatic needs of Palestine. The custom has been maintained also after the exile when Jews lived in other countries and in different climes. When a number of Spanish exiles settled in Brazil in the middle of the seventeenth century and found that the rainy season there came at a different time of the year, they turned to a rabbi in Salonica to inquire whether they would be justified in changing the recital of the prayer for rain from the winter to the summer months. This interesting question is the first recorded legal inquiry directed by Jews of the New World to those of the Old. While this was permitted to them, the *Geshem* prayer on Shemini Atzeret still remained in vogue, as this was intended to serve not merely as a prayer but also as a historic reminiscence of the indissoluble relationship of the Jews with the soil of Palestine. The special prayer is found in one form or another in all the different rites, the Sephardic as well as the Ashkenazic. In the latter ritual, a considerable number of additional *piyyutim*, describing the agricultural works to be pursued during each month of the year, each one influenced by the signs of the zodiac peculiar to it, are inserted. The crude illustrations of the signs of the zodiac may still be found in some of the older Ashkenazic festival prayer books.[3]

❧ ❧ ❧

REJOICING IN THE LAW
CECIL ROTH

There is no celebration of the Jewish year which appears to the casual eye so spontaneous and so simple as the Rejoicing in the Law. But, like all other Jewish celebrations, it has a long history behind it, apart from which it cannot be properly appreciated.

The characteristic feature of the holiday is, of course, the institution of the bridegrooms of the Law and of the Beginning. Not many of those who take on these functions nowadays realize their real significance. The modern honeymoon has robbed Jewish life of what used to be one of its most happy institutions—the "seven days of rejoicing" which followed upon every wedding, culminating in the jubilant reception of the bridegroom in synagogue on the Sabbath. On that day, he was the hero. Special hymns greeted his arrival to the seat of honor reserved for him; sweetmeats were showered down on him as he passed; and a special formula was recited when he was called up, crowned with myrtle, to the reading of the Law. With him, he bore a second *Sefer Torah*, which had been taken out of the ark specially for his benefit, and which he had with him in his place. From this, there was read the chapter in Genesis which recounts the story of the marriage of Isaac, accompanied by the Aramaic paraphrase. He then returned to his seat again, bearing his Scroll.

Our present-day institution of the bridegroom of the Law and of the Beginning follows so closely upon this model that it might almost be termed a parody of it. Special hymns are recited in the hero's honor, and he has a special seat reserved for him. Formerly, sweetmeats were showered down upon him as he passed (nowadays, the place of these is taken by a distribution to the children after the service). When he is called to the Law, a special formula is recited—that delightful, hyperbolical *Mereshut*, which asks the permission of the Almighty, of the elders, of the learned, and of the whole congregation for the formality. This is an almost exact paraphrase of a similar *Mereshut* for the ordinary bridegroom by Rabbi Simeon the Great, formerly recited in Franco-Jewish communities and found in some old manuscripts, as well as in the *Mahzor Vitry*. The original has fallen into oblivion, but the parody remains.

The bridegroom of the Law, like his everyday prototype, goes up bearing his own Scroll, from which a special portion is read. When he returns, according to the Sephardic usage, precisely the same little roundel is chanted as that with which the wedding service was enlivened. A number of other little usages, which we today consider to be typical of the Rejoicing in the Law, are similarly to be traced back to the marriage celebration on which the ceremonies are based. . . .

In the Levant, the guests of the bridegrooms were sprinkled with scent sprays. Nearer home, after the invention of gunpowder, salvoes were sometimes fired in honor of the day. As far as Italy is concerned, we may obtain delightfully intimate glimpses from the sumptuary laws, passed periodically in every community to limit extravagance and ostentation—as rife in those days as in our own. Here, it seems, the wives of the *hatanim* were known (not quite logically) as the bride of the Law and of the Beginning respectively, and received among the women much the same honors as their husbands did among the men. According to the code which was in vogue at Modena, they might not be accompanied to synagogue by an escort of more than eight ladies, excluding relatives and visitors from other towns. Those of Rome forbade the "brides" to serve any refreshments in the rooms or loggias from which they surveyed the festivities in the synagogue. Most picturesque of all, though they omit reference to this detail, were the regulations laid down in 1766 at Ancona:

xiv. On the evening when the bridegrooms of the Law (known as *hatan Torah* and *hatan Bereshit*) are drawn by lot, they may not serve either coffee or sweetmeats or any other species of refreshment. On the evenings when they exercise their functions, they may be accompanied by six torches only, in addition to the ordinary candle-bearer. Their consorts may be accompanied by only two torches. The latter, when they leave their house and return on the day of Simhat Torah, may be accompanied by only four women. Both on the eve of Simhat Torah and on the day, only coffee and a cake (*pizzola*) may be served to the women; and on the evening after Simhat Torah, only coffee both to men and to women. It shall not be permitted to any person to place a candle or torch at his window on this occasion; this shall be permitted only at the house where the function of the *hatan Torah* and *hatan Bereshit* is being held, and in a single apartment only.

This reference to illuminating the houses, and to a torchlight procession (another distinction shared also by the ordinary bridegroom, as we are informed in this same code), brings us to another forgotten but once invariable Simhat Torah practice. It was the universal custom of the *hatanim* to be accompanied to their houses by the wardens of the community, with an escort of torch-bearers. Picart's engravings of Jewish life in Amsterdam at the beginning of the eighteenth century comprise one plate which gives a vivid impression of the scene as it was enacted in northern Europe. Even in England, the same usage prevailed. The late Lucien Wolf left it on record how, as late as the nineteenth century, the bridegrooms used to be escorted home from synagogue after the evening service by a procession of congregants, singing lustily and bearing banners and torches.

Nowadays, the faint shadow of this prevails in some places in the custom of formally ushering the happy pair as far as the door of the synagogue—but no further.

England, too, appears to have known at one time (as this record shows) something of the carnival spirit which prevailed on the continent. Samuel Pepys proves it in the classical passage of his *Diary* for October 14th, 1663:

After dinner my wife and I, by Mr. Rawlinson's conduct, to the Jewish Synagogue: where the men and boys in their vayles, and the women behind a lattice out of sight; and some things stand up, which I believe is their law, in a press to which all coming in do bow; and at the putting on their vayles do say something, to which others that hear him do cry Amen, and the party do kiss his vayle. Their service all in a singing way and in Hebrew. And anon their Laws that they take out of the press are carried by several men, four or five several burthens in all, and they do relieve one another; and whether it is that everyone desires to have the carrying of it, I cannot tell, thus they carried it round about the room while such a service is singing. And in the end they had a prayer for the King, which they pronounced his name in Portugall; but the prayer, like the rest, in Hebrew. But Lord! to see the disorder, laughing, sporting, and no attention, but confusion in all their service, more like brutes than people knowing the true God, would make a man foreswear ever seeing them more; and indeed I never did see so much, or could have imagined there had been any religion in the whole world so absurdly performed as this.

It has been pointed out repeatedly that this passage obviously refers to the Rejoicing in the Law, this fact explaining the ebullience of spirit which so unfavorably impressed the diarist. But no one seems hitherto to have noticed that the service to which it alludes is nowadays unknown to the ritual of Bevis Marks, where the *Minhah* on this day is as decorous and as uneventful as on any other *yom tov* afternoon. Plainly, the community still observed then the old custom which still prevails at some Sephardic communities in Italy, where the afternoon service on Simhat Torah is one of the great occasions of the year. The Scrolls of the Law are taken out of the ark and escorted round the synagogue, to the accompaniment of various hymns chanted to exquisite Old-World Spanish tunes, brought with them by the exiles from the [Iberian] Peninsula. . . .

The congregational records provide no inkling as to when the practice was abandoned. They show plainly, however, the attempt made to prevent extravagance on this occasion. Thus in 1674, "the

Senhores of the Mahamad [standing or executive committee], considering the tumult and disorder which the decorations made on Simhat Torah . . . and on Sabbath Bereshit cause, agreed from this day henceforth it be not permitted to the Bridegrooms of the Law to decorate the Synagogue with wreaths of myrtle nor of anything, and it is only allowed them [to decorate it] with landscape tapestries or gilt leather, as also flowers on the candelabra." In the Ashkenazic synagogue in Duke's Place, Simhat Torah received statutory mention in 1735, when the sale by auction of the office of bridegroom was discontinued, and it was decided to distribute it in future by lot. In the Western Synagogue (established by the Jews of Westminster and the neighborhood in the middle of the eighteenth century) the Simhat Torah revels must have become a little too riotous at one period, and steps were taken to keep them within moderate limits. Here (we read in the regulations drawn up at the period of the Napoleonic wars) the evening circuits were discontinued "for the sake of decorum," and it was expressly laid down that no liveried servants (persons in *livery-malbushim*, is the original phrase!) might participate. Here, too, it was customary to escort the *hatanim* home with a torchlight procession. Fortunately, the majority of the members lived hard by, in and about Denmark Court; otherwise, the gay young sparks of the West End might have had a reasonable pretext for hilarity. The torches, it may be mentioned, cost the congregation half a crown!

There is, indeed, no end to the variety in local rites and usages as far as Simhat Torah is concerned. Half the communities in Italy published their own Rite of Service for the circuits on the Rejoicing in the Law; five for Ferrara alone lie before me as I write. The great Hayyim Joseph David Azulai—traveler, cabalist, and bibliophile—laid down detailed mystical prescriptions for the occasion, a copy of which I possess in manuscript. The communities of Cochin, on the Malabar Coast in India, evolved, during their long centuries of isolation from the rest of their brethren, their own characteristic rite for the afternoon service, unlike anything to be found elsewhere, and winding up with a special form of *Kaddish*, of unique interest, which stretches over four closely printed pages. In Avignon and the Comtat Venaissin a selection of scriptural readings, with their Aramaic paraphrase, was prescribed for recitation in the home on the previous evening, before *Kiddush*—similar in its way to the Passover *Haggadah*, and, indeed, sometimes found in the same manuscripts as that better-known work. The hymns recited on the following day are to be found in no other rite. Before the Scrolls were put back into the ark, an extremely elaborate form of prayer was recited on behalf of the civil power.[4]

❧ 11 ❧

THE SUKKAH

❧ ❧ ❧

BUILDING THE *SUKKAH*
JULIUS H. GREENSTONE

The only reference found in the Bible to the actual construction of the *sukkah* is in connection with the religious reformation brought about by the activities of Ezra and Nehemiah, after the return from the Babylonian exile. A proclamation was issued to the people: " 'Go forth unto the mount and fetch olive branches, the branches of the wild olive, and branches of thick trees, to make booths, as it is writ-ten.' So the people went out, and brought them, and made them-selves booths, every one upon the roof of his house, and in their courts, and in the courts of the house of God, and in the broad place of the water-gate and in the broad place of the gate of Ephraim"

(Nehemiah 8.15–16). It is further related that the ceremony was observed by all the people who returned from the exile, and the festival was celebrated in the manner unknown in Israel since the days of Joshua the son of Nun. "And there was very great gladness."

The law about the erection of booths is found only in Leviticus, although the name *Hag ha-Sukkot* is found both in Numbers and in Deuteronomy, while in Exodus the festival is designated "the Feast of Ingathering," pointing to the original agricultural character of the feast.

In later generations, the building of booths was regarded as obligatory upon every householder. It was one of the religious acts which people performed with much joy and alacrity. In many instances, the booth was built anew every year, although some would keep the same frame from year to year. The young people of the household usually undertook the labor connected with the construction, under the supervision and with the aid of their elders. There are no special provisions for the building itself except that it should be of convenient size and should have four walls. The walls need not all belong to the booth; a wall of a house or of a fence may be utilized. Great importance, however, was attached to the roofing. The roof must consist of branches of trees, detached from the trunk, sparsely spread over so that the stars may be seen through them. In the small Polish and Lithuanian Jewish towns, the peasants round about would do a brisk business in the branches which they would bring to town for the use of the Jewish population. The olive and myrtle branches of biblical days were substituted by the branches of humbler trees that were plentiful in the particular vicinity. The flimsy covering was intended to indicate the ephemeral nature of the structure and thereby emphasize its symbolic significance.

While much of the material may have been brought together weeks before the festival, the actual construction did not start until after Yom Kippur. The devout Jew, weakened by a day of fasting and prayer, would repair immediately after the fast day to place the first stake for the building of the *sukkah*. Often the booths, built by inexperienced hands out of stray boards of all shapes and dimensions, would present a most ungainly appearance. The more opulent would have an elaborate frame, made by an artisan, which they needed only to put together for the festival. In some houses, special wings were set aside for the *sukkah*, which may have been used for other purposes during the year. The roof was made movable, and

14. *Sukkah* tablet. Hand-colored woodcut. Germany. Eighteenth century.
See Chapter 9.

before the holiday it was removed or suspended and the branches were laid on top of the rafters made for that purpose. Such a room had to be either on the top floor of the house, or in a shed or bungalow built alongside the house. . . .

In the poorer neighborhoods, several families would join in the building of a large *sukkah* which would accommodate all the people of the vicinity, each family sitting at a separate table and indulging in an exchange of dishes with the other families. The housewives had to be on the alert in their culinary preparations, so as to forestall the criticism that might come to them from their sisters at the other tables.

From a home institution, the *sukkah* has been relegated in Western lands to the synagogue, serving the entire community, although many individuals still adhere to the ancient practice of having booths in their homes. The synagogue *sukkah*s are often very elaborately decorated, thanks to the women of the sisterhoods who devote much energy and ingenuity to this task. Most of these booths are portable, dismantled every year and then put up again before the festival.[1]

✡ ✡ ✡

SOME BOOTHS I HAVE KNOWN
ISRAEL ABRAHAMS

My earliest *sukkah* was my mother's. In those days—how many years ago I do not care to count!—my summer holiday lasted exactly nine days a year. We needed no train to take us to our country destination—we just stepped into our little city garden. In brief, our one and only annual outing was spent in our *sukkah*, and we young boys and girls enjoyed our change of scene far more than I have relished longer and more distant excursions in recent years. It has been said that the pleasures we make for ourselves are fuller and fairer than the pleasures which are given to us. Perhaps this is why we loved our *sukkah*—for we made it ourselves. We did not employ a professional carpenter to put in a single nail or plane a single beam. We bought rough logs and boards at the city timber yard. We planed the logs and grazed our fingers, but the pain did not count. Though all these preparatory stages occurred a fortnight beforehand, the actual building operations never began until the night, when the Great Fast was over. Old traditions clung to us, and somehow we knew it was a special merit to close the Day of Atonement, hammer in hand, putting in the first nail of the *sukkah*, passing as the psalmist has it "from strength to strength."

Our *sukkah* was much admired, but no critics were more enthusiastic than we were ourselves. It goes without saying that we had many visitors, for people in those days had a keen eye for a *sukkah*. People who neglected us all the year rubbed up their acquaintanceship as Tabernacles came around. We did not wonder that our *sukkah* was popular, for we really believed that our architectural design was an original one, and I retained that notion until only a few days ago, when an old illustrated jargon book, printed in Amsterdam in 1723, was cruelly placed in my hands, and on page 45 I beheld to my chagrin the picture of just such a *sukkah* as ours was. We put it together in this fashion: four upright beams were connected at the top and at the bottom with crossbars of wood, and thus was obtained a hollow shell of substantial strength. Our next step was to put in the flooring. How we wasted our wood by ingeniously cutting the boards just three-quarters of an inch too short! But that difficulty was overcome, after many councils of war, and we then put on the roof, not flat, but sloping. The sloping roof was a great conception. It did away almost entirely with the rain difficulty, for the water glided off the thick leaves at the top and saved us from the necessity of tarpaulins or glass superstructures. Most people make the *sukkah* roof flat and then build a sloping wooden or glass frame above the roof. Our plan was not only prettier, but it enabled us to remain in our *sukkah* without closing the top in all but very heavy showers. We had a tarpaulin ready in case of exceptional rain, but I can only recollect one or two occasions on which we scaled the garden walls and placed it in position over the greenery. But our master stroke lay in the walls. There were no walls at all. A few lines of stout string made a latticework on which we fixed thick layers of fragrant myrtle branches and laurel leaves. The effect was fairylike, and we did not spoil it by attempting to "paint the lily." The only decorations which we introduced were clusters of grapes, which trailed their luscious path along the very walls, a few citrons in their own early amber yellow, which hung from the bright roof, and an old chrysanthemum or two still growing in their mold, which added the necessary streaks of color. All this was not so costly as it may sound, for we bought in very cheap markets, and saved much of the wood from one year to the next.

Over the way, our neighbors had their *sukkah* too. This was also very pretty, and many preferred it to ours. It belonged to a more conventional and ornate type, for it was really a sort of summerhouse which stood all the year and was disroofed when Tabernacles drew nigh. We boys used to like to have a hand in their decorations as well as in our own, though it went to our hearts to see the beautiful apples and pears betinseled with wrappers of gold and silver paper. The gilder in those days was the only "proper" beautifier. Then, reams of colored papers were cut into strips and twined into chains. Finally, out came the samplers which the girls worked with their own fingers. These samplers contained the *sukkah* benedictions embroidered and crocheted in the drollest of droll Hebrew letters, but somehow as they were brought out year by year, and were hung in position on the walls with the *mizrah* facing the west, a silence of mingled gladness and tenderness fell upon them all. It seemed like a stock-taking of past memories, and a renewal of past, forgotten loves. But we loved best our own little bit of nature unadorned.

Sadly lacking in ornament, whether natural or artificial, was a *sukkah* which many of my readers will recollect. It belonged to a remarkable man now dead. He had more piety than pence. He occupied three or four rooms on the top floor of a tall house in Bevis Marks, and he had not even a square foot of open space. Must he therefore be robbed of the *mitzvah* of sitting in his own *sukkah*, nay, of sleeping in it? Perish the thought! A convenient trapdoor in one of his garrets suggested an ingenious plan. He first raised the trapdoor, removed the skylight—which was very rickety and easily detached—and hung sheets round the hole, the sheets trailing to the ground and beyond, and catching the feet of unwary visitors. Of course we all would go and see this old gentleman every Tabernacles. He refused admittance to none; whether you could comfortably squeeze yourself in was your business not his. You plodded your weary way up five or six flights of stairs and stumbled through a hole in the sheetings. If you have never before seen the sight that greets you, prepare for a surprise! You would find no furniture in the room but a simple chair bedstead. One wall contained nothing but a red handkerchief on which was imprinted a fancy picture of Jerusalem with Moses and Aaron on either side of the Ten Commandments, while olive branches figured in all possible and impossible corners of the picture. The other wall was filled with a huge scroll on which, with his own hand, he had written out at great length the wonders of the Leviathan on which the good shall hereafter feed. But the most amazing thing was the host himself. He would be so seated that his head and shoulders were directly under the aperture in the roof. He was nearsighted, but when he espied you, eagerly would he seize your arm and push *you* into the place which he vacated, so that *you* too had your head under the center of the hole while you recited the proper blessing. Of course he slept in his queer *sukkah* every night, and equally of course he had an annual cold in the head for at least three months afterwards.

Such humble constructions were almost invariably the result of poverty. One well-known case occurred in which a *sukkah* was built on a small balcony outside the first-floor window of a house in Amsterdam, if I remember accurately. The poor owner could not help himself. He could not act like our previous friend, for he did not live at the top of the house. So he just opened the window slightly at the top and slipped into the crevice half a dozen long sticks parallel to one another. (He was a stick-dealer by profession.) Then he opened the lower half of the window, squeezing it up as tight as it would go. This lower part of the window he left open the whole week, for the *sukkah* was made by covering the projecting sticks with leaves. . . .

But one unsightly *sukkah* that I knew owed its ugliness to the owner's stinginess. He was very rich, but was a thorough miser. He made his *sukkah* small to save his hoarded shillings; and he made it unattractive lest too many visitors should present themselves. He constructed the walls out of old packing-cases, and did not take the trouble to erase the inscriptions daubed upon them. As you approached his *sukkah* your eyes were greeted with the legends: THIS SIDE UP WITH CARE, EMPTY CRATE TO BE RETURNED, and so forth. . . . This miserable man was one of the first I knew to apply to Baron Lionel de Rothschild for laurel branches to cover the roof of his *sukkah*. Even in those days the Rothschilds never refused any such application, though the scale on which the branches are supplied is now far more extensive. I believe that special bushes and trees are planted at Gunnersbury to meet the ever-growing demand on Tabernacles. Many a poor East End Jew, who would otherwise be forced to forgo the pleasure, is thus enabled to build his *sukkah*. But I do not quite see why some of my West End friends also avail themselves of Mr. Leopold de Rothschild's princely generosity.

I have mentioned some humble booths, let me introduce my readers to a very beautiful one which might be seen a few years ago at The Hague.

Mr. D. Polak Daniels, a warden of the Jewish congregation in The Hague, and a member of the municipality and the county council for South Holland, is undoubtedly the owner of one of the handsomest booths that have ever been built. This notable *sukkah*, which stands in the spacious garden in his residence in the Spuistraat, was built nearly forty-five years ago by Mr. Daniel's father-in-law. It is almost square, and constructed of wood and painted glass. The internal decorations are extremely handsome and tasteful, the prevailing color being light blue. The colored glass is very fine. The *sukkah* is so constructed that when taken to pieces, the panels of two of the sides form a box in which all the other parts are deposited. There is an interesting episode in connection with this *sukkah*, the fame of which has spread beyond the confines of The Hague. During the lifetime of the late queen of Holland this *sukkah* was mentioned at Her Majesty's dinner table. Queen Sophia was well versed in Jewish history and observances, and she expressed a wish to see Mr. Daniels's *sukkah*, it being then the Feast of Tabernacles. The request was of course complied with, and on the following afternoon the queen paid her visit, which lasted half an hour. . . . Although contrary to court etiquette to partake of refreshments, Her Majesty made an exception in this case, in order to carry out the custom of eating and drinking in a tabernacle. On taking leave the queen laughingly said to Mr. Daniels, "I take your word for a great deal, but you cannot make me believe that your ancestors in the desert lived in such splendid booths as this." What a contrast this to one poor fellow I knew who turned his shop shutters into walls, and a few old flat baskets into roofing, rather than have no *sukkah* at all. Indeed, there is room for both kinds of service to God, for the wealthy and the poor. If the service is cheerfully rendered, who knows which finds the more acceptance? . . .

The *sukkah* of the Bevis Marks Synagogue is the only one I have ever seen in which a distinction was made between rich and poor. But, after all, those who paid for the *mitzvah* deserved to get something for their money. There was, in fact, a reserved compartment for the wardens and officials and the high-born aristocracy, while the plebeians flocked into a larger and less ornate *sukkah* which stood in front of the other. In my days the Sephardim did not build many private *sukkah*s, the only ones I remember were those of Mogador and Gibraltar Jews, a stately specimen being that of Dayan Corcos in Bury Street. A fine old gentlemen he was. Always dressed in Moorish costume, with a flowing white satin tunic, a crimson or yellow sash, and a red fez or a turban, he cut a splendid figure. He often welcomed me as a boy and gave me Mogador cakes, shaped like rings, the chief ingredient used in their concoction being almonds. But to return to Bevis Marks. The *sukkah* was not a permanent brick building as it is with other synagogues nowadays, still less was it used all the year round as the minister's drawing room, a use made of the tabernacle in a West End synagogue. The Bevis Marks *sukkah* was taken down piece by piece and stored in a shed through the year, side by side with an old obsolete fire engine. The *sukkah* was pieced together every year; it was very strong, but, as I hinted before, was much more like a *sukkah* than the brick constructions in the West End synagogues nowadays; but these last are yearly becoming more beautiful, more bowerlike. Well, the one I am now dealing with was painted green outside, but the inside was not pretty. The smaller reserved compartment was much more gorgeous, of course. But the larger public section had no proper greenery on the roof, for the covering was made of wickerwork. Though this was economical it was not aesthetic. I believe that it has been altered in recent years. But the most interesting feature of the Bevis Marks *sukkah* was Mr. Belasco, the beadle. His tall, burly form recalled the pugilistic heroes which his family had produced in the past ages of the glorious prize ring. This Mr. Belasco, however, was as good-humored as he was big. Naturally, as there was no other public *sukkah* in the neighborhood, many *Tedescos* (German Jews) contrived to squeeze themselves into the company of the blueblooded. Mr. Belasco enjoyed tracking out the intruders. "These *Tedescos* are welcome to enter," he said, "but they shall have none of my olives." Let me explain. Mr. Belasco used to go round with a small keg of Spanish olives—even the olives were Sephardic—and permitted every *hidalgo* to insert his fingers and take one of the tempting morsels. This would go on merrily till Mr. Belasco came to an undoubted *Tedesco*. "You are not a Portugee," he would say. "Oh yes, I am a Portugee," was the response. Mr. Belasco was not taken in by the insinuating smile of his all-confident interlocutor. "If you are a Portugee, say *Shemang Yisrael*," came the crushing rejoinder. The mere *Tedesco* would attempt to repeat the first line of the *Shema,* but would almost invariably say *Yitrael* for *Yisrael*—a common mistake of Ashkenazim who try to read in the Portuguese style. This new shibboleth of Mr. Belasco's always succeeded in weeding out the interlopers, but much ready wit was displayed, and altogether everyone enjoyed the scene immensely.

For the present I must break off here. I have forgotten to tell many things: how, for instance, one friend of mine reserved his finest tapestry for decorating his *sukkah* walls and locked it up all the year. Another man I knew made an elaborate crown of leaves and flowers and fruits and suspended it from the ceiling of his dining room to remind him of the *sukkah* which he did *not* possess. The smallest *sukkah* of the pretty type that I ever entered was Mr. Bernays's. It was one of the daintiest objects on view at the Anglo-Jewish Exhibition. But we must beware lest we allow the *sukkah* to find its way exclusively to museums. The *sukkah* is an antiquity, but it must not become a mere object of curiosity to antiquarians. It has not yet exhausted its vital possibilities.[2]

꙳ ꙳ ꙳

UNUSUAL BOOTHS IN ISRAEL
SOLOMON FEFFER

Ornament, splendor, and beauty have always been associated with the festival of Sukkot, and this tradition has inspired many constructors of *sukkot* to erect booths marked by attractive exteriors and beautifully decorated interiors.

One such *sukkah* rises annually in stained-glass splendor in Petah Tikvah. All the appurtenances in this booth are made entirely of bits of colored glass laid in mosaic patterns. It is decorated with stained-glass artifacts and pictures, among them a Hanukkah menorah in fourteen colors constructed of more than twelve thousand glass fragments, a colorful seven-branched candelabrum, suitable biblical verses, and the prayers apropriate to the Feast of Tabernacles. The creator of the "glass booth"—Abraham Bar-Oryon, who is also the originator of the process—devotes his spare time throughout the year to his hobby of beautification, and each Sukkot is the occasion for the revelation of a new *vitrage* or stained-glass portrait.

Another monument to the art of the *sukkah* was created by Isaac Weinstock, a pious stone-carver resident in Jerusalem, whose masterpiece graces the courtyard of the former Sephardic orphanage in the Holy City. This unusual *sukkah*, known as the "Booth of Wonders," is elaborately adorned with wood carvings and paintings. These include—like the stained-glass *sukkah* in Petah Tikvah—the typical Bible verses and holiday supplications. There is also a wall realistically depicting the holy places of Jerusalem as if viewed from a height, representations of the *ushpizin*, and symbols of the twelve tribes. Like his counterpart in Petah Tikvah, the pious stone-carver spends on *sukkah* decorations every moment not absolutely required to carve out a living for his large family. Also featured in this *sukkah* is a miniature East European Jewish village during the Festival of Tabernacles, the work of the artist Naftali Schreiber. Its little houses, synagogue, *sukkot*, trees, plants and flowers and grass, its tiny stream meandering through a forest—all these create an illusion of reality heightened by the bright lights shining through the tiny windows.

The *sukkah* of the Hasidic rabbi Solomon Benjamin Ashlag in Bene Berak is a magnificent example of the concretization of mystical abstractions. This scholar, whose Sukkot activity consists in intensive delving into those portions of the *Zohar* which are relevant to the festival, possesses a *sukkah* of palatial proportions and design. The decorations, in different media, are as variegated in style as in content: the traditional *ushpizin*, Abraham extending his hospitality to the angels, the binding of Isaac, Jacob's well, tiny Moses floating in his wicker basket in the Nile River (containing real water), Aaron's *ephod* and breastplate, a camel caravan on its way to Egypt, David's lyre and crown lying beside a miniature Book of Psalms, the twelve tribes, an aquarium filled with frolicking fish, a cage of multicolored birds, magnificent tapestries embroidered with pictures of animals and esoteric birds, and, in the middle, a model of Jerusalem the Golden.

The same town is the site of yet another interesting *sukkah*, the labor of love of a beauty-loving *Hasid*. This one is a bridge between generations and continents: old Satmar in Hungary and present-day Israel. The owner, Naftali Shtern, who was rescued from the Auschwitz concentration camp, had hidden his father's *sukkah* decorations before his seizure by the Nazis, and after his liberation carried them with him to Israel. The Satmar synagogue is given life again as a charming enclave in one corner. In this model are arranged, as formerly, tiny synagogue benches, the reading desk, the holy ark with its miniature Torah Scroll, all topped by a sky-blue ceiling with sparkling golden stars. The *sukkah*, which measures four square meters, is decorated in addition with artifacts of wood, paper, painted metal, multicolored mirrors, and four birds carrying the *etrog, lulav,* myrtle, and willows. A chandelier with sixty-one colored lights casts its brilliant illumination over the charming scene.

Perhaps the most interesting *sukkot* of all, however, are those erected for the seven days of the festival in the various army encampments. The office of the chief of chaplains furnishes a guide detailing the laws for the construction of a tabernacle. The military units vie with one another for the coveted title of the most beautiful army *sukkah*. During the intermediate days of the holiday a group of judges examines the booths in all units and chooses one as the most beautiful *sukkah* in the Israeli Army. The criteria for selection are strict conformity with religious regulations, and beauty of construction and decorations. Special credit is allotted to combat units engaged in field activities.

Some of the army *sukkot* are erected under the most extraordinary conditions. There are *sukkot* on wheels and mobile *sukkot* carried on special army vehicles which serve field units. There are booths—fulfilling every religious requirement—built on the decks of naval boats and ships. Indeed, the Mishnah—"If a man builds his booth on the top of a wagon [read "army truck"!] or on the deck of a ship, it is valid" (Sukkah 2.3)—comes to life in the Israeli Army.

❧ ❧ ❧

THE ADORNMENT OF THE BOOTH

While the construction of a *sukkah* for the Festival of Tabernacles is a comparatively simple matter, its embellishment with varied decorations to emphasize its significance has always been of serious concern to pious Jews. The mere fulfillment of the letter of the Law by erecting a booth was never considered sufficient. The biblical verse "This is my God and I will adorn Him" (Exodus 15.2) was interpreted by the rabbis of the Talmud to imply that one is obligated to "make a beautiful *sukkah* in His honor" (Shabbat 133b).

The Talmud discusses the adornments for beautifying the festival booth in several passages. It states that if one owns beautiful vessels and beautiful divans he should bring them into the *sukkah* (Sukkah 28b). The Talmud also describes the use of murals, fruits, and bottles of wine and oil. These decorations are not to be treated lightly, for once they are hung they play a role in the performance of the commandment. "If one covered the *sukkah* to meet its requirements, and adorned it with embroidered hangings and sheets, and hung therein nuts, almonds, peaches, pomegranates, clusters of grapes, wreaths of ears of corn, [phials of] wine, oil or fine flour, it is forbidden to make use of them [for instance, to eat any of the fruit] until the conclusion of the last day of the festival" (Sukkah 10a–b). It is still customary in Israel and in other lands to suspend from the booth's roof the seven species of Eretz Yisrael mentioned in Deuteronomy 8.8: wheat, barley, vines, figs, pomegranates, olives, and honey. Thus the *sukkah* is decorated with choice fruits and other products to symbolize gratitude for the Lord's bounty during the Festival of Ingathering.

With the passage of time new embellishments were conceived. Rabbi Jacob Molin (c. 1360–1427) in his *Sefer Maharil* described the manner of decorating the *sukkah* prevalent in his time in Germany. In oriental countries expensive rugs, colorful tapestries, and bright tablecloths were used to cover the walls. In Europe a wide variety of decorations were created; for example, embroidered samplers with verses related to the festival, artfully designed paper cutouts, paper flowers, and chains made with colored paper were frequently found in the booths. Pictures of the holy sites in Jerusalem and of

15. *Mizrah* for a *sukkah*. Colored lithograph. Tel Aviv. 1940.

Jewish sages and other personalities were hung. Birds, made with empty eggshells on which feathers were pasted for the wings and tails, were suspended from the rafters. The source of this practice is shrouded in mystery, although some claim that it alludes to the words of Isaiah 31.5: "As birds hovering, so will the Lord of hosts protect Jerusalem." Johannes Buxtorf, a seventeenth-century Christian Hebraist, wrote that he saw a *sukkah* decorated with eggs on which were inscribed verses pertaining to Sukkot. Illustrations from the Middle Ages reveal elaborate adornments in the booths, including beautiful domes, ornamental festoons, and lanterns. Indeed, in the course of centuries there developed an entire folk art of *sukkah* decoration.

Wealthy Jews engaged artists to enrich their tabernacles. A portable *sukkah*, made in Germany in the first half of the nineteenth century, with charming hand-painted murals depicting Jerusalem's holy places and other scenes, is now in the possession of the Israel Museum in Jerusalem.

Children were always encouraged to participate in the *mitzvah* of decorating the *sukkah*, and they did so with much zest and fervor. They made the paper chains and garlands, strung cranberries, and aided in hanging the twigs and leaves.

One of the popular appurtenances conspicuously displayed in many booths is the *Ushpizin*—the special prayer of invitation to "holy guests" which is recited as one enters the *sukkah*. As these sainted persons would undoubtedly refuse to dwell in a booth where the poor are not welcome, it is customary to invite indigent persons to dine and celebrate the festival. The "open door" is an integral part of the *sukkah*. It is told that Rabbi Hayyim Halberstam of Sandz, who was known for his generosity, increased the amount of charity he gave before Sukkot. He explained, "It is incumbent upon everyone to adorn the *sukkah*, which I have not done properly. Is there any more beautiful ornament for the *sukkah* than the distribution of charity to those who do not have the means to be glad in the 'Season of Our Rejoicing'?"

❧ 12 ❧

THE FOUR SPECIES

❧ ❧ ❧

A GOODLY TREE
ERICH AND RAEL ISAAC

Shortly before World War II, and well before the days of the Egyptian-Israeli conflict, the Egyptian ship *Zamzam* steamed into New York harbor with a worthless cargo which, a few days earlier, would have netted the Jewish booksellers of Canal Street and various other enterprising merchants a profit of thousands of dollars. The ship showed no gaping wounds, the log reported no accidents; the worst that had happened was a delay of a few days. But in this case time was money. The ship's cargo consisted of the "*Citrus Medica* var. *ethrog* Engl., a fragrant golden oval or oblong fruit somewhat larger than a lemon with a small stem at the base and a slight knobby projection at the head." This fruit is familiar to Jews as the *etrog*. and while it is supremely valuable to them for a single week, commanding prices ranging from six dollars for a scrawny specimen to thirty for an exceptionally handsome one, and averaging eighteen dollars apiece, it is worthless for the rest of the year. Only during the Feast of Booths, Sukkot, is the use of the *etrog* obligatory for ritual celebration. Chances are that a similar shipping delay occurred at least once before in history, for "an *etrog* after Sukkot" is a Yiddish byword for something absolutely without value.

While religious Jews today will go to considerable trouble and expense to obtain an *etrog*, their anxieties and difficulties are minor compared with the anguish suffered by Jews in previous centuries—especially those communities located north of the area where the *etrog* grew—when it came time to acquire the fruit.

The danger of the long trips from Italy, Greece, or Catalonia to Frankfort or Prague cast an aura of romance on the traders in *etrogim*. We know of one family—the Spaniers of Frankfort—who for generations were in the business of importing *etrogim* from Spain (hence the name Spanier), and whose house, occupied by the family for one hundred and fifty years, bore the title "The Golden Apple" in honor of the trade. So important economically did trade in *etrogim* become in the Middle Ages that one of the terms of the peace treaty imposed upon the defeated Republic of Pisa in 1329 by the Guelph League of Tuscany (led by Florence) forbade her to continue her commerce in *etrogim*. Presumably Florence and her allies intended to take over the flourishing trade with Jewish merchants from Germany, Austria, and Poland as one of the spoils of victory.

To what can we trace the importance of the *etrog* in the life of the Jewish community? Leviticus 23.40 says concerning the Feast of Booths: "On the first day you shall take to yourselves the fruit of the goodly tree, branches of palm trees, boughs of leafy trees and willows of the brook and you shall rejoice before the Lord your God seven days." There is no explicit reference here to the *etrog*, only to "the fruit of a goodly tree."

The Talmud advanced various arguments to prove that the traditional identification of "the fruit of a goodly tree" as the *etrog* was based on Scripture. The biblical phrase, said the rabbis, implied that both fruit and tree had to be goodly, which meant that the taste of wood and fruit must be similar; only the *etrog* lived up to both specifications. Etymological evidence was produced by several rabbis, one of whom postulated (mistakenly) that the word "goodly" (*hadar*, literally "splendor"), came from *dirah*, meaning "dwelling." The fact that the *etrog* is not a seasonal fruit, and that the citron tree can be said to provide a dwelling for the *etrog* all year round, was cited by the rabbi as proof that the *etrog* was virtually called by name in the commandment. Misguided etymological enthusiasm inspired another rabbi to conclude that *hadar* was really the Greek *hudor* ("water"); since the citron tree is often in need of irrigation, the fruit in question must be the *etrog*. The rabbi neglected to mention that many other orchard trees are commonly irrigated. An unsophisticated attempt to cut the Gordian knot was made by yet other rabbis who asserted that the word *hadar* was the Aramaic equivalent of the Hebrew word *etrog*, despite the fact that *hadar* everywhere else in the Bible means "goodly" or "glory."

Another type of interpretation was advanced by the Aggadists, who claimed that the tree of knowledge of good and evil was the *etrog* tree. This was indicated by the description of the tree in Genesis 3.6, where "the woman saw that the tree was good for eating." Said Rav Abba of Acco: "What other tree is there whose wood and fruit are both edible? It can only be the *etrog*."

In approaching the problem of "the fruit of a goodly tree," one group of rabbis, which included Maimonides, boldly converted what was apparently the chief weakness of the biblical phrase into a source of strength. These rabbis claimed that there was never any doubt that the goodly tree of the Bible was the *etrog* and that the lack of specific reference only proved the absolute necessity of oral tradition, without which we could not know the true significance of the divinely ordained command. Finally, Eleazar of Worms, a rabbi with a mathematical flair, scientifically and conclusively proved that the fruit of the commandment was the *etrog* by showing that the numerical value of the Hebrew letters spelling out "fruit of a goodly tree" was the same as of those in the word *etrogim*.

While discussion of the *etrog*'s relation to the Bible's "goodly tree" died down after the Middle Ages, the matter was never totally abandoned. In fact, only recently S. Tolkowsky, a Palestinian historian of citrus culture, has advanced the thesis that Leviticus referred not to the *etrog* but to the *dar* tree, the *ha* in front of the noun being the definite article. The *dar* tree, or *Cedrus Deodara*, is a giant cedar and a holy tree of India. The fruit of a goodly tree, on this theory, was the cedar cone, which was also used in Assyrian ritual. Tolkowsky's theory is based upon the assumption that Leviticus could not have intended the *etrog* since that tree did not grow in Palestine in biblical times. The citron, Tolkowsky holds, was introduced into Palestine in the second century B.C.E. and substituted for the cedar cone by Simon Maccabeus, in whose time a coin bearing the imprint of the fruit (the earliest evidence in Jewish records for the *etrog*) is believed to have been struck. Simon Maccabeus, according to Tolkowsky, introduced the *etrog* presumably in order to purify the Feast of Booths from the pagan implications of the cedar cone.

However, it is by no means certain that the citron was brought into the eastern Mediterranean at such a late date. Most recent findings indicate that the citron originated not in India or Southwest Asia, as was formerly thought, but in East Africa or southern Arabia, and there is ample proof of very early connections by land and sea between these areas and Mesopotamia—connections which would have permitted the introduction of the *etrog* in Palestine considerably before the fifth century B.C.E.

Internal evidence from the text of Leviticus also argues against the thesis that *hadar* means the *dar* tree. "The fruit of a goodly tree" is one of a list of items in this verse, and it is unlikely from a stylistic point of view that the definite article would be employed for only one of the objects while the others listed parallel to it are without the article. Finally, the coin bearing the imprint of the *etrog*—which Tolkowsky asserted marked the initial use of the fruit—was not struck in the time of Simon Maccabeus but two hundred years later, in the period of the first Jewish war against Rome, when, according to all available evidence, the *etrog* had already been in use for some time. . . .

By the first century C.E. the *etrog* had become so important in Jewish religious observance that it moved with the Jews outside Palestine wherever the environment permitted. In this way the tree spread through North Africa and Asia Minor, the Aegean, Greece, and Italy. To what extent the *etrog* was responsible for making Jews the expert horticulturists of Mediterranean Europe we do not know. We do know that they were noted for this art and modified the Mediterranean landscape through their practice of it.

The *etrog* played an extremely important role in the development of the entire Mediterranean citrus culture. The Jewish obsession with the *etrog* made the transition from cultivation of the *etrog* to citrus culture in general comparatively simple. It was thanks to the Jews that the peoples of Mediterranean lands grew to accept the citron as edible, and this acceptance in turn made them receptive to the rest of the citrus family. We know that when, at an early period, the citron had been encountered by Mediterranean travelers in foreign lands, it had been considered inedible. Theophrastus of Eresos, the favored pupil of Aristotle, on his trip to Babylon with Alexander the Great about 310 B.C.E., described the citron as a fruit which could not be eaten. By the second century C.E., however, the Greek physician Galen was writing recipes for its use.

In the intervening centuries the citron had spread with the numerous Jewish communities which formed throughout the Mediterranean. Up to the seventeenth century, traders who brought *etrogim* to Jewish communities in extra-Mediterranean Europe were also the traders in those other branches of the citrus family for which a European demand developed.

The further history of the *etrog* was influenced by the altered pattern of Jewish settlement in Europe. Jews established flourishing communities well north of the line where the *etrog* can be grown; at the same time, the political and economic conditions of feudal Europe made it virtually impossible for the Jews to obtain *etrogim* outside of Italy. Furthermore, it was at this period that the Jews ceased to be horticulturists, a circumstance giving rise to a new set of problems. Since Jews no longer grew the *etrog*, they no longer had confidence that *etrogim* were grown in the fashion permited by Jewish law. An indication of the growing concern over this problem can be found in the sudden rush of rabbinical responsa in the sixteenth century forbidding the use of the fruit of the grafted citron.

According to Jewish law grafting is prohibited. The prohibition is derived from a biblical command against sowing in one field seeds of different types and was applied by the rabbis to the grafting of trees. Grafting in the case of the *etrog* was particularly sacrilegious because it meant that a fruit which merely superficially appeared to be an *etrog* was employed for a holy purpose to which the *etrog* alone had been divinely designated. Italian Jews were able to detect grafted *etrogim* from their own area on sight, but not from orchards outside their immediate vicinity. Clearly the Jew beyond the growing range of the *etrog* was totally unable to determine whether the *etrog* he received was acceptable or not, and partly because of the wide practice of grafting in Italy, the attempt was made more and more to tap areas of supply beyond the offending country.

Further complications arose from the difficulties of transport and the monopolistic trading practices of Jewish merchants who obtained royal or ducal charters by paying substantial fees. The plight of many Jewish communities at Sukkot became so severe that more than one rabbi—Meir Eisenstadt I, Moses Isserles, and Benjamin A. Slonik, to cite a few examples—permitted the use of grafted or dried-out *etrogim* preserved from the previous year when others were totally unobtainable. In its extremity the entire community of Kuttenplan, now Chadova Plana in western Bohemia, went so far as to tax itself in 1576 in order to obtain a single *etrog*. . . .

There were in the seventeenth century three major sources supplying the Jews of Central and Eastern Europe with *etrogim*: Spanish Catalonia in the west; the coasts and islands of the Ligurian and Tyrrhenian Sea, especially Corsica, in the middle; and, in the east, the Adriatic shores of the Ottoman Empire and the Venetian islands of Corfu, Cephalonia, and Zante. Genoa served as the marketplace for *etrogim* from the first two areas, and Venice channeled the trade from the last. The reputation of the *etrogim* of Genoa ranked highest in the eyes of Jewish communities because the majority sold there came from Corsica, where they grew in wild and ungrafted profusion.

Beginning with the eighteenth century, when the Catalonian trade declined and trade through Genoa became more difficult, Trieste increasingly took the place of Genoa as the great central marketplace of *etrogim*. With the creation of the First Republic in France and the swift rise of Napoleon, boundary lines between French and Austrian possessions hardened, so that Jews in Austrian territories had no choice but to use the Adriatic sources. But the Adriatic trade presented problems of its own, what with the islands of Corfu, Cephalonia, and Zante, the main source for *etrogim*, changing from Venetian to French to Russian to English occupation within the space of twelve years. Of all the places supplying *etrogim*, only the coastal areas of Ottoman Albania and Epirus did not change hands. Here the sultan monopolized the growing of *etrogim* and kept close supervision over the purity of the tree stock. The *etrogim* of Parga, where the sultan maintained orchards, achieved a reputation as high as those of Corsica. These *etrogim* and others from the eastern Adriatic region were shipped largely via Corfu to Trieste.

The trouble began when the sultan let his monopoly lapse around 1840. How was it possible now to determine whether the *etrogim* had been grafted upon lemon stock? An indication of the mounting concern of Jewish communities throughout Europe, following the sultan's abandonment of his monopoly and the consequent mush-rooming of new orchards in the island provinces of Ioannina, Prevesa, and Arta in what is now Greece, was the publication in the Galician town of Lvov in 1846 of a collection of responsa on the problem. The rabbis were unanimously of the opinion that the *etrogim* received from the area could no longer be trusted. They explained that the rabbi of Corfu gave his seal of approval to the *etrogim* from the mainland, although he had no knowledge of the conditions under which they were grown. Under the circumstances the rabbis advised that tradition be followed and that Jews continue to buy only the *etrogim* of Parga, or, if available, those of Corsica or North Africa. The practical difficulty in the way of following this advice turned out to be that all the *etrogim* from the area were shipped to Corfu, where Greek traders crated them together indiscriminately. Eventually all the *etrogim* from the region became known under the single title of the Corfu *etrog*, although *etrogim* from Corfu itself were not the largest component in the trade.

The Corfu *etrog* fell into disrepute not only from the halakhic standpoint but also as a result of the practices of Greek merchants, who dumped *etrogim* into the Adriatic in order to induce an artificial scarcity and force up prices. This they were the more ready to do because the credulous merchants were convinced that Jewish super-stition dictated that a Jew who did not use a Corfu *etrog* each year would die before the next. Disgust with the Corfu *etrog* was ag-gravated in the following decades by the anti-Semitic outrages com-mitted by the people of the island. Under Napoleon, Jews had been granted full civil equality, but under English and subsequently under Greek rule outbreaks against the Jews recurred periodically with government concurrence or even connivance. Prohibitions against the Corfu *etrog* began to be issued not only by the rabbis of Eastern Europe, but also by such notables as Chief Rabbi Nathan Marcus Adler of England and the rabbis of Hamburg, Mainz, and Würzburg. Determined to end the reign of the Corfu *etrog*, Isaac Elchanan Spektor, one of the greatest talmudic authorities of the age, repeated his prohibition year after year until his death.

The ritual murder accusation of 1891 on Corfu and the subsequent pogroms clinched the case against the Corfu *etrog* for most Jews, and such famed teachers as Naftali Zevi Yehudah Berlin (head of the *yeshivah* of Volozhin) and Rabbi Shmuel Mohilever (the out-standing representative of religious Zionism) followed the example of Isaac Elchanan Spektor in prohibiting the Corfu *etrog*. An attempt was unsuccessfully made in Russia to circulate a complete list of all the rabbis who joined forces to ban the Corfu *etrog*. Traders in Corfu *etrogim*, however, managed to bribe the Russian censorship to forbid the publication of the list, so that it did not appear until 1892 when it was printed in—of all places—Newark, New Jersey.

The long debate concerning the acceptability of the Corfu *etrog* had alerted Jews to the question of grafting, and when Palestine began to replace the Corfu area as the source of the fruit, each Jew was determined to make absolutely sure that his *etrog* had not the remotest relationship to a lemon. Palestinian citrons began to figure in the European market in the late 1850s. These *etrogim*, however, met considerable opposition from certain Orthodox communities on the grounds that they were grafted. To counteract this unfavorable propaganda, a group of Palestinian rabbis investigated the situation and published a volume to inform world Jewry in which areas grafting was practiced and which exporters could not be relied upon, thus by implication putting the seal of approval upon the rest.

The rabbis denied that grafting was universal in Palestine; on the contrary, they asserted, the very desolation of the country and the lack of enterprise of its inhabitants, greatly as these must grieve a Jew, had yet the important advantage of insuring the purity of her *etrogim*. The *etrog* grew wild upon the ruins of Israel's ancient grandeur. In Jaffa, alas, it was reputed that the inhabitants were more enterprising and grafted *etrogim* grew upon the ruins. Citron cuttings had been imported from Greece and grafted on lemon stock in the environs of Jaffa. . . .

While the Palestinian *etrog* steadily climbed in popularity, the Corfu *etrog* still did not lack persistent champions. The main body of its supporters was made up of certain groups of *Hasidim* who apparently considered pogroms and possible grafting of less moment than opposition to prevailing mitnagdic views. Traders in Corfu *etrogim* embarked upon desperate propaganda campaigns to keep their market and fully exploited the rift in Jewish ranks at the same time as they instituted a search for markets in remote lands uninformed of, or at least less involved with, the Corfu debate. The United States was such a market and traders in Corfu *etrogim* hawked their wares in New York only to meet, greatly to their chagrin, the same determined resistance they had encountered in much of Europe.

16. *Sukkah* decoration. Paper cutout. Moravia. Eighteenth century.

The gauntlet was thrown down by Ephraim Deinard of Newark, New Jersey, originally of Latvian Courland, and a professional traveler and writer. He published a broadside entitled *God's War against Amalek* in 1892. It opens with an impassioned denunciation, which inevitably loses in translation from the original Hebrew:

The shriek of the children of Israel on Corfu, the island of blood, pierces heaven. These cursed beasts, these Greeks, children of Antiochus the tyrant, after two thousand years have still not gorged themselves sufficiently upon the blood of our fathers. Not a year passes, but these cannibals slander us with accusations of ritual murder in all the countries of Greece, Turkey, and Russia. Before our eyes runs the blood of our brethren in Salonica, Smyrna, Odessa, Alexandria, Port Said, and Corfu.

As for the New York traders in Greek *etrogim*, Deinard wrote:

They are traders in the blood of Israel . . . and since there is hardly a man in Europe who will touch them [the *etrogim*] they bought these *etrogim* dripping with the blood of the sons of Zion. . . . These circumcised anti-Semites . . . have connived with importers from Trieste and a group of Galician Jews . . . to mislead the people of God.

To give villainy a place and name, Deinard exposed the "robbers' hideout"—185 East Broadway.

A cautionary note was sounded by several rabbis equally concerned with the implications of the Corfu pogroms, but more thoroughly the products of Western emancipation and possessing what they considered a more comprehensive view of the anti-Semitic problem as a whole. Rabbi Hermann Adler of London, the son of the chief rabbi who had been one of the first to ban the Corfu *etrog*, argued that while the emotions which Jews now felt toward the Greeks of Corfu were entirely justified, a boycott against Corfu would merely play into the hands of the anti-Semites who warned against Jewish economic power. Rabbi Israel Hildesheimer of Berlin adopted the humanitarian assumption that all Greek merchants were not wicked and it was therefore contrary to Jewish teachings to make the innocent suffer for the sins of the others.

But their findings to the contrary notwithstanding, Jews continued to look to Palestine for their *etrogim* and at the turn of the century a Fruit of the Goodly Tree Association was set up by Palestinian Jewish citron growers. This organization was supported by Rabbi Abraham Isaac Kook, then chief rabbi of Jaffa, who sought to give a halakhic basis for the purchase of Palestinian *etrogim*. The biblical phrase says: "You shall take to yourselves . . . fruit of a goodly tree"; the Talmud amplified "you shall take to yourselves" to mean "you shall take purely—that is, not steal"; and Kook went further to say that this meant "you shall take from your own"—in other words from Jews and Jewish soil.

The wars of the twentieth century, natural limitations of supply, and the preferences of individual groups have prevented Palestine from being the sole source of *etrogim*. Today the citron is grown on Greek islands such as Crete, Naxos, and Corfu; in southern Italy in the regions of Cosenza, Salerno, and Potenza; and in California, Morocco, Tunisia, Yemen, and Israel. In the United States today we find the main importers of North African *etrogim* to be *Hasidim*. Some of the North African *etrogim* are far from living up to the early rabbinic ideal according to which both fruit and tree had to be goodly. These *etrogim* are black and shriveled. The *Hasidim* argue that the very unattractiveness of the fruit is proof of its purity: no grafted fruit could look so awful.

Although Jewish devotion to the *etrog* has not diminished over the centuries, the *etrog* itself has perhaps subtly changed in significance. No longer primarily the concrete beautiful fruit described in Leviticus and the Talmud, it has become for many an ideal, almost a schematic object. The *etrog* is often considered as a collection of attributes—i.e., it is not grafted; the fruit is flawless; the stem is intact—rather than as a single essence. It is for this reason that a dark and shriveled fruit may today be preferred over the traditionally firm and golden *etrog*.

An outsider, reading of the multiplicity of rabbinic interpretations, the endless squabbles, and the final seeming *reductio ad absurdum* of using a patently ugly object as "the fruit of the goodly tree," may well ask what the fuss is all about. Is the *etrog* just an excuse for the Jews to exercise their passion for the difficult, for the formal, and, above all, for argument? Such a view has been expressed before— in the fourth century, for example, Methodios Eubulios, a Christian bishop and subsequent martyr, wrote that it was both shameful and foolish for the Jews to make such an issue over a lemon.

But although this definition may seem adequate to other men, to the Jew the *etrog* is not merely the "*Citrus Medica* var. *ethrog* Engl.*" To the Jew the *etrog* is a tree rooted in eternity, its creation antedating man, from whose branches sprang the fruit which, in bringing the end to man's sojourn in Eden, gave us human life and history as we know it. According to one midrash the *etrog* is "the heart of man"; according to a Hasidic teacher "the orb of the world." The *etrog* is a national as well as a universal symbol to the Jew. Its fragrance was in Jacob's clothes when Isaac blessed him, bestowing upon the people of Israel, through Jacob, its identity, its rule over nations, and the favor of the Lord. Again, the *etrog* is the beloved in Israel's great poem of love, the Song of Solomon. The *etrog* calls up the glory of the Second Temple when the instrument of prayer became the fierce expression of a people's longing for freedom, hurled literally in the teeth of tyrannical power. Finally, the *etrog* symbolizes the continuity of Jewish history and its common aspiration, binding together the disparate geographic units of the Diaspora over the centuries.

As symbol of world history and Jewish national persistence within it, as the finite object in the natural world revealing God's divine and infinite mystery, the *etrog* is clearly an object of the highest significance. Man must therefore strive to make the *etrog* conform as fully as possible to its divine essence by following the specifications laid down by tradition and law. The trouble is great but the reward is high. If the fruit is the true *etrog*, for seven days each year, when the Jew takes in one hand the palm branch and in the other the *etrog*, he will be united in a chain of intimate association through Jacob with his people, through Adam with the race of man, and, ultimately, through the fulfillment of a cherished commandment, with his God.[1]

❦ ❦ ❦

THE PROCESSION OF THE PALMS
ISRAEL ABRAHAMS

Plants have a language even outside the albums of sentimental girls. Mystical fancy reads into the gift of nature a symbolism of the spirit. The palm tree—closely associated with the Feast of Tabernacles— had an emblematic virtue in ancient Hebrew poetry long before the Midrash likened the palm to the human frame and the citron to the human heart. "The righteous shall flourish like the palm tree," says the 92nd Psalm. The comparison alludes both to the beauty and the material value of the tree, to its stately height and to its sweet fruit. Jewish poets were not wanting in a healthy sense of the comeliness and utility of virtue, and as the ideal Israel represented righteousness, so the palm became a type of Israel's national and religious life. Hence though the palm was by no means plentiful in Palestine, it became a Judean emblem, and the Romans felt that the tree was so intimately connected with the Jews, that when they struck a medal to commemorate the fall of Jerusalem, Judea was represented as a forlorn woman weeping under a palm tree.

One city of Palestine was, however, famous for its palms—Jericho, now palmless, but once "the city of palm trees." It is at least a remarkable coincidence that the procession of palms on Sukkot should have another association with Jericho. For, at the siege of that city, the host of Joshua compassed the place seven times with the ark at the head of the line, and seven priests sounded seven rams' horns. The connection between this scene and the procession round the altar on Tabernacles is obvious enough, but it is impossible to say how old the circuit of the altar is. Possibly it is Maccabean; it is certainly not later. When Judas Maccabeus rededicated the altar in 165 B.C.E., the people carried branches and chanted hymns, among them the 118th Psalm, which in Professor Cheyne's version runs thus in its 27th verse: "Bind the procession with branches, step on to the altar-horns." Plutarch saw in this procession a species of Bacchanalian rite, but the only resemblance was that the celebrants carried boughs. In the time of the Mishnah any old associations with pagan processions had certainly given way to a purely religious motive. Round and round the altar went the priests, singing, "O Lord, save us now; O Lord, save us now." The wilder joyousness of the Water Drawing on the night of the 15th and the following five nights of Tishri, with its brilliant illuminations and exciting music, its frantic dances and acrobatic displays, seems indeed a survival of an Old-World nature revel. But this, too, was reinterpreted in terms of that beautiful line of Isaiah, which was foremost in the thoughts of the masses of Jerusalem as they filled the golden ewers at the pool of Siloam: "With joy shall ye draw water from the wells of salvation."

After the dispersion of Israel, it seems that some attempt was still made to continue the old procession in Jerusalem itself. This was apparently the case also in the Middle Ages. We read that in the time of Hai Gaon it was customary to make a pilgrimage to the Holy City and to walk in circuit round the Mount of Olives. At the present day the residents in and around Jerusalem fix themselves, on the three great feasts, on coigns of vantage, at windows, and on balconies, whence the old Temple wall and the Mount of Olives are visible. This mountain is associated with the Feast of Tabernacles, as indicated in the fourteenth chapter of Zechariah, a passage which the synagogue has adopted as the *haftarah* for the first day of Sukkot. Jerusalem, however, was inaccessible to the Jews in pre-Islamic times, and even later. The synagogue perforce replaced the temple, and the Torah became Israel's altar; the old procession was transferred to the ordinary houses of worship, with the Torah instead of the altar as the center of the circuit. Here, however, two kinds of procession must be distinguished. The older was what we now understand as the circuit of the palms; the later is what we may term the/circuit of the Scrolls.

The circuit of the Scrolls takes place, of course, on the ninth day of Tabernacles (Simhat Torah), and so far as Europe is concerned, is restricted to "German" congregations. On the eve of the Day of Atonement, the Sephardim, indeed, take the Scrolls from the ark, but there is no procession. Despite its connection with David's dancing exploit, which his wife so grievously misunderstood, the procession of Scrolls on Simhat Torah, like the procession of the *Hasidim* on Friday nights, is modeled rather on the marriage rites of the Middle Ages than on the Temple service of ancient days. In some places the bridegroom of the Law actually wore the crown of gold which usually adorned the *Sefer Torah,* and, as a set-off, the current bridal ceremonies were transferred to the Scroll.

How unlike to this was the procession of the palms is clear from the characteristic difference that the Scroll of the Law, which was taken out before the circuit, was kept stationary on the *bimah,* while the worshipers walked round in solemn array. This was one of the reasons why in medieval synagogues the *bimah,* or reading desk, was placed in the middle of the building, for had it occupied any other position, processions would have been robbed of their spectacular effect. "Walk about Zion, go round about her" (Psalms 48.12) was the favorite text on people's lips. "Save us now," rang the *Hosanna* cries; mingling prayer with praise. For, to cite but one of the many beautiful figures to be found in this connection in Jewish books, the *Hosanna* sounded at once a note of triumph and of wailing; the Scroll of the Law was the banner displayed in the center of the camp, while round about it marched victorious Israel, fresh from its triumph over sin won on the Day of Atonement, brandishing the palm, symbol of the righteousness by which sin is conquered, yet chanting the mystic refrain, "I and He; save us now," a phrase capable of many meanings, but not inaptly rendered by the Mekhilta, "I and He, man and God, needed both for salvation, man's effort to be like God, God's grace to remember that man is but man."[2]

❧ ❧ ❧

MYRTLE
ISRAEL ABRAHAMS

English poets have not extracted much fragrance from the myrtle, probably because the shrub does not grow in the British Isles. Byron preferred the youthful forehead garlanded with myrtle and ivy to the older brow crowned with laurel:

O talk not to me of a name great in story,
The days of our youth are the days of our glory;
And the myrtle and ivy of sweet two-and-twenty
Are worth all your laurels, tho' ever so plenty.

But Milton calls the berries of the myrtle "harsh and crude." The prettiest allusion to the myrtle in an English lyric occurs in Marlowe's "Passionate Shepherd," but here it almost seems that the exigencies of rhyme led to its introduction. The shepherd invites his fair one: "Come live with me and be my love," and among other inducements he offers:

There will I make thee beds of roses
And a thousand fragrant posies,
A cap of flowers and a kirtle
Embroidered all with leaves of myrtle.

Some attribute these lines to Shakespeare, who more than once pictures Venus and Adonis love-making in a myrtle grove. Everyone remembers, too, the beautiful lines beginning:

As it fell upon a day
In the merry month of May,
Sitting in a pleasant shade
Which a grove of myrtles made;

Beasts did leap, and birds did sing,
Trees did grow, and plants did spring;
Everything did banish moan,
Save the nightingale alone.

In Tennyson's "Sweet Little Eden" also:

Fairily-delicate palaces shine
Mix't with myrtle and clad with vine.

The Roman poets, more accustomed to the wild species of the myrtle—for it is found everywhere in the Mediterranean region—made better play with the dark green shrub. The Greeks held it sacred to Aphrodite, and crowned with it the victor in a bloodless fight. Myrtle bushes are usually low, but sometimes they attain, as in the Lebanon, to a height of twelve feet, thus qualifying for the description "tree." The most southern range of Lebanon is named "Jebel Rihan," the mound of myrtles. Myrtle flowers are white, the berries become blue black or purple; the Talmud calls the color black. The poets of Italy and Greece, however, fall far behind the Jewish in their fanciful treatment of the myrtle. And this is natural enough. The fragrant leaves of the evergreen add aroma to the entwined palm branch on the Feast of Tabernacles, and Hebrew poets of all ages have used the myrtle as a type of sensuous sweetness. There is something Eastern in this. From myrtle a wine is made, and before the introduction of other spices like pepper, it was a favorite condiment in oriental cookery. The Arab mother still stuffs her infant's couch with myrtle leaves, and bathes her babe's soft flesh in water distilled with myrtle oil. Heinrich Graetz held that the verse in Psalm 118 usually rendered "Fasten the festal victim with cords to the horns of the altar" ought to run "Bind ye garlands with myrtles unto the horns of the altar."

Whether this be right or not, the myrtle has been a favorite festive emblem with Jews. In Judah Halevi's love poems we often come across the myrtle. Myrtles were used in ancient Judea in the festoons above the bridal canopy, and rabbis danced before the marriage procession bearing myrtle branches. When the custom grew up of crowning the Scrolls of the Pentateuch on the day of the Rejoicing of the Law, coronets of myrtle as well as of silver and gold were used. It was not till after the fourteenth century that the conventional metal "crown" for the Scrolls was added as a regular ornament. The person "called up" to the Law was crowned with a myrtle wreath on Simhat

Torah, the day of the bridegroom of the Law. Though after the destruction of the Temple the bridal crowns were for a while abolished, we find the custom reappearing in the Middle Ages. On the Sabbath after the wedding, the bridegroom was crowned with myrtles. This accounts for the prominence of myrtles in Judah Halevi's songs, intended for liturgical use on such occasions. In one of these songs, he calls the happy young husband's joyous group of friends "his canopy of myrtles." When the bride's name happens to be Esther (Hadassah, or Myrtle), the poet luxuriates in the image:

To Myrtle, myrtle waft a breeze,
The pangs of lovesick love to ease.

It is said that the large Jewish betrothal rings, such as one sees at South Kensington, held sprigs of the same plant; and a keen-scented friend of mine has told me that he can still detect the faint odor of myrtle in one of the old rings. Verily, "Many waters cannot quench love." Perhaps equally imaginative are the pious Jews who reserve the myrtle from the *lulav* for use in a dried condition, as "sweet-smelling spice" at the *Havdalah* on Saturday nights.

If we go back from the medieval Hebrew poets to the Midrash, quaint thoughts on the myrtle reward our search. All of these may also be found in the liturgy for the Feast of Tabernacles. The Midrash treats the myrtle not so much from the poetical as from the emblematic and moral side. Myrtle typifies Jacob and Leah, and of course Esther. " 'Myrtle' which spreads fragrance as Esther spread grace; 'Myrtle' which fades not in winter, but is fresh always." Esther's real name (as already mentioned) was "Myrtle." Leopold Zunz long ago pointed out that Jewesses in the Middle Ages were fond of borrowing their names from flowers. Flora, Myrrha, Blümchen, Rosa, Fiori, and others of the same style often occur in early Jewish name lists. To return to the Midrash on Myrtle: "Just as the myrtle has a sweet odor and a bitter taste, so Esther was sweet to Mordecai and bitter to Haman." (Elsewhere, the rabbis speak of the myrtle as tasteless. They are thinking of different varieties, as may be seen from the Talmud, Sukkah 31b. The aromatic taste of the myrtle berry may be understood when one remembers that the eucalyptus and clove belong to the same order as the myrtle.) "Bitter and sweet will join as dainties for His palate, who stood among the myrtles," sings Kalir, in allusion to this midrash and to Zechariah 1.8, where the angel-warrior on a red horse stood in a glen of myrtles beneath Mount Olives. The liturgy also uses the midrashic parallel of the myrtle to the eye. The citron atones for heart-sins, the palm for stiff-backed pride, the willows for unholy speech, the myrtle for the lusts of the eye. The comparison to the eye is peculiarly apt. Not only does the elongated oval leaf of some species resemble the eye, but when held up to the light, it looks not unlike the iris. This effect is produced by the little oil dots in the leaf. The rabbis, like the Targum, explained the "boughs of leafy trees" of Leviticus 23.40 to mean thick-leaved myrtle with clustering berries, though for ritual use too many berries were unlawful. Nehemiah (who, however, mentions both "thick trees" and "myrtles," 8.15), and Josephus (*Antiquities* III. x. 4) bear witness that myrtles were associated with the Festival of Tabernacles. The last-named authority informs us that the myrtles were carried in the hand, a fact not clearly stated, though implied, in Leviticus. It was because of this custom that Plutarch confused the Jewish feast with a Dionysian rite, for the devotees of Dionysus, or Bacchus, carried wands wreathed in ivy and vine leaves, topped with pine cones. "Bearing wands wreathed with leaves, fair boughs and palms, after the manner of the feast of Tabernacles, they offered up hymns of thanksgiving," says the author of the *Second Book of Maccabees* (10.6) of Judas and his men.

One other talmudic thought must be mentioned, for it leads us back to Isaiah: "He who has learned and fails to teach is like a myrtle in the desert" (Rosh Hashanah 23a).

Full many a flower is born to blush unseen,
And waste its fragrance on the desert air.

Isaiah, in his picture of the return from the Babylonian exile, paints the whole desert as a garden filled with joyous men. Nature becomes a worthier scene for the redemption. The desert is not merely dotted with oases, as Marti explains; it is transformed into one vast, well-watered garden, filled with myrtles in place of thorns. Thus the wilderness stretching between Babylon and Judea was to share in the renewal of the heavens and the earth. The change was to occur on a mighty scale, that all the earth might see and wonder. If the desert was so transfigured what (though the prophet does not add this) must be the glories of the new Canaan!

I will make the wilderness a pool of water,
And the dry land flowing springs.

17. *Sukkah* decoration. By Israel David Luzzatto. Paper on canvas.
Italy. Circa 1700. Entire Book of Ecclesiastes (read during Sukkot)
is written in minute script. See Chapter 9.

I will plant in the wilderness the cedar,
    The acacia tree, and the myrtle, and the oil tree;
I will set in the desert the cypress, the plane tree, and the larch to-
    gether;
    That they may see, and know, and consider and understand to-
    gether,
That the hand of the Lord hath done this,
    And the Holy One of Israel hath created it.

                                                    Isaiah 41.18–20

And so again, when the trees wave their boughs and nature and men combine to sing a new song to the Lord,

For ye shall go out with joy,
    And be led forth with peace,
The mountains and the hills shall break forth before you into singing,
    And all the trees of the field shall clap their hands.
Instead of the thorn shall come up the cypress,
And instead of the brier shall come up the myrtle.
And it shall be to the Lord for a memorial,
For an everlasting sign that shall not be cut off.

                                                    Isaiah 55.12–13

Yet we are told that the poets of the nineteenth century first taught men the lessons of nature. The ancient prophet felt the parallel between human moods and natural phenomena. Isaiah was not the least of those who experienced this analogy, and in the lines just cited the poetry of the myrtle reaches its noblest flight.[3]

❧ ❧ ❧

THE WILLOW OF THE BROOK
JULIUS H. GREENSTONE

The humbler member in the combination of the Four Species is the willow of the brook. It grows in abundance along any body of water and is especially in evidence on the banks of the Jordan. In ancient times, the people of Jerusalem would bring large bundles of willows from Motza, a short distance away, but more recently Arabs have brought them in baskets from Hebron and other places and sold them to the pious Jews. In Temple times the altar was decorated with willows on the festival, while the procession of the people with their *lulavim* and accessories moved round about it, chanting the word *Hoshana*. The refrain was later adopted as the name of the willow itself, and we still speak of the seventh day of the feast as Hoshana Rabbah, when the willow is beaten until its leaves fall off. This is supposed to symbolize the belief in the resurrection, although other meanings have been given to it by the cabalists and folklorists.

In the rabbinic simile, the willow represented the type of people who neither study the Torah nor practice good deeds. However, by being combined with the pious and the learned (typified by the *etrog*), the learned though not pious (typified by the *lulav*), the pious and not learned (typified by the myrtle), they also will be accorded God's favor. In the union of all the various elements of Israel, the deficiencies of one kind are supplied by the others.

Because the leaves of the willow resemble the mouth, its use in the services is expected to atone for such sins as result from speech. Many other symbolic meanings were found by the rabbis in this humble plant, which has been exalted to the position of honor among the other plants of more distinguished type in the ceremonies connected with the process of praising God for the blessings of the harvest, which the festival of Sukkot has as its main purpose.[4]

℘ ℘ ℘

HOSHANOT IN A LITHUANIAN TOWN

A. S. SACHS

If one looks through the pages of the old ledgers of the various local ghetto societies, such as the Aid to the Poor Society, the Support of the Stumbling, the Visitors of the Sick, and the like, he will be sure to find under the item "income" a respectable sum under the heading of "*Hoshanot.*"

On the prospect of repaying out of the proceeds of the sale of *hoshanot,* every one of these societies would borrow and spend money in excess of the cash in the hands of its treasurer. The *hoshanot* were the best merchandise on which a *hevrah* could make profits, and the night of Hoshana Rabbah was the most opportune time for it.

For the sake of the beautiful symbolic name with which these small, half-withered willows have been favored, it behooves that they should be sold not for private gain but for the benefit of societies whose object is to help and assist the needy. More effectively than thousands of homilies, the *hoshanot* awakened the feeling of pity and made one realize that one must help his fellowman in time of need.

The Jew is thoroughly aware that in order to have God help him, he himself, who pleads and implores *"Hoshana"* (Save, please), must first aid others. One cannot brazenly come to ask for help so long as one is unwilling to help others. If we wish God to be good to us, we must be good to others. "Help us, O God!" implores the Jew on Hoshana Rabbah. "Help one another," replies an inner voice. And they do help one another.

To our fathers and grandfathers, Hoshana Rabbah meant the Day of Help. On that day particularly each felt his duties and obligations to his fellowmen and assisted them without stint or grudge.

These willow twigs, the *hoshanot,* are bound up with an important chapter of the Jewish past. Thanks to them one of the most beautiful pages in our history has been written. In the Babylonian captivity, after the destruction of the First Temple, when we had been driven out of our own land and were forced to a life of homeless wanderers in Galut, along the riverbanks of our oppressors, we hung our harps upon the willows while our hearts mutely wept for the loss of our homeland, Zion. Not upon flower plants did we hang our instruments of joy; not upon tall trees did we place our hopes, but upon these poor, humble willows: "Upon the willows in the midst thereof we hanged up our harps" (Psalms 137.2).

These plain willows that grow on the river's edge at the foot of the hill; these willows that are so mercilessly trampled upon, bring to the aching soul of the Jew more comfort than do the tall oaks that rear their haughty heads. . . . And so, when our fathers had to raise money, they would take an armful of willow twigs and make their house-to-house rounds. The *hoshanot* made it possible to render aid on Hoshana Rabbah.

On the night of Hoshana Rabbah the entire town was wide awake. No one went to bed, everyone wanted to see the skies opening. Who would miss such an important moment, such a great occasion in one's life? The elderly male folk spent the night at the synagogue reading the *Tikkun*. The women fussed all night in their kitchens. The little urchins played tag about the synagogue yard, awaiting with the greatest impatience the moment when the angel Michael would look down upon the earth. As for the young men, they did the most important work; they delivered the *hoshanot* on behalf of their societies.[5]

13

SUKKOT AND SIMHAT TORAH IN MANY LANDS

SUKKOT IN EASTERN EUROPE
HAYYIM SCHAUSS

The Jews of the town suddenly become builders in the days between Yom Kippur and Sukkot. Jews draw poles, drag lumber, hammer nails. Even those old Jews who usually sit in the *bet ha-midrash,* the house of study, reading the Torah and chanting the Psalms, desire to observe the precept in person and help erect the *sukkah.* Not that there is very much work connected with it. The erection of one wall is saved entirely, for the *sukkah* is built against the house, either in the back yard or the front yard. About half the second wall is taken up by the door, leaving only a little more than two walls to put up. These are thrown together with fence rails and odd pieces of lumber and poles. There is no need to make the *sukkah* really strong; it will surely last till Shemini Atzeret.

Sukkot are built individually, each man erecting one for his own household. Some neighbors, however, join forces and erect a great *sukkah*, in which several families eat together and are assured a religious quorum of three and sometimes ten for the purpose of pronouncing the benediction after the meal.

So Jews build *sukkot* and feel themselves fortunate in observing such an important religious precept. But the *heder* children are the happiest and most fortunate of all. It is a great occasion for them when they sit in the *sukkah*, and it is a still greater occasion for them to help build the structure. There is no school for them, so they drag planks and green branches and help erect the *sukkah*. In addition, it is a promise that Simhat Torah is almost at hand, when they will march in the procession bearing flags and will mount the synagogue *bimah* when the call comes for "all the lads."

Even the non-Jews of the neighborhood region are interested in the *sukkah* that Jews build. They learn of the approach of the day on which Jews need a certain type of branches, and they ride into town with their wagons laden with pine branches for sale. The festival is quite profitable for them financially.

The *sukkah* is complete in every detail; its roof is covered with pine branches, the floor is sprinkled with fine sand and the walls are hung with white sheets and decorated with various fruits and flowers. The decoration is the work of the girls, eager to help even though they are not enjoined to use the *sukkah*, entering it just to hear the *Kiddush*, the sanctification before meals, and to recite the benediction over the *etrog* and *lulav*.

The *lulav* and the *etrog* are ready, too, but only in certain homes, for few are wealthy enough to buy an *etrog* for individual use. All others own *etrogim* in partnership, usually in groups of six. Services are held in three places, the synagogue, the *bet ha-midrash*, and the *klaus*, the chapel, and they are not held simultaneously. While *Hallel* is being recited in the *klaus*, the worshipers have barely begun services in the *bet ha-midrash*. So it is possible to recite *Hallel* and *Hoshanot* with the same *etrog* in all three places of worship. And in each place there are two of the partners, for there is no hurry. First one partner performs the ceremony with the *lulav* and *etrog*, and then the other one. For the procession when the *Hoshana* prayers are recited the two partners in each place of worship take the *etrog* on alternate days. On Hoshana Rabbah there are seven processions around the platform, and it is easy for the partners to arrange for participation.

In this way there are six partners for each *etrog*, and the *etrogim* are continually being carried about, from early morning until midday. As soon as *Hallel* is finished in the *klaus*, the *etrogim* are taken to the synagogue. After the *Hallel* prayer in the synagogue the fruits are carried to the *bet ha-midrash*. By the time *Hallel* is finished in the *bet ha-midrash*, it is time for *Hoshanot* in the *klaus*, and so on, all morning long. The masses, the ordinary Jews, use the *klaus*, and they hurry to finish the services as soon as possible. The worshipers in the synagogue are also not overfond of prolonging the services. But in the *bet ha-midrash* the rabbi himself attends the services, and with him are the learned class, the members of the Talmud study circle. These arc Jews who have no desire to rush through the services, in order to eat sooner; on the contrary, the longer the services, the greater the satisfaction they get from them.

In addition to the fact that the *etrog* must be in the *klaus* synagogue and *bet ha-midrash* twice each day, except Saturday, it must also be in six houses every morning before breakfast. For all, including women and children, must pronounce the benediction over the *etrog* before they eat. So there is a messenger for each *etrog*, a youth who carries it about until all the services are over, and until everyone has pronounced the benediction over it. Then the *etrog* is deposited in the home of one of the six partners, where it is carefully guarded. The messenger, of course, receives payment from each of those to whom he carries the *etrog*.

There are, in town, a mass of poor people, who cannot even afford a sixth of an *etrog*. There are, therefore, a few communal *etrogim* which are utilized by the poorer Jews. The communal *etrog* passes through so many hands, and becomes so soiled and worn away that, by the time Hoshana Rabbah comes, it barely resembles the original *etrog*. . . .

On coming home from the synagogue the master of the house goes directly to the *sukkah* and, before sitting down, recites a prayer in Aramaic, in which he invites seven holy guests to come and sit with him in the *sukkah*. . . .

It is only after this invitation has been given that the *Kiddush*, the sanctification of the day, is chanted aloud, in the presence of the entire family, and in an atmosphere of tender warmth and pious fervor which pervades the *sukkah*.

Great satisfaction is derived from the *sukkah* when the weather is fair. The pines and flowers and fruit that adorn the booth send forth a delicious fragrance, and fill the hearts of the occupants with festive joy. Jews eat the holiday meal in the *sukkah*; they sing and pronounce the benediction *be-mezuman* (in groups of three or more); their joy on this holiday is boundless.

Most of the *sukkot* are small, and there is room for only the males of the family. The women of the house enter the *sukkah* just to light the candles and recite the benedictions over them, to hear the *Kiddush*, and to recite the benediction over the *etrog*. They go back into the house for their meals, for women are exempt from the precept to abide in the *sukkah*. There are, however, some larger *sukkot*, in which the entire household eats.

It happens, sometimes, that rain comes down right in the midst of the meal, ruining the festivity of the occasion. If the rain is not too heavy, the occupants stubbornly refuse to leave the flimsy booth, and rush through the meal, even managing to pronounce the grace after the meal. But sometimes it rains so hard that the very soup is watered, and the occupants hastily gather food and cloth and run into the house.

On the evening of the second day of the festival, the first evening of the half-holiday period, many lamps and candles are kindled in the *bet ha-midrash*, and the ceremony of *Simhat Bet ha-Shoevah* is celebrated by the pious Jews of the community.

The privilege of reciting the Psalms of Ascents is sold to the highest bidders, and the purchasers distribute the honor of chanting the verses to various members of the congregation. The money is used to buy apples and brandy; the participants in the ceremony partake of the food and drink, and they sing and revel in a continuation of the *Simhat Bet ha-Shoevah* in the Temple of old.

The day before Hoshana Rabbah the assistant sexton of the synagogue, accompanied by a horde of youngsters, goes to a grove on the banks of the stream and cuts willow branches. These willow branches are sold the next day in the synagogue, and the money is contributed to communal institutions.

On Hoshana Rabbah eve the women are busy baking wheaten loaves, long loaves with braided ladders on top, such as are made and served the day before Yom Kippur. The women claim that these are ladders to heaven. They also roll dough which will be filled with meat for *kreplach*.

The men stay in the *bet ha-midrash* most of the night, reciting *Tikkun*. Some of them go to the bathhouse during the night and immerse themselves in the ritual bath.

It is a strange night, filled with mysteries and curious beliefs. It is said that the heavens split on that night, and he who observes it and makes a wish at the same moment will have that wish granted. It is also believed that he who sees his own headless shadow on that night will die within the year.

On Hoshana Rabbah morning the attitude in the synagogue is a varied one. It is still part of the semi-holiday period, yet the services are as rich and impressive as on a full holiday. In addition the day is a mixture of Yom Kippur and Sukkot; there are the *etrogim* and branches of Sukkot, together with the candles, the white robes, and the chants of Yom Kippur.

The highest point of the ceremonial of Hoshana Rabbah is the procession around the *bimah*. During the first six days of Sukkot the procession winds about the platform only once and there is but one Torah Scroll on the *bimah*. On the seventh day, however, on Hoshana Rabbah, the procession makes seven circuits around the *bimah*, on which every Torah Scroll from the ark is held by members of the congregation. It differs from the Simhat Torah procession in that it is earnest and serious. The procession winds its way around and around, the men bearing the *lulavim* and *etrogim* in their hands and chanting their prayers earnestly and fervently.

After the procession the *lulav* and the *etrog* are laid aside and the willow branches taken up, five of them bound with a leaf of the *lulav*. At the close of the *Hoshana* prayers, the worshipers beat their willow branches on the ground and chant a ritual passage. According to the ritual law it is necessary to beat the branches only five times, but the mass of the congregation beats and beats, till all the leaves have been knocked off the twigs.

Everyone performs this ceremony, including the women in their section of the synagogue, but none enjoy it as much as do the youngsters. They keep beating their branches long after the others are finished and continue till their elders brusquely tell them to cease.

Many Jews carry their bundle of branches home and save them for Passover to use in the yearly search for leaven.

After the services a feast is served in the *sukkah*. There must be soup with *kreplach* served at this feast, exactly as at the meal on the day before Yom Kippur. But after the holiday services and the holiday feast the day becomes again a part of the semi-holiday period, and all go about their regular tasks.

This is the happiest day of the Sukkot festival for the youths who have been serving as messengers with the *etrog* during the week; this is the day they are paid for their work. It is a gay day for the youngsters in general. They carry around the long palm leaves of the *lulav* and braid themselves rings and bracelets of it.

Shemini Atzeret. It is raining, it is pouring outside. The streets of the town are filled with mud. Everyone hopes that the rain will cease soon, so that it will be possible to do business after the festival. In the synagogue there is a special benediction to be pronounced: in a pleading chant, accompanied by the congregation, the cantor offers up the prayers for rain!

It all seems so strange and foreign; and yet there is something heartwarming about it. As the song of prayer for rain rises the thoughts of the worshipers revert to ancient days. They are peasants in Palestine, and they wait for the new seasonal rains and for an abundant crop in field and orchard.

The rain has ceased by midday, the sun shines once more, and Jews gather for the last time in their *sukkot*. They partake of food and offer a prayer that they may merit the privilege of sitting in the *sukkah* that God will fashion from the skin of the Leviathan, when the Messiah comes.

After the afternoon prayers young and old begin to revel. Each "brotherhood" assembles for its own joyous party. The *hevrah kaddisha*, the burial brotherhood, meets in the *bet ha-midrash*. They sit at long tables, eat apples, drink beer and brandy, and sing and revel. They sing Yiddish folk songs, chants, and bits of the services and the psalms. The feast in the *klaus* is conducted by the Bible study circle, and the one at the home of the rabbi is conducted by the exalted ones, the Talmud study circle.

On Simhat Torah evening the congregation is lively and merry. There are even those who obviously took a glass too much and sway as they move about the synagogue, but they manage to recite the evening prayers properly, nevertheless.

After the evening prayers the sexton auctions off the privilege of reciting certain passages from the Bible. But the auction is more fancied than real, for there is one certain Jew who has gained the unchallenged right to it through many years of purchase. He recites only one sentence, and apportions the other sentences amongst relatives, friends, and esteemed householders. He whispers the name of his choice to the sexton, who calls out the name of the next reader. The reader recites his sentence, which the congregation repeats. He then thanks the purchaser for the honor.

After this comes the main ceremony of the evening, the procession. Even women and girls are permitted to enter in the main part of the synagogue on Simhat Torah and to kiss the Torah Scrolls as they are carried around the *bimah* seven times. But only girls and young matrons avail themselves of this privilege. The elder women look on at the ceremony from the women's gallery above.

The youngsters play a great part in the procession, for which they prepared themselves during the semi-holiday period. They bear flags mounted on sticks, and above are attached large apples or beets, hollowed out, a candle burning inside. The flags bear the inscription DEGEL MAHANEH YEHUDAH, "standard of the camp of Judah," some bearing "Ephraim" instead of "Judah." Even tiny children mounted on the shoulders of their fathers or older brothers take part in the procession around the *bimah*.

In this manner they parade about the *bimah*, older Jews bearing the Torah Scrolls, youngsters bearing illuminated flags, all chanting alphabetically arranged songs of prayer.

The morning prayers last till afternoon. But right after the early part of the services the worshipers begin to partake of food and drink. This is done in the synagogue, and also in private homes, while the last section of the Pentateuch is being read in the synagogue.

This reading of the Pentateuch drags on for hours and hours on this day. Again and again the last section is read, until every member of the congregation has been called to the *bimah* to witness the reading and to recite the benedictions. The service would never end if each member were called up individually, so two men mount the *bimah* together. There are two benedictions to be repeated over each reading of the Torah, one before the reading and one after, and the two men called up share the benedictions.

After everyone in the synagogue, adult males and boys who have been confirmed, are disposed of in this way, the call goes forth for "all the lads." This is the ceremony in which all the boys under thirteen are called up to witness the reading of the Torah. Together with them an adult Jew, usually an elderly and very pious man, recites the benedictions. This recitation, "together with all the children," is a great honor and, as a rule, a certain Jew has the privilege, gained through years of usage, and all know that it belongs to him.

The picture is wonderful to behold. The lads come forth from all sides and mount the *bimah*, ranging themselves in front of the older man, who spreads his prayer shawl over their heads and pronounces the benediction. He recites it slowly, word by word, and the children repeat it after him, the entire congregation shouting "Amen" at the end, with great fervor. Who knows how many good and pious Jews, how many rabbis and scholars of the Torah will grow up from this group of children?

Revelry goes on all day long, in the synagogue and in the homes, dancing and singing in the very streets of the town. Old, pious men, with long cloaks and gray beards, cavort about and sing, and act as if a sudden, wild joy had taken complete possession of them.

Still the Jews of the older generation claim that the joyous years

18. *Sukkah* decoration. Copper engraving and watercolor. Italy. Circa 1770. Signed: Francesco Griselini, painter. See Chapter 9.

of old, when Jews really celebrated on Simhat Torah, are gone. Nowadays, they say, nobody really indulges in revelry; in the old days they knew how.

So say these Jews, but, at the same time, they dance and sing joyously. But there is not, in all the revelry of Simhat Torah, a trace of looseness or licentiousness. They drink, but none becomes really drunk. Jews revel and pray; they drink and they read the Torah.

The final of the festival comes at night, after the official close of the holiday. The holiday feast which is the greatest and finest of the nine-day period is served to them.

This feast is not the end, however. The revelry continues on the next Sabbath, the Sabbath on which the first section of Genesis is read in the synagogue. It is only on the day after this Sabbath that one feels that the season of festivals is really over, and the cold and cloudy autumn settles on the town.

Translated by Samuel Jaffe[1]

⚕ ⚕ ⚕

SUKKOT IN KASRIELEVKY
MAURICE SAMUEL

The Festival of Booths or Tabernacles comes next to the Passover in the richness of its symbolism and the completeness of its hypnotic translation; for during that week the Kasrielevkites dwelt in booths, like their forefathers in the wilderness. Not literally, of course. Every Kasrielevkite built himself a charming, ramshackle imitation of a cabin next to his own house; the roof was of branches and leaves; the walls were hung with fruits and vegetables; and all of it suggested much more the autumn harvest huts of Palestine than the aridity of the wilderness. In this booth the Kasrielevkite took his meals with his family during the festival, wind and weather permitting. Into this booth came an odorous reminder of the Orient, a palm branch and a citron—the *lulav* and the *etrog*—imported from Palestine or Corfu, for the special prayer of the festival. And here Kasrielevky dreamed itself back into the Holy Land, or, if you like, merely assumed its other personality.

Of course not one Kasrielevkite in twenty could afford to own for himself the exotic appurtenances of the festival, the *lulav* and the *etrog* imported from Mediterranean shores. So a Jew who owned one would make the rounds of his neighbors' booths. Or else the beadle of the synagogue would perform this duty with the communal palm branch and citron. On the Festival of Booths you would see, hastening through the morning streets of Kasrielevky, bearded Jews in black capotes with a yellow citron in one hand and a cluster of palm branch in the other—fantastic apparitions to all but the Jews themselves. A Jew with a citron of his own was widely envied. Moishe Yenkel, who lived in a townlet near Kasrielevky, waited ten years before he could buy one for himself; and a terrible tragedy happened. Leibel, his little son, was so fascinated by the precious and sacred fruit that he crept down from his bed in the night, took the *etrog* in his hand, and, seized by a frightful and blasphemous curiosity, bit off the head, thereby rendering the *etrog* unfit for ritual use. Sholom Aleichem thinks the incident worth recording, and I certainly think it worth mentioning.

Echoes of the old jollity of Palestinian harvests sounded in the booths of the Kasrielevkites, and prayers of a rustic people were rehearsed with great earnestness by a nation of workers and merchants. On the last days of Booths, Leib the tinsmith and Yossie the haberdasher and Simon Ellie the tailor and Reb Melech the cantor and Reb Yozifel the rabbi—the rich and the poor, the prominent and the obscure—assembled in the synagogue, took up clusters of willows, sang Hosannas, and prayed fervently for rain; not because they had a personal interest in the rainfall, but because Palestine might need it; that is to say, not the actual Palestine which lay a thousand miles or more to the southeast, and with which they had no practical connections to speak of, but the Palestine which Kasrielevky carried around in its heart, the Palestine that once had been and was to be again. And all this elaborate make-believe, this retention of an agricultural form of self-expression by thoroughly urbanized communities, was anything but a petrified ritual. It was taken in passionate earnest and had a fantastic purposiveness. The Kasrielevkites were determined to retain, intact and ready for immediate application, the psychological modes of a life on Palestinian soil in case the Messiah should suddenly appear and lead them back to the Holy Land. Out of this retention sprang, in fact, the folk motivation of the Zionist movement. . . .

Twice a year it is meritorious to get drunk in Kasrielevky, on the day of Rejoicing for the Law, called Simhat Torah, and on Purim, the half-festival which commemorates the immeasurable devotion of Esther, the subtle wisdom of Mordecai, and the foiled villainy of Haman.

A Kasrielevkite talking of drink puts you in mind of Vikings draining gigantic flagons to the bottom. He talks big. A Kasrielevkite actually drinking is much less formidable. The first thimbleful brings a joyous light into his eyes, the second thimbleful sets him dancing, the third extinguishes him. Three healthy peasants could have downed at one sitting all the brandy consumed in Kasrielevky on Simhat Torah and Purim and walked home erect. Hence the contemptuous Yiddish phrase "A Jewish drunkard!" It is of a piece with the other folk phrase "A Jewish robber!" to which is attached the story of a Jewish highwayman who held up a merchant and demanded his life, or a pinch of snuff.

A highly suggestible people, as we have seen, they get drunk mostly on the idea of getting drunk, and become riotous with the mere thought of licence. On Simhat Torah the town is in an uproar. The lads, the boyos, the buckaroos of Kasrielevky, a round dozen of them, dance in parade through the streets and force a way into the houses of the rich, where the householder must stand treat, serve them with cake and wine, or cake and brandy, or cake and beer—or else. Or else they will take it from the sideboard without his permission; and perhaps even insult him to boot. You never know what a Kasrielevkite will do on the grand and glorious day of Simhat Torah, between his first and his third thimbleful.

The gay blades of Kasrielevky are strictly Simhat Torah blades. One neither sees them nor hears a chirrup from them the rest of the year. Just as certain American descendants of Kasrielevky are once-a-year Jews, on Yom Kippur, so the *huliakes,* the roisterers, of Kasrielevky are once-a-year roisterers, on Simhat Torah. There are other *huliakes* who choose Purim for their binge. It appears that there are no Kasrielevkites capable of mafficking twice a year. Nor do the "lads" forgather even for milder jollifications at any other time. It is a strictly annual reunion. . . .

It must be remembered, however, that all Kasrielevky rejoices on Simhat Torah, if not with the alarming abandon of the *huliakes,* at least sufficiently to give warrant to their excesses. The high point of the celebration is reached in the synagogue, where on the eve and morning of Simhat Torah, the Scrolls are taken out of the ark and carried in procession, by rounds, called *hakkafot*. Everyone has his chance to join in a procession, and the bystanders press forward and kiss the sacred objects. To give you some idea of the pandemonium of Simhat Torah, it need only be said that on the occasion of the *hakkafot* the girls are permitted to break into the men's section of the synagogue, and to join, not in the processions, of course, but in the kissing of the Scrolls. And if one girl here and there, bending down, kisses, instead of the velvet, gold-embroidered covering of the Scroll, the hand of the boy who carries it, who's to know? Such are the carryings on in Kasrielevky on Simhat Torah.[2]

❧ ❧ ❧

SIMHAT TORAH AT THE COURT OF THE KARLIN *REBBE*

WOLF ZEEV RABINOWITSCH

The period of R. Aharon the Second's "leadership" coincided with the reign of terror under the Tsar Nicolas I, with its persecutions, anti-Jewish decrees, "kidnappings," and the like. The joyfulness that R. Aharon labored to implant in the hearts of his followers undoubtedly helped them to bear the trials and tribulations of those difficult days. For a long time afterwards popular stories were told about the courage displayed, both in private and public, by R. Aharon's *Hasidim* in their time of trouble. It was thanks to R. Aharon's encouraging influence that the numbers of the Karlin *Hasidim* increased still further in his time, over and above the increase that had occurred in the days of R. Asher the First. This was the heyday of Karlin *Hasidim*. On festivals and on penitential days the *Hasidim* would leave their wives and families and make the pilgrimage to their *rebbe* in Karlin. On Shavuot and Simhat Torah as many as three to four thousand—according to an eyewitness report—would come thronging to his residence. "He who has not seen Simhat Torah in the court of R. Aharon"—so used the Hasidic elders to say—"has never seen a real celebration of Simhat Torah." Here is the scene as described by an eyewitness: R. Aharon would be sitting clothed all in white, as was his custom on Sabbaths and festivals, at the head of the long table that stood in the large courtyard next to his prayer house. Tens of canopies stretched above the court hardly sufficed as shelter for the crowds of *Hasidim* that came to their *rebbe* for Simhat Torah. When, at the evening service, R. Aharon himself led the prayers, the worshipers were carried away by spiritual ecstasy, and the circuits of the Scrolls were performed in a frenzy of jubilation that rose ever higher, circuit by circuit, song by song, and dance by dance, as the wine flowed freely. Thus transported, the *Hasidim* would spend the whole night singing and dancing in the courtyard and the nearby streets. Out of this fervent rejoicing were born many of the Karlin melodies that subsequently became famous in Hasidic circles and even throughout Jewry. . . . In addition to songs and dances, R. Aharon introduced instrumental music and had two orchestras—one of them made up of his followers from Volhynia—which used to play during *melavveh malkah,* on the intermediate days of Sukkot, and similar occasions.

During these visits to the *rebbe*'s court, the *Hasid* would forget the bitter, dreary, care-ridden reality of his daily life and find a refuge for his tired body and weary spirit. Freed for a while of his cares by the general rejoicing, he would be uplifted into a state of self-for-getfulness.

Translated by M. B. Dagut[3]

⚕ ⚕ ⚕

JOY REIGNS AT THE *YESHIVAH* OF VOLOZIN
MEIR BAR-ILAN

On Sabbath nights many *yeshivah* students remained awake all night in the study of Torah. Also on the festivals, including Rosh Hasha-nah, Yom Kippur, and even Simhat Torah, one could always find conscientious students studying the Torah all through the night. The *yeshivah* was never deserted.

The *yeshivah* students' dedication to learning did not, however, dampen their enthusiastic participation in holiday festivities. *Yomim tovim* were a time of intense joy at the *yeshivah* of Volozin, and merrymaking was maintained at a feverish pitch. It was said, "He who has not seen the *Simhat Bet ha-Shoevah* (an evening celebration, accompanied by singing and dancing during the intermediate days of the Feast of Booths) in Volozin does not know what real ecstasy is." There is much truth in this remark. The enthusiasm and abandon of youth that glowed in the hearts of five hundred *yeshivah* students caught fire on the festivals.

Even before the festival began, the students held a general meeting to select "officials" to arrange the celebration. The chosen officials were generally better students, respected by the others. Their initial task was to prepare refreshments for the occasion—something to eat, something to drink—for one cannot be gay on an empty stomach. They would also rent a spacious hall for the dancing and merrymaking for what turned out to be an ongoing day and night affair; in the frenzied rapture of the dance who cares about night or day?

No matter how large, the hall could never hold all the *yeshivah* students; therefore, some danced out into the streets. As the merriment grew more hilarious, the throng would dance to the *roshe ha-yeshivah,* the faculty members, amid yells of glee and loud singing. The ebullient students would then escort their teachers into the *yeshivah,* and the real celebration would begin.

My father, may his memory be for a blessing, joined his students in singing and dancing. He danced with such saintly fervor that all who saw his dance were drawn into its vortex.

In the interim between dances and songs, vignettes of learning appropriate to the day—biblical verses, talmudic sayings, and the like—lent a sophisticated dimension to the enchantment of the moment.

When the time came for prayers, they were sung with a merry, rhythmic cadence and with deep and tender feeling. At the conclusion of the service, the students burst out melodiously singing, "*Gut yom tov, Rebbi,*" then, "Blessed is our Lord," and finally, "Thou hast chosen us." There were no bounds to the feeling of exaltation.

At the evening service of Simhat Torah, we witnessed an extraordinary sight: Father, may his memory be for a blessing, led the service, surrounded by a group of students serving as the "cantor's choir." The betrothal of reverence and revelry was indescribable. When the concluding *Alenu* prayer was reached, the holy ark was opened and the students, prostrating themselves as they did on Yom

Kippur, chanted the prayer in the traditional Day of Atonement melody. On rising, they began to dance again, to sing again—an interminable carousal until the break of dawn.

The holiday celebration generally lasted from sunset to dawn. Yet none of the celebrants was absent from the morning service. The "intoxication" of the *yeshivah* students, in the final analysis, was not so terrible. After the service the entire *yeshivah* student body came to our house for *Kiddush*. As there were not enough chairs for all the students, only the more respected ones sat while the others stood milling about. Everyone managed to get into the house but it was a tight squeeze.

After the *Kiddush* and a brief lecture from my father dealing with the holiday, refreshments were brought into the room, to be placed on the table. A tremor of anticipation passed over the crowd, while the students mischievously interfered with the refreshments reaching the table. As the distributors vainly attempted to give each bystander his fair share, the students were setting up their own system of distribution in which the mighty reigned, good-naturedly shoving and pushing for a piece of cake. It was lively!

One of the officials of the *yeshivah*, "Eliezer the Director," a wise and shrewd Jew, used to say, "When people grab, each man has a share; and if one does not have a share it is a sign he did not grab."

Translated by Simon Raskin[4]

༥ ༥ ༥

MOURNING ON SIMHAT TORAH IN CRACOW
YEHUDAH LEB HAKOHEN MAIMON (FISHMAN)

There is a tradition that centuries ago in the old synagogue of Cracow on the night of Simhat Torah, when they were ready to start the fourth processional circuit with the Scrolls of the Law, Jesuit students invaded the house of worship and slew hundreds of Jews. On the basis of this tradition, it has been a custom in this synagogue to conduct only three-and-a-half circuits on Simhat Torah night. In the middle of the fourth procession, the Scrolls of the Law are returned to the holy ark and all present seat themselves on the floor as mourners. One of the congregants chants *"Yigdal"* to the tune of the lamentations [traditionally intoned on the Fast of the Ninth of Av], in remembrance of the martyrs who died for the sanctification of the Divine Name and of the Torah.[5]

⚘ ⚘ ⚘

SUKKOT FOLKWAYS IN GERMANIC LANDS, 1648*–1806

HERMAN POLLACK

Ezekiel Landau, in presenting a realistic picture of the unaesthetic, unsanitary physical surroundings that have to be faced when a *sukkah* is erected for the Feast of Booths, urges that precautions be taken to select a clean place where there is no refuse so that the *sukkah* can be built in hygienic surroundings. He also warns that "mosquitoes and flies will be plentiful in the booth," and advises everyone to be on the alert to protect himself against insects while sitting in the open. . . .

A local custom may express symbolically the relationship that one festival has to another, such as the *minhag* of Frankfort in using the wax that remained from Yom Kippur candles to make candles for the eve of Hoshana Rabbah, the seventh day of Sukkot, known as "the Great Deliverance." Since the final decree in the Book of Life is extended from the Day of Atonement to the seventh day of Sukkot, there is relevance in saving the Yom Kippur candle-wax for Hoshana Rabbah. The custom has acquired further significance through cabalistic interpretation, popular in its appeal to the folk: the candles for Hoshana Rabbah are to be made of five "capsules of wax," as the number five corresponds to the Five Books of Moses, the Pentateuch. Each capsule of wax must have at least three leaves; the total of fifteen leaves represents the fifteen *Shir ha-Maalot* (Psalms 120–134) and the fifteen words in the Priestly Benediction (Numbers 6.24–27).

To study on Hoshana Rabbah is regarded to be a decisive act, for

* Following the Chmielnicki pogroms.

it is also through study that people can expect to influence the "sealing of the decree" for the new year. On Hoshana Rabbah they are up all night to read from the *Tikkun*, a collection of passages selected mainly from the Bible, Mishnah, Talmud, and *Zohar*. The *Tikkun* is widely used both on Hoshana Rabbah and Shavuot, the Feast of Weeks. Joseph Kosman indicates that the *Tikkun* was introduced to European countries from Palestine, where it originated in the Lurianic cabalistic, mystical school. With regard to some of the regulations pertaining to Hol ha-Moed, the period between the first two and the last two days of Sukkot and Pesah, Ezekiel Landau adopts a lenient view. He contends that the *Shulhan Arukh* permits one to engage in any kind of work during the intervening days of the festival if he has no other way of earning his livelihood. Similarly, Landau saw no objection to an individual cutting his hair or trimming his beard during Hol ha-Moed if he expects to be in the company of civil officials or nobility. The person, Landau states, may be embarrassed or subjected to ridicule if he is not neat in his appearance. We can surmise that the association with a nobleman or official did not take the form of an informal social visit. For the Jew it meant his economic survival, as he was probably trying to interest his political superior in the wares he had for sale.

In his song for Sukkot and Simhat Torah, Elhanan Kirchan criticizes the practice of "making a fire, leaping over it, and shooting gunpowder" during the festival. There is additional evidence that in the eighteenth century Ashkenazic Jews in Central and East European lands observed the custom of exploding gunpowder on Simhat Torah as part of the holiday celebration. In his *Minhagim*, Yuspa Shammash also describes how the bonfire figured in the Simhat Torah merriment. The two "bridegrooms," *hatan Torah* and *hatan Bereshit*, who respectively recited the benedictions for the concluding section of Deuteronomy and the beginning of Genesis, would invite their friends to the wedding hall behind the synagogue. The young man who assisted the sexton then announced in the street, "Lead 'the bride and groom' to the wedding hall in the rear." Fruit and wine were served to the guests and the children were treated to delicacies. A large bonfire was built in the courtyard of the synagogue; the guests then assembled around the fire and engaged in spirited dancing. Yuspa Shammash's concluding description of the bonfire festivities conveys something of the hilarity that broke out on Simhat Torah: "At times the rabbi joined them in the joyous dancing around the fire in honor of the Torah. They would continue until *Minhah* (when afternoon prayers are recited). They drank wine by the fire: the *hatanim* gave them wine. The sexton added wood to the fire, and the *hatanim* would "let go of themselves."

There were also special customs that enabled the youth to participate in festival observances with adults. On Simhat Torah children carried flags in the synagogue, and those children who had not yet reached the age of *bar mitzvah* were called to the Torah in a group and covered with a *tallit* as though they had attained their religious majority. If the children were too young to attend Simhat Torah in the synagogue, a celebration was arranged for them at home on Shemini Atzeret. The children were assembled, fruits and sweets were thrown to them, and they scampered to gather the delicacies. Yuspa Shammash tells of a non-Jewish woman who celebrated Simhat Torah. She owned a garden near the Jewish cemetery, and in her will specified that she was giving the garden to the Jews of Worms, with the understanding that on every Simhat Torah, "until the coming of Messiah, the fruit thereof . . . must be thrown to the children behind the wedding hall." It is reported by Yuspa Shammash that the garden was destroyed during the Thirty Years' War, but seven years later, in 1655, it was rebuilt. We can assume that the adults then resumed serving fruit to the children on Simhat Torah.[6]

❧ ❧ ❧

SIMHAT TORAH IN THE SEPHARDIC SYNAGOGUE OF VIENNA
MANFRED PAPO

The most popular service of all was that held on the eve of Simhat Torah. So great was the crowd seeking entrance that the doors were always closed at 3 P.M. while those seeking admission queued up outside. At 4:30 P.M. three policemen would arrive to regulate the queue and insure that members who showed their membership cards could go in without having to wait in the queue. A quarter of an hour before the service was due to begin, the doors would be opened,

19. White tablecloth with gold brocade appliqué.
Oberzell, Germany. 1781. See Chapter 9.

and the police would admit people until all the seats and standing room were full. Very often many people at the end of the queue had to be turned away.

The reason for the extreme popularity of this service lay in its picturesqueness. Not only was the Sephardic liturgy for the occasion totally different from the Ashkenazic, but the seven traditional circuits with the Scrolls of the Law (*hakkafot*) were made in a unique way. The procession was headed by one of the beadles in full livery (complete with Turkish fez); he was followed by twenty choirboys in cap and gown, walking in pairs; behind them came the adult members of the choir, one tenor, two basses, and the choirmaster. A few steps behind them came the rabbi and the chief cantor, and then the bearers of the twenty-five Scrolls of the Law, led by the *hatan Torah* and the *hatan Bereshit*, both in tails and silk hats, and carrying Scrolls wreathed in flowers. At the end of the procession walked a group of schoolboys under *bar mitzvah* age, carrying three small *Sifre Torah* specially provided for the purpose.[7]

✤ ✤ ✤

THE FESTIVAL IN THE HASSAG LABOR CAMP

M. YECHEZKIELI

Hassag. It was called a labor camp, but it was a slaughterhouse—no more, no less. We were the remnants of the Chenstochover ghetto. Our families had been sent to their death. Only we few remained— like limbs torn from their bodies, writhing with pain, living a life without life. . . .

Sukkot, the festival which brings farmers and city apartment-house dwellers alike into temporary huts, somehow found its way to Hassag. We discovered an unused corner between two factory buildings. Lumber was piled up, as if in storage, for the *sukkah* walls, and somewhat above these walls, branches were unobtrusively stacked for the *sukkah*. We slid in and out of this temporary dwelling with our treasured crusts of bread, thinking of the protective booths in the wilderness, hoping for the *sukkah* of the Leviathan.

So we had our Sukkot in those stolen moments, for the experience of eating in the *sukkah*, no matter how makeshift it was, was a genuine experience, but what could take the place of a *le-hayyim* for the next holiday—Simhat Torah—Joy of the Law? We had no Torah Scroll, and joy was absolutely foreign to Hassag. Worse yet, on that date, just one year earlier, we were witnesses to the liquidation of the Chenstochover ghetto. Simhat Torah—a day of unbridled joy? Hardly. Yet Simhat Torah was brought to Hassag by this cobbler, who was so obscure to us that I cannot even recall his name. Here is how it happened.

One day during the week of Sukkot, a whispered message flitted around the camp: the shoemaker had been delayed in his return from the ghetto. When he finally appeared, he did not head for the kitchen for his especially generous portion, but instead he hurried into the depths of his hut. What had happened? The impossible—no, the incredible had come to pass for the second time in a month! He had successfully spirited a *Sefer Torah* out of the clutches of the dreaded Gestapo and smuggled it into our camp. How? He simply rolled it around and around his body, let his loose outer shirt hang over it, and then walked into the camp. Where he had gotten it from, he adamantly refused to reveal.

Once again, the "clean-up squad" advanced their pet theory—that he had found it in the S.S. stores of Jewish properties, from where he had procured the *shofar*—but they were at least partially wrong. It had not been nearly as easy to get the *Sefer Torah*. The S.S. maintained an extremely heavy guard on their large holdings of Jewish plunder, and were particularly careful with *sefarim* and other religious objects, regardless of their instrinsic value. Our intrepid cobbler decided to bribe one of the guards, but since he was not exactly solvent then, he offered the corporal something that he could never have purchased for any sum—a pair of officer's boots! [The Germans seem to have regarded handcrafted boots as a singular luxury and thus reserved them for high-ranking officers. Hence, too, the cobbler's privileged status.]

We later found out that he had literally saved the *Sefer Torah* from desecration because a short while later the Gestapo burned all the *Sifre Torah*, other *sefarim*, and various sacramental cloths and articles in one gigantic bonfire. This one *Sefer Torah* was the sole surviving remnant of the sacred articles of the ghetto. The cobbler selected it because of its small size, for that made it feasible for him to wrap it around his midriff without causing a telltale bulge, and later, in camp, its size permitted easy concealment.

We had instituted a regular *minyan* on Shabbat in one of the barracks, and it was there, on Shabbat Hol ha-Moed Sukkot, that the heroic shoemaker turned to us and demanded, "Who wants to hide the *Sefer Torah?*"

A companion of mine and I decided to assume the responsibility. We immediately removed a board from the head of one of the wooden cots we slept on and, in the hollow under it, concealed the Scroll.

The news of the Scroll's arrival had naturally electrified the entire camp. On Simhat Torah night we held crowded *hakkafot* in the cramped, rundown shack we called home. These *hakkafot* would have been outlandish in any other situation. The *Sefer Torah* remained safely ensconced in its hollow behind the board. We stealthily walked around the wooden cot that contained our sacred treasure. As we passed, we leaned over and kissed the board that lay directly above the *Sefer.*

We knew that if we had carried the *Sefer Torah* in our arms, as in conventional *hakkafot,* we would have been running a great risk. Don't think it was our lives that we were protecting! Of course being caught carrying the Torah would have meant sure death, but what value did our lives have, anyway? It would have been worth it! But the Scroll would have also been destroyed—God forbid!—and this was a loss we would not risk.

And so it went, far into the night. The silent "dancers" held themselves strenuously in check, as the joyous songs surged repeatedly to their lips.

One song echoed softly in our ears. Because of its obvious relevance, we could not contain it within us. And as we walked around the *Sefer,* we were almost deafened by the silent screaming of its chords that enveloped us all:

"Rejoice and be gay on Simhat Torah, because it [the Torah] is our strength and our light . . . !"

Reb Noach looked up from his cold glass of tea and peered into the faces of his listeners.

"Do you think I made up this story? Have you ever been at the Gerrer Bet Midrash in Bne Brak? Well, the Sefer Torah *is there. I brought it there after the war."*

Translated by Moshe Barkany[8]

✻ ✻ ✻

SUKKOT IN THE WARSAW GHETTO
CHAIM A. KAPLAN

October 5, 1939
Eve of Simhat Torah, 5700

Our holiday is no longer celebrated. Fear has displaced gladness and the windows of the synagogues are dark. Never before have we missed expressing our joy in the eternal Torah—even during the Middle Ages. After 7:00 P.M. there is a curfew in the city, and even in the hours before the curfew we live in dread of the Nazi conqueror's cruelty. The Nazi policy toward Jews is now in full swing.

Every day brings its share of grievous incidents. Here are some typical occurrences: Bearded Jews are stopped on the streets and abused. During the morning prayers on Shemini Atzeret, a hundred and fifty men were pulled out of the Mlawa Street synagogue, herded into a truck, and taken to enforced labor. . . .

October 17, 1940

All day long I thought it over. Should I write? Not because of a lack of impressions, but because of too many of them. Only a divinely inspired pen could describe them accurately on paper. A mere writer of impressions could not adequately record all that happened in the boiling chaos of Jewish Warsaw in the first days of the Sukkot holiday, 5701.

Today the official order was published about the ghetto, but the rulers are wary of calling a spade a spade. Instead of a ghetto, which is a medieval concept, they call it a "Jewish quarter." . . .

October 25, 1940
End of Sukkot, 5701

In the midst of sorrow, the holiday of joy. This is not a secular joy, but a "Rejoicing of the Torah," the same Torah for which we are murdered all day, for which we have become like lambs to be slaughtered, for which we have gone through fire and water. Last year there was darkness in our dwelling places, but a ray of hope still flickered in our souls. We knew the character of the murderers only by rumor, and so we suspected them of having human feelings in spite of all their cruelty and wickedness. Maybe after the first panic of war ended, life would be easier for us, because in their goodness they would grant us an opportunity for primitive human survival. After a year of physical and mental tortures never equaled in history, darkness reigns in our souls as well. The holiday was spent under the impress of the ghetto, with all the sights which accompany its creation and appearance. It is clear to us that the ghetto will be a closed one. They will push us into a Jewish section, fenced in and separated from the world outside, like sinners and criminals.

But we have not shamed our eternal Torah. This was not a raucous celebration, but an inner one, a heartfelt joy, and for that reason it was all the more warm and emotional. Everywhere holiday celebrations were organized, and every prayer group said the wine blessing. The *Hasidim* were even dancing, as is their pious custom. Someone told me that on the night of the holiday he met a large group of zealous *Hasidim* on Mila Street, and they sang holiday songs in chorus out in public, followed by a large crowd of curious people and sightseers. Joy and revelry in poverty-stricken Mila Street! When they sang, they reached such a state of ecstasy that they couldn't stop, until some heretic approached them shouting, "Jews! Safeguarding your life is a positive biblical commandment; it is a time of danger for us. Stop this." Only then did they become quiet. Some of them replied in their ecstasy, "We are not afraid of the murderer! The devil with him!"

Translated by Abraham I. Katsh[9]

⚘ ⚘ ⚘

SUKKOT IN THE SOVIET UNION
ARIE L. ELIAV

The government's war against the institutions and symbols of the Jewish faith does not stop at *matzot* and Passover. It is waged against other areas as well. Sukkot, for example, during which the Four Species—the palm frond, citron, myrtle, and willow—are used, greatly annoys the authorities, for the Four Species remind the Jews of another country, where palms and citrus trees grow. This country, with its distant, warm landscapes, arouses forbidden feelings and yearnings in the hearts of the Jews.

If a citron or palm frond somehow finds its way to the old rabbi of a community, it is regarded as so precious an object that the rabbi himself keeps careful watch over it to prevent its being damaged while it is touched by hosts of people during the festival. It is deeply moving to see the awe and reverence with which the old Jews handle a palm frond which has been cut from a tree thousands of miles away and which, by the time it gets to the rabbi, is desiccated and has lost its color and shape. To witness the elder of the community, swathed in his prayer shawl, shake the dried and withered frond reverently before the worshipers, is to realize that there is no more fitting symbol for the fate of the Jews of the Soviet Union.

On Sukkot I happened to be in the synagogue of the Mountain Jews of Baku, capital of Azerbaijan. After praying together with some two hundred Jews, I followed the crowd into the *sukkah* which had been erected in the synagogue courtyard. The *hakham* was a venerable old man who had not lost his spirit. He was a very clever man indeed.

In the *sukkah* the *hakham* showed me a small bottle of Israeli wine which he had somehow managed to obtain. The bottle was labeled "Carmel Oriental." He was very happy, for he could now make the blessing over wine from the Holy Land. I asked how he expected all the members of his congregation to share in the *Kiddush* with such a tiny quantity of wine. The old man told me not to worry about it. He asked the congregants to form a line, then instructed them to fill their glasses or goblets with the homemade wine each had brought along. Then he posted himself at the entrance to the *sukkah*, and in his hand was the tiny bottle from Israel. As each worshiper passed before him, the *hakham* dropped a few drops of the "wine from Jerusalem" into his glass. When the little bottle was empty, all the congregants joined in the benediction over glasses that had been consecrated by drops of wine from the Holy Land.[10]

❧ ❧ ❧

THE SIMHAT TORAH CELEBRATION
IN MOSCOW

ELIE WIESEL

Where did they all come from? Who sent them here? How did they know it was to be tonight, tonight on Arkhipova Street near the Great Synagogue? Who told them that tens of thousands of boys and girls would gather here to sing and dance and rejoice in the joy of the Torah? They who barely know each other and know even less of Judaism—how did they know that?

I spent hours among them, dazed and excited, agitated by an ancient dream. I forgot the depression that had been building up over the past weeks. I forgot everything except the present and the future. I have seldom felt so proud, so happy, so optimistic. The purest light is born in darkness. Here there is darkness; here there will be light. There must be—it has already begun to burn.

From group to group, from one discussion to the next, from song to song, I walked about, sharing with them a great celebration of victory. I wanted to laugh, to laugh as I have never done before. To hell with the fears of yesterday, to hell with the dread of tomorrow. We have already triumphed.

He who has not witnessed the Rejoicing of the Law in Moscow has never in his life witnessed joy. Had I come to Russia for that alone, it would have been enough. . . .

The "festival of youth" has become something of a Russian tradition since it first began four or five years ago during the period of internal easement inaugurated by Nikita Khrushchev. At first the festivals were attended by a few hundred students; then the number grew into the thousands. Now they come in tens of thousands.

Objective observers like to claim that the gatherings have no relation to Jewish religious feeling. Young people come to the synagogue as they would to a club, in order to make new friends and learn new songs and dances. If they had someplace else to go, they wouldn't come to the synagogue.

I should say this explanation is not entirely correct. There is no lack of meeting places in Moscow; young people can get together either downtown, at the university, or at the Komsomol clubs. If they come to the synagogue, it is because they want to be among Jews and to be at one in their rejoicing with their fellow Jews all over the world, in spite of everything, and precisely because they have received an education of a different sort entirely. They come precisely because of the attempts that have been made to isolate them from their heritage, and they come in defiance of all efforts to make Judaism an object worthy of their hatred. . . .

I, too, had made preparations for the night of Simhat Torah, as if for a great test or some meeting with the unknown. I was tense and restless. The many stories I had heard about the celebrations last year and the year before only increased my apprehension. I feared a disappointment. What if they didn't come? Or came, but not in great numbers? Or in great numbers, but not as Jews?

In order not to miss this meeting of three generations, I had arranged to spend the last days of Sukkot in Moscow. Unjustly, I had determined to rely neither on miracles nor on the Soviet airlines. I was afraid my plane might be delayed in Kiev or Leningrad, and I didn't want to arrive in Moscow at the last minute. I could not allow myself to miss this opportunity.

I might have seen the same thing in Leningrad . . . or so I was told. Thousands of students gather at the Leningrad synagogue on the night of Simhat Torah. In Tbilisi, too, young people crowd the synagogue even on an ordinary Sabbath. In Kiev I tried to convince myself that precisely because the Jewish leaders were attempting to suppress Jewish feeling and to drive away the younger generation, it would be worth staying to see what happened. But I was drawn to Moscow. Moscow would be the center; there the climax would occur. What would take place in Moscow could not happen anywhere else, inside Russia or abroad; so I had heard from people who had been there the past three years.

I wanted to see young people, to measure the extent of their Jewishness and discover its means of expression. . . .

It was years since I had last prepared for the night of Simhat Torah with such anticipation, such a sense of awe and excitement. I knew something would happen, something vast, a revelation. I was taut and fragile as the string on a violin. One must not force things, my friends cautioned me; you expect too much, you will never be satisfied with anything less than perfection. Patience. As the sun began to set, its rays danced in a fantasy of color over the Kremlin's gilded domes. The sky was clear blue, and there were no clouds. The weather must hold. It must not rain.

It didn't. And it did not snow. There was a cold wind that cut to the bone. That's nothing, my friends said. Young people do not fear the cold. They'll come, if only to warm up.

Apparently the Soviet authorities also expected a large crowd, and they did their best to frighten it away. It had been made known that during the High Holy Days everyone entering the synagogue had been photographed. And now in front of the synagogue two gigantic floodlights had been installed, illuminating the entire street. The Jews were not to forget that someone was watching. The Jews would do well not to become too excited or to betray an overly Jewish character in their rejoicing.

They came nevertheless. Inside, the great hall of the synagogue was crammed with more than two thousand men and women. Many brought their children, for children, too, were to see that the Jews knew how to rejoice. The atmosphere was festive. Young girls stood among the men on the ground floor. The balcony was overflowing. People smiled at one another. Wherefore was this night different from all other nights? On all other nights we live in fear; tonight we are free men. Tonight one is permitted even to smile at strangers.

The old rabbi seemed calmer than he had on Yom Kippur. The hall buzzed with conversation. Eyes reflected hope and well-being. "Would you give your flag to my grandson?" an elderly man asked an Israeli child who held a pennant in his hand. The boy smiled and nodded. "Here you are." The Russian child took the Jewish flag and kissed it. An informer came up and demanded that the old man return the gift. He hesitated a second, took courage, then said no. His friends stood at his side. The informer bowed his head. Tonight he was alone.

When would the processions begin? They had long since finished the evening prayers. Why were they waiting? It seemed that they were just waiting; they had no special reason. They waited because it was pleasant to wait, because it was good to be in the midst of such a large and living crowd, in such a joyful place. If they didn't begin, they wouldn't have to end; they could treasure the perfection of the holiday. Expectation itself became part of the event. They drew it out, trying to expand the holiday past the limits of a single evening or a single day. If one could only remain here, united, until next year.

"Festivities are already under way outside," we were told by new arrivals.

The *gabbai* decided they had to begin. It was already late. One could not stay here all night, or even if one could, it would be dangerous. There was no knowing what people might do or say once they had been given a chance to release their feelings. There was no knowing what the repercussions would be from above.

They had to start. The *gabbai* banged on the table and shouted for silence. Useless. Thousands of whispers grew into an overwhelming roar. The *gabbai* continued shouting, but only those standing nearby, as we were, could hear him. The congregation had come to hear cries of a different sort, or perhaps not to hear anything, just to be present, to partake of the sacred joy of the holiday.

They began. Rabbi Yehudah Leib Levin was honored with the first verse, "Thou has caused us to know. . . ." He seemed to have recovered his youthful energy. His deep, sorrowful voice seemed more melodious. How many Jews in that hall fully understood his meaning when he sang, "For God is the Lord, there is no other beside Him"?

"The celebrating outside is incredible," we were told.

Inside, too, it was the same. The Israeli ambassador, Mr. Katriel Katz, was given the honor of reciting a verse, "Thy priests shall be clothed in righteousness, and Thy faithful ones rejoice." His voice, too, was lost in the roar of whispers, but his title was known, and the enthusiasm mounted. People stood on tiptoe to see the representative of the sovereign state of Israel. His presence made them straighten up; they seemed taller.

The Scrolls of the Torah were taken from the ark and the dignitaries of the community invited to lead the first procession. The night before, I had participated in this ceremony in a small side chamber where the *Hasidim* pray. All the guests had been called for the first procession. Rabbi Levin had also been there, and we danced and danced until our strength gave out. We sang Hasidic and Israeli songs in Yiddish and Hebrew. A tall, awkward, red-faced Jew had suddenly broken into the circle and caught the rabbi's arm. "Come, Rabbi, let us fulfill the commandment to dance! We must gladden our hearts for the Torah!" The two of them danced as we clapped our hands in time. The rabbi grew tired, but his partner goaded him on, more, more! They danced not for themselves but for the entire house of Israel. The tall one's happiness was mingled with

20. *Sukkah*. Woodcut.
From *Sefer Minhagim*,
Amsterdam, 1723.

21. *Hoshanot*. Woodcut.
From *Sefer Minhagim*,
Amsterdam, 1723.

22. The headless man on
Hoshana Rabbah. Woodcut.
From *Sefer Minhagim*,
Amsterdam, 1723.
See Chapter 9.

rage. He could not sing, and he danced without rhythm in little jumps. His eyes shone with unworldly wrath, and I knew that his joy was real, flowing as it did out of an anger long contained. All year one is forbidden to be angry and forbidden to rejoice. Tonight one is permitted to rejoice. He was crying, too. Why, I do not know. Why does a man cry? Because things are good; because things are bad. Here the question is different; why does a man rejoice? Where does he get the strength to rejoice?

But that was last night, and they were *Hasidim*. The people crowding into the synagogue tonight were simple Jews who had come to learn that is was possible to be a Jew and to find reasons for rejoicing . . . or to rejoice for no reason at all. Longbeards and workers, old and young, widows and lovely girls, students and bureaucrats. Among them there were many who had never prayed but who had come to watch the processions and to honor the Torah.

Processions? How could they lead a procession through this mob? The Jews formed an impenetrable living mass. No matter. Here everything was possible. It would take time, but no matter. They had the time, and patience too. Somehow the parade would pass. In the meantime they sang, louder and louder. They were all looking at us, the guests, as if to say, "Well, what's with you? Let's hear something from you." The entire Israeli diplomatic corps was present, together with their wives and children. We sang, "Gather our scattered ones from among the nations, and our dispersed from the corners of the world." Five times, ten times. A number of the diplomats belonged to left-wing parties. In their youth they had scorned religion, and religious people in particular. Tonight they celebrated the holiday with Hasidic enthusiasm and abandon. Differences of opinion and class were left behind. An American writer once told me, "As I stood among the Jews of Russia, I became a Jew." He was not alone; many who come here as Israelis also return home as Jews.

"Outside they are turning the world upside down."

Should we go out? There was still time. Here, too, the world was in uproar. Men who had not sung for a year were raising their voices in song. Men who had not seen a Torah all year long were embracing and kissing it with a love bequeathed to them from generations past. Old men lifted their grandchildren onto their shoulders, saying, "Look, and remember." The children looked in wonder and laughed, uncertain what was happening. No matter; they would understand later, and they would remember. Tzvikah, the vocalist in the Israeli corps, assembled his chorus and gave them the pitch: "David, king of Israel, lives and endures." There was not a Jew in the hall who was not prepared to give his life defending that assertion.

The dignitaries had made their way back to the pulpit. The first procession was over. The *gabbai* announced that all guests were to take part in the second, and the congregation responded with new bursts of song. From one corner came an Israeli tune, "*Hevenu Shalom Aleikhem*, We have brought peace unto you"; from another, "*Havah Nagilah*, Come let us rejoice." A third group preferred a traditional song, "Blessed is our God who created us in His honor and separated us from the nations and implanted in us eternal life." Instead of resisting one another, the various songs seemed to fuse into a single melodic affirmation. Those who had spent years in prison or in Siberia, those who had only recently become aware of their Jewishness, now proclaimed their unity: one people, one Torah. Each of them had stood once at the foot of Mount Sinai and heard the word, "*Anokhi*—I am the Lord thy God." Each of them had received the promise of eternity.

We held the Scrolls tightly to our chests and tried to make our way through the congregation. But instead of opening a path for us they pressed in closer, as if to block the way completely. They wanted us to stay among them. We were surrounded by a sea of faces, creased, joyful, unmasked. Hats of all kinds, skullcaps of every color, handkerchiefs in place of head covering. A young girl clapped her hands, an old man lifted up his eyes as if in prayer, a laborer sighed joyfully. Old men and their children and their children's children—everyone wanted to touch the Torah, to touch us. Everyone had something to whisper in our ears, a blessing or a secret. I have never in my life received so many blessings, never in my life been surrounded by so much goodwill and love. One pressed my hand, a second patted my arm, a third held my clothing. They would not let us move forward. They seemed to be trying to stop the progress of time. Through us they became freer, came closer to the reality of their dreams. They looked upon us as redeeming and protective angels. The fact that we were different, unafraid, was sufficient to elevate us in their eyes to the stature of saints and wonder-workers. When I was young, we used to surround the holy *rebbe* in this fashion, begging him to intercede for us before the heavenly tribunal. But here, they asked for nothing. On the contrary, they brought us their gifts, their love, their blessings. Hundreds of them. Be healthy! Be strong! Be courageous! May we see you in the years to come! May we all live until that day! May you prosper! And may you sing! Do you hear? Just sing! A few went further, giving vent to their inmost feelings, but always in a whisper: I have a brother in Israel, a sister in Jerusalem, an uncle in Haifa. Short notices: brother, sister, grandfather, uncle, grandson. No names. They simply wanted us to know that a part of them was there, in the land of Israel. Others used clichés that in any other context would have produced smiles of condescension or contempt. "The people of Israel lives"; "The eternity of Israel shall not prove false"; "The redeemer shall come to Zion soon in our days." A Jew with a laborer's cap falling over his brow pushed forward and announced that he had something to tell me but no one was to hear. He began to hum in my ear the words of *Hatikvah,* finished the first stanza, and disappeared, his face alight with victory. . . .

Our procession lasted about an hour. Pale and drenched with sweat, we relinquished the Torah Scrolls to the next group of marchers and returned to our seats in the visitors' section. I was out of breath and exhausted. I wanted to rest, close my eyes, and wait for my strength to return. The third procession had begun. The singing reached me as if from a great distance or from behind a curtain, as in a daydream. I had never imagined that the weight and power of this experience would stun me as it did. If I had come for this alone, it would have been sufficient.

"They're going crazy out there. We must join them."

We went. The remaining processions we would celebrate outside. Luckily there was a side door; we did not have to pass through the congregation. They would never have let us go. Two or three "agents" got up to follow us. Let them. The Prince of the Torah protects those who come to rejoice in His Name.

The street was unrecognizable. For a second I thought I had been transported to another world, somewhere in Israel or in Brooklyn. Angels and seraphim were serenading the night; King David played his harp. The city burst with gladness and joy. The evening had just begun. . . .

I do not know where all these young people came from. They didn't tell me, although I asked. Perhaps there is no one answer, but tens of thousands that are all the same. No matter—they came.

Who sent them? Who persuaded them to come running to spend a Jewish holiday in a Jewish atmosphere and in accordance with traditional Jewish custom? Who told them when and where and why? I was unable to discover. Perhaps they knew but preferred not to say in public. Fine. Let them preserve their secret. All that matters is that they have one and that they came.

Still, there is something strange about it. Tens of thousands of youngsters do not suddenly emerge from nowhere at a specified time and place. Someone had to organize and direct them; someone had to make the contacts, maintain the necessary spirit, and inform them of the date and time. Who made all the preparations? Who breathed the spark into a flame? I didn't ask; they wouldn't have answered. Perhaps it is better for me not to know.

They came in droves. From near and far, from downtown and the suburbs, from the university and from the factories, from school dormitories and from the Komsomol club. They came in groups; they came alone. But once here, they became a single body, voicing a song of praise to the Jewish people and its will to live.

How many were there? Ten thousand? Twenty thousand? More. About thirty thousand. The crush was worse than it had been inside the synagogue. They filled the whole street, spilled over into court-yards, dancing and singing, dancing and singing. They seemed to hover in midair, Chagall-like, floating above the mass of shadows and colors below, above time, climbing a Jacob's ladder that reached to the heavens, if not higher.

Tomorrow they would descend and scatter, disappear into the innermost parts of Moscow, not to be heard from for another year. But they would return and bring more with them. The line will never break; one who has come will always return.

I moved among them like a sleepwalker, stunned by what I saw and heard, half disbelieving my own senses. I had known they would come, but not in such numbers; I had known they would celebrate, but not that their celebration would be so genuine and so deeply Jewish.

They sang and danced, talked among themselves or with strangers. They were borne along on a crest that seemed incapable of breaking. Their faces reflected a special radiance, their eyes the age-old flame that burned in the house of their ancestors—to which they seemed finally to have returned.

I was swept along in the current, passing from one group to

another, from one circle to the next, sharing their happiness and absorbing the sound of their voices.

It was after ten. The cold brought tears to one's eyes. But it was easy to warm up; one had only to join in the singing or start talking with someone.

A girl strummed her guitar and sang a Yiddish folk song. "Buy my cigarettes, take pity on a poor orphan." A few steps away, a boy played *Hevenu Shalom Aleikhem* on the accordian. Further on, others were dancing the *horah*. . . .

A dark-haired and vivacious girl stood in the middle of a circle, leading a chorus of voices in a series of questions and answers.

"Who are we?"

"Jews!"

"What are we?"

"Jews!"

"What shall we remain?"

"Jews!"

They laughed as they chanted their responses. Someone translated the dialogue for me, urged me to join in the laughter and handclapping. It was a splendid joke. The Kremlin was ten minutes away, and the echos of the Jewish celebration reached to the tomb of Stalin. "It's too crowded here!" a boy cried. "Next year we celebrate in Red Square!" His audience burst into applause.

"Who are we?" asked the dark-haired girl.

"Jews!" . . .

The songs they sang were mostly products of the nineteenth century. The most popular Yiddish folk song, "Come let us go together, all of us together, and greet the bride and groom." But they had updated the lyrics, substituting for the last phrase, "Come let us greet the Jewish people," or "the people of Israel," or "the God of Israel and His Torah."

One group of students had formed a human pyramid. The young man at the apex was yelling defiantly, "Nothing can help them! We shall overcome them!" His audience roared back, "Hurrah! Hurrah!"

More cheers came from a nearby group that was celebrating the holiday in a manner decidedly Russian, tossing one of their number into the air. Five times, six, seven. Higher, higher. A girl pleaded with them to stop, but they paid no attention. Eight times, nine, ten.

Nothing would happen. Nothing did. A carpet of outstretched hands was waiting to catch the hero upon his return from on high. "Hurrah! Hurrah!"

This is how Russian soldiers celebrated their victory over the Germans, and how the Jews celebrate their triumph over despair.

"What does anyone in America or Israel care if my passport is stamped 'Jewish'? It doesn't matter to me, and it doesn't matter to these young people here tonight. So stop protesting about things that don't bother us. We have long since ceased being ashamed of our Jewishness. We can't hide it anyway. Besides, by accepting it we've managed to turn obedience to the law into an act of free choice."

The man I was talking to had served as a captain in the Red Army and had been decorated in Berlin. Like his father before him, he was a sworn Communist. But like all the rest, he suffered on account of his Jewishness. Were he Russian he would have long ago been appointed a full professor at the university. He was still holding an instructorship in foreign languages. One day, he said, he decided that as long as they made him feel like a Jew, he might as well act accordingly. It was the only way to beat them at their own game. "Two years ago I came to the synagogue on the night of Simhat Torah. I wanted to see Jews, and I wanted to be with them. I didn't tell my wife, who isn't Jewish, or my sixteen-year-old son. Why should I burden him with problems? There was time enough for that. I came back last year for the second time. The youngsters were singing and dancing, almost like tonight. I found myself suddenly in the middle of a group of youngsters, and my heart stopped . . . I was standing face to face with my son. He said he'd been coming for the past three years, but hadn't dared to tell me.

"Would you like to see him?" he asked me.

"Yes, very much."

"He's here, somewhere," he said, gesturing at the crowd as if to say, "Look closely, they are all my son." . . .

This evening gave me new hope and encouragement. We need not despair. The Jews in Kiev, Leningrad, and Tbilisi who had complained to me about the doubtful future of Russian Jewry were wrong. They were too pessimistic, and apparently did not know their own children or the hidden forces which prompt them, at least once a year, to affirm their sense of community. Everyone has judged this generation guilty of denying its God and of being ashamed of its

Jewishness. They are said to despise all mention of Israel. But it is a lie. Their love for Israel exceeds that of young Jews anywhere else in the world.

If, on this night of dancing, gladness finally overcame fear, it was because of them. If song triumphed over silence, it was their triumph. And it was through them only that the dream of freedom and community became reality. I am still waiting to see tens of thousands of Jews singing and dancing in Times Square or the Place de l'Etoile as they danced here, in the heart of Moscow, on the night of Simhat Torah. They danced until midnight without rest, to let the city know that they are Jews.

Translated by Neal Kozodoy[11]

❧ ❧ ❧

SUKKOT IN MY NATIVE SALONICA
BARUCH UZIEL

Soon after the conclusion of Yom Kippur, the square near the Jewish market (*La Plaza Judía*) was filled with piles of reeds. Jews hurried to buy them as coverings for their *sukkot*; porters made their deliveries, and reeds were visible as far as the eye could reach. . . . When the festival began, all the booths were in a state of readiness: walls of wooden beams draped with snow-white sheets, ceiling of reeds, curtained door. They were decorated with yellow flowers called *conchas de Succot*, resembling marigolds in size and shape, and chains of colored paper called "Bar Yohai." Why "Bar Yohai"? This was a reference to Lag ba-Omer, when such paper chains together with lighted lanterns, would decorate the windows of the houses. These were the "standard" booths, but there were also others decorated with tapestries, mirrors, rugs, and draperies.

The booths were erected in courtyards or porches, and even on "laundry roofs." Every roof in town consisted of two parts: one made of red tiles covering the house proper which, like all roofs, was slanted, and the other covering the extensive kitchen wing. This was flat, made of zinc and used for hanging laundry.

After *Kiddush* on the first night of the holiday the evening meal would be served. At that moment traditional choruses of joy began to resound from neighbor to neighbor across courtyards and roofs, from booth to booth, although those who called could not see one another.

"*David, donde tienes la mano?* (Where is your hand?)"

"*A l'cena.* (In my plate.)"

This conversation was repeated annually for generations, steeped in hidden allusions whose meaning and humor never wore off. These simple words evidenced a pervasive friendship and joy that permeated the entire city that night.

The first two days of the holiday were called *Los Primeros*, the last two, *Los Traseros*, and the intermediate days *Los Medianos*. These terms were also applied to Passover. *Los Primeros* were devoted to prayer and to family visits, because all the men participated semi-annually in these official festive visits. The women stayed at home to receive the relatives while their men and children went visiting. Sometimes three generations could be seen marching off together—grandfather, sons, and grandchildren. From morning to noon the streets were filled with a joyous crowd, divided into groups strolling at ease. All were arrayed in their holiday best; a few, parading pompously, swung their canes and displayed their new shoes; and from everyone came the tuneful, drawn-out, loud and festive greetings expressing joy and revelry:

"*Moadim le-Simhah!*"

"*Haggim u-Zemannim le-Sason!*"

This was without doubt a Jewish city, and these people had deep roots here. They felt uninhibited and happy, because at the end of the holiday they would engage in their trades and occupations without hindrance. Every business and activity was open to them, including seamanship and fishing.

Arriving at their destination the guests greeted their hosts warmly and respectfully in a special tune transmitted from generation to generation: "*Moadim le-Simhah!*"

The women hurried toward them, excited and smiling, replying to their greetings. . . .

La musa de la casa, the oldest unmarried daughter, serves the sweet table (*la tabla de dulce*). This is a silver or copper tray with two handles, with a glass or crystal jar of sweet preserves in the center. These are usually the traditional *naranjas*, tiny citrus fruits imported from unknown exotic regions. Around the jar are arranged, in a semicircle, glasses of cold water as a "chaser" after the preserves. The young lady, shy and festive and redolent of myrrh, moves among the guests according to age and prominence—the older people being served first. She tarries patiently while each guest takes some preserves, extends holiday greetings and cordial wishes for good health and a happy marriage, and sips from a glass of water after reciting the benediction. Her cheeks sweetly blushing at the mention of a bridegroom, she passes on to the next guest.

The men hurry on; there are many visits to complete. During the first two days of the festival all the relatives must be called on. An oversight would be regarded as an insult, especially if the neglected relative is poor or widowed. Moreover, these visits had to be completed by noon—there is no visiting in the afternoon hours—and it is sometimes necessary to tour the whole city in order to reach everybody. The men therefore start on their way while the women complain coyishly:

"Why must you go? It's still early!"

The men make their excuses and the women, realizing they must not detain them, pronounce their blessings and extend regards to the womenfolk. The guests receive the traditional gifts: for the adults hard-boiled eggs colored brown by boiling in water containing onion skins, and for the children apples (on Passover, oranges). The more distinguished ladies present duck eggs instead of chicken eggs, especially to an important guest or one whom they wish to impress particularly.

The holiday preparations and the holiday itself allay somewhat the solemnity of the Penitential Days. But the atmosphere is rife with the pall of approaching autumn and the cold north winds blowing across the Vardar River. Nevertheless, one is eager to be merry during the intermediate days of the festival, and the elation of these hard-working Jews erupts during the afternoon hours. Groups of strollers gather at every corner and horse-drawn carriages carry the town's young blades, gay and not infrequently inebriated. At times there is an unbroken row of carriages headed by musicians—the traditional trio with fiddle, trumpet, and drums—as in marriage and circumcision ceremonies.

This celebration is but the prelude to another, more jubilant celebration, that of Simhat Torah—it is the secular rejoicing preceding the sacred observance.

The intermediate days, however, are not entirely secular. In addition to prayer and the fulfillment of the commandment of *sukkah*, the synagogue beadle carries the *lulav* and *etrog* to each house so that the women may recite the benediction. It is noteworthy that, unlike the

Ashkenazim, the Sephardim do not purchase individual *etrogim;* the *hazzan* discharges the obligation for the entire congregation.

The festival has now reached its zenith. The doors of the ark are opened and the circuits begin:

Lift up your heads, O ye gates,
And be lifted up, ye everlasting doors
That You, King, may enter in song,
May enter the sacred precincts!

Hymn follows upon hymn and circuit succeeds circuit. The singing begins placidly but soon bursts into rapturous enthusiasm, first in Hebrew and then in Ladino:

From the mouth of God,
From the mouth of God,
May blessings come to Israel!

The Torah Scrolls in their embroidered coverlets are paraded round and round in the arms of the dancing Jews. The beadle circles among them with a silver decanter and sprinkles rosewater over the sacred Scrolls and over the worshipers.

Then the sublime words of Ibn Gabirol are sung to an ancient stirring melody:

Return, O Shulammite, return
To Zion's sacred mount,
Escorting Elijah the prophet
To God's holy fount!

The Jews marching around the reading desk grow more and more enraptured as they intone unceasingly:

Amen, amen, amen,
O awe-inspiring Name,
Amen, amen, amen!

With each "amen" they genuflect, almost turning into dervishes as they peer into one another's eyes for a sign of accord.

The singing surges out into the streets, into the boisterous Jewish city. The bridegrooms of the Law and of Genesis are accompanied to their homes, where lavish refreshments await the guests. They are followed by groups of children, who taunt them with the familiar Ladino tune:

He has no money at all—
The poor poor bridegroom.

This is an ancient song, as indicated by the Arabic word for "poor," *muflus*—a language unknown to the inhabitants of Salonica—and not understood by the children. However, the children know one thing: when the *hatan* hears their teasing, he throws them their favorite white sugarplums (*confites*) to prove that he is neither poor nor miserly. They, in turn, grab at the dainties, competing for the largest share, and the general joy mounts as each synagogue sends forth another *hatan* followed by a similar group.

Sometimes, when two such groups meet on their way from different synagogues, they walk off in opposite directions, "insulting" each other with peculiar epithets nobody understands. This incomprehension derives from the fact that Salonica was settled by Jews who came from various countries—Palestine, the Greek Islands (the authentic "Romaniotes"), Bavaria, Hungary (during the Crusades), Italy, Spain, Portugal, and North Africa. Every wave of immigration established its own community and erected a synagogue according to its own rites and customs. . . .

Toward evening the rejoicing gradually comes to a halt as the weekday mood approaches and the north winds blow from the Vardar River.

Among all the gay Simhat Torah melodies the children note the minor key of *Adon Olam* and, sensitive to its pensive mood, invoke it as an accompaniment to the holiday's end. They alter its text, however, by fitting Ladino words to the tune. The result is elegiac:

O Eternal, Sukkot has come and gone:
Yet Thou art our God, O Eternal!

Across the Vardar the wind soughs on a subdued note; yet it is sure to emerge with greater vigor.

O false north wind! Why did we not see that out of the north the evil would erupt upon this happy community, that out of the north would outpour the evil Teutonic hordes to wreak destruction upon it?

Translated by Solomon Feffer[12]

23. The procession of palms in the Amsterdam synagogue.
From *Cérémonies et coutumes religieuses*, by Bernard Picart,
Amsterdam, 1723. See Chapter 9.

※ ※ ※

SIMHAT TORAH IN THE
MEDIEVAL VENICE GHETTO

ERIC WERNER

We possess an enthusiastic report about that "Accademia Musicale"
and its performances on Simhat Torah under the leadership of Leon
da Modena. The writer is his former disciple, the apostate Giulio
Morosini (alias Samuel Nachmias del Salonicco). He says: "I remember well that at the time of my successes in Venice during 1628 or
thereabouts, if I am not mistaken, the Jews fled from Mantua because
of the war, and some came to Venice. At that juncture Mantua flourished in many fields of study. Also the Jews applied themselves to

music and to the playing of instruments. Upon their arrival in Venice, they organized an academy of music in the ghetto where I was living, and sang there twice a week in the evenings. It was chiefly certain leading personalities and the rich men of the ghetto who supported that institution. I also was to be found among those there assembled. My teacher, R. Leon da Modena, was the *maestro di cappella*.

"In that year, two rich and brilliant personalities were elected bridegrooms of the Law—one of whom was a member of the academy. With the help of the musicians, there had been arranged for our benefit two choirs in the Spanish Synagogue, which was beautifully decorated and adorned with silverware and jewels. On the two evenings, i.e., on the "Octave" [sic] of the feast Shemini Atzeret and Simhat Torah, these choirs sang figural music [that is, music in artistic settings] in the Hebrew language, also a part of *Arvit*, several psalms, and the *Minhah*: that is to say, also the afternoon service of the last holiday was solemnized by music. Thus, during some hours of the evening, a throng of noblemen and ladies gathered amid such great applause that many officers and policemen had to guard the gates to secure quiet and safe passage. Among the instruments, an organ also was brought into the synagogue; which is not permitted by the rabbis, because it is the instrument usually played in our churches. . . ."

Elsewhere Morosini emphasizes the great part choral singing played on Simhat Torah. He reports that rhymed *piyyutim* with references to Jerusalem and the coming of Elijah and of the Messiah were sung, sometimes in Spanish or Turkish. In the center of the festivity are the *hatan Torah* and *hatan Bereshit* in whose praise are rendered hymns, encomia, and eulogies. Their names are celebrated in poems created *ad hoc*, and all the arts (above all, music) have to contribute to their glorification. When reading such reports, we need not be surprised that the strict Orthodox of Venice tolerated such secularistic activities. We learn that Simhat Torah was not considered a full holiday, inasmuch as the prohibition of work on that day was somewhat flexible. Already in the early sixteenth century, the rabbis had permitted dancing in the synagogue on that occasion.[13]

✴ ✴ ✴

THE HARVEST FESTIVAL IN ENGLAND
BENJAMIN DISRAELI

The vineyards of Israel have ceased to exist, but the eternal Law enjoins the children of Israel still to celebrate the vintage. A race that persists in celebrating their vintage, although they have no fruits to gather, will regain their vineyards. What sublime inexorability in the Law! But what indomitable spirit in the people!

It is easy for the happier Sephardim, the Hebrews who have never quitted the sunny regions that are laved by the Midland ocean—it is easy for them, though they have lost their heritage, to sympathize, in their beautiful Asian cities or in their Moorish and Arabian gardens, with the graceful rites that are, at least, an homage to a benignant nature. But picture to yourself the child of Israel in the dingy suburb or the squalid quarter of some bleak northern town, where there is never a sun that can at any date ripen grapes. Yet he must celebrate the vintage of purple Palestine! The Law has told him, though a denizen in an icy clime, that he must dwell for seven days in a bower, and that he must build it of the boughs of thick trees; and the rabbins have told him that those thick trees are the palm, the myrtle, and the weeping willow. Even Sarmatia may furnish a weeping willow. The law has told him that he must pluck the fruit of goodly trees, and the rabbins have explained that goodly fruit on this occasion is confined to citron. . . . His mercantile connections will enable him, often at considerable cost, to procure some palm leaves from Canaan, which he may wave in his synagogue, while he exclaims . . . "Hosanah in the highest!" There is something profoundly interesting in this devoted observance of oriental customs in the heart of our Saxon and Sclavonian cities; in these descendants of the bedouins, who conquered Canaan more than three thousand years ago, still celebrating that success which secured for their forefathers for the first time grapes and wine.

Conceive a being born and bred in the *Judenstrasse* of Hamburg or Frankfort, or rather in the purlieus of our Houndsditch or Minories, born to hereditary insult, without any education, apparently without a circumstance that can develop the slightest taste or cherish the least sentiment for the beautiful, living amid fogs and filth, never treated with kindness, seldom with justice, occupied with the meanest, if not the vilest, toil, bargaining for frippery, speculating in usury, existing forever under the concurrent influence of degrading causes which would have worn out long ago any race that was not of the unmixed blood of Caucasus, and did not adhere to the laws of Moses—conceive such a being, an object to you of prejudice, dislike, disgust, perhaps hatred. The season arrives, and the mind and heart of that being are filled with images and passions that have been ranked in all ages among the most beautiful and the most genial of human experience; filled with a subject the most vivid, the most graceful, the most joyous, and the most exuberant—a subject that has inspired poets and which has made God—the harvest of the grape in the native regions of the vine.

He rises in the morning, goes early to some Whitechapel market, purchases some willow boughs, for which he had previously given a commission, and which are brought probably from one of the neighboring rivers of Essex, hastens home, cleans out the yard of his miserable tenement, builds his bower, decks it, even profusely, with the finest flowers and fruits that he can procure, the myrtle and the citron never forgotten, and hangs its roof with variegated lamps. After the service of his synagogue, he sups late with his wife and his children in the open air as if he were in the pleasant villages of Galilee, beneath its sweet and starry sky.[14]

✳ ✳ ✳

THE FESTIVAL OF BOOTHS IN COLONIAL AMERICA
JACOB R. MARCUS

The Jewish life of Barbados was a full-fledged one. The communal cabana, a loose framework of planks covered with foliage to commemorate the fall harvest festival of the ancient Hebrews, was decorated within by palm branches tied together with gaily colored ribbons. Through the open spaces in its roof the twinkling stars could be seen at night. Lanterns were hung, and in addition the members who crowded into the frail structure by the dozens all carried lit candles. Refreshments included olives and fruits, while the conviviality of the festival was further stimulated by the flow of wine. . . .

It was during this autumnal harvest festival that some of the synagogal officers were elected for the ensuing year and that the cycle of pentateuchal readings was recommended. At New York the newly elected officers were evidently expected to provide liquid refreshments in the cabana erected in the synagogue courtyard—with the result that the celebrants returned to their homes in a very exhilarated mood. The Sukkot celebration at Newport was an equally joyous occasion. The cabana was beautifully decorated with yellow, green, purple, and red ribbons, pinned to the walls or hanging as streamers, while the *lulav* was carefully wrapped in yards of colored ribbon. A table in the cabana held ample servings of fruit, bread, and rum.[15]

❧ ❧ ❧

THE FEAST OF REJOICING IN THE LAW IN A MONTREAL SYNAGOGUE
ABRAHAM M. KLEIN

I was ten years old, it was the Feast of Rejoicing in the Law. . . . The synagogue was brightly illuminated throughout, even in those parts where no service was going on. On the tables reserved for study there lay holy books, some of them still leafy with twigs of myrtle between the pages, last remnants of the Sukkot ritual, serving now as bookmarks; but in the center of the synagogue, about the *almemar* and before the ark of the covenant, there was sound and exaltation. Wine had been drunk, and the Torah was being cherished with singing and dance.

As every year, the old Kuznetsov was already ecstatically exhilarated; his beard awry, his muddy features shiny pink, his very pockmarks hieratic like unleavened bread, he was dancing—a velvet-mantled Scroll in his arms—with a fine otherworldly abandon, as his friends clapped hands in time. The cantor kept trilling forth pertinent versicles, answered by the congregation in antiphon. A year of the reading of the Law had been concluded, a year was beginning anew, the last verses of Deuteronomy joined the first of Genesis, the eternal circle continued. Circular, too, was the dance, a scriptural gaiety, with wine rejoicing the heart, and Torah exalting it to heights that strong wine could not reach.

My father, a copy of the Pentateuch before him, stood watching the sacred circle, smiling. Not a demonstrative man, he felt that joy had worthier means of expression than hopping feet; a shrewd man, too, he could not resist the reflection that most of those who were now jubilant with Torah either did not see Torah from year's end to year's end or, seeing, looked on it as knowingly as did the rooster on the page of the prayer of *Bne Adam*. Nonetheless, my father stood there smiling, smiling and happy, happy to see Torah honored even if only by hearsay.[16]

❧ ❧ ❧

A *SUKKAH* BY COURTESY OF
U.S. ARMY ENGINEERS
OSCAR M. LIFSHUTZ

"Chaplain," the voice on the telephone asked, "what in the Sam Hill is a *sukkah*? You sure you spelled it right?"

"Certainly," I answered the lieutenant from the engineering section. "It's spelled right."

"But it's not in the book, Chaplain. How about changing the nomenclature?"

Thus began my friendly encounter with the U.S. Army Engineers to build a *sukkah* for the Feast of Tabernacles in Munich, Germany. Now don't get me wrong. The army can build anything, but they have to know what they are building, and there are always a few technicalities to be complied with if you want to have it done right or at all. GIs call it red tape. But that's not true. It's a matter of getting the right idea to the right place in proper form—and, of course, with proper approval. The Army will build a 500-foot TV tower if you can prove you're entitled to it, or build a bridge across the deepest gorge if you can assure them that you have to cross it. But when it comes to building a *sukkah*—that's another matter.

A few weeks before Rosh Hashanah of last year I conferred with Chaplain Terry, my administrative chief, and laid out my plans for the High Holy Days and Sukkot. He was enthused with the entire program and told me to make sure to put my requisitions in on time. Thus I had gotten across the first hurdle when I cleared my program and the other chaplain concurred.

Then I called in my assistant, Sam Roth, and told him to type up a 447, which is the army way of putting in a work order. We dispatched it immediately to the Engineers for action. A few days later a German civilian called on the phone and asked for the chaplain. When I answered the phone he asked, "Chaplain, *was ist das—sukkah?*" I explained to him the nature of the *sukkah* and gave him a brief idea as to its construction. "Oh, *zie wollen ein* chapel annex *haben,*" he answered. "This is *verboten: Keine*-building. Military economy."

I again explained to him that this *sukkah* didn't have a roof and was only a temporary structure. He quickly answered that this would make no difference, but if I would hang on for a moment he would check it with the boss. After waiting for a while I heard his voice again, and he told me that the boss might go along with me but added with a chuckle, "*Warum keine* roof? For the same money and approval *sie kennen ein* roof *haben.*"

"But I don't want a roof," I answered heatedly. "I just want a *sukkah.*"

It was then that the lieutenant in charge of the Engineering Section got on the phone and asked me what a *sukkah* was.

"Long ago when the children of Israel came out of Egypt and traveled in the desert, they lived in booths," I started to tell him. And after a few moments of scriptural history I conveyed to him the significance of the *sukkah.*

"We'll approve it, Chaplain," he answered, "and I'll send my representative out to see you."

We were still far from having a *sukkah* but were over the major hump. The next morning a representative came out to see me, and we visited the chapel grounds. "How large do you want it?" he asked as we surveyed our possible location. I gave him a rough idea as to our needs. "Ah, come on, Chaplain," he said, "as long as we're building a *sukkah,* let's build a big one!" I tried to explain to him that I didn't want to overdo it, and every time I measured, he added on a couple of feet for good measure.

"Now, Chaplain," he said, "let's understand something. Maybe you were a little modest; let me give you a roof."

"But we don't want a roof," I said. "It would be contrary to Jewish law, and it wouldn't be a *sukkah* if it had one."

"It rains awful bad here in Bavaria, and I for one am well acquainted with the liquid sunshine we have been receiving."

"Don't worry," I told him, "it never rains on Jewish holidays."

With a mirthful look he assured me it would be accomplished according to our plans and religious directives.

Next I had to get permission from the supervisor of grounds in order to put up the structure. Then we called the fire department to get their concurrence. They assured us it would be approved if they could come in and fireproof the place before it was used. Then we called the utilities to get permission to put an electric extension line from the chapel into the *sukkah*. Permission was granted.

A few days later as I left my home across the street from the chapel, I witnessed a beautiful sight. There by the chapel was a huge army truck being unloaded by its crew. I went over to see what was going on and found to my extreme satisfaction that the U.S. Army Engineers were ready to tackle the problem—one deluxe *sukkah* for the Jewish chaplain. While the crew began to lay out materials, one of the German civilians assisting came over to me and whispered quietly, "*Ya*, I know *was ist ein sukkah*. Years ago there was one of your people who used to build a *sukkah* behind his house."

"Years ago?" I asked him.

He answered in a mournful tone, "It was before they took him away."

By midafternoon our *sukkah* was completed. It was a delight to behold. Several of the Jewish GIs came out and gave it their approving nods. We were happy, but we still had some problems to overcome. We needed the covering for the *sukkah*. Although we cover the top with foliage, it must allow those inside to peer through and see the stars. My delegation of Jewish boys went to see the forester of Perlacher Forst, the area in which we reside. When I explained to him what we needed, he not only gave us his immediate approval but asked us if we would like to have a few trees planted around it. I told him that it wasn't necessary and thanked him profusely.

The Jewish Women's Club came down and decorated the *sukkah* with fruit, candy, tinsel, the bright autumn foliage, and the aromatic pine cones. Army folding tables and chairs were brought in. Sam Roth stood on a ladder and hung up strings of bright red apples handed to him by my wife, Miriam, Frieda Kolieb, and Mrs. Cill Reitler, who also filled little paper bags with sweets, nuts, and surprise gifts for the children.

Then we ran into a most hilarious situation. The schoolchildren on their homeward way stopped to take notice. They asked why couldn't they have a *sukkah* too. The children of our neighbors wanted to know if they could have a party in it after the Jewish children were through. Our neighbors arrived to congratulate us. I arranged with the Christian chaplain to take the Sunday school children into the *sukkah*. The Sunday sightseers came by in droves. One commented that at last the army had begun to build a chapel annex.

But little did they know that out here in southern Bavaria, across the street from Stadleheim Prison of Nazi infamy—on the edge of a forest, a *sukkah* was filled with joyous sons and daughters of Israel who were commemorating the Feast of Tabernacles. The walls hid from our sight the tyranny and terror that once lived here. They now encompassed the merry throng and hid from sight the dread reminders of the past—we looked upward in song through the roof and saw the stars.[17]

❧ ❧ ❧

THE ECONOMICS OF SUKKOT IN HASIDIC WILLIAMSBURG
SOLOMON POLL

Although not all the *Hasidim* sleep in a *sukkah*, it is essential that every male person have all his meals in one during the seven days of Tabernacles. In the metropolis of New York, especially Williamsburg, where space is a problem, some members of the community sell a portable *sukkah*. This can be erected in back yards, on fire escapes, roofs, or any space under the open sky, as required by the law. A person in the portable *sukkah* business will advertise in the following way:

A New Model of Ready-Made Tabernacles

Water and fireproof. Can be erected in 15 minutes. You can put the whole tabernacle together yourself—ready-made. Tools are not needed; hammer, nails, or screws are not needed. If you have complained about our last year's tabernacles, we are ready to help you.

Zeiger and Farkas Corp. 181 Marcy Avenue, Corner Broadway, Brooklyn.

There is another firm producing prefabricated tabernacles. The firm's name is *Sukkat Shalom*, Shelter of Peace, or Perfect Shelter. . . .

There are special dealers who sell *sekhakh* throughout the community and who advertise before the holiday in the Hasidic newspapers and on placards posted in the various houses of worship. . . .

The competition in the *sekhakh* business is so great that there is even a business establishment selling *sekhakh* that calls itself S'chach Incorporated. . . .

Not only are the ready-made tabernacles and the *sekhakh* merchants concerned with the building of a tabernacle, but the linoleum merchant as well has gone into the tabernacle business. He, too, sells merchandise that beautifies the tabernacle. He advertises that for a really beautiful *sukkah*, there should be a linoleum rug on the floor. Linoleum has nothing to do with the *sukkah*, nor is there any requirement of having a floor covering in the *sukkah*; nevertheless, he appeals to the members of the community in terms of having a "beautified *sukkah*." He also calls to the attention of the community that if one does not have a linoleum rug in his *sukkah*, he may transgress a prohibition of *The Code of Jewish Law*. According to this law, one is not allowed to sweep the uneven dirt floor on the Sabbath and holidays. Since the dirt floor is not even, there may be some small holes in the ground, and by sweeping the floor one may cover the holes. Such "covering of holes" is considered "working on the holiday." But if one has a smooth linoleum rug on the floor, he cannot "cover holes" on the Sabbath and holidays. . . .

Jewish law requires that for the holiday of Tabernacles a Jew must have "four kinds of plants." . . . The most important of these "four kinds" is the *etrog*, "the fruit of a goodly tree." The most zealous religious Jew is very careful that even the most minute blemish shall not mar his *etrog*. Before he buys an *etrog*, he gives it a microscopic examination. During the *etrog* season, Hasidic Jews are seen in front of the *etrog* stores with magnifying glasses in their right hands and *etrogim* in their left hands, turning them, twisting them, looking for the tiniest blemish. . . .

The dealer knows exactly how to take advantage of the detailed and complicated interpretations of the religious laws concerning *etrogim*. For example, many Hasidic Jews will not use Israeli *etrogim*. The laws "concerning the land" are applicable only in the "land of Israel." Hasidic Jews believe that these laws are not being observed in Israel today, and consequently, they buy *etrogim* imported from Yanev, Greece, or Arizona, where the biblical law does not apply. The Hasidic *etrog* dealer must have all kinds of *etrogim* to satisfy different views.

Because almost all Hasidic adult males will have an *etrog* for the holiday, this becomes a "big business" in Hasidic circles. Merchants hang their circulars on the walls and doors of the houses of worship far in advance, telling the community about their "beautiful *etrogim.*" . . .

The *etrogim* are usually sold in stores carrying religious articles. This is the most appropriate place, one where the customer will automatically look for *etrogim*. However, there are people who are not in the religious article business but who enter the *etrog* business just before the holiday because of the profitable economic return and because of the short duration of the season. These dealers sublet a store or part of a store in a "good" neighborhood for two weeks until the season ends.[18]

℘ ℘ ℘

THE SUKKOT OBSERVANCE IN COCHIN
DAVID G. MANDELBAUM

For the Feast of Tabernacles there is a small shelter of thatched palm leaves erected by each Jewish house. There meals are eaten and hymns sung. Citrons and palm leaves, the ceremonial paraphernalia of the holiday, are to be had for the plucking and are used to adorn the booth. On the wall of some booths, a great six-pointed star, the *magen David*, is pinned. The symbol is often to be seen in Jewtown; many women wear a gold *magen David* as a neck pendant.

On the festival of Shemini Atzeret, the six-year-old son of a leading family reads the portion from the Prophets, for the first time. This occasion marks the advent of a boy into the ranks of those who are able to read from the sacred books before the congregation. It is celebrated in lavish style. The boy's relatives dress in their finest costumes. The women bring out the dresses which they reserve for weddings and for special celebrations. The boy himself was attired in neatly tailored white jacket and shorts and ascended to the lectern draped in a long prayer shawl. After he had bravely piped through the liturgy, he descended from the balcony and made the round of the synagogue, being blessed by each man. He held out a corner of his prayer shawl; when the adult had touched it he brought the corner

24. Torah shield. Fashioned by Master J. Kogler of Prague. 1708. See
Chapter 9.

to his lips; the one who blessed him kissed the fingertips which had touched the shawl. As he came around to his uncles and his grandfather, he was garlanded and his girl cousins came shyly forward to present him with gifts. Later in the day his parents gave a grand feast for the entire community. The importance of this event in the life of a six-year-old cannot be overstressed. It is a day when tokens of approbation pour in on him, when he becomes the cynosure of the community, his world. It furnishes him, when his character is yet plastic, with moments of personal triumph which leave an ineradicable impression. And the medium of his triumph and the scene of his success is the synagogue. Small wonder, then, that the synagogue holds the loyalty and devotion of the individual throughout his life.

The festival of Simhat Torah, the Rejoicing of the Law, climaxes the series of holidays. In vivid contrast to the low pitch of the Day of Atonement, it is a day of exuberant release, of hilarious celebration. The synagogue is fragrant with long strings of jasmine wreaths, and aglow with many candles. In front of the synagogue entrance, a great pyramid of coconut oil lamps, taller than a man, blazes forth. The interior of the synagogue is adorned with a dress of ark curtains and China silk. The curtains are commemorative donations, and have as a centerpiece the rich ceremonial waistcloth of the person in whose memory the curtain was given. The Scrolls, in their brightly polished silver cases and gleaming gold crowns, are taken out of the ark and set up on a platform in front of it, flanked by tall silver pillars which support a canopy.

On this day the tears in the social fabric are mended. All quarrels are supposed to be patched up on Simhat Torah, and many dissensions really are smoothed over in the general merrymaking. The least of the congregation enjoys the honor of reading the blessings before the Law together with the most distinguished. Women are allowed to come into the synagogue hall to kiss the sacred books. At noon the young people dine in houses other than their own. Wine and arrack flow copiously, and some men become gloriously tight. Like drunken men the world over, they crack muddled jokes and bawl out catchy tunes. But in Cochin the tunes that they sing in their groggy animation are synagogue melodies, hymns, and paeans to the Lord of Israel.

The great moments in this great day come when the seven Scrolls are taken from their places and carried around the synagogue. The younger men try hard to have the honor of carrying them. There are two small Scrolls which are carried by boys. I noticed one little fellow tearfully pleading with his father that he might have the privilege of bearing the *Sefer*. The privilege must be purchased, and when the father finally nodded his assent, the boy went bounding off in an about-face of emotion, to tell his friends of his luck.

When a hymn is begun, the silver cases are taken up and slowly carried around the ambit of the hall. The men walk backward before the advancing bearers of the Scrolls, shouting the hymns as lustily as they can. The women remain at the back of the hall; some of the black Jewesses emit a high ululating call as the Scrolls are carried past them. Boys jump up and down before the holy books, and their enthusiasm infects the younger girls, who begin to bob up and down in their places at the rear. In the afternoon a carpet is laid over the granite flagstones of the outer walk, and the Scrolls are ceremonially carried around the outer circumference of the synagogue. The scene is one of unbridled exaltation in which all take part.

The services are not concluded until it is dark. Then the eldest man of the congregation is escorted home. With slow gait he walks down Jewstreet, all his people singing before him, clapping their hands, paying homage to him. The twin rows of holiday lights which shine at every door parallel his homeward course and flicker over the crowd of rejoicing Jews. When he reaches his door, he turns and blesses his escort, then goes into the house. A last loud cheer follows him in and the holiday is over. Within the province of the festival, the community has let itself go, has given vent to pent-up drives, and now is ready to settle down to the round of everyday affairs once again.[19]

✌ ✌ ✌

CALCUTTA'S SUKKOT QUEEN OF BEAUTY
IDA G. COWEN

Driving from Dum Dum airport to India's sprawling metropolis of Calcutta was an introduction to the sounds and sights and smells of India. . . . I walked that first evening directly into the midst of a mass of people already settled down for the night on the pavement stones fronting the hotel. Intermingled with the people were cows who had also chosen the precincts of the Great Eastern Hotel for their night's rest. I beat a hasty retreat indoors.

Another night, however, I did go out—for *Kiddush* in a *sukkah* of a Jewish family. *Kiddush,* in true oriental Sephardic fashion, turned out to be dinner. The home was an apartment chosen because its open terrace lent itself to the making of a *sukkah.* Braided palm leaves were used for walls and roof of the *sukkah.* Multicolored balls, lights, and flowers were strung along one side, half open to the street. A hanging lamp with seven glass containers for oil held the customary holiday lights.

In one corner was a lectern on which an open Bible had been placed. According to tradition, a very special "worthy guest" is welcomed to the family feast. On the first night it is the patriarch Abraham who is the worthy guest, the second night Isaac, and third night Jacob; then in turn Moses, Aaron, Joseph, and David. Each night the Bible is opened to a selection bearing on the life of the "worthy guest" of the evening.

The silk *hallah* cloth was embroidered with the words *le-shanim rabbot,* wishing one many years. To the wine in the *Kiddush* cup some water was added, my host told me, "so that the words of the 23rd Psalm, 'my cup runneth over,' might be fulfilled." On the menu that evening in Calcutta was roast chicken. As the old skilled *shohet* had died, and the new one was not sufficiently trained for the ritual slaughter of mutton (the government forbids the importation of beef), the observant Jews of Calcutta were limited to the use of chicken. Custard apples and a drink made of cut beets and lime juice closed the meal.

After the recitation of Grace after Meals, the children kissed the hands of mother and father. Then the father, placing his hand on the child's head, blessed and kissed each one.

My host in that *sukkah* was a sixth-generation member of a family that had come from Baghdad. Most of the Jews in Calcutta trace their ancestry to Baghdad or Syria. . . .

It was to the Maghen David Synagogue that I went that Simhat Torah eve of 1961, accompanied by its minister. . . . A thrilling sight met my eyes as I entered the synagogue. Ranged across the wide pulpit were the Scrolls of the Law, about fifty in number, each one encased in silver—altogether a glittering, gleaming display.

The mantles in which the Scrolls are usually enveloped had been removed and were hung in tiers on the synagogue columns or suspended from the women's gallery. Their silks and satins and velvets, multicolored and richly embroidered or textured, made a breathtaking scene that made me think of jousting fields when knighthood was in vogue. But the only armor these twentieth century "knights" had were their embroidered velvet *yarmulkes* and the Scrolls they carried in glad procession, an honor won by an auction held in the Arabic tongue.

For this special occasion women were permitted on the main floor of the synagogue. All were in holiday finery, most in saris, making a colorful sight as they moved about gracefully. One of the women, her dark brown skin set off by a blue silk sari over a gold lamé blouse, made a particularly enchanting picture.

"Make a wish and kiss the Torah. Then your wish will come true," the women advised me. There was a constant surge of women and children to the pulpit all through the course of the seven circuits. Starting at one end of the pulpit, they advanced from Scroll to Scroll —kissing each in turn—proceeding rhythmically until they reached the far end of the pulpit. . . .

Holiday festivities closed with the choice of a Queen of Beauty at the annual Simhat Torah Ball held at the Judean Club.

"Every Queen of Beauty has been married in the year following her selection," said Ezra Nissim, president of the Judean Club, as he asked me to join the judges for this important event for unmarried young women. Our choice, a unanimous one, was lovely seventeen-year-old hairdresser Sheila Joshua. Shining-eyed, winsome, tall Sheila had to bend her head so that I could crown her Queen of Beauty.

But over the joyous occasion hung an air of poignancy, of melancholy. The lineup of participants for the procession from which a Queen of Beauty is chosen was becoming smaller and smaller with each passing year, an indication of what was happening in Calcutta. In 1945 there had been 4,000 Jews there. In the early 1960s only a thousand remained.[20]

❧ ❧ ❧

THE FEAST OF TABERNACLES AMONG BUKHARAN JEWRY

DEVORA AND MENAHEM HACOHEN

The prescription for the Feast of Tabernacles was very much to the liking of the Bukharan Jews; the more intricate the commandment, the better they liked it. They decorated their booths with gay splendor: the walls were hung with tapestry and adorned with colorful paper garlands, and the ground was covered with thick carpets. "Elijah's chair," a symbol of welcome to the patriarchs, since according to tradition they visit the booths in spirit, stood in one corner, decorated with silks and laden with sacred books.

On Hoshana Rabbah they were careful not to leave their homes, for they believed—as the *Zohar* intimates—that anyone venturing abroad on that night who does not see his shadow would meet with tragedy.

Simhat Torah was a day of pure rejoicing. The walls of the synagogue would be adorned with tapestry and drapery. Each Scroll of the Law was wrapped in seven coverlets. Removal of the coverlets, and the bringing to light of the written parchment, was considered a great honor and worthy of considerable sums to be donated to the synagogue. Removal of the last coverlet was naturally the highest honor, and the wealthy worshipers bid for it hotly, much to the merriment of the congregation. The winner would later treat his friends and relatives to a feast.

Immediately after Sukkot, the trustees would make the rounds of the homes of the wealthy for funds to buy fuel to tide the poor over the long and bitterly cold winter.

Translated by Israel I. Taslitt[21]

※ ※ ※

SUKKOT IN YEMEN
DEVORA AND MENAHEM HACOHEN

Sukkot was such a festive and popular celebration that many houses were built with one room without a ceiling so as to provide a permanent *sukkah*; the room was covered the rest of the year with mats, to keep the rain out. The *sukkot* covering consisted of durra or corn stalks or green cacti leaves. Inside, the floor was covered with mats and carpets, and bowls of myrtle leaves hung in the corners.

Possession of a *lulav* and *etrog* was an imperative. Some fathers used to acquire them for all of their sons who were capable of holding them. Yemen, incidentally, grew two kinds of *etrogim*: one, edible, weighed up to fifteen pounds; the other, much smaller and inedible, was used for the Sukkot ritual.

It was customary, in some areas of Yemen, for several families to buy jointly an ox or a sheep, so as to have an abundance of meat for the holiday. On Sukkot nights, everyone slept in the *sukkah*.

Hoshana Rabbah differed from its observance elsewhere in the Diaspora in one major item: between each *hakkafah* (circling of the pulpit), the ram's horn was sounded. . . .

The Yemenite boy was formally introduced to his community when his father took him to the synagogue, at the first Simhat Torah in his life, and had the worshipers bless the child—a joyful ceremony which culminated with a festive *Kiddush*.

Translated by Israel I. Taslitt[22]

⚘ ⚘ ⚘

A TORAH PYRAMID IN AFGHANISTAN
ERICH BRAUER

At Simhat Torah all the Torah Scrolls are taken out of the ark to build a high pyramid on the lectern. The pyramid, which often reaches to the ceiling, is covered with silk cloths. The synagogue is also decorated with brightly colored cloths. The processions are made around one of the Scrolls which stands in "Elijah's chair," and the celebration lasts far into the night. In the pauses between the circuits the people eat and drink. Simhat Torah is the gayest of the festivals among the Afghan Jews.[23]

⚘ ⚘ ⚘

SUKKOT IN A NORTH AFRICAN *MELLAH*
MOSHE DLUZNOWSKY

On the day after Yom Kippur, the marketplace in the *mellah*, which is usually full of merchandise, rags, garbage, donkeys, camels, fish, and whatnot, has the appearance of a skinned hide crawling with flies which suddenly turns into a garden. Every corner is filled with foliage to cover the *sukkot,* with *etrogim* and *lulavim* and the willow branches required for the ceremony in the home and the synagogue. The balconies of the houses are transformed into tabernacles—*sukkot,* hung with rugs and fruits. On the first night, the master holds the door of the booth open to welcome the patriarchs, Abraham, Isaac, Jacob, and King David, who comes to play the harp, according to legend. In the daytime, when the menfolk are at prayer, the women-folk come to the *sukkah* to welcome Mother Rachel.[24]

⚹ ⚹ ⚹

THE TABERNACLE FEAST OF THE FALASHAS
WOLF LESLAU

The Feast of Tabernacles (in Ethiopic *ba'ala masallat*) is celebrated from the fifteenth to the twenty-second of the seventh moon in com-memoration of the exodus of the Jews from Egypt and corresponds to the Jewish Feast of Tabernacles. There are special prayers, but the Falashas do not make the booths required by Scripture. The reason given for the disregard of the ordinance is that the huts in which they live may be regarded as booths symbolical of Israel's sojourn in the wilderness. They spread leaves of various trees, such as the palm or a variety of weeping willow, over the floors of their houses and the synagogue. As at the Passover, the first and the last days are called holy, and no work is allowed during the whole festival. On the last day the priests or the deacons carry the Torah in the syna-gogue, and the people dance in the synagogue.[25]

⚹ ⚹ ⚹

MYRTLES FROM EGYPT
CHAIM WEIZMANN

A curious incident has stayed vividly in my memory. . . . It occurred just as I was leaving Palestine for England at the end of September 1918. My train was due to pull out of Lydda in a couple of hours;

my luggage was packed and was being taken out to the car. I was following it when I noticed two venerable gentlemen—their combined ages must have been in the neighborhood of one hundred and eighty years—bearing down upon me. What struck me at first, apart from their great age, was that I had not seen them before. By this time I was under the impression that I had met every man, woman, and child in the Jewish community of fifty thousand, most of them several times. Slowly and with dignity they advanced to meet me, pausing to give close scrutiny to the car, the luggage, and the other indications of departure. Then they turned to me and said, "But you are not really going away? You can't go yet. There are still some matters of importance to be settled here."

I was only too conscious that there *were* matters of importance still unsettled—many of them to remain so for many years—but I did not at once grasp what was meant. Sensing my ignorance, the elder of the two gentlemen proceeded to enlighten me.

"Do you know that the Feast of Tabernacles is almost upon us, and we have no myrtles?" (At the Feast of Tabernacles certain prayers are said by Orthodox Jews while they hold a palm branch adorned with myrtles in one hand and an *etrog,* or citron, in the other.)

Though I was familiar enough with the need for myrtles at Sukkot, it had somehow slipped my mind, and it had not occurred to me to include this particular job among the many chores of the Zionist Commission, operating in the midst of a bloody war.

A little startled, I said, "Surely you can get myrtles from Egypt."

My friends looked pained. "For the Feast of Tabernacles," one of them answered, reproachfully, "one must have myrtles of the finest quality. These come from Trieste. In a matter of high religious importance, surely General Allenby will be willing to send instructions to Trieste for the shipment of myrtles."

I explained carefully that there was a war on, and that Trieste was in enemy territory.

"Yes, they say there is a war," replied one of the old gentlemen. "But *this* is a purely religious matter—a matter of peace. Myrtles are, indeed, the very symbol of peace. . . ."

The conversation showed every sign of prolonging itself indefinitely; I thought of my train from Lydda—the only one that day— and steeled myself to firmness. "You will have to make do," I said, "with Egyptian myrtles."

At this stage my interlocutors brought out their trump card. "But

25. *Etrog* container.
Silver gilt. Augsberg,
Germany. Circa 1670.
See Chapter 9.

26. *Etrog* container.
Silver. Austria.
Nineteenth century.
See Chapter 9.

27. *Etrog* container.
Polished cut glass.
Germany.
Nineteenth century.

28. *Etrog* container.
Porcelain. Galicia.
Nineteenth century.

there is a quarantine imposed on the importation of plants from Egypt; the military authorities do not permit it."

We seemed to have reached a deadlock. I had to go, and with some misgivings handed the two rabbis over to my colleagues, assuring them with my parting breath as I climbed into the car that every possible effort would be made to secure the myrtle supply in time for Tabernacles, by some means or other. (By what means I would have been hard put to it to explain.)

I traveled down to Egypt genuinely worried over this question of myrtles and the quarantine; and even more worried by the responsibility for some thousands of people living, like these two old gentlemen, in a world of their own so remote from ours that they seemed as unreal to us as the war did to them. By the time I fell asleep in the train I was no longer sure what was, in fact, real, the war or the Feast of Tabernacles.

The business of renewing contacts in Cairo—there were many of them—drove the myrtles from my mind. But when I went to take leave of General Allenby just before my boat sailed, and we had finished our business talk, he suddenly said, "By the way, about those myrtles!" He pulled a letter out of his pocket, glanced at it, and added, "You know, it is an important business; it's all in the Bible; I read it up in the Book of Nehemiah last night. Well, you'll be glad to hear that we have lifted the quarantine, and a consignment of myrtles will get to Palestine in good time for the Feast of Tabernacles!"[26]

❧ ❧ ❧

A CLUSTER OF SUKKOT CUSTOMS IN JERUSALEM

YOM-TOV LEWINSKI

It was a Jerusalem custom after the destruction of the Second Temple to ascend on Sukkot the Mount of Olives opposite the Temple and to pray there. On Hoshana Rabbah it was the practice to encompass the mount seven times and to direct the eyes toward the Temple. In the gaonic period, Jews would stream to this site from the nearby countries and even from across the seas to celebrate the holiday. In order to accommodate them, the erection of large communal tabernacles in synagogue courtyards and on roofs was sanctioned, although normally every man was enjoined to put up a *sukkah* by himself wherein he was to eat, drink, study Torah, and sleep. Only in Jerusalem were communal *sukkot* permitted, and the authority for them was adduced from the passage relating to the return to Zion: "And all the congregation of them that were come back out of captivity made booths, and dwelt in the booths" (Nehemiah 8.17). Since then, it became a tradition in Jerusalem to erect communal tabernacles for pilgrims.

It was also a tradition to recite the *Musaf* prayer on the first day of Sukkot at the Western Wall. On the second day of Hol ha-Moed groups of pilgrims from the different cities and from abroad would circle the wall of the Holy City, with their eyes focused on the Temple ruins and their hearts yearning for the redemption. As they slowly circumambulated the wall, they chanted the psalms of David. All this was in order to fulfill that which is written: "Walk about Zion and go round about her; count the towers thereof. Mark ye well her ramparts, traverse her palaces" (Psalms 48.13–14).

The Sukkot pilgrimage to Jerusalem was suspended during the several centuries preceding the rise of Zionism, for various causes, but when Jewish youth began to come to Eretz Israel and to renew their ties with the soil of the homeland, there was a strong desire to resume the pilgrimage to Jerusalem. In 1904, in the days of the Second Aliyah, a group of farm workers from Petah Tikvah, Rehovot, Nes Tzionah and Hederah made a joint pilgrimage to the Holy City for the Festival of the Harvest. The city elders came out to greet them and received them warmly. The rabbi of Jerusalem, Rabbi Shmuel Salant, also sent them money (five napoleons) to buy provisions for the holiday, but they refused all aid, since they had saved up from the toil of their hands to cover their expenses. They erected a large *sukkah* from mats on the roof of the house where they stayed, in the Bet Israel quarter. On the eve of the holiday they went in a group to the synagogue and after the service returned to their *sukkah,* where the oldest among them, Aaron David Gordon— who was destined to become the spiritual leader of the Jewish workers in the country—recited the blessing over the wine in a voice so strong and clear that many inhabitants of the quarter gathered about them and later joined in the dancing.

The custom of circling the Old City wall was also adopted by the young pioneers. Every Sukkot many bands of pilgrims from the colonies could be seen making their way over the rocks and walking around the wall while singing songs of Zion. Today [1955] with the Old City in alien hands, the devout go up to Mount Zion and from there direct their gaze and heart toward the Temple site.

An important custom in Jerusalem was the display of a napkin in front of the tabernacle door, thereby indicating that guests might come in and partake of the meal. The removal of the napkin was a sign that the meal was finished and that guests should no longer enter. But visitors would always enter the *sukkah* without paying attention to whether or not a napkin was spread, because among those who come to the *sukkot* are the seven *ushpizin*, the guests "who see but are not seen": the beloved Abraham, the bound Isaac, the patriarch Jacob, the faithful pastor Moses, Aaron the holy priest, Joseph the righteous, and David the messianic king.

Every day, as it is known, one of them takes his turn at the head of the holy company which visits the tabernacle. The Sephardic Jews in Jerusalem therefore leave one place vacant at the head of the table, where they set a beautifully decorated armchair in honor of the chief of guests. Some also hang thereon a tablet upon which is very handsomely written the name of the guest of the day, while others place holy books on the chair in his honor. And in their minds' eye the assembled see the hidden *tzadik* enter the *sukkah* and take his seat. The *Hasidim* and pious ones, even in our own day, bring musical instrumnts to the tabernacle on Hol ha-Moed, and play selections from the Songs of Ascent as they set the chair in honor of the *ushpiz*.

In the tractate Sukkah it is stated: "Thus the Jerusalemite would do: when he came to the synagogue he would carry his *lulav* in his hand; when he read the Torah or recited the prayers on behalf of the congregation, he would hold his *lulav* in his hand; when he left the synagogue, it was with a *lulav* in his hand; when he went to comfort mourners, he would have his *lulav* with him."

This custom was current in Jerusalem until the last generation. And even today it is possible to meet members of the Bukharan or other communities strolling about on Sukkot carrying an *etrog* and *lulav*.

Simhat Torah is a special day in Jerusalem. Although the Shemini Atzeret prayers (which are said in Israel on Simhat Torah and are recited in the tunes of the Days of Awe) lend a note of solemnity, they fail to dampen the rejoicing which prevails in full force. . . .

The Sephardim do not stop with the *hatan Torah* and the *hatan Bereshit*; they also call up a third "bridegroom," *hatan Meonah*, who reads the passage, "The ancient God is a refuge" (Deuteronomy 33.27), and a fourth "bridegroom," *hatan Va-Yaal*, who reads, "Moses went up from the steppes of Moab to Mount Nebo" (Deuteronomy 34.1). All four "bridegrooms" treat the youngsters in the synagogue to peanuts and roast nuts, sweetmeats and candy, and after the service the congregation carries them home to the public meal prepared by the "brides."

At the end of Simhat Torah, at night, the people again assemble in the synagogue. The pulpit is decked out with all the Torah Scrolls and their crowns, with gold and flowers, fruits and spices. The prominent members of the congregation are dressed in their special festive robes, and the entire building is filled with candlelight. On this occasion the synagogal honors are sold for the entire year; for example, the raising and the rolling up of the Torah Scrolls, the opening and closing of the ark, the privilege of lighting candles on Sabbath eves, the furnishing of wine for *Kiddush* and *Havdalah,* etc. The women purchase the honors of cleaning the synagogue floor and giving drink to those who study in the House of God. Musicians provide gay music at this ceremony. Every purchaser of a *mitzvah*—whose contribution goes to the upkeep of the synagogue—is treated to drinks and fruits, and he on his part donates drinks and cookies. The rejoicing goes on late into the night.[27]

❧ ❧ ❧

SIMHAT TORAH IN JERUSALEM
HAROLD FENTON

Simhat Torah in the unified Holy City was, in this year of 5728 (1967), Jewry's unique and unforgettable festival. We, who were privileged to have celebrated the joy of the Torah, the *raison d'être* of our people, still talk and revive memories of the experience which in its verve, and uplifting, edifying satisfaction acted and acts still as a therapy for whatever strain we might have left over from the exhausting previous days.

The night of Simhat Torah found Jerusalemites pursuing their annual round of visiting as many synagogues of as many sects as possible and the streets in the area of Mahaneh Yehudah and Meah Shearim were crowded with excited people doing their rounds in methodical pathways. As night descended and the air became cool as on a March day in Britain, the streets were temporarily cleared as *Maariv* time approached and *hakkafot* followed. And then after a synchronous pause throughout Jerusalem, the echoes swelled as the arks were thrown wide open and refrains of traditional songs floated out of colorful hallways, or stained-glass windows along narrow ill-lit cobbled passageways and up or down crumbling staircases. The floating song wooed the stones to life and they too appeared to hum and sing in tune. The chanting oriental strains of songs, combined with rhythmic clapping, was at once a contrast and accompaniment to the Hasidic repetitious joy to the background of stamping feet. The vibrant chants meeting in the middle of a street or halfway on a stretch of stairs seemed to intertwine and become wafted away by a sudden dart of air to titillate the shadows of an arch or the shutters of a window, so that the shadows melted and the shutters opened to reveal lit candles awaiting their guests after prayers. I began my evening somewhere in East Asia, prayed *Maariv* in Bukhara, had first *hakkafah* in North Africa, another *hakkafah* in Italy, a final *hakkafah* in Hungary and Poland with the evening ending on the Polish-Russian border! The bright neon lighting of the Sephardic synagogues was matched by burning and twinkling eyes of piles of children, who seemed to stand on each other's backs and in a well-rehearsed chorus shouted the verses of song, whilst sweat shining on red cheeks and foreheads reflected the sparkle of lights around. This contrasted with the candle illuminated small *shtiblech*, where depending on the sect different colored long silk festive overgarments, *kapotehs*, and fur-trimmed wide hats, *shtreimlech*, replaced the open-necked shirts and sports clothes and gaily embroidered skullcaps of the oriental Jews.

The silver- or gold-encased Sephardic *Sifre Torah* were taken and handed from one person to another who executed a few steps, intricate in their timing to the background Eastern chant. I managed to do a between mixture of an old-fashioned conga, a tango, and the Lancers and tried not to appear too foreign before handing on to a waiting boy who in a supreme ecstasy put me to shame by leaping almost to the roof with glee. With foot movements too quick for the eye to follow he gyrated as only a Yemenite could. As the evening wore on and my forehead had a few rivulets of sweat, each depicting a different community, the dance tempo slowed as we approached Europe, and finally I was in a large circle of velvet-covered *Sifre Torah* borne by black-clad *Hasidim* of Reb Arele Levin. Here there was less emphasis on foot movement and more on pouring out one's heart in hoarse song in a hypnotic *hitlahavut,* a trancelike detachment which was so comfortable that we wanted the song to go on forever. We clutched the *Sifre Torah* close, wet with perspiration of effort, so that not only figuratively but also somewhat literally we clung to our *Sifre Torah* as a drowning man to a lifesaving raft.

Thus passed the night of Simhat Torah, which in normal years would have been a climax in itself; but this was just a foretaste to what, in our hearts, we were saving for the morrow, which would bring us in daylight, in singing and rejoicing before our "friend," the *Kotel ha-Maaravi,* waiting patiently in the cold night air for sunrise.

Various synagogues in Jerusalem beginning earlier than in previous years at 7 or 7:30 A.M. had "agreed" to meet in front of Bet Hillel, the student center, at 10:30 for a Simhat Torah *hakkafah* through new and old Jerusalem to the [Western] Wall. As each synagogue finished their own services and celebrations, they came bearing their *Sifre Torah* at the head of a procession of congregants. They came from all directions singing and clapping, and Jerusalem's streets were filled with song and rejoicing. We formed naturally into rows, some wearing their prayer shawls, others bearing Scrolls, others holding up prayer shawls as a canopy for one bearing a *Sefer Torah* beneath. With our arms around each other's shoulders or waists, or with hands held aloft clapping in unison we sang and marched. The sun shone on a joyous multitude and beads of sweat glistened as the hundreds seemed borne floating along the wide Rehov Agrippas in front of the Kings Hotel down toward the Old City. Gone were the gray border walls, gone the evil-smelling rubbish where no one trod for fear of one's life, gone the terror of the sniper. Ahead lay the wide thoroughfare of what was a no-man's-land and at the end of the newly laid road the gap made by Kaiser Wilhelm in the 300-year-old wall next to the Jaffa Gate. We lost all sense of time. We do not remember how long it took; we remember the smiling crowds running alongside, the clouds of dust at our feet, the echoes of our songs, and the hundreds of people on balconies above us who threw sweets among us. And thus singing and stamping, skipping or jumping we passed through Jerusalem's wall and turned right, squeezing through the alleys and past the Jewish quarter on the left with its new Hebrew street signs and its signs of reconstruction. The sun grew hotter and so did the fever of our excitement as we danced down the long slope toward the large clearing ahead, bordered at its eastern side by the warm golden rows of stones of the Western Wall. There it was waiting for us, already greeting us with echoes of our own song, which it had somehow made its own by a subtle addition of a timeless quality. The wall had heard the words of our songs before, for their author was David.

We almost charged down in front of the wall and at our head, all our *Sifre Torah*. In the large clearing danced students, professors, laborers, Sephardim, Ashkenazim, *Hasidim,* and the nonreligious. The headgear included dark trilby hats, *tembel* hats, knitted skull-caps, large hombergs, American straw, and knotted handkerchiefs. There at the *Kotel* we were all religiously happy, all rejoicing and felt, as suggested by Rav Yosha Ber Brisk, that not only should we have been rejoicing with the Torah, but that the Torah was rejoicing with us. We crossed and recrossed in song and dance, or formed in a long sinuously winding row or circled within circles. We felt no tiredness, nought but elation, and with our happiness we urged almost telepathically that all Jews everywhere taste the *simhah* and feel our throbbing hearts and beat together with us at that time. We danced and sang for the years and years of not being allowed to dance, and we danced and sang for the overwhelming realization that we had come with no foreign permission for us to do so. Our movements of the men in the clearing were mirrored by women and girls on the surrounds and the square before the *Kotel*. Further back, Arabs watched us and smiled, shouting to us a *"Shalom"* as we passed, but this time they knew it was our *simhah*—by right and not by condescension.

I suspect too that a few Arabs joined us as well. I certainly could not tell any difference, and even if I could, "My house is a house of prayer . . . a call to all peoples."

There had been the capture of Jerusalem in war—at Simhat Torah its capture in peace with the Torah entering the Old City at the end of singing legions. "For its ways are pleasant and all its paths are peace." All our song and all our dance—and we found it had lasted for four hours!—was also a prayer that in a continued peace we may continue to renew the joy annually retracing our footprints during this first historic year of Jerusalem's redemption.[28]

❦ ❦ ❦

YIZKOR AND SIMHAT TORAH IN ISRAEL
ARYEH AVIVI

The festival of Sukkot is over. Since, according to tradition, there is no doubt as to the identity of the day on which a holiday occurs in the Land of Israel, the two festivals of Shemini Atzeret and Simhat Torah fall on one and the same day. On the eve of Simhat Torah the atmosphere of the synagogue is, by custom, festive; the procession of the Scroll-bearers and the dancers, including Bar Yoseph, are twined in a circle in honor of the Torah.

"The service tomorrow morning will begin at eight o'clock," the *gabbai* proclaims, trying to give his announcement a festive form. "The prayers should begin earlier," someone interrupts, "because we must recite *Yizkor*." When Bar Yoseph heard the notice about the memorial prayers he was at once transformed into another person enveloped by the atmosphere of the departed.

It is Simhat Torah. The order of the Torah procession is at hand. The spiritual environment in the synagogue is exultant and exhilarating. All are dancing and rejoicing; likewise Bar Yoseph is joyous with the joy of the Torah. The order of the reading of the Torah begins. The bridegroom of the Law and the bridegroom of Genesis chant their portions in accordance with the tradition. Suddenly, a voice is heard, accompanied by a bang on the desk, calling for the *Yizkor* service. The merriment stops overpowered by a change in the climate; nevertheless, here and there, are still seen signs of "rebellion" against the acceptance of the yoke of the kingdom of tears. The people obligated to recite *Yizkor* gather in the vicinity of the reader's lectern; and in the western part of the synagogue others are assembled and drink, toasting each other "for life." Life and death are face to face; there is rivalry between tears and mirth. At one moment mourning seems dominant, at another gladness. From the women's gallery is heard solemn sobbing which calms for a moment, and even turns aside, the glee of the festivities. However, Bar Yoseph is the sole individual who is withdrawn from the celebration and is enveloped in mourning. He has abandoned the world of jollity and has entered the region of the sacred souls that hover before his eyes. Wrapped in his prayer shawl, he calls to them, one by one. "The soul of my mother who was killed for the sanctification of the Name; the soul of my oldest brother with his family"; again "my brother" and once more "my youngest brother." Teardrops roll down his face. And in the midst of this tragic ceremony which tears the heart apart are heard the sounds of merriment from groups of dancers and singers joined together with Torah Scrolls cradled in their arms.

The worshipers of a neighboring synagogue, responding before they were invited, come to participate in the joyous celebration for "in the multitude of people is the king's honor" (Proverbs 14.28). They clear a way for themselves and come into the inner sanctuary. The dances and the songs, full of enthusiasm, captivate the host congregation, and the noise of the merrymakers increases. . . . The doleful *Yizkor* prayers are suspended in favor of the dancers "so that the people could not discern the noise of the shout of joy from the noise of the weeping of the people; for the people shouted with a loud shout and the noise was heard afar off" (Ezra 3.13).

The circle of dancers is enlarged, and the *Yizkor* lament is silenced in accord with the injunction that "we turn aside the funeral cortege before a bride." And now a hand took hold of Bar Yoseph and tugged at his *tallit,* urging him to join the circle of rejoicers with the joy of the Torah. Bar Yoseph hardly feels the hand which drags him; he was far away from the world of the dancers; like a mourner among the bridegrooms, the bridegrooms of the Torah. He found himself in the fold of his family, those that were slain for the sanctification of the Name. His heart was still weeping bitterly, and the list—the list of the murdered, the slaughtered, and the massacred for the sanctification of the Name—is long, bringing back to life the terror, the atrocities, and the terrible memories.

So it is, life and death meet, joy and sorrow are coupled, a tear and glee kiss. The order of life and the shadows of the dead are mingled. The recalling of the souls of the departed and the rejoicing of the Torah are as one. Is that possible? Indeed, it is possible. Shemini Atzeret and Simhat Torah—are there greater opposites than these two? Nevertheless, the reality of the Land of Israel proves it possible.

Translated by Herbert Parzen[29]

✼ ✼ ✼

SUKKOT IN THE BET SHEAN VALLEY
TZVI GIVONE

The settlements of *Ha-Kibbutz ha-Dati* (the religious *kibbutz* move-ment) can take pride in the fact that they build the largest *sukkot* in the world. It is doubtful whether even the East European Hasidic rabbis, to whom thousands of *Hasidim* flocked in days gone by, had *sukkot* larger than these, which may comfortably seat some four hundred persons around the tables. . . .

During the intermediary days of the festival the workday is short-ened, and many members take their annual vacation then. In the *kibbutz* compound there is a great bustle created by the visitors com-ing and going. In this period the *Simhat Bet ha-Shoevah* celebration is held. While the four *kevutzot* of the Bet Shean bloc hold a joint celebration, mainly for their members, the chief attraction of our settlements is the colorful pageant that Kvutzat Yavneh holds once

29. *Etrog* container.
By Ludwig Wolpert
(Tobe Pascher Workshop).
Silver. Contemporary.
See Chapter 9.

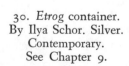

30. *Etrog* container.
By Ilya Schor. Silver.
Contemporary.
See Chapter 9.

every several years. This celebration attracts a country-wide audience, and as many as ten thousand people at one time have already attended these festivities, to commemorate the Water-Drawing ceremony in Temple times.

The eve of Hoshana Rabbah is devoted to study. Lectures on Torah subjects are held, followed by a study class which is in session until the small hours of the morning. The *aravot* which are used on Hoshana Rabbah grow mostly on the banks of the nearby streams and ponds.

On Shemini Atzeret and Simhat Torah there exists a confusion of customs today in Israel, where both holidays are observed on the same day. The joy of Simhat Torah, the sorrow of *Yizkor* and the solemn prayer for rain combine in one service. The Bet Shean valley settlements devoted a lot of thought to this problem, and, with the consent of the rabbinate of the city of Bet Shean, decided to institute a change in the order of prayers of this day. After *Hallel,* three Scrolls of the Law are taken from the ark. Only five men are called up to the first, followed by the *hatan Torah.* The *hatan Bereshit* is called up to the second Torah, and the *maftir* is read from the third. *Yizkor* is said right after that, followed by the prayer for rain. After the service, *Kiddush* is made and a light meal served. Only then do the *hakkafot* take place, and the dancing can continue uninterrupted for many hours. After the *hakkafot* the readings from the *Sifre Torah* take place in different corners of the dining hall and the *sukkah,* until all the men and boys have been called up, down to the kindergarten children.

Translated by Aryeh Rubinstein[30]

❧ ❧ ❧

THE SIGNIFICANCE OF SUKKOT
IN THE *KIBBUTZ*
MEIR TAMARI

The summer heat has passed. All over the farm stand the signs of a successfully completed and abundant harvest. In front of the storage bins lie mounds of sacks of wheat and barley which are the overflow of the silos filled with part of this year's crop. Every day trucks pull up before the cold-storage plant to be loaded up with the pomegranates, dates, and olives brought in from the fruit plantations. Trailers are piled high with the fluffy white-gold cotton on their way to the nearby gin.

These are the signs to be seen of the completion of a successful agricultural year as Sukkot draws near, so that it is not difficult for us to celebrate with fervor and after much preparation this festival of rejoicing and of the ingathering of the harvest.

Immediately on the completion of Yom Kippur work is begun on the building of the communal *sukkah* of our *kibbutz*. What a *sukkah*! Large enough to seat in comfort the four hundred souls of our settlement and all the guests, this *sukkah* is to be our home for all the days of the festival, and therefore much work and care are lavished on its erection and its decoration.

There is hardly a branch of the settlement's economy that does not contribute something to it. From the fruit plantations are brought the choicest pomegranates and small olive branches laden with fruit to be hung from the roof. The art group has been busy for many weeks preparing drawings, posters, and illustrated biblical verses, to be placed on the walls of the *sukkah*. Naturally, these reflect the communal and agricultural basis of our *kibbutz*, so that they will depict scenes of our harvest and those prayers for successful crops and protection against pests and disease which appear in the traditional prayer book. There is one important difference, in that for as long as we were cut off from our own soil and from agricultural work they were expressions of a glorious past and a yearning for a messianic future, whereas for us today these prayers reflect a vital part of our lives and are given added meaning by our daily work.

The children, too, have their role in the erection of the *sukkah*. In order to allow their maximum participation in this work, each children's house and each Youth Aliyah group has its own *sukkah*. Obviously they will be helped to erect them by the older members. However, the decorations are the work of the children themselves, and weeks are spent on drawings, cutouts, and paintings, in all the various children's groups. Above all, being the children of Jewish farmers, they decorate their *sukkot* with plants, fruits, and branches picked by themselves and artistically arranged in many original forms.

Although the *sukkah* is the most obvious and familiar symbol of Sukkot, there are of course many other customs connected with the festival. The most important of these are the Four Species—namely, *etrog,* myrtle, palm, and willow, which are used during the reciting of *Hallel* and during the daily processions round the *almemar* of the synagogue. Unfortunately our *kibbutz* has not been successful in its attempts to grow its own *etrogim,* so each year we have to buy a sufficient number of the finest from one of the farmers who specialize in growing them. Our fishermen have made it their tradition to bring palms from a neighboring old Arab grove. Each children's house has its own *arbaah minim,* and the children after their morning prayers recite the benedictions over them in unison.

During the intermediate days of Sukkot a special program of hikes and tours is arranged. Tractors laden with *haverim* and their children, all dressed in their best clothes, leave the gates of the settlement each day bound for another spot in the vicinity. The Youth Aliyah groups also go out accompanied by their leaders on prolonged tours.

The festival also presents us with an opportunity for an intensive cultural program. Both serious and lighter cultural activities are prepared by the cultural committee for the week. Scholars and communal leaders are invited to spend the festival with us, together with their families, and they deliver a number of lectures on various topics to the different study groups. These include history, Judaism, literature, and politics. Concerts, folk dancing, choir recitals, and a chess contest with neighboring settlements are also features of this program.

Agriculturally the climax of the festival is the recital of the prayer for rain on Shemini Atzeret. This prayer and the prayers of thanksgiving for the divine bounty recited during the whole of the festival have nothing symbolical or allegorical about them for us. Growing crops once more on the soil of Eretz Yisrael make a reality of the message of Sukkot and these prayers, recited by Jewish farmers working their own soil, possess a grandeur and awesomeness which they lacked when land and people were separated.[31]

❧ ❧ ❧

SECOND *HAKKAFOT* IN ISRAEL

MOSHE KOHN

The Talmud, describing the Sukkot celebrations in the Second Temple period, says: "He who has not seen the *Simhat Bet ha-Shoevah* (Rejoicing of the Water Drawing celebration) has never seen rejoicing in his life." In our own time, the same may be said concerning the pervasive Jewish exultation at the Simhat Torah *hakkafot* at Israeli synagogues and *yeshivot* generally, and particularly at the "Second *Hakkafot*" in many places in Israel on the night after Simhat Torah—when it is just beginning everywhere else in the Jewish world. Probably the greatest such celebration since the *Simhat Bet ha-Shoevah* of Temple times was the "Second *Hakkafot*" before the Citadel ("David's Tower") of Old Jerusalem on Thursday night, October 26, 1967, 141 days after the Israel Defense Forces liberated the Old City and reunited Jerusalem under Jewish rule for the first time since the Destruction. That night an assembly estimated at 100,000, embodying the unity of Jerusalem, filled the area before the Citadel and the streets leading to it across the former border that had divided Israeli Jerusalem from the Jordan-occupied sector.

Except for the location and the size of the throng, the celebration that night was typical of the "Second *Hakkafot*" held in other parts of the country in the years before and since. In the first circuit, the Torah Scrolls were carried by the president of the State of Israel, the chief rabbis, the cabinet ministers, and other dignitaries, and the mayor of reunited Jerusalem. The chants and songs, as well as the music played by the *klezmer* brought for the occasion, were the more familiar ones. In the ensuing circuits, the Scrolls were carried and the chanting and singing led, in turn, by men of the Ladino-speaking community, by Yemenite Jews, by Jews of Kurdish origin, then Bukharans, then Habad (Lubavitch) *Hasidim*, and so on. And each time the *klezmer* produced a suitable repertoire of music, sometimes bolstered, for example, by a Kurdish drummer with the syncopation to which his fellow Kurdish Jews did their slow rhythmic dance with the Torah Scrolls.

In other years and other places in Israel, the circuits would be performed by members of other communities. In 1970, for example, the most moving moment of the "Second *Hakkafot*" in Jerusalem was the circuit conducted by a group of new arrivals from the Soviet Union, who sang some of the tunes chanted at the Simhat Torah services at the Moscow Choral Synagogue. Another "community" honored at the 1970 "Second *Hakkafot*" was the police force, a number of whose uniformed commanders and lower-echelon officers carried the Torah Scrolls and led the singing.

The celebrations described above were organized by Hechal

Shlomoh, the headquarters of the Chief Rabbinate. One of the main objectives of the Hechal Shlomoh management in organizing "Second *Hakkafot*"—originally held in the street outside the Hechal Shlomoh building close to downtown Jerusalem where most of the tourist hotels are situated, and lately held in Independence Park across the street, which can accommodate the bigger throngs that have been coming—was to serve the growing number of Jewish pilgrims from abroad who come to spend the High Holy Day and Sukkot season in Jerusalem. For them, as noted above, Simhat Torah begins when it is ending in Israel. But for some of Jerusalem's Orthodox Jews and for like-minded Jews from abroad—ranging from those who support the Agudath Israel brand of Zionism to the followers of the Neture Karta brand of anti-Zionism—Hechal Shlomoh, regarded as Mizrahi (National Religious party) property, is off limits. Accordingly, the Agudath Israel annually organizes its own "Second *Hakkafot*" in the Meah Shearim quarter's central plaza, the intersection of Strauss and Meah Shearim streets, popularly known as "Sabbath Square." Here, too, thousands of persons participate, including many who go first or afterwards to the Hechal Shlomoh celebration. At both celebrations one sees large numbers of people obviously not of Orthodox backgrounds, but who link themselves to the dancing circles spurred by an eagerness to become an integral part of the "celebration of the Torah." Others watch it with a wistful look indicating they would join at the slightest hint from an "insider" that they were welcome to do so.

Another of Israel's major "Second *Hakkafot*" celebrations is that held in the Florentine Quarter of Tel Aviv's poorer section, settled mainly by Sephardic Jews and Jews from Arab lands. These circuits are presided over by the widely beloved rabbi of the area, Rabbi Yitzhak Yedidya Frankel, who settled in Israel in the mid-1930s from Poland. The participants include the mayor of Tel Aviv, and usually the chief of staff of the Israel Defense Forces, the inspector-general of police, cabinet ministers, and other dignitaries living in the Tel Aviv area. The honored guests will also frequently include—as at the Hechal Shlomoh celebration in Jerusalem—foreign diplomats living in the area. But the chief joy here, of course, is that of the many thousands of residents, largely members of the struggling urban proletariat. Most of those are striving to maintain and pass on to their children and grandchildren the Jewish traditional ways of life. For them Simhat Torah and the "Second *Hakkafot*" are probably the one time of the year when they identify and celebrate their sense of unity with the entire Jewish people.

"Second *Hakkafot*" in Israel; first *hakkafot* at the Moscow Choral Synagogue and at Lubavitch in Brooklyn—perhaps this great "Torah link" encircling the world *has* become, after the obscure origins of Simhat Torah in medieval times, the great affirmation of the oneness, the indivisibility and the eternity of the Jewish people.

✿ 14 ✿

SUKKOT AND SIMHAT TORAH
IN POETRY

✻ ✻ ✻

SIMHAT TORAH:
THE REJOICING OF THE LAW
JUDAH LEIB GORDON

a leading exponent of the Haskalah movement, Hebrew essayist,
fiction writer, and poet of stature (1830–1892)

Le-hayyim, my brethren, *le-hayyim,* I say!
Health, peace, and good fortune I wish you today.
Today we have ended the Torah once more,
Today we begin it anew, as of yore.
Be thankful and glad and the Lord extol,
Who gave us the Law on its parchment scroll.

The Torah has been our consolation,
Our help in exile and sore privation.

Lost have we all we were wont to prize,
Our holy Temple a ruin lies.
Laid waste is the land, where our songs we sung,
Forgotten our language, our mother tongue.
Of kingdom and priesthood are we bereft,
Our faith is our only treasure left.
God in our hearts, the Law in our hands,
We have wandered sadly through many lands.
We have suffered much, yet, behold, we live
Through the comfort the Law alone can give.

Come, my dear brethren, come, let us look!
Quick, let us open an historical book!
See, all the tales and the chronicles old,
They tell but of robbers and bandits bold.
Worldwide is the scene of *our* story, and still
'Tis traced with a sword-point, instead of a quill.
The ink is of blood, mixed with tears of distress,
In exile, not Leipzig, it passed through the press;
No gilding it shows, and in iron 'tis bound.
Come, find me a corner, the universe round,
Where we met not with suff'ring and fierce oppression,
For the sake of the Torah, our sole possession.

In the very beginning, a long time ago,
We held up our heads with the best, as you know,
When householders sitting at home we were,
Nor needed the strangers' meal to share.
May none have to bear at the hands of men,
What we from our neighbors have borne since then.
How bitter, alas! was the lot we knew
When our neighbors to be our landlords grew,
And we were driven, by fate unkind,
Our lodging beneath their roof to find.
How did we live then? How did we rest?
Ask not, I pray you, for silence is best,
Like cabbage heads, hither and thither that fall,
With the holy Law, that we treasured through all.

Two thousand years, a little thing when spoken,
Two thousand years tormented, crushed, and broken!

Seven and seventy dark generations,
Filled up with anguish and lamentations.
Their tale of sorrow, did I unfold,
No Simhat Torah today we'd hold.
And why should I tell it you all again?
In our bones 'tis branded with fire and pain.
We have sacrificed all. We have given our wealth,
Our homes, our honors, our land, our health,
Our lives—like Hannah her children seven—
For the sake of the Torah that came from heaven.

And now, what next? Will they let us be?
Have the nations then come at last to see
That we Jews are men like the rest, and no more
Need we wander homeless as heretofore,
Abused and slandered wherever we go?
Ah! I cannot tell you, but this I know,
That the same God still lives in heaven above,
And on earth the same Law, the same Faith that we love.
Then fear not, and weep not; but hope in the Lord,
And the sacred Torah, His holy word.

Le-hayyim, my brethren, *le-hayyim,* I say!
Health, peace, and good fortune I wish you today.
Today we have ended the Torah once more,
Today we begin it again as of yore.
Be thankful and glad and the Lord extol,
Who gave us the Law on its parchment scroll.

> Translated by Alice Lucas and Helena Frank[1]

❦ ❦ ❦

SIMHAT TORAH
MORRIS ROSENFELD

*a Yiddish poet of social protest who limned Jewish ghetto life in
Russia and New York (1862–1923)*

Simhat Torah! skip and hop
On your feet till down you drop!
In your mouth a merry jest—
And a burden in your breast.

—*Old Song*

So frisky and fit,
At table we sit,
We eat what we choose,
We drink and are gay.

31. Simhat Torah flag. Lithograph on paper. Poland. Nineteenth century.
See Chapter 9.

Sing, brother Jews,
Be merry today!
Cup after cup—
Drink it all up
No need to fear.
Lift up your voice,
Today we rejoice,
Sing, brothers dear.

Alas, Jewish singing!
And alas! Jewish gladness,
What means it; O tell me,
And whence is the sadness
That weighs on my heart when I hear?
I hang down my head
Like a child that is chidden.
And oft, ere I know it,
Uncalled for, unbidden,
Falls bitter and burning,
A tear!

Not always with sorrow
Our hopes are requited;
And often the sunshine
Has brightened our way.
We once were a nation
Both strong and united,
And yet, O my brothers,
And yet, to this day
We keep not one feast day
But still doth remind us
Of swords that lie shivered
And broken behind us.
And old tattered banners,
Now useless and furled,
Of all our dead heroes,
Our great ones who perished,
The altars forgotten,
The ruins uncherished.
And scattered abroad o'er the world
No song but contains but
Two words of rejoicing,

In which we discern not
The jesting below,
An echo of laughter,
Of false bitter laughter,
A cry half-despairing
Of shame and of woe! . . .

O great and happy feast day, Simhat Torah!
    High above your head thy bright star flashes
To win such a feast day, one such feast day,
        Ten we spend fasting in sackcloth and ashes.[2]

❧ ❧ ❧

A TABERNACLE THOUGHT
ISRAEL ZANGWILL

British novelist, playwright, poet, and Jewish communal leader
(1864–1926)

Lovely grapes and apples,
And such pretty flowers,
Blooming in the *sukkah*,
That in the back yard towers.

Green leaves for the ceiling
Sift the sun and shade
To a pretty pattern,
As in forest glade.

Cool retreat and dainty
For a little child,
Toddling in, by prospect
Of its joy beguiled.

Round he casts his blue eyes,
Stretches hand in haste;
Darling baby, all this
Just is to his taste.

But his eyes brim over
Soon with sudden tears.
Ah, he learns the lesson
Of the coming years.

For the fruit is gilded
And the flowers are wax.
Life's a pretty vision,
Only truth it lacks.[3]

❧ ❧ ❧

FOREIGNERS

HAYYIM NAHMAN BIALIK

*the most eminent of modern Hebrew poets and leader of the Hebrew
literary renaissance (1873–1934)*

The moon a pallid light is shedding
And through the *sukkah* roof it creeps;
In silver case, on fleecy bedding,
The citron like an infant sleeps.

The palm, as watcher by its pillow,
Still leans against the fragile wall,
Bound up with myrtle twigs and willow,
Then slips and o'er the citron falls.

The twain lie sleeping, but apart
Each dreams his dream in moonshine dim,
And who can know the stranger's heart
Or what his dreaming means to him?

Dream they of brighter moons that shone?
The splendor of their native sky?
Or are they sick of journeying on,
All travel-stained and dull and dry?

Dream they with fright: the feast is ended,
And brief their union fate ordained;
The broken bond will ne'er be mended,
Their fragrance gone, their beauty stained?

We cannot tell! . . . from overhead
The pallid beams of moonlight creep
To where the citron on its bed,
The palm beside it, lies asleep.

Translated by Helena Frank[4]

❧ ❧ ❧

THE *SUKKAH*
SAUL TCHERNIHOVSKY

*a Hebrew poet of distinction who ranked next to H.N. Bialik, who
composed idylls and sonnets, wrote stories and philological studies,
and translated many classical works (1875–1943)*

In my *sukkah* I take great pride;
It is built as specified.

Comrades, come, you must not miss
An enchanting sight like this.

All its board, while I looked on,
Father joined them, one by one.

On the hinges he fixed a door,
Sparkling sheets he spread all o'er.

Mother hung first fruits and flowers,
Washed in dew and bathed in showers.

I strewed sand around, around,
On the threshold, on the ground.

Finished is the task, come see
The *sukkah* father built for me. . . .

From the roof of boughs of pine,
Through the foliage of my shrine,

Who is winking? Is it true? . . .
Golden stars are peeping through.

Translated by Harry H. Fein[5]

❧ ❧ ❧

HAKKAFOT

SAUL TCHERNIHOVSKY

There's crowding in the house of prayer,
    There's light and warmth a-glowing;
The house is filled with festive folk,
    All pews and aisle o'erflowing.
The tumult's great and loud the noise,
Against old men are crowding boys,
    They even swamp the east wall.

Both girls and women stand penned up,
    Each chair and bench invading,
With turbans, kerchiefs of all sorts,
    And Sabbath clothes parading. . . .
"Come, cantor, start," a voice rings clear,
And soon, behold! some boys appear,
    Judeans captivating.

The vanguard marches leisurely,
    In rhythmic measure pacing,
Each youth with flag whose gilded top
    An apple red is gracing.
They raise their flags, they raise them 'loft,
And sister calls to brother soft,
    And brother calls to sister.

The cantor starts. Behind him trail
    Old men (their hands they're clapping),
With Torah Scrolls close in their arms,
    Encased in embroidered wrapping,
On whose gilded crowns bright, manifold,
The tiny tinkling bells of gold
    Are ringing and are jingling.

The cantor struts, the cantor chants,
    The choir raise their voices;
The treasurer and deacon sing,
    The merry crowd rejoices.

Tra, ra, ra, ra, and bim, bim, bom—
Both young and old are frolicsome,
    The rabbi's no exception.

The Torah-bearers slowly tread
    Through crowds exultant, thronging,
Who stop them, and kiss ardently
    The Torah with great longing.
"God grant you life this coming year!"—
"Peace be with you, abundant cheer!"—
    The maidens, too, are shouting.

The house is filled with light and warmth
    And mirth and laughter's buoyance;
One talks, one sings, one shouts: "Please, hush!"
    Each count'nance beams with joyance.
The cantor sings as he marches on:
"Hosanna, Savior, Holy One!"
    With all the crowd responding.

                    Translated by Harry H. Fein[6]

❧ ❧ ❧

DANCE HASIDIC

ABRAHAM M. KLEIN

*Canadian attorney, novelist, and pioneer of authentic Jewish poetry
in English (1909–1972)*

Twist each sidecurl; form the symbol
Of a quaver; comb the beard;
Let the prayer make all toes nimble. . . .
The Lord loved and the Lord feared
In your attitude, the pendules dangled
Ecstatically, defiantly the fingers snapped—
In such wise is cursed Satan to be wrangled,
In such the *Hasid* to be rapt.

Let the *rebbe* take the mantled Scroll;
You, *Hasidim*, lift your caftans, dance;
Circle the Torah and rejoice the soul,
Look God-wards and He will not look askance.

Let this be humility;
Back bent in the pious reel,
Head inclined imploringly,
And palms upward in appeal.

And let this be pride;
Beard pointed upwards, eyes aflame like *yahrzeit* lamps.
And right hand stretched as if it held God's left hand in it,
Marching as into paradise, while each foot stamps,
Crushing eternity into a dusty minute. . . .

Thus let the soul be cast from pride, gesticulating
Into humility, and from humility
Into the pride divine, so alternating
Until pride and humility be one,
Until above the Jews, above the Scroll, above the cherubim,
There broods the Immanence of Him. . . .[7]

❧ ❧ ❧

REB ABRAHAM
ABRAHAM M. KLEIN

Reb Abraham, the jolly,
Avowed the gloomy face
Unpardonable folly,
Unworthy of his race.

When God is served in revel
By all His joyous Jews,
He says the surly devil
Stands gloomy at the news. . . .

Reb Abraham loved Torah
If followed by a feast:
A *milah*-banquet, or a
Schnapps to drink, at least. . . .

On all Feasts of Rejoicing
Reb Abraham's thick soles
Stamped pious meters, voicing
Laudation of the Scrolls.

Averring that in heaven
One more Jew had been crowned,
Reb Abraham drank even
On cemetery ground.

And when Messiah greeting,
Reb Abraham's set plan
Is to make goodly eating
With roast Leviathan.

When God is served in revel
By all His joyous Jews,
He says the surly devil
Stands gloomy at the news. . . . [8]

❧ ❧ ❧

A WEEK WITHIN THE *SUKKAH* GREEN
ISABELLA R. HESS

A week within the *sukkah* green
We've sung Thy boundless praise,
Now ended is the autumn feast,
The golden harvest days.

Again we lift up voice in pray'r,
Oh send Thy blessed rain,
That when another harvest comes
We may rejoice again![9]

❦ ❦ ❦

THE HUT

AVIGDOR HAMEIRI

*Israeli editor of literary magazines, playwright, novelist, and poet
who wrote several volumes of verse; recipient of the Bialik Literary
Prize*

Fruit of the goodly tree, leaves of the palm tree,
Branch of the myrtle, and willows of the stream—
God of every fearful hour,
In this forest of horrors, guard Thou my hut,
Hut of young shoots, hut of creativity,
From the conjurings of men, and men that come of lions.

Fruit of the goodly tree, branch of the myrtle,
Willows of the stream, and leaves of the palm tree—
God of every pleasant hour,
In this forest of horrors, never fête for victory,
No exulting over spoils, and no paean after battle;
Here in the straits, guard Thou this hut of mine.

Fruit of the goodly tree, willows of the stream,
Leaves of the palm tree, and branches of myrtle—
God of each eternal hour,
In this forest of horrors, only this coign is for me,
In all of the earth, and in all of heaven.
Perhaps, perhaps, perhaps, Thou'llt not move me again?

Translated by Jacob Sloan[10]

32. Simhat Torah flag. Lithograph, black on light blue paper. Poland. Nineteenth Century. See Chapter 9.

※ ※ ※

SIMHAT TORAH
RUTH F. BRIN

short story writer, poet, and interpreter of Jewish liturgy

We have finished the Torah now,
reading of the days of our teacher, Moses,
and we have begun at the beginning once more.

We have moved from the story of Israel
to the creation of light,

resolved to make a new and better beginning
in our study of Torah.

Before He created man,
God created time, evening and morning.

He created the stars and the planets whirling in their courses,
and the patterns of motion for earth and sun and moon.

He created plants and birds, animals and the creatures of the sea,
each with its beginning, its flowering, and its ending,
its rhythm of death and of birth.

Though we move in cycles, like every work of Thy hand,
we are not bound to a wheel revolving on a fixed axis;
we can move forward in the path Moses taught us.

Inspire us, O Lord, to continue the cycle of Torah,
strengthen us to renew the life of Israel,
help us to bring Thy light to the lives of men;
speed us toward the bright morning of peace.[11]

❧ ❧ ❧

SIMHAT TORAH
MOLLIE R. GOLOMB

instructor of English and creative writing and literary advisor

The sculptured grief beneath the prayer shawl's edge
This night is warmed to joy, as craggy ridge
Can be transformed with sun.
Humbly he chants his praise:
Reading completed, once again begun,
Law and prophecy;
Submerged the corrugating hurt.
Scratched kiss on velvet gold-embossed,
Beard skyward in an ecstasy
Of prayer, bending ancient knees
In unaccustomed dance, possessed,

Clutching the precious burden of his heritage:
Tree of life, rooted in the heart,
Child, mother, wife and bride
Of mystic marriage—
He thrills his thanks to God.

Gone are the wooden benches, narrow walls;
Stilled are the lightning thunders. Sinai smiles.[12]

SUKKOT AND SIMHAT TORAH IN THE SHORT STORY

THE DEAD CITRON
SHOLOM ALEICHEM

(pseudonym of Shalom Rabinowitz), the great humorist of Yiddish literature; born in 1859 in Russia and died in 1916 in New York; a most prolific writer, known as the "Jewish Mark Twain," his masterful stories were extremely popular among the Jewish masses and have been translated into many languages

Whenever you see the name Leibel in this story, it refers to me.

I am short and fat and soft as down. But if you look at my body closely, you'd find that I am not as chubby as I appear. I am really rather scrawny, but I wear thicklined trousers, thicklined underwear, and a thicklined coat. My mother, you see, wants to keep me warm.

She's afraid I might catch pneumonia, God forbid, so she wraps me in wool padding from head to foot. She thinks that it's all right to wrap a boy in wool but it's wrong to use wool for stuffing balls. However, I have my own ideas. I pulled the wool out of my coat and trousers and distributed it to all the boys until she caught me. She slapped me and pinched me and whacked me. But Leibel went on doing as he pleased—handing out wool to his pals.

My face is red, my cheeks are blue, and my nose is always running.

"What a nose!" shouts my mother. "If he had no nose, he'd be all right. He'd have nothing to freeze in the winter."

I often try to picture myself without a nose. If people had no noses, what would they look like?

But I was going to tell you the story of the dead citron and I have digressed. So I'd better get back to my story.

My father, Moshe-Yankel, has been a clerk in an insurance firm for many years. He is paid five-and-a-half rubles a week. But he is expecting an increase. He says that if he gets more wages this year, please God, he will buy a citron. But my mother, Basse-Beila, thinks he is daydreaming. She says that the military barracks will crumble before father is given more pay.

One day, just before the New Year, Leibel overheard the following conversation between his father and mother.

"Even if the world turns upside down," he said, "I must have a citron this year!"

"The world will not turn upside down," she replied, "and you'll have no citron."

"That's what you say. Suppose I tell you, though, that I've already been promised something with which to buy a citron?"

"That belongs in a joke book. In the month named after the town of Kremenitz a miracle happened—a bear died in the forest. So what? If I don't believe it, I won't be a great unbeliever."

"Believe it or not, I'm telling you that for this Feast of Tabernacles we will have a citron of our own."

"Amen! I hope it's true. From your mouth into God's ears."

"Amen, amen," repeated Leibel to himself. He pictured his father entering the synagogue, like one of the rich men, with his own citron and his own palm branch. When the men walked around the ark with their citrons and their palms, Moshe-Yankel, though only a clerk, would follow them with his palm and his citron. The idea made Leibel very happy.

When he was in *heder* that day, he told everyone that this year his father would have his own citron and palm. But nobody believed him.

"What do you say to his father?" asked the young rascals of one another. "A beggar like that wants a citron of his own. He must think it's a lemon or a crab apple!"

Those are the remarks the boys made. They pushed Leibel around and gave him a few good whacks and punches. Leibel began to believe that his father was a beggar. So you can imagine his surprise when he came home and found Reb Hensel sitting at the table, in his Napoleonic hat, facing his father. In front of them stood a box of citrons whose fragrance filled the room.

Reb Hensel's hat was the kind worn in the time of Napoleon the Great. Over there in France these hats had been long out of fashion. But in our village there was still one to be found—only one, and it belonged to Reb Hensel. The hat was long and narrow. It had a slit and a button in front, and two tassels hung from the back. I always wanted these tassels. If the hat had gotten into my hands for two minutes—only two—the tassels would have been mine.

Reb Hensel spread out his delightful stock. He picked up a citron with his two fingers and passed it to father to examine.

"Take this citron, Reb Moshe-Yankel. You'll enjoy it."

"Is it a good one?" asked my father, checking the citron from every angle as one might examine a diamond. His hands trembled with joy.

"The best," replied Reb Hensel, and the tassels of his hat shook with his laughter.

Moshe-Yankel played with the citron. He smelled it, and could not take his eyes off it. He called his wife and with a happy smile he displayed the citron as though it were a priceless gem or an only, dear child. Basse-Beila came close and put out her hand slowly to take the citron, but she did not get it.

"Be careful of touching it. Just smell it."

Mother was satisfied with a sniff. I couldn't get even a sniff. I wasn't allowed to get near or even look at it.

"Look," said she, "he's here too. If he gets near the citron he'll bite the stem off it."

"God forbid!" cried my father.

"God preserve us!" echoed Reb Hensel, and his tassels shook again. He gave Father some wool in which he could nest the citron. The fine fragrance spread to every corner of the house. The citron was wrapped up as if it were a precious gem. It was placed in a beautiful round, carved and decorated sugar box. The sugar was emptied out and the citron was nestled in, like a beloved guest.

"Welcome art thou, Reb Citron. Into the box—into the box!"

The box was carefully closed and tenderly placed in the glass cupboard. The door was closed over it and—good-bye!

I heard my mother whisper to my father, "I'm afraid the heathen" —that was meant for me—"will get at the citron and bite off its stem." She took me by the hand and hustled me away from the cupboard.

Like a cat that has smelt butter and jumps down from a shelf for it, straightens her back, walks round and round rubbing herself against everything, looks into everyone's eyes, and licks herself, so did Leibel, poor boy, go round and round the cupboard. He gazed through the glass door, smiled at the citron box until his mother saw him. She remarked to his father that the young scoundrel wanted to get his hands on the citron and bite off its stem.

"To school, you scamp! Make yourself invisible!"

Leibel bent his head, lowered his eyes, and went off to school.

What his mother said about biting off the stem of the citron burned itself into Leibel's heart and ate into his bones like deadly poison. The top of the citron buried itself in his brain. It did not leave his thoughts for a moment. He dreamed of it at night. It worried him and almost dragged him by the hand.

"Don't you recognize me, foolish boy? It's I—the citron stem."

Leibel turned over on the other side, groaned, and fell asleep. It worried him again.

"Get up, fool. Go and open the cupboard, take out the citron and bite me off. You'll enjoy yourself."

Leibel got up in the morning, washed himself, and began to recite his prayers. He ate his breakfast and started to leave for school. On the way he passed the cupboard and stopped to look at the citron box. He imagined the box was winking at him. "Over here, over here, little boy," he seemed to hear. Leibel walked out of the house quickly.

Early one morning Leibel found himself alone in the house. His father had left for work, his mother had gone to the market. The servant was busy in the kitchen. Leibel again looked inside the glass cupboard and saw the box. It seemed to be beckoning to him.

"Over here, over here, little boy." Leibel opened the glass door softly, took out the beautiful box, and raised the lid. Before he had time to pick up the citron, the fragrance filled his nostrils—a pungent, heavenly fragrance. Before he had time to turn around, the citron was in his hand and the top of it close to his eyes.

"Do you want to enjoy yourself? Do you want to know the taste of paradise? Take hold and bite me off. Don't be afraid, little fool. No one will know. No one will see you. No bird will snitch on you."

You want to know what happened? You want to know whether I bit the top off the citron or held myself back from doing it? I should like to know what you would have done in my place—if you had been told ten times not to dare bite off the top of the citron. Would you not have wanted to know what it tasted like? Would you not also have thought of a plan—to bite it off and stick it on again with spittle? You may believe me or not—that is your own affair—but I do not myself know how it happened. Almost before the citron was in my hands, the top of it was between my teeth.

The day before the festival, Father came home a little earlier from his office to untie the palm branch. He had put it away in a corner, warning Leibel not to go near it. But it was a useless warning. Leibel had his own troubles. The top of the citron haunted him. Why had he wanted to bite it off? What good had it done to taste it when it was as bitter as gall? It was for nothing he had spoiled the citron and made it unfit for use in the synagogue. That the citron could not now be used, Leibel knew very well. Why had he spoiled this beautiful creation, bitten off its head, and taken away its life? Why? Why? He dreamt of the citron that night. It haunted him and asked, "Why have you done this thing to me? Why did you bite off my head? Now I am useless—useless." Leibel turned over on the other side, groaned, and fell asleep again. But the citron plagued him. "Murderer, what did you have against me? What had my head done to you."

The first day of the Feast of Tabernacles arrived. After a frosty night, the sun rose and covered the earth with delayed warmth, like that of a stepmother. That morning Moshe-Yankel got up earlier than usual and practiced by heart the festival prayers, reciting them to a beautiful festival melody. That day also Basse-Beila was very busy cooking the fish and the other special dishes. That day also

Zalman the carpenter came to our tabernacle to make a blessing over the citron and palm before anyone else so that he might be able to enjoy the festival.

"Zalman wants the palm and citron," Mother told Father.

"Open the cupboard and take out the box—but carefully," said my father.

He himself stood on a chair, took the palm from the top shelf, and brought it out to Zalman.

"Here," he said, "make a blessing. But be careful, in heaven's name, be careful!"

Our neighbor Zalman was a giant of a man—may no evil eye harm him! Each finger of his two huge hands could knock down three such Leibels as I. His hands were always sticky and his nails red from glue. When he drew one of these nails across a plank, there was a mark that might have been made by a sharp iron.

In honor of the festival, Zalman had put on a clean shirt and a new coat. He had scrubbed his hands with pumice stone, but had not succeeded in making them clean. They were still sticky, and the nails were still red with glue. Into these hands fell the dainty citron. There was good reason for Moshe-Yankel to get excited when Zalman gave the citron a good squeeze and the palm a good shake.

"Be careful, be careful," he cried. "Now turn the citron head downwards, and make the blessing. Carefully, carefully. For heaven's sake, be careful!"

Suddenly Moshe-Yankel threw himself forward and shouted "Ooh!" The cry brought his wife running into the tabernacle.

"What is it, Moshe-Yankel? For God's sake, what is it?"

"Fumbling ninny! Dope!" he shouted at the carpenter and looked as though he were ready to kill him. "How could you be such a fumbling fool? Is a citron an ax? a bore? You have cut my throat without a knife. You've spoiled my citron. Here is the stem here, look! Fumbling ninny! Dope!"

We were all paralyzed. At this moment Zalman resembled a corpse. He could not understand how this misfortune had happened. How had the stem broken off the citron? Surely he had held it lightly, with the tips of his fingers? It was dreadful—a misfortune.

Basse-Beila was pale as death. She wrung her hands and moaned.

"When a man is unlucky, he may as well dig a grave and bury himself alive."

And Leibel? Leibel didn't know whether he ought to dance with joy because God had performed a miracle for him, or whether he should cry for his father's agony and his mother's tears, or whether he should kiss Zalman's thick hands with their sticky fingers and red nails because he was his good angel. Leibel looked at his father's face, his mother's tears, the carpenter's hands, and at the citron that lay on the table, yellow as wax, without a head, without a spark of life, a dead thing.

"A dead citron," said my father in a broken voice.

"A dead citron," repeated my mother, gushing tears.

"A dead citron," echoed the carpenter, looking at his hands. He seemed to be saying to himself, "There's a pair of hands for you! May they wither!"

"A dead citron," said Leibel, in a joyful voice. But he caught himself, fearing that the tone of his exclamation might proclaim that he, Leibel, was the killer, the murderer of the citron.

Translated by Leo W. Schwarz[1]

❧ ❧ ❧

THE FEAST OF TABERNACLES
SHOLOM ALEICHEM

Yom Kippur passed, and with it the tears. There began the days of rejoicing and happiness, the Feast of Tabernacles.

The first stave of Grandfather's tabernacle was raised on the evening following Yom Kippur. Uncle Itzie built the booth with the help of the orphans, but it was Grandfather who gave the commands, like an experienced architect. "This goes here! . . . That goes there! . . . This will do! . . . That won't do! . . ." Oddly enough, Grandfather and Uncle Itzie were not on speaking terms. They were angry with each other, and this caused Grandmother no end of grief. An only son, the only heir "in a hundred and twenty years," and he didn't speak to his own father! Who ever heard of such a thing?

In this communal tabernacle, two large tables were prepared, one for Grandfather and one for Uncle. On each table there were wine for the blessing, bread, and candles, arranged separately. Aunt Sossie blessed the candles at her table, and Grandmother Gittel (who was carried in on her bed) blessed hers. Then Uncle came from the synagogue. He had to wait for Grandfather to arrive and be the first to pronounce grace. One could not be rude to one's father, for it is written: "Honor thy father and mother. . . ." From time to time, Uncle Itzie would leave the house to peek into the tabernacle, each time with a different excuse. "Isn't he here yet? . . . This time the *Hasidim* are later than usual! . . . Hmmm! The candles are burning out, and we'll have to eat in the dark. . . ." The children secretly gloated over their uncle's discomfort, for he was a harsh, heartless man—it wouldn't hurt him to experience the sensation of hunger!

But at last Grandfather comes, dressed in his holiday coat and flourishing the thick prayer book of Rabbi Jacob Emden. Sonorously he greets them and starts citing the prayer *Ushpizin*. He chants and chants and chants. . . . As if out of spite, from the kitchen comes delicious aromas of fish, peppered stuffing, and fresh crisp bread, which tickle the palate and seem to tease, "If you'd dip us into hot fish sauce, you'd taste something heavenly!" And Grandfather is still chanting. The candles are burning down, and Grandfather is still chanting. The children are expiring with hunger, they are nodding with sleepiness, and Grandfather is still chanting! . . . Suddenly he stops, runs to the table, and quickly rattles off the grace. They begin to come to life. Uncle Itzie repeats grace after his father, at his own table. When he finishes, it's the turn of Haya Esther's orphans to say grace, one by one, and Grandmother Gittel sheds a tear. It is a long, long time before they are finally able to dip a piece of bread into the honey and to make the acquaintance of the fish and taste the pepper with the tips of their tongues!

It was even worse on the last days of the feast, and finally, one evening, on the Feast of the Rejoicing of the Law, Uncle Itzie could stand it no longer. He called the children and said, "Youngsters, do you want to see something interesting? Go to the synagogue, and you'll see a sight!"

He did not have to urge them, and, taking each other by the hand, they were off. It was pitch black in the street. All the other Jews were already at home having supper. Every synagogue had been closed and darkened long ago, but in the Old Synagogue there was still light. Quietly the children opened a crack in the door and saw something they could scarcely believe. There was only one man in the whole synagogue—Grandfather. He was wrapped in his prayer shawl; he held his fat prayer book in one hand and a Scroll of the Law in the other. Tightly pressing the Scroll to his breast, he walked slowly around the pulpit and, like a cantor, recited loudly, in a sing-song, the *Hakkafot*: "Aid of the poor, save us!"

After he had gone round the pulpit once, he stopped in front of the ark and began to dance by himself, hugging the Scroll to his breast and singing:

"Moses rejoiced in the Torah!
Lamtedridom, haida!
Be joyful and happy with the Torah!
Lamtedridom, dom-dom-dom!
Haida, dridada!
The Torah of Moses, ha!"

The children were awestruck, and at the same time they wanted to laugh. Taking each other by the hand, they ran headlong home.

"Well, what did you see there? Wasn't it a nice spectacle?" With these words Uncle Itzie greeted them and burst out laughing until tears came to his eyes. But at that moment, the children felt a profound dislike—not for Grandfather, but for their uncle.

Translated by Tamara Kahana[2]

✠ ✠ ✠

THE NIGHT OF *HAKKAFOT*
SHOLOM ALEICHEM

If I were Goethe, I would not describe the sorrows of young Werther; I would describe the sorrows of a poor Jewish lad who was madly in love with the cantor's daughter. If I were Heine, I would not sing of Florentine nights; I would sing of the night of Simhat Torah, when Jews make the rounds of *hakkafot* and when young women and pretty girls mingle with the men in the synagogue—the one night when this is permitted. The women kiss the Scroll of the Law. They jump up and down, squealing in every key, "Long life to you!" The answer is "Same to you, same to you!"

An hour or two before the *hakkafot* ceremony, the smaller children

33. Simhat Torah. By Jossi Stern. Color lithograph. Contemporary. See
Chapter 9.

gathered in the synagogue and climbed upon the benches. Flags fluttered in their hands, flags topped with red apples in which candles were burning. But the apples were not redder than the cheeks of the children, and the candles shone no brighter than their eyes. The older boys strolled in the synagogue yard, and there the air was soft and clear, the sky star-studded, and one had the sensation that the whole world was enjoying a holiday. Even the silence was festive, and nothing dared to mar the holiness of this night, the night of the Rejoicing of the Law, when the chosen people celebrated the heavenly gift of the Torah throughout the earth.

Did it matter that a peasant cart clattered by, raising a cloud of fragrant dust? Or that the post chaise rumbled past, breaking the stillness with the ting-a-ling of its bells? . . . The dust settled, the sound of the bell died in the distance, and the night remained as holy and as festive as before, for the holiday of the Rejoicing of the Law was being celebrated throughout the world. . . .

A black cat ran past on its soft, velvety paws; it cut across the synagogue yard and disappeared. A dog howled in a melancholy key and then was quiet. Yet the night remained holy, still festive, because this holiday of the Rejoicing of the Law reigned, and it was being celebrated everywhere.

It was easy to breathe in such clear air. One's heart almost burst with joy, and one's soul, was light. . . . One felt proud—this was the night of the Rejoicing of the Law! Above was the sky, and God was there—your God, your heaven, your holiday!

"Children, they're starting the *hakkafot!*"

They darted into the synagogue, but it was a false alarm. The men were still engaged in the evening prayer. Tzali, the cantor of the Cold Synagogue, stood at the altar with his two choirboys: one a swarthy lad with thick lips, the bass; the other a slender boy with a pale face, the soprano. The cantor, Reb Tzali, Tzali of the golden voice, was a tall, blond man with a nose hooked like a bull's horn. He had thin curly earlocks and a blond wavy beard that looked as if it had been tied to his face. Was it possible that this freak had such a handsome daughter? The cantor's daughter, you must understand, was *his* daughter, Cantor Tzali was *her* father! . . . His daughter, he often boasted, was unique. There was only one trouble with her—she didn't want to get married. "Anybody we suggest, she turns down. But, of course, that's just nonsense. When the right man comes along, she'll have to say yes. If not, we'll drag her to the wedding by her braids. And of course there's always a cane!" the cantor would say jokingly, flourishing his reed cane with its old yellow ivory knob.

And then at last the evening prayer was finished, but it was still a long way to the *hakkafot*. Now they were intoning the hymn, "Unto thee it was shown that thou mightest know that the Lord He is God. . . ." Stanzas of the hymn were being distributed among the most distinguished members of the congregation. Everyone recited his stanza, but each in a different key and with a different melody. Actually, the litany was the same the world over, but, since people have different voices and timbres and are a bit frightened of the sound of their own voices, the tune emerged not quite as expected, and the trills which should have come at the end of the stanzas were entirely lost.

The Cold Synagogue was large, wide, and lofty. It had no ceiling —just a roof; that was why it was called the "Cold" Synagogue. . . .

Where did all these men come from? All the women, girls, young men, and children? Sholom was visiting the Cold Synagogue for the first time, and he could not help thinking of the verse "How goodly are thy tents, O Jacob. . . ." It was not easy to find a place. Happily, the beadle recognized him—why, wasn't he the son of Nahum Rabinowitz? Room must be made for him among the members of the congregation on the "mirror" side!

What were they reading now? The noise and confusion were so great that neither the cantor nor the choirboys could be heard. In vain did everyone shout "Quiet!" In vain did the beadle pound his fist on the table. Women were shouting, girls giggling, children squealing. . . .

Here was a little boy crying. "Why are you crying, little boy?" Someone had knocked the apple off his flag and crushed it with his foot. What would he do without an apple? . . . A big boy, standing next to the child, grinned, showing all his teeth. The child's tragedy seemed to amuse him. This annoyed Sholom, and he asked angrily, "What are you laughing at?" The lad replied, still showing all his teeth, "That kid's weak in the head!" His answer irritated Sholom even more. "Were you any brighter at his age?" The fellow stopped grinning. "I really don't remember, but one thing I do know—I have more brains in my heel than you have in your head, even though you do go to the County School and are the son of Nahum Rabinowitz!" Had the son of Nahum Rabinowitz not been among strangers in a strange synagogue, he would have known what to do. But he managed to keep his temper. . . . Besides, through the terrific din, he heard the dear, familiar words with which the beadle invited the congregation to the rite of *hakkafot*.

"The learned Reb Shimon Zeev, son of Reb Hayyim Tzvi, the Cohen, is invited to honor the Torah!"

"The learned Reb Moshe Yaakov, son of Nahum Dov, the Levite, is invited to honor the Torah!"

Each man so honored received a Scroll of the Law with which he paraded around the synagogue.

And so the *hakkafot* ceremony began. But where was the cantor's daughter? . . .

"O Lord! I beseech thee, save us. . . ." The first round had finished with the chorus "*Hai-da!*" and with a dance. The beadle again called out in his hoarse voice, "The learned Reb so-and-so is invited to honor the Torah. . . ." Thus ended the second round, the third, the fourth. . . . Each was followed by dancing and singing, and the cantor's daughter was nowhere to be seen!

Sholom could not sit still. He twisted and turned in his seat. Would he ever find her? Could she have deceived him so shabbily? Or had their tryst been discovered and had she been kept at home under lock and key? One could expect anything of Cantor Tzali, a man capable of pulling a girl by her braids and caning her! . . .

Apparently the beadle, noticing Sholom squirming in his seat and looking restlessly about, thought he must be eager to be called. Or perhaps it was one of the trustees who wanted to give Rabinowitz's son a treat. In any event, Sholom suddenly heard his name called. "Sholom, the son of Menahem Nahum, is invited to honor the Torah!"

The blood rushed to his head. All eyes seemed to be fixed upon him. He felt as every young man feels when he is summoned for the first time to read from the Torah. Almost before he knew it, the beadle had brought a Scroll to him, and, standing among the others, he hugged the large Scroll in his arms. The procession had already begun. Cantor Tzali, at the head, sang, "Helper of the poor, save us!" Women and girls crowded about to kiss the Scrolls, calling out, "Long life to you!" It was strange to be treated with so much respect. The unexpected honor thrilled Sholom. He was very proud to be the only youth among men—and all because he was somebody. He was the son of Nahum Rabinowitz! . . . Suddenly someone kissed his hand. "Long life to you!" He raised his eyes and saw the cantor's daughter, standing next to her friend. . . .

The heavens opened; angels descended singing hymns. They praised the world God had created—this good, beautiful world; praised the people He had created—good, kind people! Everything was so beautiful, Sholom wanted to weep, and his heart sang to the angels.

He was astonished and bewildered—instead of kissing the Scroll, she had kissed his hand. Had it been an accident? It could not have been! Her smiling eyes told him. He almost dropped the Scroll. He wanted to pause, to look again in her eyes, to say a word or two. . . . But he could not. He had to move on. The Scroll had to be passed to another. Only when he had reached the altar and returned the Scroll to the beadle was he able to glance back. But she was no longer there. Again he was in the procession, straggling after the men, but this time without a Scroll. His eyes searched for her everywhere, but she had disappeared. Perhaps it had only been an illusion. But he still felt the kiss on his hand. As he left the synagogue, he felt that he had wings; he was flying. . . . Angels were flying with him.

In the Big Synagogue, the ceremony was still going on. Father was in high spirits. Dressed in an old satin coat which was cracked at the seams, showing its yellow lining in places, he nevertheless looked noble and handsome. Lazar Yossel and Magidov stood beside him. Father smiled as he listened to them. "Where have you been?" he asked Sholom, not angrily, but out of curiosity. "In the Cold Synagogue," Sholom replied, and boasted that his name had been called to honor the Torah. "That was very nice of them!" Father said, pleased, and the superior sons-in-law teased Sholom. One of them asked whether he had been introduced to the Helper of the Poor. The other remarked, "How could he have met the Helper there? It's only the Helper's grandson who's at the Cold Synagogue!" Everyone laughed. What a night that was! Such a night could only come on Simhat Torah!

Translated by Tamara Kahana[3]

※ ※ ※

DAVID, KING OF ISRAEL
SHOLOM ALEICHEM

Old Dodi had snow-white hair and curly sidelocks, which he covered with an old-fashioned Napoleon-style hat. He was always seen holding a long thick staff with a carved ivory handle and carrying a sack on his bent back. On Friday afternoons and the eves of holidays he always went from house to house collecting Sabbath loaves for the poor Jewish prisoners.

Old Dodi, who was almost one hundred years old, was a town celebrity better known as David, King of Israel. Since everyone knew that he merely wanted bread for his poor prisoners, no one argued with him. There were those who had bread and the will to share, as well as those who had neither. But Old Dodi did not take it amiss if he was turned away empty-handed. If everyone had bread and the will to share, he asked, what would happen to the takers? And without givers and takers what would become of compassion, righteousness, and good deeds? Then what need would there be for the world-to-come and paradise? And if there would be neither world-to-come nor paradise, where would the righteous souls go?

Such were the questions that ran through Old Dodi's mind. His view was that whatever God did was right; there had to be takers and givers, haves and have-nots, prisoners and free men who cared for the prisoners by collecting white loaf on Friday afternoons and on the eves of holidays. . . .

Why was he called David, king of Israel?

Because once a year during Simhat Torah he became a king, the king of the Jewish children.

At Simhat Torah you would not recognize Old Dodi. His bent back was straight, his beard and sidecurls were combed. His Napoleon-style hat was turned inside out. His broad white collar was smooth and neat. And he no longer carried his staff and sack. Old Dodi was transformed. His face shone, his eyes sparkled. Having taken a drop of liquor in honor of the holiday, Old Dodi became spirited and gay—he became a new man with a reanimated soul.

He gathered all the small fry from all the synagogues, lined them up in circles around him, then walked about in the midst of the circle, stretched his hands heavenward and sang, "Holy little lambs!"

"Baa-baa," replied the youngsters.

"Tell me now, who's leading you?"

"Our King David, baa-baa."

"What's his full name?"

"David, king of Israel, baa-baa."

"Then shout it out, Jewish children, with a pretty melody: David, king of Israel, is still alive!"

"David . . . king . . . of Israel . . . is still . . . alive!"

"Once again. Holy little lambs!"

"Baa-baa."

"Tell me now, who's leading you?"

"Our King David, baa-baa."

"What's his full name?"

"David, king of Israel, baa-baa."

"Then shout it out, Jewish children, with a pretty melody: David . . . king . . . of Israel . . . is still . . . alive!"

"David . . . king . . . of Israel . . . is still . . . alive!"

More children joined the troupe. The cavalcade grew. The on-lookers kept increasing. The sound of tumultuous voices surrounded the village. David, king of Israel, stopped at every *sukkah,* where he was given a drink by the householders and a piece of cake by their wives. He drank the whiskey and distributed the cake among the children, singing, "Holy little lambs!"

"Baa-baa."

"What have I got in my hand?"

"Honey cake, baa-baa."

"What blessing is said over it?"

"Blessed is He who creates various kinds of foods. Baa-baa."

"Tell me now, who's leading you?"

"Our King David, baa-baa."

"What's his full name?"

"David, king of Israel, baa-baa."

"Then shout it out, Jewish children, with a pretty melody: David . . . king . . . of Israel . . . is still . . . alive!"

"David . . . king . . . of Israel . . . is still . . . alive!"

You might wonder what harm was there in a poor old centenarian's taking a drop of liquor once a year on Simhat Torah, becoming cheerful and gay and posing as a king, while young merrymakers trailed after him bleating, "Baa-baa"?

But here's what happened.

Just before Rosh Hashanah, during the season of the Penitential Prayers, a new police chief was sent to our village (the old one had dropped dead). As usual, the new police chief, sporting a personality all his own, instituted brand-new procedures. First of all, it was said that he was a scrupulously conscientious man—too conscientious, in fact. Meeting a Jew he would straightaway ask him, "What's your name and where are you from? Got a passport?" Secondly, his palms were absolutely ungreasable. He took nothing. Neither cash nor goods. Talk of being ethical! He was clean as a whistle. The news spread like wildfire through town. Bad business! A rat! A Haman!

The next morning he was already strolling through the village. He ran through the marketplace, inspected all the stores and butcher shops, poked his nose into the synagogue courtyard, sniffed here and there. . . . But, poor fellow, what illicit business could he have found during the holiday season? The Hebrew teachers had already released the schoolchildren, and counterfeit money was not our stock in trade. So we dismissed the police chief from our thoughts.

But God provided him with grist for the mill. The holiday of Sukkot! Just listen. He didn't like the way the Jews built their booths. Said they were a fire hazard, dangerous to life and limb. Get the picture? For thousands of years Jews have lived in these booths and feared absolutely nothing. Now all of a sudden there was a fire to worry about!

"Well, your lordship, what exactly is it you want?"

"I don't want you to build your booths this way, but in the following manner."

Of course they paid as much attention to him as Haman does to the Purim rattle-clacker. And they began building their Sukkot booths in the age-old traditional way. So the police chief got wind of this and had them torn down.

A delegation was sent to him. "Your lordship," they said, "how can we celebrate Sukkot without our booths?"

"Nothing doing," he said.

So go knock your head against the wall. For if you really insisted he'd demand to see your passport and take down your name.

To make a long story short, we were in hot water. We went into hiding. Several families shared one booth, scared to death lest—I don't have to spell it out for you! But the good Lord had mercy on us and most of the holiday passed by without incident. All our fears had been in vain. But then came the final day of the holiday, Simhat Torah.

On the last day, Simhat Torah, Old Dodi and his troupe of merry-makers came into the synagogue courtyard.

"Holy little lambs!" he called out in his usual fashion.

"Baa-baa," replied the holy little lambs.

Suddenly the police chief materialized as though out of nowhere. He gazed at the scene in utter amazement, apparently seeing such a show for the first time. Since Old Dodi had no reason to fear the new police chief, he continued.

"Tell me now, Jewish children, who's leading you?"

"Our King David!"

"What's his full name?"

"David, king of Israel."

"Then shout it out, Jewish children, with a pretty melody: David . . . king . . . of Israel . . . is still . . . alive!"

"David . . . king . . . of Israel . . . is still . . . alive!"

The police chief then demanded an explanation. What did all this mean? Who was the old man? And what were the youngsters singing?

Reb Shepsel the teacher, who had a reputation for his knowledge of Russian, stepped forth. He brushed his sidecurls behind his ears and volunteered to be the interpreter.

"He is David the Jewish tsar and the children are his serfs," said Reb Shepsel in Russian.

At this the police chief slapped his hands in glee and began to laugh. But do you think he just chuckled? He held his sides and laughed so hysterically he almost went into convulsions. David, king of Israel, did not stop singing, "Holy little lambs!" and the holy little lambs did not stop shouting, "Baa-baa." After a while the police chief got sick of the performance. He chased the troupe of children and, in his usual fashion, took David, king of Israel, to task.

"Where are you from?" he demanded. "Got a passport?"

It turned out that the old man himself did not know where he was from. And so, alas, he was sent to jail, where he joined his poor prisoners.

"He'll sober up there," said the police chief, "that old sot!"

A year later, Jews dwelled in their Sukkot booths, as usual. They made merry at Simhat Torah as they did every year. But one element was missing. David, king of Israel, was gone. And his little song, "Holy little lambs," which elicited the reply, "Baa-baa," was heard no more.

Translated by Curt Leviant[4]

❧ ❧ ❧

"BETWEEN TWO CLIFFS"
Based on the story by I. L. PERETZ
MAURICE SAMUEL

born in 1895, died in 1972; leading writer, translator, and lecturer in America, author of many books; a foremost interpreter of Yiddish literature, his The World of Sholom Aleichem *and* The Prince of the Ghetto *brought to the fore two of the greatest Yiddish authors; in the latter book, he recounts folk tales and Hasidic stories of Isaac Loeb Peretz (1852–1915), who together with Mendele Mocher Seforim and Sholom Aleichem are considered the three modern Yiddish literary classicists*

So these two mighty cliffs came face to face, and I was caught between them. It was a miracle that I wasn't flattened out.

He of Biale—his memory be our blessing—followed a custom of his own on the Day of the Rejoicing of the Law. He would send his *Hasidim* out of the study house and tell them to go strolling in the open air, and he himself would sit on the veranda and take pleasure in the sight.

Biale is no longer what it was. In those days it was little more than a village—clusters of tiny, low houses, with the synagogue and the rabbi's study house standing out in their midst. The veranda was on the second story, and below it the village and its surrounding lay as in the palm of your hand, enclosed between the hills on the east and the river on the west. The rabbi sits up there and looks down. If a group of *Hasidim* passes without singing, he throws them the opening notes of a melody, which they take up and carry away with them. So group after group goes by and, singing, spreads out into the fields, filled with true happiness, as is proper on the Day of the

Rejoicing of the Law; and the rabbi would remain up there and never stir from his place.

The rabbi must have recognized our footsteps, for on this occasion he rose and came forward in salutation.

"*Shalom aleikhem*, greetings, Rabbi," he said modestly, in his low, sweet voice.

"*Aleikhem shalom*, Noah," answered he of Brisk.

The rabbi of Brisk sat down, and he of Biale stood before him.

"Tell me, Noah," said he of Brisk, lifting his eyebrows, "what made you run away from my *yeshivah*? What did you lack there?"

"Air, Rabbi," said he of Biale gently. "I lacked air. I couldn't catch my breath."

"Come, come, Noah; how can that be?"

"I mean my soul lacked air," said he of Biale in the same voice. "It was being stifled."

"Why, Noah?"

"Your Torah, Rabbi, is only law and judgment, without compassion. It is a Torah without a touch of tenderness. And therefore it is without joy; the breath of life is not in it. Only iron and bronze, iron laws and tablets of bronze: a lofty and majestic Torah, for scholars and for choice spirits."

He of Brisk was silent, and my rabbi continued. "But tell me, Rabbi, what Torah have you for the common people—for the wood-gatherer, the butcher, the laborer, the ordinary, everyday Jew? And particularly for a sinful Jew. What have you, Rabbi, for those who are not scholars?"

He of Brisk still remained silent, as if he did not know what was being said to him. And he of Biale went on again, in his sweet, low voice.

"Forgive me, Rabbi, but I must be truthful with you. Your Torah was hard, hard and arid, because it had only the body and not the soul of the Torah."

"The soul?" said he of Brisk, and rubbed his forehead.

"Indeed, Rabbi. Your Torah, I said, was only for scholars, for the elect, for a few chosen spirits, and not for the masses of Israel. But the Torah was given to all Israel, and the divine glory must rest on all Israel, for the Torah is the soul of Israel."

"And your Torah, Noah?"

"Do you want to see it, Rabbi?"

"*See* it? See the *Torah*?"

34. Sukkot in Jerusalem. By Reuven Rubin. 1926. Oil on canvas.

"Come, Rabbi, I will show it to you. I will show you the glory of it, the joy that streams out from it for all Israel."

The rabbi of Brisk remained seated.

"Come, I beg you, Rabbi. It is not far."

And he led the rabbi of Brisk out on the veranda. I followed silently. Nevertheless my rabbi heard me, and he turned and said, "You may come too, Shmaya. Today you will see, and the rabbi of Brisk, too, will see, what the Day of Rejoicing of the Law is—a true rejoicing in the Torah."

That which I saw differed in no way from what I had seen on previous occasions; but the manner of my seeing it was different. It was as if scales had fallen from my eyes.

I saw the wide, enormous heavens, infinite in extent, and blue, radiant blue, so that the eye was filled with delight. A host of little silver clouds floated up there, and if one looked closely one could really see that they quivered with happiness, as if they were dancing in the Rejoicing of the Law. Below, within the circle of the hills and the river, the townlet lay embedded in green, a dark and living green; one would have said that a living spirit breathed among the grasses. The spirit broke out here, there, elsewhere, like an odorous flame, which danced between the bushes, kissing and caressing them. . . .

On the meadows, among the flames and grasses, little groups of *Hasidim* walked to and fro. Their satin gabardines—and even those of plain cotton—glittered like mirrors: all of them, even those that were ragged. And the flames that danced among the grasses touched the holiday attire of the *Hasidim* and played with it; it was as if every *Hasid* was surrounded with exultant, joyous fire. And the *Hasidim* turned their longing eyes to the veranda, and the light in their eyes was drawn from the eyes of their rabbi. And as the light grew, their songs became louder, gayer, and even more sacred.

Every group sang its own melody, and the melodies mingled in the air and came to us in a single harmony. And not only they sang; the heavens sang too, the upper spheres sang, and the earth under their feet sang; the soul of the world sang—everything sang.

Lord of the world! The sweetness of it melted my heart!

And yet the moment I had hoped for did not come.

"It is time for evening prayer!" exclaimed he of Brisk sharply. In that instant everything vanished.

The scales covered my eyes again. I looked and saw an ordinary sky, and under it ordinary fields. On the fields wandered beggarly *Hasidim* in tattered gabardines. The flames were extinguished.

I turned to my rabbi. His face, too, was extinguished.

No, they did not come to an understanding. He of Brisk remained an opponent of *Hasidim*. But the visit was not without effect. From that time on he no longer persecuted the *Hasidim*.[5]

✹ ✹ ✹

THE STORY OF THE MELODY
SHMUEL YOSEF AGNON

born in Galicia in 1888 and from 1924 on resident of Jerusalem, where he died in 1970; master of an original style and a prolific pen, he authored several novels, hundreds of short stories and anthologies of Jewish folklore; recognized as the foremost modern Hebrew writer, he received the Nobel Prize for Literature, the first author in the holy tongue to be so honored

It was the evening of the Festival of Rejoicing in the Torah. That evening the rabbi's house of study was full of bright lights, every light fixture glowing with a radiance from on high. Righteous and saintly *Hasidim* clothed in white robes of pure silk, with Torah Scrolls in their arms, circled the pulpit, dancing with holy fervor and enjoying the pleasures of the Torah. A number of *Hasidim* as well as ordinary householders get the privilege of dancing with them, and they cling to the sacred Torah and to those who selflessly obey the Torah, and they forget all anger and all disputes and all kinds of troublesome trivialities. And their young children form an outer circle around them, each child carrying a colored flag, red or green or white or blue, each flag inscribed with letters of gold. On top of each flag is an apple, and on top of each apple a burning candle, and all the candles glow like planets in the mystical "field of sacred apples." And when young boys or girls see their father receive this honor, carrying a Torah Scroll in his arms, they immediately jump toward him grasping the Scroll, caressing, embracing, kissing it with their pure lips that have not tasted sin; they clap their hands and sing sweetly, "Happy art thou, O Israel," and their fathers nod their heads toward the children, singing, "Ye holy lambs." And the women in the outer lobby feast their eyes on this exalted holiness.

When the seventh round of the procession around the pulpit is reached, the cantor takes a Torah Scroll to his bosom and calls out to the youths: "Whoever studies the Torah let him come and take a Torah Scroll," and a number of fine youths come and take Scrolls in their arms.

Then the cantor calls out again. "The distinguished young man, Raphael, is honored with the honor of the Torah, and with the singing of a beautiful melody."

Raphael came forward, went to the ark, accepted the Scroll from the cantor, and walked at the head of the procession. The elders stood and clapped their hands, adding to the rejoicing. The children stood on the benches chanting aloud, "Ye holy lambs" and waving their flags over the heads of the youths. But when Raphael began to sing his melody all hands became still, and everyone stood motionless without saying a word. Even the older *Hasidim* whose saintly way in prayer and in dancing with great fervor is like that of the ancient sage Rabbi Akiba—of whom it is told that when he prayed by himself, his bowing and genuflecting were so fervent that "if when you left him he was in one corner, you found him in another corner at the next moment"—even they restrained themselves with all their might from doing this. They did not lift a hand to clap because of the ecstatic sweetness, even though their hearts were consumed with fire. The women leaned from the windows of the women's gallery, and their heads hung out like a flock of doves lined up on the frieze of a wall.

Raphael held the Scroll in his arm, walking in the lead with all the other youths following him in the procession around the pulpit. At that moment a young girl pushed her way through the legs of the dancers, leaped toward Raphael, sank her red lips into the white mantle of the Torah Scroll in Raphael's arm, and kept on kissing the Scroll and caressing it with her hands. Just then the flag fell out of her hand, and the burning candle dropped on Raphael's clothing.

After the holiday Raphael's father brought an action before the rabbi against the girl's father in the matter of Raphael's robe that had been burned because of the girl. The rabbi, indulging himself in the pleasure of a wise remark, said to the girl's father, "God willing, for their wedding day you will have a new garment made for him." Immediately they brought a decanter of brandy and wrote the betrothal contract. And for Raphael's and Miriam's wedding a new garment was made for him. This is the story of the melody.

Translated by Isaac Franck[6]

❧ ❧ ❧

THE BIG *SUKKAH*
ABRAHAM REISEN

writer with a wide reputation among Yiddish readers for his sensitive lyric poetry and his numerous short stories and sketches of life in the Jewish ghetto (1876–1953)

Baruch's cottage was the smallest on the street. It was really more like a village hut than a town cottage. Only the roof with its rotting shingles showed that it belonged to the town, and the *mezuzah* on the doorpost that it was a Jewish home.

The little cottage consisted of a single room. Baruch's older daughter once called the rear half, which was separated from the front by an unpainted wooden cupboard, "the dark chamber," but somehow she couldn't impress this name on the family. Twice she called it "the dark chamber," but when the others remained indifferent she began to doubt the propriety of her phrase and went back to calling it, like everyone else, "the dark corner."

In such a crowded cottage a cupboard is hardly a welcome guest. Tall, proud, wholly self-assured, it stood there in the middle of the single room, without regard to the discomfort it caused every member of the family. But the cupboard was an inheritance from Baruch's parents and had to be tolerated, though secretly everyone hoped it would somehow vanish.

The oven was an even greater nuisance, a tyrant that occupied almost three-quarters of the cottage. The cupboard was its close neighbor, but it was plain that between them little love was lost: they kept staring at each other like old enemies. Only on the eve of Passover, when Tzivyeh, the mistress of the house, would whitewash the front of the oven, would it deign to look upon its neighbor with any friendliness.

How such a huge oven had managed to squeeze into such a small cottage no one knew. The cottage must have been a hundred years old, but what its former proprietor could have had in mind was still a mystery. Anyway, its present owner hadn't bought the cottage himself. Right after Baruch's wedding his father had settled him there, and there Baruch had remained for some twenty years, never troubling to learn the history of the cottage. There were more important things to do. Baruch was a man with a wife, a man with many children and little income.

Naturally, one of the biggest troubles in his household is the overcrowding. His wife, Tzivyeh, is an able housekeeper, and their older daughter is an even better one; the two of them try hard to get some order and roominess in the cottage. But no matter how hard they work they seem to accomplish very little. . . .

Not only did the crowding cause physical hardship to Baruch and his family, it also caused spiritual hardship, and indeed the spiritual was by far the greater.

Baruch, to be sure, was a poor Jew, and yet, as was fitting for a man of his origins, he was a householder. Itche Zlates, for example, was a close relative of his, and Itche was a wealthy man. Besides Itche, Baruch had many other relatives. Nor did Tzivyeh have anything to be ashamed of—her origins were also far from lowly. The two sides of the family had aunts, uncles, nephews, and nieces aplenty. And it was precisely because of these many relatives that Baruch, Tzivyeh, and their older daughter quarreled so often.

It happens, and not seldom, that Tzivyeh gives birth to a son, and naturally that's a time for celebrating—even if it's the third boy. In the cottage it's quite crowded, but for the first week the newborn baby lies near its mother and takes up little space. Even later, when it needs a crib, there is no problem. Tzivyeh has brought up all her children in hanging cribs, which take up room only in the air, forming a kind of second floor. But there is no room for the circumcision, not even for a quorum of men to hold the prayers. And, as has been mentioned, Baruch and Tzivyeh both have large families, all of whom must of course be invited.

That's when the quarreling starts. The wealthier aunts and uncles, the shining lights of the family, are the first to arrive, and even they don't come in a group, but in pairs. Baruch apologizes to them for the lack of room, and he throws complaining looks at the walls, as if to say, Stretch, you oppressors, stretch!

Still more bitter is their humiliation during the holidays, when the relatives, as is the custom, invite one another to their homes.

"Remember now," they all say to Baruch, slapping him on the back after prayer. "Don't make me coax you to come with your whole family—remember, do you hear me?"

Baruch listens and wonders. What can he do? Not go, and create ill feeling in the family? So, of course, he and his wife and their children make the rounds of the relatives. They have a sociable drink and a bite to eat, and then, when the time comes to invite them to his house, which is the polite thing to do, his tongue loses the power of speech and he can only mumble, "It would be nice to ask you to my house, but—"

"Of course, when you have a bigger house. God will help."

Baruch would like to say, "Why not now? After all, in a happy home it's never too crowded." Could there be a cleverer answer? Yet it remains in his throat, never leaving his lips no matter how hard he tries.

Forgetting to thank his relatives for their hospitality, Baruch slinks out, his family trailing behind him, and he is plagued by the feeling that he has gone not so much for the holiday as to be given a meal by a rich man who pities him. And his face burns with shame.

In this way he visits a second relative, a third, and a fourth. What else can one do?

But to accept the hospitality of his relatives every holiday and never return it is simply unthinkable to Baruch. No matter how poor he is, that low he has not fallen.

Passover, Shavuot, Hanukkah with pancakes, Purim with its delicacies—out of the question, the cottage is simply too small. But that's why there is another holiday—Sukkot. And on Sukkot, Baruch has the laugh on the whole world.

His cottage, to be sure, is the smallest on the street, but the yard next to it is the largest. Nor is there a lack of vacant space. The trick is to build, and while Baruch hasn't the means to put up a big house he can patch together a *sukkah* larger than any other. The rest of the year he may be cramped and miserable, but for these seven days he wants to live like a prince of the land. An hour of good living is worthwhile, but seven days! Think of it, seven days of comfort, when there is no need to be ashamed before one's relatives!

Right after Yom Kippur, Baruch begins to build his palace. First he sends his oldest boy to the garret, where there are four or five boards, also an inheritance from his father. Naturally, these boards wouldn't even "cover a tooth" on an ordinary *sukkah*, least of all one so huge as Baruch plans. But one must remember that Baruch is a very thrifty planner. He does not build his *sukkah* in the middle of the yard, where he would have to put up four walls; he builds it against a wall of his cottage. And since the *sukkah* must be bigger than the cottage, he attaches the few boards to his wall so that they touch his neighbor's fence, which is, fortunately, also made of boards. Thus Baruch has two walls, almost ready-made, and he now has to build only another wall and a half. Then he takes down the three storm windows from the garret, the two doors of the cupboard, and borrows the rest of the necessary materials from his neighbors, who are already familiar with his plight and lend him this and that, as they have done before. Now the *sukkah* has three-and-a-half walls and an opening for a door. The door is made not from wood but from quilts, actually two quilts, since a big *sukkah* must have a big door, and one quilt would of course not be enough.

When the shell of the *sukkah* is finished and there is no further need for man's work, the women go to it—that is, Tzivyeh and her older daughter. They sweep the ground, cover it with yellow sand, carry all the furniture from the cottage—that is, the table with the two benches and the two stools—to the *sukkah*. The cottage is empty and feels offended, and the four walls can almost be heard to murmur, Eh, fancy people! But who has time to pay attention to the cottage, when in the yard stands such a grand *sukkah*. Everybody laughs at the cottage and wants to forget that after Sukkot they'll have to return to it.

Who, indeed, when things go well, considers what will come later?

The *sukkah* is now the dwelling of the family, while the cottage serves merely as a kitchen. "As a kitchen," says Tzivyeh bitingly, "it is really quite large."

The cottage hears all this and almost bursts. The four walls think to themselves, Wait, wait, we'll settle accounts with you!

But who listens to them? Now the grand lady is the huge *sukkah*, and the relatives will come to her, not to the cottage.

And, true enough, the second day of the holiday, Baruch invites the shining lights of the two families.

"Will you see a *sukkah*!" he says to them with a proud smile. "A *sukkah*—a field! a prairie!"

"Yes, yes," say the various members of the family, "on Sukkot you are king."

The family enjoys his lavish hospitality, which Tzivyeh has prepared with their last penny, and Baruch serves everyone, his face beaming. He just can't resist the temptation to say to at least one relative, "I incline to think that my *sukkah* is bigger than yours."

The "incline," of course, is used merely out of politeness. Baruch is positive that his *sukkah* is the biggest in town. And great is his joy when the wealthiest relative says to him, in a somewhat dejected manner, "My *sukkah* is a bit of a thing. There's hardly enough room to move around."

This is the reply that Baruch remembers all year long, and it gives him the courage and the brass to accept the hospitality of his relatives on the other holidays. It's not so terrible—on Sukkot he repays them many times.

Translated by Charles Angoff[7]

❧ ❧ ❧

WINGS
LAMED SHAPIRO

author of short stories and translator of English classics into Yiddish; while most of his original writings deal with Jewish life of the past, his meticulous style was completely modern (1878–1948)

My father never built a *sukkah* for Sukkot; nevertheless, we still had a *sukkah* for the sacred festival. What's more, it was a beautiful one. All year long it was simply a plain pantry room, where one could find a sack of potatoes, a string of onions, a barrel of borscht, and other edibles. It bore not even the slightest trace of holiness, and no one ever dreamt that it served as a *sukkah*. If anyone had looked up to the ceiling, he would have seen a clever device that could convert the pantry to a *sukkah*: the ceiling was made of bars and crates. But who would glance up to the ceiling in the middle of the year? Therefore, everyone thought it was simply a pantry.

Still, each year on the day before Sukkot, the room became a *sukkah*. My older brother climbed up on the roof, fussed with something, and suddenly two big black wings opened up above the pantry. The bars were immediately covered with green boughs and thatching, the potatoes and onions vanished, a white cloth was draped over the borscht barrel, and a table, chair, and couch appeared. My father faithfully fulfilled the precept of residing in the *sukkah*— eating, drinking, and sleeping there. The entire house, usually higher than the pantry, was now lower than it. The pantry now proudly spread its wings over the house as though to say, "I'm a *sukkah*," seemingly ready to fly to the blue sky and bright sun.

One year, the first day of the festival passed without incident. The *sukkah* felt like home: we ate and slept in it; we lived there. Most importantly, the *sukkah* was privileged to hear sacred discussions concerning itself. My father and brother chewed over the laws concerning the *sukkah*—how high it may be, with what it may be covered, and many other details. The *sukkah* heard all this and no doubt thought that it could even satisfy the most pious Jew. And it was absolutely right.

But the second day brought misfortune.

From early morning a huge, dark cloud hung low and heavy over the *sukkah*, as though about to crash down on it and crush it. The wind moved the *sukkah*'s wings and they squealed softly and plaintively. Everyone in the house was vexed. Father kept looking gloomily and anxiously through the window, shaking his head.

Nevertheless, we ate lunch in the *sukkah*. We were still hopeful. But in the midst of the meal we heard some sort of noise on the roof, as if a tiny creature were scampering around on the thatching. We looked up and then silently stared at our own plates. Everyone ate quickly and quietly. A minute later one of us wiped his cheek. Then something wet and shiny splashed down into a bowl, followed by another drop, and a third. Father rose.

"It's no use! Moishe, lower the wings."

My brother stood and untied the rope that hung down from the ceiling. A creaking noise—and then with a slam something fell over our heads.

A gray workaday shadow entered, expanded and covered the entire length and breadth of the *sukkah*. The snow-white tablecloth, the silver candelabra, and the entire festival-set table looked odd and strange, like new silver embroidery on a dirty prayer shawl. Near the wall, beneath its white covering, the borscht barrel seemed to mock us, like a truculent slave humiliating his master. And, avoiding one another's glances, we swiftly slipped out of the *sukkah*.

The *sukkah* had become a pantry again.

Translated by Curt Leviant[8]

⚘ ⚘ ⚘

THE *PARNAS* IS TAUGHT A LESSON
JACOB PICARD

a native of a South German village who vividly portrayed the Jewish communal life of his birthplace in a series of legendary novelettes and stories (1883–1967)

They were both named Moishe: the proud *parnas*, Moishe Levy, with his big farm and his six daughters, of whom he had already married off three with proper dowries, two of them as far away from home as Baden—whence you may learn concerning his prosperity—and also the little man Moishele, who was so poor that people had forgotten his family name and whose age no one knew. He might have been forty or even sixty or, if you like, more. And it seemed to everyone as though he had always been around.

You may well ask why the two were called Moishe and not Maushe, as everywhere in Germany, especially in the south. Well, it is because of the dialect spoken in upper Alsace, not too far from Basle, and the name derives from the French word Moïse, which is the name of Moses, our great teacher. Yes, the scene of the story which is to be told here is in upper Alsace; it is to be the image of happy and serene days and also as a sign of the possibility of a Christian teaching a lesson to Jewish people as a rare recompense for that which our holy commandments have given them through the millennia, and how the Jews involved were grateful for the lesson and glad of the oneness and community of moral attitudes.

It was in that part of the country which was the homeland of that good and true poet Johann Peter Hebel, the same in which, on the other shore of the Rhine, there was born several centuries ago that good man and great helper of our ancestors, Jossele von Rosheim, and whence he set forth whenever it was necessary to protect his Jewish brethren anywhere in the great realm of the Germans. And the time of the story is that period of French dominance when the second Napoleon, who called himself the third, and his vain wife, Eugénie, produced turmoil in his great country, to which Alsace belonged at that time and brought trade and activity to it but also restlessness and finally the misfortune of war, as his uncle had done before him. But the Jewish people of Alsace lived very well. They culti-

35. Simhat Torah. By Reuven Rubin. 1967. Oil on canvas.

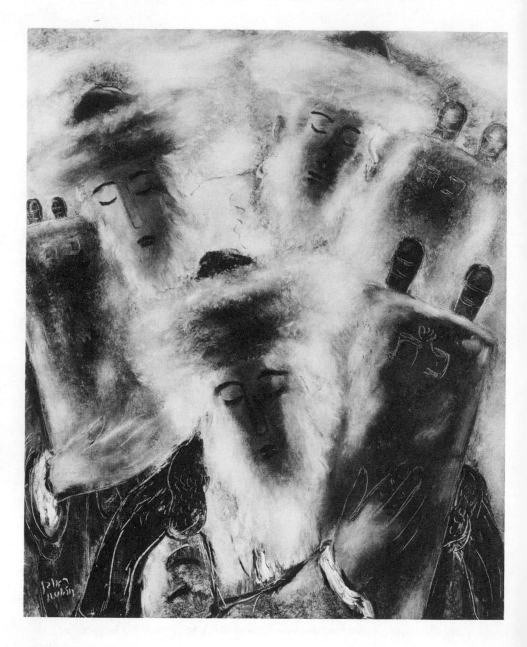

vated the land just like their fellows and had had time by virtue of many decades of peace and freedom and equality to attain prosperity. Nevertheless, though no one was in want, yet there were some who had no more than what was barely necessary, no more and also no less; and it is ever thus among us that there are those who, despite pains and industry, have no particular luck. They never truly prospered, and this applies to whole families who seem to lack luck and the favor of heaven. Thus, while most members of the *kehillah* were able annually to lay aside several hundred golden napoleons, yet there were a few who managed just to live and not to go hungry. This was the best they could do and ready money was always lacking to them. To the latter group belonged Moishele, as you may have suspected.

Ready cash? He was the village barber, the barber of the Jews. What is that? Well, to put it precisely, he was the hairdresser. But even that does not define it correctly, as must be done if the people of today are not to receive a false impression. If you imagine that he ever used a razor, you are wrong. A pious Jew and a razor—those things don't go together. So what am I telling you? Yet you must know. But if you imagine that in those days and in that village even the most honorable man in the *kehillah* employed the barber on weekdays, on ordinary weekdays, you are mistaken. Not even the *parnas* indulged in such luxury. It was on the eve of the Sabbath that this thing was done, and then only with a bent, dull pair of scissors which rattled through the thick beards of the men.

They could always see Moishele coming from afar in his wooden boots and his blue linen smock which reached down to his knees and which had two wide-open pockets on his chest from which one could see protruding the scissors and a whitish yellow comb of bone. First he went to the house of the *parnas*, Moishe Levy, and this was the little man's most important moment of the week. He seemed to himself indispensable then and was delighted when the mighty president of the congregation asked him, "Well, what is there new among the people, Moishele?" And he could answer and tell all he had heard. He always made a point of knowing something, even if he had to make it up. To come back to the practical matter, you will realize that there wasn't much ready cash involved in this service which Moishele rendered. He was, in fact, the poorest man in the *kehillah*, if you omit the two feeble-minded sisters Bloch, who, like himself, lived in the Bach alley in little one-storied huts. So he could barely buy himself garments, although those he had lasted for decades; far less could he indulge in any luxuries, not even in tobacco in order to use it, as the other did, in a clay pipe or to roll cigarettes.

One day—it was the first day of the Hol ha-Moed Sukkot—Moishele sat early in the morning on the milestone that stood in the bend of the road which led from the lower to the upper village on the way to the synagogue. It was a solid white piece of sandstone from the champagne country. He sat there in his blue smock, his hands on his knees and gazed before him. He wasn't cheerful, to be honest, under the black pointed cap which they all wore in those days. His hair fell down a little over his forehead and his gaze was absentminded. It needn't have been the good Hans Brohme, the *maire* of the village, as they call the burgomaster in that part of the country—who was placed above both Jews and Christians by the prefect and who took notice of everything, even as his office demanded—it needn't, I say, have been he. Anyone else would have turned to Moishele and asked him why he looked so miserable and downcast. But the *maire* considered it his official duty to find out what was wrong and approached the little man with mighty tread. "Well, Moishele, what ails you? What's the matter with you? You sit there as though the hail had killed your crops."

To begin with, Moishele was silent. He just sat there and looked up at the maire with melancholy eyes. After a little while he shook his head and struck his knees repeatedly with the palms of his hands.

"Well, come on! Answer me, man!" the *maire* said impatiently.

Finally the other replied.

"They didn't call me up to the Torah on the holy days, not on Rosh Hashanah and not now again on Sukkot."

"Why didn't they, Moishele? You're a Jew, the same as the others."

"That's true. But it is because I can't make a contribution for good causes, because I have no *mezuman*, like the other people, the rich ones."

"Because you have no *mezuman*! But that won't do at all! Our dear Lord doesn't care about that; what He cares about is the heart and faith. Aren't you a pious Jew?"

"That I am. But there's nothing you can do about it."

The *maire* reflected briefly.

"Oh yes, there is something to be done about it. Let me see to it.

And don't tell anybody that I know. Are there any more days of *yom tov?*"

And Moishele with a dazed look at the *maire* told him that on the next Thursday it would be Shemini Atzeret and the following day Simhat Torah. And the *maire,* who was a peasant, had a pretty good idea of this festival and its meaning, because for nearly a week now the booths had been standing in front of the Jewish houses, covered with foliage and adorned within by the fruits of the harvest. He patted the shoulder of Moishele, who had risen, and said, "Have patience, Moishele, we'll attend to that!"

And he went on his way.

Now came the penultimate day of the festival and next that happy day on which we rejoice in the Law and hopefully seek to forget all evil. From all the streets men and women walked to the *shul* that morning. So, also, Moishe Levy, the *parnas.* He wore a broad-brimmed gray top hat, which grew narrower at the peak, the black coat with the high collar that reached almost to his ears behind, and the trousers checked in gray and black. It was the Parisian fashion before the last. The top hat he had recently bought in Strasbourg when his daughter, who knew how to manage horses, had driven him there for the purpose of selling his wheat in the big city. Next to him strode his wife, Henriette, a member of the Bloch family in Gebweiler, known to everyone in the land, with her distinguished, broad East Indian shawl over her shoulders, which was held together by a great brooch of twisted gold woven like a bird's nest, and from under whose wig hung down the appropriate earrings of blue enamel on gold like handsome heavy fruits. And the others were clad, even as these were, in more or less sumptuous garments. They were all in a happy mood. And it seemed to the men as though they were still carrying the festive *lulav* with the green willow wands from the edges of their own brooks, as well as the rare *etrogim* in their silver bowls. For there had been a rich harvest this year, which was equally favorable for trade. The grapes had had enough sun as well as rain at the proper time, so that the clusters had become sweet all over the land and as far as Baden; the ears of the wheat had been fuller than for long, and the maize and hops had been rich. On the slopes of the nearby hills the foliage was still green, and as far as eye could reach were the pines and fir trees on the dark summits of the Vosges Mountains. Moishele the barber also had donned his holiday garment, which wasn't even of the fashion before the last.

In happy mood they stood between the pews of the *shul*. And who can describe their amazement when suddenly—the *hazzan*, Shloime Ruef, had just begun to intone the prayer—they saw a strange and yet familiar figure enter the House of God with their own people. Unquestionably, it was Hans Brohme; it was the *maire*. For a moment they were of two minds, hesitating between the scruple of a Christian in the house of the one and only God—a thing much rarer in those days in the country than in the cities, although Christians and Jews were not ill-informed concerning each other's customs—and, on the other hand, their satisfaction in that the *maire* considered it important to stand with them before God on an important holiday. In the end their pleasure in the community of faith overcame their scruples. They smiled and nodded to him, especially his friend Moishe Levy who was, next to him, the most important man of the community. And, as they observed, Hans Brohme, too, was festively attired and, moreover, had about his neck the silver chain of his office and in the buttonhole of his black morning coat the gleaming red ribbon of the Légion d'Honneur.

Had anyone ever heard of such a thing? In no other village, in no other country was that possible. Only among them, where all men lived in peace with each other. And how tactful, how significant it was that for this sign of goodwill the *maire* had chosen precisely the feast of Simhat Torah. They were not likely to forget this.

The service proceeded. Brohme stood with a serious and even solemn expression near the door, while the Jewish men about him, led by the *hazzan*, sang the old holy prayers with such fervor that he, too, was moved.

Then the Torah Scrolls were lifted from the ark in their white silk coverings and were carried about the synagogue with the ringing of bells and with singing and finally there began the reading of the Scripture portion of the day. The first one called to the Torah was naturally Moishe Levy. Slowly and loudly he sang the blessing, as one had not heard it done for a long time, as though it were a question of showing their friend and through him the whole of Christendom how the Jews here in this village, and indeed everywhere, praised the greatness of God. Already the rich *parnas* had named his contributions: five livres for the *hevrah kaddisha* and five livres for this and five livres for that, so that they all looked at each other and nodded at each other because they had so generous a *parnas*. Already the *hazzan* was calling, "*Yaamod sheni*," and the latter, the second one called up, was the fat Jacques Brunshwig with his little black Napoleonic beard, who was the second most powerful member of the *kehillah,* needless to say. He was already on his way to the *almemar,* when a sudden voice arose.

"Why don't you call up Moishele? Moishele must be called up. I'll contribute for him. He can contribute today as much as Moishe the *parnas.*"

It was the *maire.* No doubt about that. Consternation seized upon them all. So that was why he had come. First they hardly knew how to treat this unheard-of and painful situation, that someone interfered in the accustomed course of their service. They didn't even at that moment consider whether it was a sin which was being committed here. But they would not have had the best and best respected *parnas* in the whole of upper Alsace if he hadn't found a way out. Swiftly he went up to Jacques Brunshwig, who was about to intone the blessing, conferred in whispers with him and next with the *hazzan,* Shloime Ruef, whereupon the former left the *almemar* with a smile and returned to his seat, while the latter, commissioned by the *parnas,* hastened to the good Moishele and whispered to him.

He had probably been the only one in the synagogue who had been morally uncomfortable during the incident, at least so soon as he felt that what was taking place here concerned him. Indeed, a feeling of guilt came over him.

But immediately the voice of the *hazzan* rose again and cried, "*Yaamod sheni.*"

Nevertheless, after a moment of hesitation, Moishele, finally not without pride, walked up to the consecrated Scroll and spoke—no, sang—clearly and without a trembling of the voice, the blessing as he had probably not sung it since his own *bar mitzvah.* And the whole congregation perceived the special quality of the moment and were delighted with the experience which had been given them.

Was it because, in the person of Moishele, Hans Brohme had in a sense been called to the Torah, one of the other faith and in him, too, the prefect of the region and thus the whole government, including the Emperor Napoleon in Paris? Or was it that they received a satisfaction from this particular Simhat Torah because a Christian friend had taught them a lesson which they were bound to remember, that the value of a man was not to be gauged by his ability to contribute for causes, however good, but by the sanctity of his will, by his being a pious and honorable man who did well his day's work, however humble it may be?

We would like to believe that both motivations were active.

What is certain is that, in the succeeding years on Simhat Torah, it was always the poorest man in the *kehillah* who was called third to the Torah, after a *Kohen* and a *Levi*. The *mitzvah* was bought for him by one of the rich men. But neither the name of the latter nor the amount of his contribution was ever revealed. Such was the fruit of the lesson which the *parnas*, Moishe Levy, learned for himself and for the others and which was motivated by poor Moishele. For, when at the end of the service, the *parnas*, with his wife between himself and the *maire*, had proceeded on his way home and they had shaken hands all around, he had promised himself never to forget the lesson he had received.

Translated by Ludwig Lewisohn[9]

✻ ✻ ✻

SIMHAT TORAH
JOSEPH OPATOSHU

one of the major Yiddish literati of this century, having contributed several historical novels and hundreds of short stories and sketches of Jewish life; two of his novels and many stories have been translated into English (1887–1954)

The golden days set in, the season of the festival of Simhat Torah, when the sun warms but does not scorch, and wild geese rise aloft in the autumn haze to fly honking to warmer lands.

Simhat Torah.

In the small Gerer synagogue where ten-year-old Joseph worshiped with his father, the *Hasidim* formed in groups after the Simhat Torah festive meal and left to gladden their hearts with wine. Those who had rich kinfolk washed down roast geese and duck in foreign wines. Those who were keen of mind visited the homes of the most influential and eldest of the *Hasidim*, where, between one melody and the next, between one dance and the next, there were learned discussions in the style of the *rebbe*.

Only Joseph's father, David, a tall man in his late twenties, remained at home. Though David worshiped in the Hasidic synagogue, he had no dealings with the *Hasidim*—nor they with him. Under their breath they insisted that David was a covert rationalist, who ought to be expelled from the synagogue. But they did not expel him. This was not because David was a man of learning, somewhat of a cabalist, to whom one appealed for help in interpreting a particularly difficult teaching of Hasidism from the school of Pszisha or Kotsk. Rather, what was important was that David's grandfather, Master Favesh Shraga, had supported Rabbi Mendel Tomashover, and that David's father, Master Israel Leizer, an old adherent of the rabbi of Kotsk and one of the first followers of the rabbi of Ger, was highly respected by the learned author of the *Sefat Emet*. Who would wish to bring shame upon Master Israel Leizer, lay his soul desolate, and shatter his heart?

David sat at a table strewn with holy volumes. He had just finished the last reading in the Book of Deuteronomy, which begins with the verse "This is the blessing wherewith Moses blessed the children of Israel" and had immediately gone on to the first reading in Genesis: "In the beginning God created." Now it occurred to him that the death of Moses was not really the end; it was a new beginning, it was Genesis.

This thought pulled him out of his chair. Thrusting a thumb under his sash, he paced the room, humming the tune of the hymn beginning, "Bridegroom of Genesis," which he had just been teaching his ten-year-old son, Joseph. David had a curly blond beard. His green eyes, the shade of water plants, were hazy. There was such a melancholy in his pacing and humming that if someone had rapped on the windowpane—"David, what are you doing at home on Simhat Torah? Come, and rejoice with us!"—he would not have hesitated a second, but would have gone out immediately.

Ten-year-old Joseph sat at the window. The boy was unhappy, pained because his father was so strict. Weekdays, early in the morning when it was still dark, Father was already studying. Business came after prayer. On the Sabbath and holidays, Father sat over the holy volume night and day. No one from the little synagogue ever came to visit him, nor did he go to visit them.

Joseph looked out the window—not a friend was in sight. They had all gone out with their fathers. Every now and then snatches of a lively tune issued from the wide courtyard where the wagoners sat in "Big-Bones'" tavern, singing, "Whatever we may do, Jews is what we are."

The boy was fascinated by the singing. The words called to him, "Even the wagoners are enjoying Simhat Torah. They are sitting at table over glasses of beer and platters of fruit, while your father stays all alone, humming, as though he were not a proper Jew."

The father sensed his son's unhappiness and took him by the chin.

"What are you doing sitting at home, Joseph? Why don't you go out into the street for a while?"

"Where am I to go?" the boy burst forth. "Everybody else is with his father—but you always sit at home, even on Simhat Torah."

David felt guilty. He smiled and said, "Very well. Do you want to go out? Come now, we'll go somewhere together!"

The lump in Joseph's throat melted. Delighted, he touched all the objects on the ledge of the open window. Seeing the *etrog* case, he remembered that the children would be making torches tonight, and he pulled out the hemp.

A company of the older children who were too grown-up to carry flags like the small fry gathered in the synagogue courtyard. One boy held a hollow turnip that had been stuffed with hemp. He soaked the hemp in kerosene, then waved the turnip like a torch. Sparks flashed here and there as other boys set fire to wax candles with spurts from bottles of kerosene. Still other boys sprinkled the tips of broken matches on burning candles, then blew until the match heads lit up with a crackle, like Bengal lights.

The tumult in the courtyard increased. Elderly *Hasidim* danced in a circle, their sashes around their hips. Younger men whirled, their sashes flying, as the song pealed to the sky:

"Although, although, although Israel is desolated
Still, still, still. . . ."

Rising above the fires, the singing expelled the melancholy that autumn, harbinger of the coming winter, had laid upon the shoulders of Jews. Carried away by the lights and singing, Joseph forgot all about his father, who accompanied several *Hasidim* to Master Bunem's wine cellar. The latter was a great-grandson of the preacher of Koszhnitz, and so thin with constant fasting that he was nicknamed "the Last Breath."

A group of *Hasidim* were going from one synagogue to another. They stood in the middle of the courtyard, and soon a new melody interrupted the first. Other *Hasidim* joined in; legs wove a dance:

"Ah, ah, ah,
With Thy commandments, sanctify us."

At Master Bunem the winemaker's there was much drinking and talking of Torah. There was also a tacit agreement to make that personage David drunk, so as to discover once and for all whether the silent one was really a heretic. After his second glass of mead mixed with whiskey and beer, David could no longer keep his chair, and stretched out on a sofa.

Samuel-David the slaughterer, one of the most respected *Hasidim* of Ger, whose preparations for prayer took twice or three times as long as the prayer itself, went over to David.

"Well, young man, what do you think? Was the Torah revealed on Mount Sinai?"

"On Mount Sinai." Hazily, David gathered what was happening and murmured, "Although, although, although . . ."

"The lad is in his cups," someone cried.

"Go away, let me alone." Samuel-David the slaughterer would allow no one to come near. "What has happened to you? Your grandfather, God rest his soul, was close to the court of Kotsk, your father is one of the household of the author of *Sefat-Emet*—and you David, why are you never to be seen in Ger?"

"Although, although, although." David screwed up his eyes and mumbled into the sofa.

Joseph entered. He saw his father, pale-faced, and was terrified. "What's the matter, Father? Aren't you feeling well?"

"He'll sleep it off, nothing will happen to him."

"It doesn't matter, today is Simhat Torah!"

David opened his eyes, and gave Joseph a lost, apologetic look. "It's all for your sake, my son."

Suddenly David rose from the sofa. Laying both hands on his son's narrow shoulders, he stammered, "Listen, Joseph, they think I'm drunk. You know, son, they wanted to put me over the barrel, thinking when wine comes in, the secret comes out. Well, what are you standing here for, Joseph?" He began to clap his hands. "Today is Simhat Torah. We have finished 'And Moses died there,' and now we must begin from the beginning all over again with Genesis. Sing Joseph, sing, boy.

"And still another virtue
Hath Thy people Israel."

Joseph could not look at his father, was unable to understand what had happened. His father—usually so quiet, so reserved, never agitated—now all at once this way! Could they have made him drunk? The boy could have thrown himself at the *Hasidim* who were standing around making fun of his father.

The cloud that had hung over David, the melancholy that had been lifted by the wine, flooded his brain again. His tall body tottered; he looked so pitifully sad that the boy burst into tears.

"Come, Father, come home."

Ten-year-old Joseph led his father home. And in the cool, dark Simhat Torah night a hoarse voice kept insisting:

"And oh, another virtue,
Still another virtue,
Hath Thy people Israel.
Oh, oh, oh. . . ."

Translated by Jacob Sloan[10]

❦ ❦ ❦

TWO LEGACIES

MYER JACK LANDA

British Jewish author of short stories and, in collaboration with his wife, of novels and plays; also served as editor of the Jewish World
(1874–1947)

"Shebeens and sheenies!"

An interpolation by the lawyer, quoting his quondam client. The harsh inelegance of the alliteration, contemptuous and complementary in its implication, jarred on the supersensitive soul of Mr. Septimus Lovelace. He was in a terrible quandary. His fleshy outer casing was already seared, tingling under the damning revelation that the "expectations," long awaited, from his uncle—just interred but not lamented—were tied up in brewery shares and slum property inhabited by Jews! Two topics that had drawn frothy anathema from him for years. His patience cracked.

"You quoted my uncle with relish," he snapped.

36. "Rejoicing on Simhat Torah." By Mark Chagall. See Chapter 9.

"You meant to say 'sauce,'" returned the lawyer, pointedly.

Mr. Lovelace gazed blankly at the solicitor, who had paused in his reading of the eagerly awaited document. He detected an unholy gleam in the legal eye bent on him.

"Well, it's—er—awkward, for me," he managed to gasp.

"Your uncle," murmured the lawyer, in his most professional tone, "was a shrewd businessman. Invested his money with acumen. He used to say Cohens and cocktails were certain coin collectors."

Lovelace exploded.

"Drop that impious irrelevance," he growled, irritably. "I could rattle off that sort of expression, if I so forgot myself as to descend to vulgarity."

"As for instance," returned the solicitor, sceptical and provocative.

"Levites and licensed libertines, if you will have it," hissed Mr. Lovelace, red with indignation and shame at his inability to resist the serpent. Joyous, however, to relieve himself of a phrase which had taken some compilation in many difficult efforts to imitate his uncle's coarse felicity.

The lawyer beamed approval. It meant business to see men in that mood.

"Of course," proceeded Mr. Lovelace pontifically, "when I enter into this inheritance, I can dispose of these properties—transfer the money to—er—more reasonable—that is, legitimate—I mean, more worthy enterprises."

"Wait," commented the lawyer, with something like a chuckle. "Let me conclude the reading of the will."

And to the legatee's horror he proceeded to recite, with extreme unction, a clause which intimated that no attempt must be made to dispose of either the shares or property within ten years!

A thunderbolt could not have had a more stunning effect than this edict upon Mr. Lovelace. He seemed to have been suddenly surrounded by a horde of grinning brewers and jeering Jews. His uncle had detested his views, he knew, and had thus planned a post-humous, fiendish revenge. He groaned, he fumed. In his heart, he cursed. Almost on his lips were words of rank blasphemy.

"What do you advise?" he asked, appealing helplessly.

"Grin and bear it," was the heartless reply.

"I don't see why I should grin," exclaimed Lovelace, fiercely.

"There's no compulsion," returned the lawyer, imperturbably. "It's not in the bond," he supplemented, purporting to examine the will closely.

That was a deliberate turning of the blade of Lovelace's own knife against him—an application of one of his pet platform phrases. He winced.

"It's a wanton insistence of the dead hand," he tiraded. "Can't the courts be induced to set it aside?" It was a cry from the depths of an agonized soul.

"My profession," answered the lawyer, with solemn gravity, "will pass you a hearty vote of thanks if you decide to contest the condition. It will be profitable—to us."

"It's—it's intolerable wickedness on the part of the old—scou—. I mean, he meant to humiliate me, to hound me out of the public position I have gained for myself as a temperance advocate—"

"And as a rabid Jew-hater," added the lawyer, quietly. "I daresay you have guessed right. He—ahem!—as you correctly suspect, despised your views, thought them hypocritical, assumed as the only avenue to notoriety possible to a man of your extreme opinions."

Mr. Lovelace shuddered. He pulled himself together.

"Of course," he sneered, "a worldly minded materialist like my uncle could not appreciate sincere, righteous motives."

"He called it downright humbug," pursued the lawyer.

"Stop," screamed the luckless heir. "How dare you talk to me in that insulting fashion?"

"I am using language less strong than you have done of your uncle, who has been exceedingly generous." The lawyer's tone gave the impression that he was thoroughly enjoying the spectacle of Mr. Lovelace in the toils and increasing the constriction. "Your uncle was my friend, as well as my client. He knew you—through and through."

Mr. Lovelace squirmed.

"Go on," he muttered. "I must bear my cross."

"Yes," murmured the lawyer, drily, "your uncle predicted that you would use those words. I had my instructions to convey his opinion of you, with his profound compliments."

That staggered Mr. Lovelace; completely sobered his intemperate spirit for a moment. His uncle was astute to devise these pinpricks from the grave.

"Didn't it occur to you," he said, acidly, attempting the superciliously reproachful strain, "that it was a gross iniquity?"

"None of my business."

"And you connived, I see. You are taking a positive delight in rubbing in my uncle's contempt."

The lawyer rose.

"Mr. Lovelace," he said, with ominous quietness, "I am neither a Jew nor a publican. I don't propose to put up with your cant, nor to turn the other cheek. Your uncle's business was profitable to me; I collected his rents. But I decline to serve you. Candidly, I cannot afford the risk of losing my Jewish clients. Nor have I the least desire to insult them."

Mr. Lovelace collapsed. He apologized profusely, sought sympathy.

"It's a bitter pill," he whined.

"A well-gilded dose," was the brutal rejoinder.

"But," with some effort at hauteur, "Midas long ago discovered that gold was indigestible."

"And Midas had asses' ears," concluded the lawyer, scornful of the specious display of classical knowledge.

Mr. Lovelace walked out into the wilderness. A world of sharp unsparing thorns. Public obloquy. Unanimous glee at his discomfiture. His long serial dream, during his hard struggles in a small business, and his overzealous labors to gain publicity, had ended in a wild nightmare. He had conjured up visions of the day when he would be free from financial worries, when his name would be in all men's mouths. But he had not anticipated such a gross travesty. It was a cruel joke on the part of fickle fortune.

"Ought to give up the legacy, if he's honest." That summed up the hints and innuendoes.

He had wrestled with the wickedly generous angel—and had been worsted, as a public remark, obviously intended for his overhearing, had affirmed would be the case. He was incapable of the strength to repudiate the heritage. Oh, yes, he was fain to confess—to himself, at any rate—that his critics and detractors had a gorgeous banquet of his cooked-up phrases. It was so easy to fling them all back at him. And how he suffered! Plangent night thoughts robbed him of sleep. They ebbed and flowed through the day. He saw a tidal wave of reproof in every public frown. There was a weird, diabolical playfulness in the trick of fate. It was the brewery that was most discussed in public, but it was the Jewish tenantry who haunted him mainly in the secrecy of his own despair.

Vivid in his memory was the idyllic picture he had drawn of himself as a landlord. It was the height of his ambition, the supreme mundane happiness, to his thinking, to go round each Monday morning to collect his rents. To be hailed as "the landlord" had been his most ardent longing.

What a fiasco was the realization! The furtive looks of his tenants, their ill-concealed loathing—they called him "Haman," he knew— and yet their calm confidence in their power to resist him was galling. He could forgive the brewers and the publicans. They were but the victims of historic, albeit misguided, human habits—if you looked at it closely. But the Jews! To his overwrought fanaticism, they were Satan's appointed myrmidons of evil and God's chosen scapegoats. And, despite his fulminations, his threats, his warnings, they did not fear him! Under his own roof! His one effort to impress his importance on them was a ludicrous failure. He had tried it on a meek-looking woman. She had listened patiently. Had then yawned.

"I am afraid," he said, with a simulation of dignity, "that you do not show a proper respect to me—your landlord."

"Where does it say in the English law that you must show respect to a landlord?" she had replied, with the ghetto habit of putting questions.

To be snubbed by a Jewess! To have the English law calmly expounded to him from Semitic lips! She had intimated, too, that his Jewish tenants would remain law-abiding—and defy him. It maddened him.

His hatred quickened. He swore unto himself a violent rather than sacred oath that he would seize the first opportunity to make the Jews suffer. Yea, he would persecute. He did not flinch. Had he not historic warrant? Curious how he appealed to history—in the solitude of his own ignorance. His first fierce impulse was to evict his Jewish tenants —after due notice, naturally. But he speedily learned, to his dismay, that the consequences would be queer. And to himself disastrous.

Once the area had been thief-infested, criminal, insanitary, a plague spot. The Jews had driven out the jailbirds, had transformed an underworld. The facts were on record in the reports of the police and the medical officer of health. The Jews were the one sure safeguard against a relapse of the neighborhood!

"There's something wrong with destiny," he moaned. "It's got bitten with the modern craze. It's jazzing. Here am I, devoting my life to unselfish service and everything goes wrong, while my uncle, the reprobate, is actually made to appear a public benefactor!"

He plunged into dejection, brooded, planned, schemed. Fed his bigotry on the cankered fruits of disappointment. It flourished like a foul weed in the forcing house of his miasmic stupidity. It was his ghoulish delight to inflict pain by his weekly visitation to the ghetto. Besides, it saved the fees of an agent.

And thus it came to pass that one Monday morning a strange sight met his gaze. Startling! Surely the hateful Jews were meditating the destruction of his property. So blatantly, so impudently. Actually with laughter!

They had collected timber and straw in all the back yards. Were piling them into sinister-looking structures. Dry inflammable material. Incipient bonfires! Monstrous!

He asked no questions. He acted on intuition. Precipitantly. He prided himself on promptness.

"Take these things down," he commanded, sternly.

"Why?"

"Because I, the landlord, order you," he screamed, infuriated by their irrepressible questioning habit.

They refused. They shrugged their shoulders. They offered no explanations. Ignored his presence. Went on with their mysterious labors.

He rushed off to a lawyer. Dashed from there to a magistrate. Would have swooped down on the police had he not been prevented. In his frenzy he would have had all his Jewish tenants immediately arrested. But the English law was so obtuse, so slothful—"subsidized by the Jews," he had once dared to assert. Here was proof!

He writhed under the official delay, but summonses had to be served and it was the third day before his peremptory demand for punishment was heard in the magistrate's court. The Jews were there in festive finery. They were beyond understanding. Not a scrap of fear did they betray. Not a sign of alarm. They were animated and happy.

But grasping tightly a copy of the terms of tenancy, he was sure.

"Even," as his lawyer put it—rather mildly, he thought—"if there is no incendiary intent, the material is highly inflammable, and the conditions expressly prohibit the erection of out-houses or structures of any kind, temporary or permanent, without the permission of the landlord."

A Jewish lawyer put the case for the tenants. He, too, had the ghetto habit of asking questions.

"Has my friend ever heard of the Feast of Tabernacles?" he inquired.

"What has that got to do with it?" asked Lovelace's lawyer.

"Rather a good deal," was the reply, and he launched into a disquisition on the Mosaic ordinance to build booths in remembrance of the shelters in the wilderness, and the modern interpretation that the structures were probably the old harvest homes of Israel. Perhaps the magistrate knew something about it.

"Oh, yes," was the response from the Bench. "I know all about the practice of the Jews celebrating Tabernacles, the harvest festival, by setting up wooden booths with straw roofs in gardens and back yards, and taking their meals in them.

"A quaint idea," he added, "but I believe Disraeli has elaborated it beautifully by saying that a race that persists in celebrating their vintage, although they have no fruits to gather, will regain their vineyards."

"Yes, in *Tancred*," corroborated the Jewish lawyer.

"Don't you know of the Jewish Festival of Tabernacles and its customs?" the magistrate asked Mr. Lovelace. There was a note of pitying censure in the question.

"I know nothing of vintages and modern tabernacles," answered the landlord stiffly.

"Strange, isn't it," commented the Jewish lawyer—again that exasperating ghetto peculiarity—"for one who is well known as a heavy holder of liquor shares and has only Jewish tenants?"

Mr. Lovelace could only glare, speechless.

"But—but the covenant of the tenancies," pleaded his advocate, desperately. "More important, at the moment, I submit, than the scriptural covenant applicable to Palestine centuries ago."

"Ah, yes," returned the magistrate suavely, "since you insist on that, I cannot overlook it. Seeing that the tenants have hitherto enjoyed the privilege of erecting these booths unmolested, Mr. Lovelace has, in the opinion of the Bench, acted arbitrarily, even foolishly, and has unnecessarily disturbed these inoffensive people in the practice of their religion, in what is an ancient and picturesque custom that preserves tradition and brings romance into their dull lives. It does no harm and has some value.

"But the tenants have committed a technical breach of their agreements, and the court must mark its sense of that infraction, without, however, mulcting them in costs. The decision of the Bench is that these structures must be removed within seven days."

Then a strange thing happened. The Jews tittered, swelled the cachinnation into a roar of laughter, then stood up and cheered lustily. They were turned out of court, but to Mr. Lovelace's utter bewilderment, they were inordinately cheerful. Their demeanor denoted triumph. What a singular and stubborn people! When he had just succeeded in having them publicly admonished and in asserting his power as landlord!

But the evening papers enlightened him. Made merry at his expense by pointing out that the magistrate was evidently aware that the festival would be over in seven days!

Many a non-Jewish visitor was entertained in the back yard

tabernacles that joyous, permissive week. The wise cadi was freely toasted in beverages from which Mr. Lovelace drew his dividends, and the final day of the festival, which coincided with the magisterial limit, was never more aptly celebrated as the Rejoicing of the Law.

Two legacies—and that of Lovelace, with public approval, was made to conform with that of Leviticus![11]

❧ ❧ ❧

WHOSE SUKKAH?

ABRAHAM SOYER

faculty member of Yeshiva University Teachers Institute for many years; wrote numerous short stories in Hebrew, both for adults and children (1868–1940)

Reb Samson was truly appreciative of life.

Every single moment of living was precious to him, and he tried hard not to waste it.

He used to say, "The Holy One, blessed be He, wanted to benefit His people, so He gave them this world, which is as full of opportunities for *mitzvot* [good deeds] as a pomegranate is full of seeds. At every step there are oodles of *mitzvot* which can be performed with all of our 248 organs and 365 sinews. As a matter of fact, with every motion, with every sigh, with every nod and glance we can do a *mitzvah*.

"The moment you look at the sunshine, at the blue sky, at the constant renewal of creation, and you exclaim, 'How numerous are Thy deeds, O Lord!' you have already performed a *mitzvah*. As you walk along idly, apparently not doing anything, just looking around, noticing a beautiful field, a row of pretty flowers, newly ripened fruits, a forest, a hill, a flower-strewn valley, a swift stream, a bird flying, a butterfly fluttering, a fly humming—as your eyes light up with joy and your lips open involuntarily to celebrate all this beauty and glory and you express your gratitude to the Creator of all, again you have performed a *mitzvah*!"

Reb Samson was especially fond of the practical commandments, of those which involve physical activity. "The spiritual *mitzvot*," he would say, "are reserved for angels and saints! We simple humans are concerned with the active *mitzvot*: sharing a ritual meal, eating the unleavened bread, blowing the *shofar*, waving the *lulav*." But his favorite *mitzvah* was building the *sukkah*.

"The *sukkah* is a *mitzvah* . . . a *mitzvah*"—and he would grow silent for a moment in search of the proper description—"a *mitzvah* that envelops you completely. You are entirely wrapped up in it! The space that surrounds you, the very air that you breathe—they are part of the *mitzvah*!"

Reb Samson would begin to busy himself with his *sukkah* the day before Yom Kippur. His *sukkah* was built of storm windows. There was a special reason for this. "This beautiful *mitzvah*, which surrounds me on all sides, must not separate me from the world of the Holy One, blessed be He. . . ."

"When I sit in the *sukkah* I must gaze at His beautiful world, at the sky, at the sun, at the birds and butterflies and flies—I must see everything." That was why he made the walls of storm windows. "My *sukkah* is a showcase," he would say; "in my *sukkah* I both see and am seen."

But since he owned three little storm windows (there were only three windows in his house), he needed help. He would borrow a window here and a window there until he had enough for his walls. On the day before Yom Kippur, as he made the rounds among his friends and neighbors to wish them a good year and to beg their forgiveness according to custom, he would ask in passing for a window or two. On this day all hearts are softened—and no one could refuse him. . . .

Immediately after the blessing for the moon at the conclusion of Yom Kippur, he hurried home, briefly greeted his family, recited the *Havdalah*—and soon he stood on his little courtyard not far from the tall birch, now in its autumnal dress, head dropping, bending to every breeze, and dropping, one by one, its yellow, withered leaves. Near the birch he stuck a peg into the ground—the beginning of the *sukkah*.

The following morning Reb Samson was fully occupied. He cleared the ground, put up poles, ran from neighbor to neighbor carrying storm windows, his face flushed, all smiles, eyes gleaming, sparkling, his bones trembling with a deep inner joy.

The next day the *sukkah* was completely finished and decorated.

All the beautiful dishes and furniture that he possessed were brought into the *sukkah*. It was now his very own "thing of beauty." All the boys in town came to see the "clouds of glory" he made out of paper, the pomegranates and apples and birds he fashioned out of wax and hollow eggshells—an art that only Reb Samson had mastered.

On Hoshana Rabbah my grandfather, accompanied by the town's elders and scholars, would visit Reb Samson, sit in his *sukkah*, and observe everything with delight. Reb Samson served them himself. He carefully set on the table a bottle of his special wine—raisin wine, preserved since the previous Passover for this occasion. This wine was made by Reb Samson from his personal recipe, and tasted—according to all his guests—of paradise itself. Deborah, his wife, a saintly and charming woman, brought in pancakes fried in chicken fat. This fat was rendered from a chicken which she had bought right after Tishah be-Av and fattened up for these honored guests. Now they were drinking the wine and praising it, eating the pancakes and extolling them, and Reb Samson was full of happiness and delight, his eyes sparkling and all his bodily organs expressing his joy.

"Sir," he observed to my grandfather, "if my little tabernacle may be called beautiful, how much more beautiful is the divine Tabernacle of Peace!"

"Spread over us," one of the guests would begin, intoning the melody made popular by Reb Avigdor, Grandfather's cantor, and the rest would chime in, "the tabernacle of Thy peace, O Lord!"

Reb Samson would grow excited, his soul yearning for tenderness and holiness, and with eyes and voice raised aloft, he would sing out, "Once more, my friends, 'Spread over us, heavenly Father, the tabernacle of Thy peace!'"

As the guests emerged from the *sukkah* they would wish him an even more beautiful *sukkah* the following year. And Reb Samson was delighted with the wish because the *sukkah* never quite measured up to his standards. The windows were of different sizes—large and small, wide and narrow—and there were never enough for all the walls, so he pieced them together with boards and shelves. This troubled him, and he longed for a really complete *sukkah*.

Once, as the guests were leaving and wishing him, as usual, a beautiful and complete *sukkah*, Reb Samson smiled and said that their blessing had already come true and he hoped that the following year he would have a really beautiful *sukkah*. His erstwhile pupil, Yehiel the son of Hannah, who was building a large new house, had offered him just before Yom Kippur the windows of his old house, more than a dozen large and beautiful windows.

And, to tell the truth, those who did not see Reb Samson's new *sukkah* have never beheld a beautiful structure: it was long and wide, the windows uniform in size, the panes gleaming brightly. In the daytime it was bathed in sunlight and at night, after Deborah had lit her seven candles and his married daughter—who, with her husband, took her meals with him—kindled her three, the *sukkah* shone like a beacon of light. Reb Samson would recite the *Kiddush* with a beaming face, illumination within illumination. . . .

But this *sukkah* did not last even the seven days of the holiday; on the eve of Hoshana Rabbah it was gone.

And this is how it came about.

That night Reb Samson went to the synagogue as usual to recite the psalms and the midnight prayers. All night until daybreak, he stayed in the synagogue. At dawn he performed his ablutions and read his prayers with the first *minyan*. Then he studied several chapters of *Eyn Yaakov* and the Mishnah. When he came home he found his *sukkah* completely destroyed—not a single window was left, not a single pole was in place; everything was in ruins.

On Hoshana Rabbah a fair was held in our town. From all the neighboring towns and villages the peasants gathered with their horses and wagons, and during the night a number of them, passing by Reb Samson's *sukkah*, thought it would be great fun to throw stones and to break all the windowpanes.

Once Esau starts destroying, he is not satisfied until destruction is complete. After smashing the window panes, they broke the windows and pulled up the poles until only a heap of splinters and bits of glass were left. This act of barbarism frightened all the Jews in town, who thought that a pogrom was in the making. When it was discovered that the peasants were sated with their destruction of the *sukkah*, they all breathed a sign of relief, although everyone was sorry that the beautiful *sukkah* was gone together with Reb Samson's holiday joy.

Grandfather did not know what to do; it had been his habit to visit Reb Samson's *sukkah* on Hoshana Rabbah. His friends came to consult him—Samuel "the dreamer," Jacob who used to recite enthusiastically the blessing "who has not made me a heathen," Joshua "the greedy"—but no one had an idea what to do.

As they were conversing, the door opened and Reb Samson

entered. In one hand he held a bottle of his special wine and in the other a trayful of fried pancakes, and his face shone with joy as if some great miracle had befallen him or he had won a fortune.

"Gentlemen," he said, "here are the goodies that I prepared in your honor. Let's eat in celebration of the holiday in the rabbi's *sukkah*."

Reb Samson sat down near Grandfather and the guests recited the blessings, drank, and ate.

Reb Samson was so happy that he actually trembled with delight and his face was surrounded by a halo of joy.

At first the *sukkah* was not even mentioned; they all wanted to spare his feelings. But when Grandfather saw how happy he was, he could not restrain himself. "Tell us, Reb Samson, what are you so happy about?"

"My dear rabbi," Reb Samson replied happily, "whose *sukkah*

37. "The Rejoicing of the Law." By Solomon Alexander Hart (1806–1881). Oil on canvas. Interior of synagogue at Livorno. See Chapter 9.

was destroyed? Was it the divine *Sukkah,* the tabernacle of God's peace? Why should I grieve for my poor little *sukkah* when His tabernacle is complete and fully equipped and no one in the world can harm it. Let's not talk about my *sukkah.* Let's have another drink, gentlemen, of my special wine and another taste of my pancakes. Today is God's festival!"

They refilled their glasses, wished one another life and happiness, and, above all, wished that Reb Samson would merit the building of his *sukkah* the following year in Jerusalem.

"Spread over us," began one of the guests, and soon he was joined by the others, their voices uniting in a tune of melody and warmth until it filled the *sukkah,* filled every corner. And after each pause could be heard Reb Samson's voice intoning; "Again, my friends: 'Lord of the Universe! Spread over us the tabernacle of Thy peace, Thy peace!'"

Translated by Solomon Feffer[12]

🌿 16 🌿

SUKKOT AND SIMHAT TORAH MISCELLANY

🌿 🌿 🌿

THE NOMENCLATURE OF
THE FESTIVAL

The Bible records several names for the Sukkot festival: *Hag ha-Sukkot*, the Festival of Tabernacles or Booths (Leviticus 23.34); *Hag ha-Asif*, Festival of the Ingathering (Exodus 23.16); *Hag Adoshem*, Festival of the Lord (Leviticus 23.39), and *Ha-Hag*, The Festival (1 Kings 8.2). The designation of Sukkot as *The Festival* connotes its preeminence in the cycle of the Jewish year.

Although there are three major Jewish festivals—Pesah, Shavuot, and Sukkot—only the last-mentioned is termed in the liturgy *Zeman Simhatenu*, Season of Our Rejoicing. A number of reasons have been advanced for this special designation. The Pentateuch thrice enjoins, only regarding Sukkot, that one rejoice on this festival

(Leviticus 23.40, Deuteronomy 16.14–15); the harvest period is a joyous one; the *Simhat Bet ha-Shoevah*, Rejoicing at the House of the Water Drawing, during the festival was publicly observed with great jubilation; and only four days prior to Sukkot—on Yom Kippur —the Jews atoned for their sins against God.

The seventh day of Sukkot, known as Hoshana Rabbah, Great Hosanna, refers to the liturgy of the *Hoshanot*, invocations for forgiveness and redemption. This liturgy derives from the belief that judgment decreed on the Day of Atonement was finalized on Hoshana Rabbah. The Talmud denominates this day as *yom hibbut ha-aravot*, "day of beating the palm twigs," and as *yom shevii shel aravah*, "seventh day of the willow" (Sukkah 4.3,6). The willows, termed *hoshanot*, are beaten at the conclusion of the service to symbolize the shedding of sins, just as leaves fall when beaten.

While the precise meaning of *atzeret* is uncertain, Shemini Atzeret is generally translated Eighth Day of Solemn Assembly or Gathering. Atzeret (Leviticus 23.36) was considered by some rabbinical authorities as the last day of Sukkot; therefore it became known as the Closing Festival. Others maintained that it was a separate festival. Hence, in the prayer book we find this designation: *Yom Shemini Hag ha-Atzeret ha-Zeh*, Eighth Day, This Festival of the Atzeret, an attempted compromise between the disparate viewpoints.

The term *simhat Torah* first appears in a seventh-century book but it may refer to the actual rejoicing upon the conclusion of reading of the Pentateuch and not to a festival. In the gaonic period, Simhat Torah was known as *Yom ha-Berakhah*, Day of the Blessing, since the blessing of Moses in the last pentateuchal portion was read on that day. It was also called the Second Day of Shemini Atzeret, the Ninth Day of Sukkot, the Last Day of the Festival, and the Day of Completion (of the Torah). The name Simhat Torah, most expressive of the day's spirit, finally found general acceptance.[1]

✹ ✹ ✹

THE SIGNIFICANCE OF SEVEN

The frequent use of the numeral seven in Jewish lore is invested with particular significance. The Sabbath occurs on the seventh day. Seven is related to both Sukkot and Simhat Torah; Sukkot occurs in

Tishri, the seventh month of the Jewish calendar, and Sukkot without Shemini Atzeret is observed for seven days. Seven celestial guests—*ushpizin*—are invited to the *sukkah*. The more devout *Hasidim* light seven candles every evening in the *sukkah* to honor these fancied visitors. The bouquet of the Four Species includes seven items: one *lulav*, one *etrog*, two willows, and three myrtle branches. On Hoshana Rabbah, the seventh day of the festival, the worshipers hold aloft the palm and citron and make seven processional circuits in the synagogue, emulating the ancient priests who circled the Temple altar seven times on this day. Likewise, seven *hakkafot* are conducted with the Scrolls of the Law on Simhat Torah. The number of sacrificial animals offered during the festival totaled ten times seven.[2]

❦ ❦ ❦

GEMATRIAS—NUMERICAL EQUIVALENTS

A gematria is an evaluation of Hebrew words by their numerical equivalents, each letter in the Hebrew alphabet having a different value. Ingenious gematrias have been devised by Jewish sages and mystics, not merely as pleasant pastimes but also to adduce ethical concepts and homiletical lessons.

Equating the fulfillment of the *mitzvah* of holding the *etrog* with the observance of the 613 commandments in the Torah is deduced as follows: the Hebrew letters of *etrog* total 610; adding the other three species (palm, myrtle, and willow) brings the total to 613.

The Hebrew numerical equivalent of *lulav* is 68, the same as for *hakham* (wise man) and for *hayyim* (life). Hence, the *lulav* is held in the right hand opposite the heart, in conformity with the biblical statement that "a wise man's heart tends toward the right hand" (Ecclesiastes 10.2). Likewise, the similar numerical value of *lulav* and of *hayyim* denotes that the *lulav* must be fresh and not withered; also, it intimates that he who acquires a beautiful palm merits life in this and the next world.

It is customary to spread branches of a tree for the booth roofing, since the Hebrew word for tree, *ilan*, is equal to 91, the identical number as for *sukkah*.

In the verse "On the eighth day a solemn gathering shall be unto you" (Numbers 29.35), referring to Shemini Atzeret, the numerical sum of the Hebrew word *lakhem* (unto you) is 90, the same as for *mayim* (water). This indicates that on Shemini Atzeret the prayer for rain is to be recited.

꙰ ꙰ ꙰

THE BOOK OF ECCLESIASTES

On *Shabbat Hol ha-Moed* (the intermediate Sabbath) of Sukkot or on Shemini Atzeret, the biblical book of Kohelet (Ecclesiastes) is read. This practice is derived from the verse adjuring us to "Distribute portions to seven or even eight" (Ecclesiastes 11.2), which is regarded as alluding to the seven days of Sukkot and to Shemini Atzeret, the Eighth Day of Solemn Assembly. Another interpretation maintains that, just as Ecclesiastes preaches pessimistically on the transitoriness of material possessions and optimistically on the attainment of happiness in fulfilling God's commandments, so Sukkot evokes the austerity of living in a temporary shelter amid rejoicing over the harvest, while contemplating divine omnipotence. Indeed, the reading of Ecclesiastes in itself, with its emphasis on vanity, tempers excessive exultation.[3]

꙰ ꙰ ꙰

THE KARAITE SUKKOT

The Karaites, who accepted the Bible literally but rejected the rabbinical Oral Law, use the Four Species for the construction of the *sukkah*, claiming that this fulfills the commandment in Leviticus 23.40. The fifteenth-century Italian rabbi, Obadiah of Bertinoro, reported that the *lulav* and the other plants were hung in the synagogue for all to gaze upon.

As the Karaites did not follow the calendar adhered to by world Jewry, their observance of festivals occurred on different days. An account from Samuel Jemsel, a Karaite who visited his brethren in Cairo in 1641, demonstrates that they did not observe Sukkot on the fifteenth day of Tishri:

> There we were able to celebrate at our ease the second Festival of Tabernacles, on the fifteenth day of the month of Marcheshvan. It is both a fitting and seemly thing thus to keep the feast days consecrated to the Lord when the fruits of the earth are already producing the harvests of a new season in the Land of Israel—the land that God was wont to look upon as His most holy place.[4]

❧ ❧ ❧

YUCHI INDIANS OBSERVE A "FESTIVAL OF BOOTHS"

Scholars have recently revealed a strange coincidence in the close similarity between the Jewish observance of Sukkot and the "Green Corn" ceremony of the Yuchi Indian tribe. This tribe was expelled from Georgia in 1836 and settled in Oklahoma, where they continue to maintain their ancient religious traditions. Dr. Cyrus H. Gordon, head of the Mediterranean studies department at Brandeis University, draws this parallel based on evidence supplied by Dr. Joseph B. Mahan, Jr., a specialist on the Yuchis:

> As in Leviticus 23, the Yuchis celebrate (1) an eight-day festival, (2) that starts on the fifteenth day (or full moon) of the holy harvest month; throughout the holiday, they (3) live in booths, (4) at the cultic center, where (5) they nurture a sacred fire. To this day the Jews also observe the first three of these features. They have given up the fourth, because after the destruction of their Temples in Jerusalem and their dispersal throughout the world, they had no cultic center to which the pilgrimages could be made. The Jews have also discontinued the fifth point, the fire, because it is associated with the sacrifice, all of which have been suspended since the loss of the Second Temple in 70 c.e.

Like the Yuchis, observant Jews start their holiday on the full moon and dwell in booths. The latter are constructed with open spaces in the roof which are covered during the festival with branches, foliage, fruits, and vegetables, much like the Yuchi booths with open spaces in the roof covered with branches and foliage for the holiday.

Both the Jews and Yuchis form processions making circumambulations on the festivals. The Jews do this in the synagogue, the Yuchis, around the fire in the sacred cultic area. In the Yuchi processions, a couple of men carry each a large, foliage-crested branch, as they accompany the community in their circumambulations. At other times during the celebration, larger numbers of men shake such foliage-crested branches. The Jews have a similar custom; on Tabernacles they shake the *lulav*.

According to Dr. Gordon, the comparison is not intended to prove that the Yuchi Indians are descendants of the "Ten Lost Tribes," but that the Yuchi celebration, like the biblical Festival of Booths, had its origin in the ancient Mediterranean area. Substantiating evidence is derived from the discovery in Georgia, in 1966, of the Metcalf Stone, inscribed with ancient Aegean writing, believed to have reached America through the Mediterranean and the Gulf of Mexico.[5]

❀ ❀ ❀

SUKKOT AND HANUKKAH

During the Maccabean revolt, the Jews were unable to observe the Festival of Tabernacles owing to battle conditions and to the inaccessibility of the Temple in Jerusalem. However, when they recaptured the Temple on the twenty-fifth day of Kislev, 165 B.C.E., they celebrated Sukkot for eight days. This is confirmed in the Apocrypha, which states that the Festival of Tabernacles was observed in the month of Kislev. Here we also learn that Hanukkah was celebrated in the same manner as Sukkot. (See chapter 2, "Sukkot in Postbiblical Writings.") Hence, it is not surprising that Sukkot and Hanukkah share common features: both are celebrated for eight days, and the complete *Hallel* (Psalms 113–18) is recited on both.

❧ ❧ ❧

THE *SUKKAH* COMPARED TO THE LAND OF ISRAEL

Rabbi Elijah, Gaon of Wilna, maintained that there are two commandments the Jew fulfills with the totality of his being—living in a *sukkah* and living in Eretz Israel. When one is in the *sukkah*, his complete being consummates the fulfillment of the precept to live in a booth. Likewise, when one dwells in the land of Israel, his entire being is daily linked to the commandment of living in the Holy Land. He found support for this interpretation in the verse "In Salem [literally, "complete," "whole"] His tabernacle is set and His dwelling-place in Zion" (Psalms 76.3). The gaon interpreted the passage thus: "Man is whole when he dwells in a booth and also when he lives in Zion." Furthermore, he linked the construction of a booth with the rebuilding of the Land of Israel as a sine qua non for the ultimate redemption of the Jewish people. Citing the phrase "You shall make" (Deuteronomy 16.13) in the biblical injunction to build a *sukkah* as implying that one already made is disqualified (Sukkah 11b), the gaon adduces that "you shall make" applies equally to the rebuilding of Zion.[6]

❧ ❧ ❧

THE *SUKKAH*MOBILE

Inasmuch as the Talmud sanctions the erection of a *sukkah* on a wagon,[7] it is not surprising to find in recent years a festival booth mounted on a truck. Sponsored by the *Hasidim* of the Lubavitcher *rebbe*, a "*sukkah*mobile" tours New York City during the intermediate days of the Feast of Booths, stopping at schools, hospitals, shopping centers, and other public institutions. Passersby are invited by members of the Lubavitch Youth Organization to enter the walnut-paneled *sukkah*, where they may pronounce the blessing on the *lulav.* All visitors are presented with a publication describing the Sukkot traditions.[8]

⚘ ⚘ ⚘

THE USEFULNESS OF THE *ETROG*

The citron served several purposes after its use on Sukkot, one of which was to be made into a delicious preserve. The *etrog,* whose scientific name is *citrus medica* according to papers found in the Cairo Genizah, was also utilized to concoct a medicine.[9] A belief prevailed that this prescription was especially potent for women who had difficulty in giving birth. Pregnant women would bite off the protuberance (*pitma*) of the *etrog* on Hoshana Rabbah, distribute charity to the poor and recite this prayer:

"Lord of the universe, if one woman, Eve, tasted the apple, shall Your wrath fall on all women? If I had been in the Garden of Eden at that time, I would not have listened to the snake and I would not have tasted the apple. *I* did not eat and *I* did not reap the benefit of the *etrog* during the seven days of Sukkot, as it was then ordained to fulfill a commandment. Even today, Hoshana Rabbah, when the time is passed for the observance of the commandment, it is not my wish to enjoy its use. In the same manner, as I had only slight benefit of this *pitma,* so in the Garden of Eden I would have used the tree of knowledge that was forbidden to be eaten."

There was a popular legend in Germany that Princess Louise, the daughter of Prince Charles of Mecklenburg-Strelitz who married the crown prince of Prussia, bit off the *pitma* of an *etrog* on Hoshana Rabbah and recited the above supplication. Subsequently, she gave birth to a male child who became Frederick William IV, king of Prussia.[10]

The above story accords with the belief among the masses in Eastern Europe that a pregnant woman who bit off the *pitma* would bear a male child.

These superstitions may have originated from a talmudic legend: "One who eats an *etrog* will have fragrant children. The daughter of King Shapur, whose mother had eaten an *etrog* [while she was pregnant] with her, used to be presented before her father as his principal perfume."[11]

❦ ❦ ❦

THE OPEN ARK

Obadiah of Bertinoro (1450–1520), an Italian rabbi noted for his classic commentary on the Mishnah, reported that on a visit on Simhat Torah night in 1487 to the synagogue in Palermo, Sicily, he observed that "after the prayers are finished, the two officials open the doors of the ark and remain there the whole night; women come there in family groups to kiss the roll of the Law and to prostrate themselves before it; they enter at one door and go out by the other, and this continues the whole night, some coming and others going."[12]

❦ ❦ ❦

TORAH READING ON SIMHAT TORAH EVENING

It is forbidden to read the Torah in the synagogue after nightfall, but an exception was made on Simhat Torah eve. This custom was introduced at the end of the fourteenth century, when the processional circuits with the Scrolls of the Law were made on the night of the Rejoicing in the Law. As it was considered improper to remove the *Sifre Torah* from the ark without reading from at least one of them, the Torah reading was permitted. This is the only evening throughout the entire year when this practice is sanctioned.[13]

38. Simhat Torah in the Amsterdam synagogue.
From *Cérémonies et coutumes religieuses,* by Bernard Picart,
Amsterdam, 1723. See Chapter 9.

☙ ☙ ☙

BRIDEGROOMS AS CONGREGATIONAL OFFICERS

As early as 1663, the ordinances of the Spanish and Portuguese Synagogue of London provided for the election of the "bridegrooms of the Law" on the eve of Rosh Hashanah. The importance of the role played by these bridegrooms is attested by the still extant record of those who served in these capacities.[14] Similar records of Simhat Torah bridegrooms are found in the eighteenth- and nineteenth-century minute books of the Spanish and Portuguese Congregation

Shearith Israel of New York, where the *hatan Torah* and *hatan Bereshit* were also chosen at annual elections. These assignments were not only honorary, but they imposed special responsibilities such as serving as the *parnas* (leader of the community) when he was unavailable. In the minute book of the Congregation Shearith Israel, this resolution, dated September 8, 1771, is found:

Att a full meeting of the Parnasim and Adjuntos [board members] it was unanimously agreed, that whereas, much difficulty has Arisen from the inconveniencey of Electing two Parnassim with Hatanim Torah and Bereshit annually, Occasioned by the small number of persons, who are proper, and willing to Accept of the said offices, it is Resolved for the tranquility of our Congregation, to return to the first institution dated 5466 [1705] & 5489 [1728] of Electing one Parnas for the whole year with the Hatan Torah, and Hatan Bereshit, to Serve for the same time, During which term they are to set in the Bench with the parnas, and be his Assistants, and in his absence to act in proper turn as Parnas, with this further addition, that after the Parnas has compleated the year, the Hatan Torah is then to become Parnas, Hatan Bereshit to become Hatan Torah, and only a new Hatan Bereshit to be nominated annually.[15]

In the latter half of the eighteenth century, the German Jews who had settled in Philadelphia and had organized Congregation Mikveh Israel included among their regulations the following provision (translated from the Yiddish):

If it should happen that a person has been a *hatan Torah* and a *hatan Bereshit,* and his turn arrives to become president, and it is known that he is quarrelsome and tyrannical, then that man is not to be made president. The Board of Five shall then elect another person, one who is respected here, to serve as president, even though he has not been either *hatan Torah* or *hatan Bereshit.*[16]

❧ ❧ ❧

SIMHAT TORAH HATS

On Simhat Torah in some Galician Jewish communities, it was customary to place a hat adorned with many small bells on the head of everyone called to the Torah reading. At the synagogue of the Dinover Rabbi, Tzvi Elimelekh Shapira (1785–1841), the cantor for the additional service, donned a hat fashioned like a large paper bag decorated with feathers and bells. In Wilna the *hakkafot* were led by the most prominent members of the congregation wearing special hats for the occasion.[17] In Spain during the thirteenth century, a bizarre head-covering was used on Simhat Torah—a crown of a Scroll of the Law set on the head of the bridegroom of the Law and on the head of every man called to the reading of the Torah. Nor were the children neglected. Rabbi Solomon Ben Adreth wrote: "I still remember, when a child, the crowns [of the Torah Scrolls] were placed on the heads of children, and they were then put back under guard to the place where they were stored for safety."[18]

✹ ✹ ✹

ELEGIES ON SIMHAT TORAH

In Babylon during the tenth century and later in other countries, it was a practice on Simhat Torah to recite elegies for Moses, whose death is recorded in the last pentateuchal portion read on that day. In Provence, two "mourners" were appointed to chant the dirges or to stand on the Torah reader's sides and weep when he read about Moses' death. Among Italian Jews and those of North Africa, the conclusion of the reading of the Torah evoked a cacophony of joyous hymns and plaintive elegies, with the latter predominating. When the institution of *hakkafot* with the Scrolls was established, the mournful melodies gave way to gay songs and hymns that accompanied the circuits.[19]

✹ ✹ ✹

SIMHAT TORAH DEMONSTRATIONS IN AMERICA

The annual massive assemblage in recent years of Jewish youth in front of synagogues in Moscow and other cities of the Soviet Union on Simhat Torah has stimulated Jewish communities the world over to express solidarity with their Russian fellow Jews during the Festival of Tabernacles. Since 1968 Jewish communities in the United States have sponsored Simhat Torah rallies and other demonstrations to protest the treatment of Soviet Jewry, especially the harassment of those desirous of immigrating to Israel. In 1970 nearly one hundred communities in North America conducted a variety of demonstrations, according to reports received by the National Conference on Soviet Jewry.

On Hoshana Rabbah in 1971, despite a heavy downpour, an impressive "Simhat Torah Freedom Procession" marched to the residence of the Soviet Union Mission to the United States in Glen Cove, Long Island. Representing scores of congregations and other Jewish institutions, and singing Hebrew songs and shouting freedom slogans, the paraders bore aloft about one hundred Torah Scrolls, protected from the rain by transparent plastic covers, and a large number of flags and signs. On the same day, the Jewish community in Washington, D.C., conducted a march and rally in protest of the treatment of Soviet Jewry. Here scores of demonstrators carried *lulavim* and *etrogim* and five Nazi concentration camp survivors held Scrolls of the Law in the procession, while the rally was marked by prayer, song, and dance.[20]

Some synagogues converted the Simhat Torah *hakkafot* into demonstrations, with young people carrying appropriately worded placards following the Scroll-bearers. Prior to or following the synagogue services, the entire congregation led by those with the Scrolls and placards marched in a public demonstration either in front of the synagogue or in a public square, to publicize their concern for the plight of the Russian Jews.

17

SUKKOT AND SIMHAT TORAH HUMOR

※ ※ ※

RENTAL FOR A SUKKAH

Berel and Shmerel reached an agreement whereby Berel would construct a *sukkah* in his backyard, and Shmerel would pay rent for using it during the festival of Sukkot. After the holiday Berel claimed the stipulated rental fee. Shocked when Shmerel refused to fulfill his agreement, Berel summoned him for a hearing before the local rabbi.

When the rabbi heard Berel's story, his decision was that Shmerel need not pay.

Both plaintiff and defendant were astonished at this judicial decision. Noting their amazement, the rabbi explained.

"The Talmud says that the obligation to dwell in a *sukkah* should be fulfilled in the same manner as dwelling in one's house. Last week you, Shmerel, appeared before me on the complaint of your landlord. If you do not pay rent for your house, why should you pay rent for the *sukkah*?"

❧ ❧ ❧

"THIS *ETROG* IS AN *ETROG*"

The wise men of Helm were elated with the *etrog* the president of their congregation had purchased for Sukkot. This was not an ordinary *etrog*. It came from the Land of Israel. It was yellow as the color of an *etrog*. It was fragrant as the odor of an *etrog*. It was without a blemish as an *etrog*. It had a firm and dainty *pitma*. In short, this was an *etrog*!

The president reluctantly entrusted the sexton to take the *etrog* to all the Helm householders so that they could recite the traditional blessing over it. Apprehensive of the sexton's carelessness, the president warned him.

"Remember! This *etrog* is an *etrog*! Handle it with tenderness. Be especially careful that the *pitma* should not be spoiled by handling and thereby render the *etrog* unsuitable for use. Remember! This *etrog* is an *etrog*."

The wise sexton joyfully embarked on his holy mission. Clutching the *etrog* in both hands, he started out through the streets of Helm, when a sudden inspiration stopped him in his tracks. He looked at the *etrog*, held it level with his eyes, and scrutinized it from all sides. Shutting his eyes in devout meditation, the sexton recalled the president's instructions to take extreme precautions that the *pitma* should not be spoiled. Ah, he was shrewd! But what was the inspiration that brought him to a sudden halt? Had he forgotten his clever device? No! No! He knew what he had to do. No sooner said than done!

The sexton took a sharp knife from his pocket and carefully cut out the *pitma* from the *etrog*. The president had ordered him to take good care of it, and he would never dare disobey the president. He wrapped the *pitma* in a clean handkerchief and gently placed it in his pocket. He then proceeded to the homes of the wise Helmites to allow them to recite the blessing over the *etrog*.

As the sexton entered each home, he reiterated the president's admonition.

"Remember! This *etrog* is an *etrog*!"

❦ ❦ ❦

THE CONSCIENTIOUS MISER

The Jews of a small town decided to share the cost of an *etrog* and a *lulav*. Only Kamtzan, the local miser, refused to contribute his share. On the first day of Sukkot, when the sexton was carrying the *etrog* and *lulav* from house to house so that all could pronounce the benediction, he bypassed Kamtzan's house. The miser, however, was hiding near a neighbor's house, and as the sexton came along, Kamtzan grabbed him from behind and lifted him into the air. Holding the sexton aloft, Kamtzan waved him heavenwards, earthwards, and to the four winds, while reciting the blessing for "taking the *lulav*." He then turned the frantic sexton upside down and pronounced the benediction "and He has preserved us."

Concluding the ceremony, the miser put the sexton back on his feet and said, "Now you should understand why I didn't give money for the *etrog* and *lulav*. I don't like to fulfill the commandment of the Torah in an easy way."

❦ ❦ ❦

A PRAYER FOR RAIN IS ANSWERED

A severe drought wrought havoc with the crops, and unless rain fell soon, the farmers would suffer great losses. To demonstrate the efficacy of prayer, the rabbi decided to utilize the approaching festival of Shemini Atzeret, when it is customary to recite the prayer for rain. To this end, he engaged a cantor to officiate for the festival.

On Shemini Atzeret morning the rabbi preached a soul-stirring sermon on prayer. Emphasizing that God always answers prayers emanating from the heart, he urged the congregants to worship fervently for a favorable response to the prayer for rain. With deep emotion the cantor chanted the special prayer and the congregation responded in like vein. Never before was such a prayer for rain heard.

No one was therefore surprised that a heavy rain fell as the services were concluded. So abundant was the downpour, that it seemed the very heavens were emptying. Surely, the rabbi was being vindicated; their prayers were answered.

However, whatever had been left of the crops was completely destroyed by the plethora of water.

Two neighbors who had left their houses in the rain to examine their ruined fields met on the road. With a deep sigh of anguish, one said to the other, "The rabbi really knows how to get answers to his prayers."

The other rejoined, "That is quite true, but he certainly doesn't know how to irrigate a field."

❧ ❧ ❧

A CANTOR'S SUCCESSFUL PRAYER

At the Shemini Atzeret services, the cantor exploited every word of the prayer for rain, in order to display his vocal talents. No sooner was the prayer concluded than there was a teeming downpour.

After the service, the cantor bragged to the rabbi.

"I am pleased that God listened to my prayer and that I caused rain to fall."

The rabbi quickly retorted, "I am not at all surprised. Some time ago people like you caused a flood."

❧ ❧ ❧

REJOICING WITH THE TORAH

A Jew who never found time to study was rejoicing hilariously in the synagogue on Simhat Torah. He sang and danced enthusiastically, ate and drank abundantly, fully observing the festival of Simhat Torah.

Unable to fathom this sudden ebullience for the Torah, the rabbi remarked sarcastically, "My friend, I study the Torah all year and I have reason to be gay on this festival. Have you studied Torah all year that you should now celebrate so ardently?"

The exhilarated Jew replied, "On the Day of Atonement I beat my breast and ask forgiveness for the sin of bribery. Am I guilty of this sin? Why, then, should I confess to a sin of which I am blameless? The reason is obvious. It is written: 'All Israelites are responsible for one another.' If I am culpable for the sins of others, why shouldn't I also participate in their rejoicing?"

❧ ❧ ❧

NO TIME FOR DANCING

In the general synagogue hilarity on Simhat Torah, the town's pauper danced with a rich man. The following day, confident that he had established a friendly relationship with the man of wealth, the pauper went to his palatial residence for a loan.

As the poor man entered the home, the owner said to him, "Did you come to dance with me? I'm sorry but I'm very busy today."

≝ ≝ ≝

PREPARING THE WINE FOR
SIMHAT TORAH

On the night following Simhat Torah, an emergency meeting of the members of the Tailors' Synagogue was convened to cope with a depressing situation—there had been insufficient wine to celebrate the festival properly. Many proposals were presented to avoid the recurrence of such a predicament, but none met with the approval of the tailors, and the debate continued far into the night.

39. Chairs for the bridegrooms of the Torah and Bereshit. Synagogue, Mantua, Italy. 1775. See Chapter 9.

Finally, one of the tailors offered this suggestion: "Let an empty barrel be placed near the synagogue, and every Friday each tailor will pour a cup of his Sabbath wine into the barrel. Thus, by next Simhat Torah we will have more than enough wine to observe the festival fittingly."

This plan appealed to the tailors, and they readily accepted it. Each tailor promised to bring his cup of wine regularly on the eve of every Sabbath.

On the first Friday that the plan was to go into effect, each tailor thought to himself, "I'll pour a glass of water in the barrel and no one will know the difference."

The year passed. It was again Simhat Torah. The tailors were in their synagogue. They prepared to drink *le-hayyim*. The barrel was opened. Drinks were poured for all. They recited the blessing for wine, sipped their cups, and lo and behold, they had pronounced a blessing in vain!

❧ ❧ ❧

COMMUNAL DISPUTATION IN HELM

The Jews of Helm planned to erect a new synagogue building, and had already resolved many weighty problems concerning its architecture.

As they were about to commence the actual construction, Berel, one of the most sagacious of the Helmites, suggested that the synagogue flooring be planed smooth. In support of his proposal he pointed out that on Yom Kippur the worshipers did not wear shoes, and if the boards were not smooth they might get splinters in their feet. Shmerel, another of the town's wise men, countered that if the flooring was smooth, the Jews might slide and fall when they danced in the synagogue on Simhat Torah. He urged that the flooring should not be planed, but should be left unfinished.

The sages of Helm, recognizing the seriousness of their dilemma, did not take the matter lightly. The clash of opinions generated deep divisiveness in the city of Helm. One group supported Berel, and the other, Shmerel.

The Berelites importuned, "Do you know what will happen if you get a splinter in your foot? It will become infected, and you will have to limp and perhaps fall. We must have a smooth floor!"

The Shmerelites protested, "Do you know what will happen if you slide and fall on Simhat Torah while dancing with the Torah? You will drop the Torah and then you will have to fast for forty days. We must have a rough floor!"

The construction was held in abeyance while the two factions engaged in a bitter dispute. Days, weeks, months went by, but there seemed no hope of reaching an agreement. Both factions finally appealed to the rabbi, who listened to forceful presentations by both Berel and Shmerel. He then retired to his chambers and deliberated for seven day and seven nights. On the morning of the eighth day, he summoned the leaders of both factions and announced his decision.

"For seven days and seven nights I considered your claims. I consulted the books of law, the responsa of the rabbis, and the chronicles of Helm. I invoked divine guidance. As a result I have come to the conclusion that both groups are right. I therefore decree that both plans must be used: the floorboards shall be smooth on one side and rough on the other. To avoid splinters on Yom Kippur, the smooth side of the board shall be used. To prevent falling on Simhat Torah, the flooring shall be reversed so that the rough side is on the surface."

And peace reigned once more in Helm.[1]

18

THE FESTIVAL DELICACIES

※ ※ ※

Sukkot, a season of thanksgiving for the Lord's bounties, was always celebrated as the most joyful of the three pilgrimage festivals. The biblical injunction "You shall rejoice in your festival" (Deuteronomy 16.14) implies a duty to enjoy festive meals. However, we are also reminded that good fortune and felicity need to be shared with the disadvantaged and the stranger. In this spirit guests are always welcome in the *sukkah*. According to Jewish tradition, it is obligatory to have one's meals in a *sukkah* throughout the festival. The Talmud states: "Rabbi Eliezer said: 'A man is duty-bound to eat fourteen meals in the *sukkah*, one every day and one every night.'

But the Sages say: 'There is no fixed number [of meals], except [that he must eat in the *sukkah*] on the first night of the festival' " (Sukkah 2.6). Observant Jews generally eat two full meals in the *sukkah* on each day of Sukkot. The bread is dipped in honey as an omen for a sweet year. Not only is fasting proscribed throughout Sukkot, but opportunities are afforded for enjoyment of delicacies.

Hoshana Rabbah, the seventh day of the festival, is considered the last day of the New Year season, on which divine judgment is finally sealed. As on Rosh Hashanah, round *hallot* and honey are eaten on Hoshana Rabbah. *Hallah* and cake are baked in different symbolic shapes: a ladder for the ascent of prayers to heaven, a key for the opening of the heavenly portals, and a hand for receiving the divine decree for the New Year. Pious Jews devote the entire night preceding Hoshana Rabbah to study at the synagogue, at which coffee and cake are served.

Marking the completion and renewal of the yearly Torah-reading cycle in the synagogue, Simhat Torah is a day of revelry and feasting. Some maintain that it is permissible to imbibe a bit more strong drink than usual, although the rabbis frowned upon any excesses. In German congregations during the circuits with the Scrolls of the Law, candy is given to the marching children, and many come prepared with large bags to hold their loot. In some communities, cake, fruit, wine, and other refreshments are provided at the services for both young and old to enhance the festivity.

In many lands the *hatan Torah* and *hatan Bereshit* show their appreciation of the signal honor bestowed on them by hosting the congregation at a sumptuous meal. Tossing nuts, raisins, and candy on the bridegrooms when they stood at the reading desk, as was done to a bridegroom on the Sabbath preceding his wedding, was a widespread practice on the part of the women in the synagogue gallery. Even in staid England, women reportedly threw sugarplums from the balcony, which the children would eagerly gather up, until it was prohibited as a breach of decorum. In other places, women threw small paper bags containing raisins and nuts. In Salonica the bridegrooms distributed candy to the children.

Maimonides, in his codification of laws, states that on a festival children should be given roasted ears (popcorn?), nuts, and sweetmeats.

Culinary customs for Sukkot have varied from country to country. In Yemen a number of families would jointly purchase a sheep or an ox, to assure sufficient meat for the lengthy festival. In the south of Russia a favorite dish was cabbage leaves stuffed with chopped meat. On Hoshana Rabbah in Berlin a type of cabbage called *vasser kal* was eaten, because on this day the liturgical hymn *Kol Mevasser* is recited as one strikes the willows. Elsewhere cabbage is eaten on Simhat Torah; its Hebrew term is *cherub*, an allusion to the cherubim carved on the ark of the covenant (Exodus 25.18–22).

Kreplach, triangular pieces of dough filled with chopped meat, are the traditional *pièce de résistance* for Hoshana Rabbah. According to folklore, *kreplach* are eaten on those days on which there is "beating": on Purim, when Haman is "beaten" as his name is read in the Scroll of Esther; on the eve of the Day of Atonement, when men are flogged with forty stripes; and on Hoshana Rabbah, when the willow branches are beaten. In some communities the *etrog* was eaten on Simhat Torah; in others, jam was made from this citrus fruit. *Teiglach*, honey balls, are the most typical of the Sukkot delicacies.

❧ ❧ ❧

RECIPES FOR SUKKOT
HANNA GOODMAN

STUFFED CABBAGE

1	large cabbage (4 pounds)	1	clove of garlic, mashed
1½	pounds chopped meat	2	onions, sliced
2	onions, grated		28-ounce can tomatoes in puree
¼	cup bread crumbs		meat bones
2	eggs	½	cup brown or light sugar
	salt and pepper	2	bay leaves

juice of 1 lemon

With a sharp knife core the cabbage, removing as much as possible of the center.

Bring a big pot of water to a boil. Immerse the cabbage in the water with the core down. Take off each leaf with a fork. When all the leaves are removed, put them back into the water and turn off the heat. Let stand until the filling is prepared and then drain the water.

To make the filling, add the grated onions, bread crumbs, eggs, salt, pepper, and the mashed garlic to the chopped meat, and mix well.

Lay each cabbage leaf flat on a plate. Cut off the hard part of the cabbage leaf. Put some of the filling on each leaf. Cover the filling by folding two sides of the leaf over it and roll up like a blintz.

In a large roaster or pot, put the sliced onions, tomatoes, and bones. If any cabbage leaves remain, shred and place them in the roaster. Lay the stuffed cabbage leaves end down on top. Cover the roaster and bring to a boil. Lower the heat and cook for 1 hour. Add the sugar, bay leaves, and lemon juice, and continue to cook for 1 hour longer. Taste for seasoning and add more sugar or lemon juice as may be required. The cabbage can also be cooked in the oven at 325°.

The stuffed cabbage improves in taste if left standing for a day. If this is done, reheat slowly. It may be served with rice as a main dish.

If small stuffed cabbage portions are preferred, use a small head of cabbage, or cut big leaves in half.

KREPLACH

Meat Filling
½ pound chopped meat
1 egg
1 small onion, grated
1 tablespoon bread crumbs
salt and pepper to taste

Dough
2 eggs, beaten
1½ cups flour (approximately)
½ teaspoon salt

Prepare the meat filling by mixing well the chopped meat, egg, onion, bread, salt, and pepper.

To make the dough, beat the 2 eggs in a bowl, add the flour and salt, and knead until the dough is elastic. A little warm water will help to form a soft dough.

On a floured board or floured wax paper, roll out the dough into a very thin oblong. Cut in squares to size desired. On each square, place a small ball of the filling and quickly fold into a triangle, pinching the edges together. Allow the finished *kreplach* to stand for 15 minutes.

Bring a large pot of salted water to a boil, add the *kreplach*, and cover the pot. Cook for 25 to 30 minutes, depending on the thickness of the *kreplach*. Drain and add to soup.

NUT CAKE

¼	cup margarine	
½	cup sugar	
4	eggs, separated	
1	cup flour	
1	teaspoon baking powder	
1	teaspoon cinnamon	
2	cups chopped walnuts	

Syrup

½	cup sugar
¼	cup water
½	cup honey
1	teaspoon cinnamon
2	tablespoons rum

Cream the margarine, then add the sugar and beat until fluffy. Add the egg yolks one at a time. Beat the egg whites until stiff. Fold the beaten egg whites into the egg yolk mixture.

Combine the flour with the baking powder and cinnamon and add to the mixture. Add the nuts, mixing well.

Pour the batter into a 9 x 9-inch greased pan and bake in a 350° oven for 30 minutes.

While cake is baking, make the syrup. Boil together the sugar and water for about 10 minutes until syrupy. Stir in the honey and cinnamon. Cook for 5 more minutes and then add the rum. Pour the hot syrup over the hot cake. Let the cake stand overnight before serving.

SIMHAT TORAH CAKES (LEKACH)

2	eggs
½	cup sugar
1	tablespoon margarine

1¼	cups flour, sifted
1	teaspoon baking power
1	teaspoon vanilla

coarse sugar

Beat the eggs with the sugar until light in color. Add the margarine.

Sift the flour with the baking powder, and add to the egg mixture. Add the vanilla.

Grease a foil-lined cookie sheet. Drop batter onto foil, about a tablespoon at a time, leaving 4 inches between each cake.

Sprinkle with coarse sugar.

Bake the cakes in a 350° oven until light brown, about 15 to 20 minutes.

PARAVE COFFEE CAKE

3 cups flour, sifted	1½ cups sugar
2 teaspoons baking powder	5 eggs
1 teaspoon baking soda	1 cup orange juice
1 cup margarine	2 teaspoons vanilla

Sift the flour. Sift again with the baking powder and baking soda.

Cream the margarine with the sugar and add the eggs, one at a time. Mix well. Add the flour mixture, one cup at a time, with the orange juice. Add the vanilla and mix well.

Pour half the batter into a greased 9 x 12½-inch pan. Sprinkle with half the topping mixture. Cover with the rest of the batter, and sprinkle the rest of the topping mixture on top of the cake.

Bake the cake in a 350° oven for 1 hour or until done.

Topping

1 cup walnuts, chopped	1 teaspoon cinnamon
2 squares cooking chocolate, grated	¾ cup sugar

Mix all the ingredients together and use for the topping.

STRUDEL

½ pound strudel leaves	1 cup jellied candy slices, cut in small pieces
2 cups coconut	
1 cup white raisins	1 cup mixed candied fruits
2 cups walnuts, chopped in large pieces	4 cups sugar
	2 teaspoons cinnamon
1 cup candied pineapple, cut in small pieces	corn flakes crumbs or bread crumbs
1 cup candied cherries, cut in quarters	½ pound margarine or butter
	1 pound dried apricots
2 oranges	

Prepare the filling first. Mix the coconut, raisins, nuts, pineapple, cherries, candy slices, and candied fruit with 2 cups of sugar in a large bowl.

Mix the cinnamon with the corn flakes crumbs or bread crumbs.

Put the dried apricots and the oranges through a grinder. Add 2 cups of sugar. Mix well. (Any kind of jam can be used instead of the apricot-orange filling.)

Line baking sheets with foil and grease well.

On a slightly damp towel place two sheets of the strudel. (Keep the strudel leaves not being used wrapped well to prevent drying.) Spread some of the melted margarine or butter over the strudel leaves. Scatter some of the corn flakes crumbs over the entire surface. Scatter some of the coconut-fruit mixture. On the end of the strudel leaves nearest to you make a row of the apricot filling and then roll it up like a jelly roll. Place carefully with the seams down on the baking sheets. Brush with some more melted margarine or butter, and sprinkle with sugar. With a sharp knife, cut down into slices, but do not slice all the way through. Bend the ends under.

Bake in a 375° oven for 25 to 30 minutes or until light brown. While still warm, cut all the way through. Cool. If stored in a tin box, the strudel will keep a few weeks.

APPLE STRUDEL

6 strudel leaves	grated peel of 1 lemon
1 can apples for pie	1 cup corn flakes crumbs or
¾ cup sugar	bread crumbs
1 teaspoon cinnamon	1 cup almonds, chopped
melted margarine or butter	

Mix the apples with the sugar, cinnamon, and lemon peel.

Remove 3 strudel leaves and spread some melted margarine or butter over the top leaf. Sprinkle with half the crumbs and almonds.

Spread half the apple filling across one end of the strudel, a few inches from the edge. Fold the dough over the filling and roll up the strudel.

Place the filled strudel on a greased cookie sheet, brush with more melted margarine or butter, and sprinkle with some sugar. Cut the strudel in portions, but do not cut all the way through.

Continue with the other 3 strudel leaves, repeating the same process as above.

Bake the strudel in a 375° oven until browned. Cool and cut in portions.

BAKLAVA

1 pound strudel leaves	*Syrup*
3 cups walnuts, chopped	1 cup water
1 cup sugar	1 cup sugar
1½ teaspoons cinnamon	1½ cups honey
1 teaspoon allspice	1 teaspoon vanilla
1 pound margarine, melted	1 teaspoon cinnamon
whole cloves	

Grease a 12 x 9-inch baking pan.

Mix the chopped walnuts with the sugar, cinnamon, and allspice.

Place four sheets of the strudel leaves in the pan, brushing each sheet with the melted margarine. On top of these four sheets put a sprinkling of the walnut mixture. Then place one sheet and cover with a layer of walnut mixture. Continue this procedure, making sure to brush each sheet with the margarine, until there are 4 to 6 leaves remaining, which are to be placed on top.

For easier slicing, dip a knife in melted margarine, cut the pastry into 2-inch strips, and then cut these strips to make diamond-shaped pieces. Pour some of the melted margarine with a teaspoon between the cut strips, and pour the rest over the entire surface. Stud each piece with a whole clove.

Bake in a 300° oven for 30 minutes, and then slowly pour half of the hot syrup on top. Increase the oven temperature to 400° and continue baking until the syrup has been absorbed.

Remove from oven and pour the rest of the syrup on top. The baklava should be made the day before serving so that all the syrup will be absorbed.

To make the syrup, mix the water and sugar in a saucepan, and boil over a low heat for 12 minutes. Then add the honey, vanilla, and cinnamon, and simmer for 5 more minutes.

APPLE CANDY

2 pounds apples   1 teaspoon rose water
sugar

Cut the apples in quarters and core but do not peel. Place them in a saucepan. Cover with a little water and bring to a boil. Lower the heat and simmer the apples until very soft.

Blend the apples in a blender or put through a sieve.

For every cup of apple pulp, use 1 cup of sugar. Bring the sugar and the apple pulp to a boil in a pot, lower the heat, and simmer for about 1 hour, stirring every few minutes. When the consistency is like a very thick jam, add the rose water and pour the mixture into a 9 x 9-inch dish that is sprinkled with sugar. Allow the candy to cool. Cut into squares and sprinkle with more sugar. Let the candy dry at room temperature for a few days.

The same procedure can be followed for peaches, pears, or quinces.

40. The spouses of the Law conducted home.
From *Cérémonies et coutumes religieuses*, by Bernard Picart,
Amsterdam, 1723. See Chapter 9.

19

CHILDREN'S STORIES FOR SUKKOT AND SIMHAT TORAH

A STREETFUL OF FRIENDS
SADIE ROSE WEILERSTEIN

author of eleven books for Jewish children in a successful writing career; in 1956 and 1962 the recipient of the Jewish Juvenile Award of the Jewish Book Council of the National Jewish Welfare Board

(age level four to seven)

Once upon a time there was a street with many houses and many children in the many houses. Ruth and Debby lived in one house; Joan and Edward in another; Hilda and Edgar in another. But Ruth and Debby didn't know any of the children, not a single one. They hadn't lived on the street very long.

"Go out and play," said Mother.

"We don't know anyone to play with," said Ruthie.

"We haven't any friends at all," said Debby sadly.

Then Sukkot time came. Ruth and Debby and Mother and Daddy and Cousin Judith and great big Cousin Danny were out in the yard watching the carpenter put up the *sukkah* walls.

Bang! Bang! Bang! went the carpenter's hammer.

"Hello!" said a voice over the fence.

There were Joan and Edward from the house next door.

"What's the carpenter making?" asked Edward. "Is it a garage?"

"Oh, no," said Ruthie. "We haven't any car."

"Is it a playhouse?" asked Joanie.

"No," said Debby. "You can play in it, but it isn't a playhouse."

"Then what is it?" asked Joan and Edward together.

Ruth and Debby laughed.

"Wait and see! Wait and see!
Something lovely soon will be."

And that's all they would tell Joan and Edward that day. But that night when Mother was tucking them into bed, Ruth and Debby whispered, "We have two friends, Mother—Joan and Edward."

Next morning Ruth and Debby and Joan and Edward were standing at the curb looking down the street. They were watching for old Mr. Solomon. Mr. Solomon always brought the branches to cover the *sukkah*. A *sukkah* hasn't a roof, you know, just green branches.

Clatter, clatter, clatter! Down the street came Mr. Solomon with his wagon and his old gray horse. The wagon was piled high with fresh pine boughs.

Danny jumped on top of the load and threw the branches down. Ruth and Debby and Joan and Edward carried them to the back yard.

"We'll help you," said a voice.

There were Edgar and Hilda dragging a big branch.

"Are you going to plant these?" asked Hilda.

"Goodness, no!" said Ruthie. "They haven't any roots."

"Then what are you going to do with them?" asked Edgar.

Ruth and Debby smiled.

"Wait and see! Wait and see!
Something lovely soon will be."

Danny leaned a ladder against the *sukkah* wall and climbed up. He had to lay the branches across the top. Joan and Edward and Hilda and Edgar handed the branches up. Ruth and Debby stood inside the *sukkah* to see that everything was done the proper way.

"Move the branches nearer together," Ruthie called up to Danny. She knew there had to be more shade than light.

"Not *so* close together, Danny," said Debby. "We won't be able to see the stars."

Danny moved the branches this way and that, until he got them exactly right. Then down he came. The *sukkah* was ready.

"A snug little house
With a roof of green;
Look up through the branches;
The sky can be seen."

"You call it a *sukkah*," said Ruth and Debby.

"Why?" asked Hilda.

"Because a *sukkah* is a booth," Cousin Judith explained. "The Israelites lived in booths forty years when they wandered in the wilderness, so *we* live in booths on Sukkot—to remember those days."

"But we don't live in them forty years," laughed Danny. "Just seven days!"

"Do you sleep in the *sukkah*?" asked Edgar.

"No, just eat there, and sing songs, and thank God for the fruit and all. It's like Thanksgiving."

And that night Ruth and Debby whispered to Mother. "We have four friends now, Joan and Edgar and Hilda and Edward."

Well, the next day Ruth and Debby were coming home from the store. Each had a bag in her hand. Joan and Edward and Hilda and Edgar and the Twin were playing hopscotch on the sidewalk.

"What have you got?" asked Joanie.

"Cranberries," said Ruthie.

"Going to cook them?" asked the Twin.

"No, string them," said Debby. "Do you want to help?"

"Can we help, too?" asked Joanie and Edward and Hilda and Edgar together.

They all went to Ruth's and Debby's yard. Cousin Judith gave each one a needle and a long thread. Through the needle, down the thread, through the needle, down the thread went the cranberries. There were yards and yards of them like bright red beads. Danny wound them in and out the green pine boughs. They hung down into the *sukkah* in loops and clusters and six-pointed stars.

Mother sent down rosy apples. The children rubbed them until their fat cheeks were shining. Judith tied strings to them and Danny hung them from the roof. He hung up pears, too, and oranges and purple grapes. He hung up seven little eggshell birds with bills of dough and paper wings. They twirled on their long strings.

"Seven little birds,
  Bright and gay ;
One for each glad
  Sukkot day."

Then it was time to carry things from the house to the *sukkah*. Dan and Edgar carried a table; Ruth carried the cloth; Debby, the candlesticks and candles; Joanie, the holiday twists; Judith, wine; Hilda, cookies; the Twin, fruit. Edgar and his cousin carried chairs. Down the stairs they marched, through the yard, into the *sukkah*. Two little boys, sitting on the fence, jumped down from the fence and marched along, too.

"Oh, oh," said Joanie, when everything was in place. "You said something lovely soon would be, and it is! A *sukkah* is the nicest thing in the world."

"A wee little house
  With a roof of green;
The loveliest place
  That ever was seen."

They all stood quiet for a moment, looking at the snowy cloth with the candles and *hallah* and wine, at the green branches overhead and the blue specks of sky, at the cranberry strings and the colored fruits. They smelled the good pine smell.

"I wish my little sister could see it," said Hilda. "May I bring her over?"

"May I bring my big brother?" asked Joanie.

"May we ask our cousins?" said the Twin.

"You may bring everybody," said Ruth and Debby.

When Mother came into the *sukkah* to light the candles, how surprised she was! There were children around the table. There were children in the corners. There were children peeping in through the window and standing on the fence.

"They're our friends," said Ruth and Debby. "We invited them."

Mother looked at Joan and Edward and Hilda and Edgar and the Twin, at the children peeping in the window and the boys standing on the fence.

"I'm glad you've come," she said, "You must stay for *Kiddush*."[1]

❦ ❦ ❦

HOW K'TONTON PRAYED FOR RAIN
SADIE ROSE WEILERSTEIN

(age level four to seven)

K'tonton [a little Jewish Tom Thumb] rolled up his Simhat Torah flag and tucked it under his pillow—the wee Simhat Torah flag Father had made out of a bit of wood and a slip of paper. "Rejoice and be merry," said the little flag. How could anyone help being merry on a week so full of holidays? First came Sukkot, then Hoshana Rabbah. Tonight was Shemini Atzeret. Tomorrow night would be Simhat Torah.

"Mother," said K'tonton, "I'll surely go to synagogue on Simhat Torah, won't I?"

"Of course," said Mother, "if it doesn't rain."

If it doesn't rain! K'tonton hadn't thought about rain before. Suppose it DID rain! Suppose he could not go to synagogue and wave his flag. He looked anxiously out of the window. The sky was clear and cloudless, twinkling with stars. But you never could tell. A cloud might come up as big as a fist, and grow and grow.

All night K'tonton dreamed of clouds and storms, of wind and sweeping rain. He awoke to a pattering sound under his window. Rain!! But it wasn't rain. It was only the wind rustling the dried leaves on the *sukkah* roof.

Twice that morning during the synagogue service K'tonton forgot to say "Amen." He was so busy looking at the sky through the window. "It must not rain! It must not rain! It must not rain!" he kept whispering.

The cantor had gone out for a moment. He returned now dressed in a white robe, the same robe which he wore on Rosh Hashanah and Yom Kippur. K'tonton looked questioningly at his father.

"It's for *Geshem*, the prayer for rain," Father explained. "Have you forgotten?"

Geshem! The prayer for rain! K'tonton had forgotten. Soon all the congregation would be praying for rain. The cantor in his white robe would be praying for rain. He, K'tonton, would be praying for rain. But it must not rain. It must not!

The ark was opened. The congregation arose. "Thou makest the wind to blow and the rain to fall." The cantor began his solemn chant.

"Remember one who followed Thee
As to the sea flows water!
For Abram's sake send water!"

And all the congregation cried aloud, "For Abram's sake send water!" All but K'tonton. K'tonton shut his lips tight and made no sound. On and on went the cantor, and the people followed.

"For Isaac's sake send water!
For Jacob's sake send water!
For Moses' sake send water!
For Aaron's sake send water!"

Not a word did K'tonton say.

"For Israel's sake send water!" It was the last verse.

"Amen! Amen! Amen!" cried the congregation. K'tonton's mouth opened to form an Amen but he shut it quickly. It mustn't rain! He would not let it rain. The sky would be clear and he would go to synagogue and stand on Father's shoulder and throw kisses to the *Sifre Torah* and wave his flag. K'tonton looked defiantly at the sky.

But deep down in K'tonton's heart was something that had not been there before, something troubling and uncomfortable.

"Why, K'tonton, you haven't eaten a thing," said Mother at dinner as she looked at K'tonton's plate. It was piled high with chicken and *kugel* and carrot *tzimmes*. "Is anything wrong?"

"Nothing," said K'tonton. "I guess I'm tired. I'll take a little rest."

He climbed into his bed near the window. The sky was clear and cloudless. His wee flag crinkled comfortingly under his pillow, but K'tonton took no joy in the sky or in the flag. Something had gone wrong!

At last K'tonton slept. In his sleep he dreamed. He dreamed that he was in Eretz Yisrael, in the Land of Israel. But it wasn't a goodly land, a land of brooks of water and fountains that spring out of valleys and hills, a land of wheat and barley and vines and figs and pomegranates. It was a wasteland, a land parched and withered—a land that mourned. In this parched and barren land K'tonton heard the sound of prayer.

"Thou who causest the wind to blow and the rain to fall,
Send water!
Send water!
Send water!"

Startled, K'tonton looked about. It was the trees who prayed, the palm and the cedar, the olive and the citron, the myrtle, the willows of the brook. They rustled their withered leaves. They bowed and swayed. K'tonton saw that the tree which led in prayer was his own almond tree.

"Send water! Send water!" cried the almond tree. "For Israel's sake send water! For Israel's land send water!"

A sigh ran through its slender branches and set its dry leaves quivering.

Then a heavenly voice sounded in the still air. Two words spoke the heavenly voice.

"K'tonton shut his lips!
K'tonton would not pray!"

K'tonton awoke with a start and sprang from his bed. The little flag crinkled, but he pushed it firmly aside. He must pray for rain. He must pray at once. But how did one pray without a congregation? He remembered a story Father had told him. It was about Honi the Circlemaker. Long, long ago in the Land of Israel there had lived a righteous man named Honi. When the earth was parched and the springs dried up and no rain fell, Honi drew a circle on the ground. He stood in the center of the circle and cried to God for rain. And the rain fell.

K'tonton climbed quickly to his little grove on the windowseat. With his finger he drew a circle on the ground. He paused. Honi had been a righteous man and he was a sinner. But wasn't it written somewhere that if one were truly sorry and repented, he could stand even in the place of the righteous? No one, K'tonton thought, could be more full of repentance than he. He could feel the repentance in his throat, at his heart. He stepped firmly into the center of the circle and prayed.

"Thou who makest the wind to blow and the rain to fall,
For Israel's sake send water!
For Israel's land send water!
For my almond tree send water!"

He looked anxiously at the sky. A gray spot had appeared, a cloud as big as a fist. It grew. It spread. The whole sky turned leaden. A drop of rain splashed against the windowpane and came rolling down. K'tonton leaped into the air with a shout of joy.

That evening as K'tonton sat in his little grove watching the rain through the window and thinking of his almond tree—a green, fresh almond tree sucking up rain through its roots—he was interrupted by Father's voice.

"Where are you, K'tonton? Get your flag and hurry. We'll be late for synagogue."

"But the rain," said K'tonton.

"Never mind the rain," said Father. "I'll tuck you into my pocket."[2]

41. The Four Species.

❦ ❦ ❦

HOW K'TONTON REJOICED AND WAS MERRY ON SIMHAT TORAH

SADIE ROSE WEILERSTEIN

(age level four to seven)

"Let me see your flag, K'tonton."

It was David who spoke. You remember David, don't you? The sick little boy who lived next door! He wasn't sick anymore. He was quite well now and came in often to play with K'tonton.

K'tonton [a little Jewish Tom Thumb] showed him his flag. It was a Simhat Torah flag. Father had made it out of a match stick and a slip of paper. There were golden lions on it and Hebrew words in beautiful tiny letters: "Rejoice and be merry on Simhat Torah."

But K'tonton wasn't merry. He wasn't the least bit merry. There was something in his heart that wouldn't let him be merry. K'TON-TON WANTED TO BE BIG! As big as other boys—as big as David— big enough to march on Simhat Torah! K'tonton sighed. It was such a big, deep sigh that David jumped up in his seat.

"Goodness, K'tonton, what's wrong? It isn't Yom Kippur coming! It's Simhat Torah. Don't you like your flag?"

"Of course I do," said K'tonton. "It's a very good flag."

"Then what is the matter? We're friends, aren't we? You can tell a friend, can't you?"

So K'tonton told him. He told him all that was in his heart; how he wanted so much to march on Simhat Torah, and how he couldn't because he was too small.

"David," he said when he finished, "I was thinking—do you suppose I might happen to grow big enough by tomorrow? It says in the *siddur*, 'Thy miracles that are daily with us.' Daily is now, isn't it? And in the Bible it says, 'The low He makes high and the high He brings low'; and it says, 'Thy beginning shall be small, but thy end great.' It might happen, mightn't it?" He looked up eagerly at his friend.

"Y-e-s—it might," David said, "but I wouldn't count on it too much if I were you." Just then David's mother called him home.

"Better go to bed, David," she said, "you'll have to be up late tomorrow night."

So David went to bed, but he didn't sleep. Thoughts and verses kept running around in his head. Thoughts of K'tonton standing up on his father's shoulder watching the boys march by, when he wanted so much to be marching himself. Verses about "Miracles that are daily with us," and "The low He makes high," and "Thy end shall be great."

"He's GOT to march! He's got to!" thought David. "There must be a way." His forehead was puckered in thought.

Suddenly his face broke into a big smile. "I've got it!" He said. "I've got it!" He turned over on his pillow and went to sleep.

Next day there was such whispering going on, in K'tonton's house. David whispered to K'tonton's father, and K'tonton's father whispered to David, and Mother whispered to both. But nobody whispered to K'tonton. I don't know why K'tonton didn't notice, but he didn't. Perhaps because he was too busy trying to be merry, when he didn't feel merry.

Night came at last and they all started out for the synagogue. David carried his big flag and K'tonton carried his little flag. Father didn't need a flag because he was going to carry a *Sefer Torah* and Mother didn't have one, because all that mothers do, is kiss the *Sifre Torah* and wave their hands. When they reached the synagogue the lights were all lit and the grown-ups were smiling and whispering. All the children were hurrying down the aisles with crinkly new flags.

"You'd better hurry, David," said K'tonton, "if you want a good place."

He was trying not to remember how much he wanted to march himself.

"Have to fix my flag first!" said David.

He sat down on a bench beside K'tonton and his father. K'tonton watched him carefully. First he took out of his pocket a big rosy apple with a hole in the middle. Then he stuck the apple into the stick at the top of his flag.

"I know what it's for," said K'tonton. "It's for a candle."

"Is it?" said Father, and the next minute he had picked K'tonton up and stuck HIM inside the apple, right in the hole in the apple where the candle belonged. K'tonton's feet fitted snugly inside. Then David lifted the flag with K'tonton at the top of it and hurried along the aisle. "The low He makes high," laughed David.

Oh, how astonished K'tonton was! On they went, straight toward the *bimah* with the brightly lighted candlesticks and the crowds of boys and girls.

"K'tonton! It's K'tonton!" called the children. "K'tonton will be our leader! Let K'tonton lead." They waved their flags so hard it sounded like the wind in the forest.

So K'tonton marched on Simhat Torah after all, high up on David's flag at the head of the line. The beautiful *Sifre Torah* were so near he could touch their velvet covers with his hand. Once, twice, three times, four times, five times, six times, seven times round they marched. High above them all, higher than the children, higher than the flags, almost as high as the *Sifre Torah* moved K'tonton waving his little flag.

"Rejoice and be merry on Simhat Torah."[3]

✻ ✻ ✻

GITA MEETS SOME FRIENDS
MORRIS EPSTEIN

editor of World Over, *a magazine for Jewish children, and professor and chairman of the Department of English at Stern College for Women of Yeshiva University; in addition to scholarly work, he has written extensively for children.*

(age level six to nine)

Never was the synagogue so crowded. It was Simhat Torah eve. All the Torah Scrolls, clothed in their beautiful mantles, were taken out of the ark. Around and around the synagogue they were carried —once, twice . . . seven times. Gita and Jerry and all the other pupils of the Hebrew school marched along with the grown-ups. They held high their little flags topped by shiny freckled apples.

The big people sang and clapped their hands and celebrated. Gita and Jerry paraded and ate the chocolate bars given out by the principal. Tomorrow night the holiday would be over. In the morning, the reading of the Torah would come to an end and would be begun all over again from the very first word: "*Bereshit*."

At last, the dancing and the singing drew to a close. Gita and Jerry went home with Mother and Father. When they got into the house, Mother looked at the kitchen clock. "My it's *very* late," she exclaimed. "Into bed with you, Jerry and Gita."

The children undressed, washed, and brushed their teeth. They said their prayers with Mother and tumbled into bed. "I bet I'll be asleep in one minute," said Gita, yawning. "I bet I'll be asleep in one second," cried Jerry, curling up like a caterpillar.

But somehow, Gita couldn't find a comfortable spot. She tossed and turned. She rolled over and called softly, "Jerry!" But Jerry was fast asleep. Gita tried lying on her back, then on her stomach, and then on her side, but it was no use. She lay there a long, long time, staring into the dark. . . .

Suddenly she heard a faint scratch at the door. She sat up in bed and beheld a most amazing procession marching into the bedroom. First came a fat yellow *etrog*, with two twinkling eyes and a pair of stubby legs. Next strode a lanky *lulav*, with a long face and a pointy skull. He was followed by three myrtle twigs and two willow branches, rustling in a whispery sort of way. A cluster of five willow twigs, forming a *hoshana*, entered and curtsied to Gita. Bringing up the rear was a stocky *sukkah*, which squeezed and huffed and puffed until it just managed to get through the doorway.

All the visitors formed a neat line and looked to the *sukkah* for a sign to begin. He nodded, and they all said, "Hello, little Gita!"

Gita was so startled that she had to open her mouth twice before anything came out. "Wh-what are *you* doing here?" she finally blurted.

"We're very sad," said the *lulav* with the long face. "And we've come to make a request. But first, let us introduce ourselves."

"I-I know who you are," said Gita, rubbing her eyes in wonder. The visitors did not even seem to hear her and went right on talking.

"I'm the *sukkah*," said the stocky one in a deep voice. "I remind everyone of the forty years of wandering of the Israelites in the desert. After they left Egypt, you know, they lived in booths like me. And later, in Palestine, they built booths every Sukkot. They put twigs on me for a roof, so that they could see the stars in heaven shining through. And they decorated me with fruits and vegetables and thanked God for the fine harvest He had given to them. They brought the *lulav* in to me—"

"I'll speak for myself, thank you," broke in the lanky *lulav*. "Each day of Sukkot, I, a noble palm branch, am waved to the north, south, east and west, to show that God rules everywhere. I am carried around the synagogue by all the men . . ."

"And so are we!" chimed in the fat *etrog* and the myrtle twigs and the willow branches. "We are the *hadasim* and the *aravot*."

"All of us, except the *sukkah*, represent the *Arbaah Minim*, the 'Four Kinds' of growing things," said the *etrog*. "I am like the heart, without which man cannot live. The *lulav* is the spine, the myrtle is the eye, and the willow leaves are lips. We declare that a human being ought to serve God with all his soul and body."

"Ho, there, what about me?" cried the cluster of five willow twigs. "I'm important, too! I'm the *hoshana*. On Hoshana Rabbah, people strike me on a bench till my leaves fall off. I remind them that just as leaves fall and grow again, so God always gives people life and new hope. And I want to say—"

"Stop! Stop!" cried Gita, holding her hands to her ears. "I know *who* you all are. I learned *all* about you in Hebrew school. And Daddy uses you, and . . . and . . . But, won't you please tell me *why* you are here?"

"Well, as my friend said," remarked the *sukkah*, "we have a request. Sukkot and Shemini Atzeret and Simhat Torah are almost over. Where shall *we* be the day after tomorrow? I, for one, will be demolished!

"Our request is—can't you please keep us with you?" pleaded the *sukkah*. "We want to stay all year round!"

"Yes!" all the visitors cried in a chorus. "*We want to stay with you!*"

"You poor things!" said Gita, full of sympathy for them. "I love you all! I'll take care of you. I'll take care of you! I'll . . ."

Suddenly Gita felt a hand shaking her. She opened her eyes and found Mother standing over her bed.

"Gita!" said Mother. "Wake up, dear. Why are you shouting so? It's morning. Jerry's been up for more than an hour. Don't you want to go to synagogue with Daddy?"

Gita blinked. The sun was streaming in through the window. Then she remembered her visitors. "Mother!" she cried. "What's going to happen to the *etrog* and *lulav* and everything after Sukkot?"

"Why," said Mother, "We'll take the *sukkah* apart and put it neatly into the cellar. We'll put the *etrog* into its soft nest of straw and Daddy will keep it along with the spices when he says the *Havdalah* on Saturday night. And the *lulav* will stand tall and straight in the corner of the sun parlor."

"But—will they *like* that?" asked Gita. "Will they be happy?"

"What a strange question!" exclaimed Mother. "I suppose they will. They've done their job, and we have treated them carefully. I can't very well *ask* them though, can I?"

Just then, through the open bedroom door, Gita spied Father's tall *lulav*, standing in the corner of the sun parlor. A gust of wind blew in through the screened half-open window. And the lanky *lulav* rustled and quivered, his leaves scraping against each other, saying "Y-z-z, y-z-z, y-z-z!"

"Look, Mommy, look! The *lulav* is saying 'yes.' They will be pleased! They *really* will!"

Mother said, "Wonderful, dear. Now won't you get dressed?" And Gita did, thinking, "Golly, sometimes parents just *don't* understand the most important things of all!"[4]

❧ ❧ ❧

THE BIG AND THE LITTLE *ETROG*
HERMANN SCHWAB

historian of German Jewry, particularly concerned with traditional Jewish life; also author of a collection of stories for children that were first published in German in 1908 and since then translated into five languages (1879–1962)

(age level seven to ten)

It was just before Sukkot. The little Hebrew book shop was busy. People came and went as at no other time of the year. Yom Kippur was over, and those who had not yet bought their *lulav* and *etrog* made haste to get them, because the best went first, and those who came late had to take what was left.

The shop window had been specially decorated for Sukkot. All the year round it had a display of books and pictures, prayer shawls and Hanukkah lamps, cedarwood spice boxes, Esther scrolls on parchment, *seder* dishes, and Torah ornaments with little tinkling gold bells.

Now the window was full of nothing but *etrogim*. They lay there in little and big boxes, and every hour the number of boxes grew less, and then new boxes took their place; but the fruit was no longer so choice.

For no *etrog* is like the other. There are *etrogim* whose color is a happy blend between green and yellow, with the slowly rising shape of a tower, and without any spots or patches, and there are others which are round like lemons and are full of spots and patches.

They had come from overseas in big ships, from countries where the sun is warmer than here, and the sky is cloudless. Now they were lying in the window of the Hebrew book shop waiting for buyers.

In one box, right in front, against the windowpanes were two *etrogim,* one a real beauty, the other a poor-looking thing, so yellow that it looked almost dried up. They seemed to have been forgotten. They were the last left in their box.

The little one hid himself humbly in a corner, while the bigger one rolled as near as he could get to the glass panes, and sunned himself proudly, showing himself to all who passed.

He had taken no notice till now of his poorer neighbor, but as hour after hour went by, he swallowed his pride and turned to the little *etrog.*

"Not much hope for you," he said. "You look such a poor specimen. You would have done better to have stayed at home. No one will want to buy you here."

The other looked up startled. He had been dreaming of his home, the palms and pomegranates, oranges and almonds, blue skies and bright sunshine. What did this big fellow want? He did not know him. And what right had he to scoff at him?

The other went on. "We shan't be left here together for long. I am only waiting till the richest man in the town comes to buy an *etrog.* Then I shall be in a beautiful house, in a silver box, and when they say the blessing for the *lulav* in the synagogue I shall be right in front, and I shall lead the procession."

"You mustn't be so proud," said the little *etrog.* "You did not make yourself beautiful, and beauty can be lost."

"Lost?" said the other arrogantly. "Don't you worry about me. I can look after myself."

Just then the shopkeeper opened the inside window. He was talking very respectfully to a dignified looking gentleman.

"Certainly," he was saying, "I have kept the finest *etrog* for you. You will be delighted with it."

He leaned over to catch hold of the big *etrog,* but it had rolled too near the windowpane, and he could not reach it. The shopkeeper called his youngest son and told him to get up into the window and fetch out the *etrog*. "Careful," he called after him.

The youngster climbed lightly into the window, walked right up to the glass, took hold of the big *etrog*, and came back with it. The gentleman held out his hand to take it with a pleased smile at the sight of the beautiful *etrog*. But the boy tripped. The *etrog* fell out of his hand, and when he picked it up again, its crown, the *pitma*, had broken off.

All three stood aghast. The *etrog* was unusable. The bookseller shouted at the boy; the youngster cried; and the gentleman shrugged his shoulders and said, "Give me another one, please."

"But I haven't any other as good as this," said the bookseller. "I kept it specially for you. I have only one *etrog* left, and it isn't good enough for you. I hadn't thought of selling it at all. It's such a poor specimen."

42. The *etrog* and *lulav* market in Tel Aviv.

He leaned over and brought out the little *etrog* which had been lying patiently in its corner.

The little *etrog* saw his big neighbor looking glum. The bookseller held him for a moment and then threw him into a box of discarded *etrogim*.

The little *etrog* looked down at him with pity. He had a kind heart and had already forgotten how arrogant the other had been. And his pity for the other *etrog* suddenly beautified him. The spots and patches disappeared, and he seemed to grow in size. The gentleman held him in his hand and said, "It's quite a nice *etrog*."

The bookseller looked at the *etrog*, surprised. It seemed to have changed completely.

The gentleman paid for the *etrog* and took it away with him. The bookseller stood for a while shaking his head. He still did not understand what had happened to the little *etrog*.

Translated by Joseph Leftwich[5]

❧ ❧ ❧

TWO FEASTS FOR SUKKOT
HELEN FINE

teacher in both public and religious schools and author of several books for Jewish children

(age level eight to eleven)

"On Sukkot those who know the best
Will point the *lulav* east and west.
To north and south, to earth and sky,
To show that God is always nigh."

Debra chanted her poem as the car sped smoothly over the country road. Debra and David and Daddy and G'dee were winging their way to the Blue Hills to gather branches to decorate the walls and cover the roof of the Temple Israel *sukkah*. Behind the school, in the garden, the carpenters had built a *sukkah*. On Sukkot the children were going to have a party. How they looked forward to the Sukkot fun.

Mr. Mann spied a good place to stop the car. They piled out. Into the woods they tramped until they came to a mossy carpet. Huge branches were everywhere. Soon they were gathering great heaps of fragrant branches, and carrying them to the car. When the back of the car was full Daddy opened the trunk, and used that space too.

G'dee was helping too. David thrust a branch into G'dee's mouth.

"Here, G'dee, take this to the car, please." Off scampered G'dee with the branch held firmly in his mouth. He was back in a few minutes. Debra did the same thing. G'dee liked this game. It was such good fun. He was being an obedient goat. He was anxious to please his family, especially Daddy.

Everything was fine until—whisk! A bushy-tailed squirrel scooted suddenly in front of G'dee, frightening him within an inch of his goat life. G'dee's ears stood up like Indian wigwams. His whiskers flew up like a shelf. His mouth opened and the branch fell out. With a quick leap he was after the squirrel. No whisky, frisky squirrel was going to insult him!

He almost had the squirrel by the tail when it scampered up a tall tree—up, up, up, to the tippety-top branch. There it sat toasting its tail in the sun, staring boldly down at G'dee.

G'dee tried to climb the tree. My—how he tried. But the bark was too slippery for him. Patiently he stood at the foot of the tree, glaring at his enemy, waiting for the squirrel to come down again. But Bushy Tail frisked through the sunny branches chattering away to the sky. G'dee waited and waited and waited. He was going to catch that scoundrel if it took all day and night.

Meanwhile, the twins and Daddy filled every bit of space in the car with spicy branches. They looked around for G'dee.

"G'dee," shouted Debra, "we're ready to go home."

"Now where could he have disappeared?" worried David.

"Ma-a-a-a-a," came an angry bleat from the direction of a tall tree. What a relief to find their goat safe! They coaxed and coaxed him to come with them, but the goat wouldn't budge. David and Debra couldn't understand G'dee's stubbornness. He had been so helpful all day.

"Let me be," bleated G'dee, "I'm going to teach that squirrel a lesson he'll never forget!"

Finally, David grasped G'dee by the right horn, and Debra grasped him by the left horn. Tugging at him with all their might, they dragged the unwilling goat to the car.

But when G'dee saw those tempting branches he forgot to be cross. Nestling in the soft branches he had the time of his goat life munching away. It was a feast fit for a crown prince, that is, a crown prince goat.

And that was G'dee's Sukkot feast number one.

The next day dawned crisp and clear. After school Mrs. Mann picked up the twins in the car. They were going to the temple *sukkah* to help decorate it. She drove them home quickly for some milk and cookies. When they came out to get into the car again, G'dee was waiting. The twins looked wistfully at Mother. G'dee looked wistfully at Mother. Mrs. Mann put them out of their suspense with a smile.

"All right, put G'dee in the back of the car, and hurry. We're late already. I do hope G'dee behaves himself."

G'dee nodded his head up and down. "Why do you always put ideas into my head?" he bleated, as the twins pushed him into the car.

When they arrived they found five mothers inside the *sukkah*. Susan and Jonathan, classmates of the twins, were there too. When they saw G'dee they rushed over to hug him. G'dee felt very important.

The twins looked at the long tables. They saw shiny peppers and fat string beans and curly yellow squashes. They saw red twinkly apples and green Seckel pears and bunches of deep purple grapes. On the walls and over the roof the mothers had already hung the spicy branches. How fragrantly everything smelled!

"It's like an enchanted forest," said Debra.

The mothers hung the fruit and vegetables among the branches. Mr. Kirkman was up on a tall ladder hanging fruit and vegetables on the branches in the highest part of the *sukkah*.

"How would you four children like to string these cranberries on this string?" asked Mrs. Mann, pointing to a pile of cranberries on the table.

David and Jonathan bored the holes with thick needles. Debra and Susan threaded the juicy berries on the long strings. G'dee was running about everywhere. He stood close to Debra, as close as could be. Pop! Into his mouth slid a cranberry. He ran to Susan. Pop! Into his mouth went another cranberry. Another and another and another —the fruit flew into G'dee's mouth faster than it went onto the string. His beard was streaked with red juice. Some of the juice stained his face in spots.

"Look!" said Debra, "G'dee has the measles!" But G'dee didn't let that bother him. He was having a cranberry good time.

When the cranberry strings were threaded, Mr. Kirkman hung them in loops on the beams running across the ceiling, high, high up in the *sukkah*. G'dee kept glancing up at the delicious berries so far out of his reach. How he longed to be able to reach them. But how?

Debra looked up to the holes in the roof where the boards separated.

"Mother, why are the holes there?"

Mother smiled at her. "Our ancestors wandered about the desert for forty years, living in small huts called *sukkot*, before they became a free nation. These huts were not their real homes. They could be swept away with a sudden gust of wind, and no longer shelter them. But our ancestors felt safe because they knew God was helping them. They felt protected no matter what happened. Today we leave holes in our *sukkah* roof to remind us that God is still near us."

Jonathan had something to add to Mother's story. "When they came to the Promised Land, our ancestors lived in *sukkot*, too. They lived in them while they gathered in the harvest."

David had a question too. "Why do we hang fruits and vegetables in the *sukkah*?"

"The fruit and vegetables are God's gifts to all of us. This is how we show our thanks to God for everything He gives to us," said Mother.

David remembered about the Pilgrims. "Our teacher told us that the Pilgrims took their idea for Thanksgiving from our holiday of Sukkot. Our ancestors celebrated Sukkot by bringing the finest fruits and vegetables of the harvest to the Temple in Jerusalem."

Debra thought of a poem.

"Gather in our *sukkah* cosy,
Hung with grapes and apples rosy,
Pretty flowers gaily spread,
Leafy branches overhead.

Thanking God we pray together
For our blessings day by day,
Here in sunny autumn weather,
In our *sukkah* bright and gay."

Everybody clapped. Debra blushed. David was so proud he almost burst. Mrs. Mann just beamed all over.

"My uncle Joseph who lives in the State of Israel sent us a *lulav* and an *etrog*," said Debra, changing the subject. "The *lulav* is a sheaf of palm leaves tied together with three twigs of myrtle, and two branches of willow. All these trees grow in Uncle Joseph's garden. He has an *etrog* tree too."

Jonathan's mother asked, "Why do you suppose they chose those special trees?"

All the children were ready with the answer. They had studied it in religious school.

Jonathan said, "Miss Baron said it happened so long ago that no one really knows. But the rabbis said the *lulav* reminds us of the kings and prophets in the Bible."

"The myrtle reminds us of the wisdom of the Torah," said Susan.

"The drooping willow reminds us of the years our ancestors wandered over the face of the earth," said David.

"The *etrog* is the Jewish hope for the future," said Debra. All the mothers clapped again.

"I just love to hold the *etrog* close to my nose. It smells like French perfume," said Debra, closing her eyes and breathing in deeply.

David laughed and said, "Debra keeps sniffing and sniffing at the *etrog* just like G'dee."

"Which reminds me, where is G'dee?" asked Debra, looking about the *sukkah*.

"He must have wandered into the garden," said David.

The children ran into the garden. They looked everywhere but G'dee was nowhere in sight.

"Ma-a-a-a," came an unhappy bleat from the top of the *sukkah*.

The children stared in amazement. Coming closer to the *sukkah*, David saw that G'dee had fallen into a hole in the roof, his feet dangling inside. His hind feet were standing on a broad roof beam covered with branches. G'dee was wriggling the front of his body back and forth, but he couldn't budge his front legs.

"He must have climbed the ladder leaning at the side of the *sukkah* wall," thought David, wincing at his goat's cries of pain.

"I'll call Mr. Kirkman," said Debra, running inside the *sukkah*.

Mr. Kirkman and Debra came out, followed by all the mothers.

"Can you save my goat?" asked Debra. The lump in her throat was like a rock.

"Don't worry," promised Mr. Kirkman. "I'll figure something out." He climbed up on the ladder while the twins held it in place so that it wouldn't wobble. Everyone watched breathlessly.

Mr. Kirkman reached the roof. He saw that G'dee had fallen into a hole close to the side of the *sukkah*. With his long arms he leaned over and grasped G'dee's front legs where they joined his body. With a quick jerk he pushed G'dee straight up into the air. Pulling the trembling goat toward his chest, he came down the ladder. Placing G'dee on the grass, he wiped the beads of perspiration from his face. G'dee wobbled unsteadily.

"Oh, thank you, thank you," cried the twins, giving Mr. Kirkman a hug on both sides. The twins kneeled down and hugged G'dee, too.

"Thank Mr. Kirkman, G'dee," said Debra. Shaking his cranberry beard, G'dee tottered over to the janitor.

"Thank you for saving my life, Mr. Kirkman," he bleated. "Those cranberries almost ruined me."

Mrs. Mann decided that her family had had enough excitement for one afternoon. She bundled them into the car. G'dee stretched himself out on the back seat. He yawned a great yawn, and fell alseep.

Mrs. Mann and the twins left him in the car when they arrived home. He slept in the car all night. And that was the end of G'dee's Sukkot feast number two.[6]

❦ ❦ ❦

SIMON'S FIRST REAL SUKKOT
DOROTHY F. ZELIGS

psychologist who received her doctorate in education; author of a series of Jewish history texts and other children's books

(age level ten to thirteen)

Simon was holding a bright-colored gourd in his hand, trying to decide just where to hang it. He looked thoughtfully all around the large synagogue *sukkah*, which he and his classmates at religious school were decorating. Simon felt very lucky because his group had been chosen for this pleasant task, while other classes were busy with their regular lessons. The *sukkah* looked lovely, he thought. The walls were covered with the green branches of trees and trailing vines. Against this background were hung fruits of many kinds and colors, and other products of the harvest season. Large, rosy apples, ruddy pears, and clusters of luscious dark grapes hung by their stems on the walls and from the roof. A small bunch of bananas made a splash of golden color near the pale green of quinces. From the roof, which was made of fragrant pine branches, hung festoons of strung popped corn, a vivid white against the green. On the floor, in a corner, stood an autumn sheaf of cornstalks, and right beside it lay a large, bright-colored pumpkin. Green and red peppers, also strung on cord, made a gay arc across one of the walls.

Simon looked around critically but with a pleasant feeling of accomplishment. His classmates were still dashing about here and there, putting on the finishing touches. He wondered where he should hang the large, gaily colored gourd which he still held in his hand. He had to find just the right place for this final bit of decoration. Then he spied a bare spot on the roof, at the front of the *sukkah*. The very place, he decided, for everyone would see it there. He dashed for the ladder, climbed up, and tied on the gourd. His teacher, a pleasant young man of about twenty-two, stood watchfully at the foot of the ladder. He breathed more easily when the boy came down.

And now it was time for the whole school to gather in the *sukkah*, for the general assembly was to be held there.

The admiring exclamations of the children who came flocking in at the sound of the bell was sweet praise to those who had done the task. Simon looked up at his own special gourd and gave it a friendly smile.

The assembly service began with a song of thanksgiving for the bountiful harvest season. In the fragrant and colorful atmosphere of the *sukkah*, even the city children felt the breath of fields and orchards and the richness of the fertile earth. As the rabbi began to talk about the significance of this festival, Simon listened intently. This was the first real Sukkot of his experience, and he found it tremendously interesting.

"Many, many centuries ago," the rabbi was saying, "our ancestors lived as farmers in the land of Canaan. Long before America was discovered, centuries before Christianity was founded, the ancient Hebrews were plowing the soil of Palestine and planting seed. They lived in small villages, in huts of sun-baked clay. Their most joyous holiday of the year was the Festival of Ingathering, when the harvest was completed and the people gave thanks to God for His goodness. That was Sukkot in ancient days, the festival which we still celebrate today.

"As we look about this beautiful booth, we ask ourselves what it means, and why the Jewish people have followed the interesting custom of the *sukkah* for hundreds of years. The commandment to build the *sukkah* is given in the Bible, which says, 'The Lord had commanded by Moses, that the children of Israel should dwell in booths in the feast of the seventh month; and that they should publish and proclaim in all their cities, and in Jerusalem, saying, "Go forth unto the mount and fetch olive branches and myrtle branches, and palm branches, and branches of thick trees, to make booths, as it is written." So the people went forth and brought them, and made themselves booths, every one upon the roof of his house, and in their courts, and in the courts of the house of God, and in the broad place of the water-gate and in the broad place of the gate of Ephraim. . . . And there was great gladness. . . . And they kept the feast seven days; and the eighth day was a solemn assembly, according unto the law.'

"A number of reasons have been given to explain this custom of the *sukkah*. The Bible tells us that the *sukkah* reminds us of the days when our ancestors lived as nomads in the desert, wandering

43. Examining willows in Jerusalem.

about from place to place, and dwelling in tents. The *sukkah* also serves as a reminder of the small booths which the farmers of Palestine would often erect in their fields and vineyards during the harvest season. There they would sleep, guarding their crops from thieves and wild animals. We can imagine them lying on their mats within their loosely built booths made of the branches of trees. Through the boughs fell the bright rays of the brilliant Palestine moon, just as in this *sukkah* the sun is dropping its golden shafts at this moment.

"Other explanations have been added by Jewish scholars and teachers concerning the meaning of the *sukkah*. Some say that it is a symbol of our faith in God, for even though we leave our sturdy homes and dwell in these frail booths, we feel confident that God will protect us, just as He did our ancestors who wandered in the wilderness and lived in tents. The *sukkah* may also be a symbol of the insecure lives which the Jewish people have led during the past two thousand years, as they wandered from land to land, seeking a safe place in which to live. And yet, throughout their hardships, the Jews have survived. Thus, the *sukkah* reminds us of our own weakness and of the goodness of God, who protects us. But, chiefly, it recalls the happy harvest season in Palestine."

After the rabbi was through speaking, a group of children came to the front of the *sukkah*. They were each carrying a green, slender palm branch, known as a *lulav* in Hebrew, and a fragrant, yellow citron, called an *etrog*. Each palm branch had some small branches of a willow tree fastened to it on one side, and some myrtle branches on the other side. These four kinds of plants are used at Sukkot to represent the fruitfulness of the earth at this harvest season. Orthodox Jews recite a blessing over them every morning of the Sukkot festival.

The children displayed their plants. They sang songs and recited poems about them. Within that colorful *sukkah*, everyone felt the presence of the happy harvest season.

After the assembly, Simon and the Jonathon children walked home together, talking about the *sukkah* and the interesting things the rabbi had told them. Mrs. Jonathon met them at the door. "I have a surprise for you," she cried. "We've all been invited to spend the second part of the Sukkot festival with Aunt Bess and Uncle David. You know, Simon, they haven't seen much of you since your arrival, and they're eager to have you. Grandfather lives with them, and he is looking forward to your visit."

"I'll bet Cousin Danny is too," put in Ruthie excitedly. "Oh, Mother, I'm so glad Maury and I are going too."

"I'm so glad I'm going too," echoed Naomi, beginning to hop around the room on one foot, as she usually did when excited.

"I think Sukkot is a grand holiday," Simon declared. "I like the way it's divided into two parts, with half-holidays in between."

On the afternoon of the seventh day of Sukkot, several hours before sunset, the Jonathon family and Simon started on the trip for the distant suburb where their relatives lived. "We want to get there before evening," Dr. Jonathon said, "or Grandfather will have left for the synagogue. You know, tonight is *yom tov*.

"Aunt Bess and Uncle David are very Orthodox," Maury informed Simon. "That's one reason why Grandfather lives with them."

"They have a *sukkah* all their own," Ruthie chimed in eagerly. "It's in their back yard. And we'll eat our meals there and everything."

Dr. Jonathon stopped his car in front of a simple two-family brick house. Twelve-year-old Danny, who was waiting for them on the porch, gave a whoop of delight. Aunt Bess, glowing with welcome, hurried to the door and gave each child a big hug and a kiss in her warmhearted fashion. "It's so good to see you all," she cried. "Come in. Here is Grandfather. He's been talking of nothing but you children all day. I think he's been even more impatient for your coming than Danny."

"Of course I was." Grandfather smiled as he embraced them. "And look at them—why shouldn't I be proud to be their grandfather!"

The men and boys now had to hurry off to the synagogue. Ruthie and Aunt Elsa helped to set the table in the *sukkah* for the evening meal. "It's beautiful," Ruthie cried as she stopped with a pile of plates in her hands and looked around admiringly. The green-covered walls of the *sukkah* were generously decorated with fruits and flowers of all kinds and colors. Through the green branches of the roof glinted the warm rays of the setting sun. The air was fragrant with a mingling of delightful odors—the smell of fresh flowers and pine branches. The table looked very nice, Ruthie thought, with its shining white cloth, sparkling silver, and dainty-stemmed glassware. The candles, which had just been lit, glowed in the silver candlesticks. At the head of the table lay two long twists of golden white bread, covered with an embroidered cloth. Nearby stood a goblet for wine and a filled decanter. Ruthie arranged the dinner plates, handling them very carefully, for they were her aunt's best dishes.

Now Aunt Bess came in to say the blessing over the candles. Ruth enjoyed the lovely scene. Aunt Bess spread her hands over the lights and then covered her face as she said the following prayer in Hebrew. "Blessed art Thou, O Lord our God, King of the universe, who hast sanctified us by Thy commandments, and commanded us to light the festival lights."

Very soon the front door was flung open and the sound of merry voices filled the air. "Good *yom tov*, Good *yom tov*," everyone cried.

They gathered around the table and remained standing while Grandfather filled the goblet with wine and chanted the *Kiddush* in a beautiful melody. Then came the ritual washing of the hands, which is customary before every meal by Orthodox Jews. Simon did as the others, pouring a glass of water first over one hand and then over the other. As he dried them on a towel, he repeated the Hebrew prayer after his grandfather. "Blessed art Thou, O Lord our God, King of the universe, who hast sanctified us by Thy commandments and commanded us concerning the washing of the hands."

When they were all seated at the table, Grandfather repeated a prayer over the bread. "Blessed art Thou, O Lord, our God, King of the universe, who hast brought forth bread from the earth." Each one repeated the prayer and ate a piece of the bread which was passed around.

Then came one of Aunt Bess's delicious holiday dinners.

After grace was said, the children followed Grandfather into the living room and gathered around his chair. "This is one time when you get a vacation, Phil," smiled his wife. "It looks like Grandfather will be doing the talking tonight."

"Perhaps I shouldn't admit it, Elsa, but I think I shall miss being the center of their attention. It's rather fun, you know."

Simon promptly spied a *lulav* and *etrog*, which were standing on a table. He picked them up and examined them. "The willow branches are a bit faded, Grandfather," he said critically, "and the twigs of myrtle are losing some of their leaves. But your *etrog* is very nice, and so is the *lulav*."

"Well, you seem to be quite an expert on the subject," Grandfather replied, with a twinkle in his eye. "But this happens to be the seventh day of Sukkot. The blessing over these species is recited only on the mornings of the first seven days of the festival, so these plants have already served their purpose."

"You see, little boys shouldn't be so clever," Maury put in teasingly.

"Come, I'll show you just how it is done," Grandfather suggested. "The *etrog* is held in the left hand and the *lulav* in the right. The following blessing is recited: 'Blessed art Thou, O Lord our God, King of the universe, who has sanctified us by Thy commandments and commanded us to take the *lulav*.'"

"Does everybody here say it too?" asked Naomi.

"Every member of the family," her grandfather replied.

"All sorts of interesting meanings have been given to these four species of plants," the old man went on. "You see, the *etrog* has both beauty and fragrance. The *lulav* has beauty but not fragrance. The myrtle has fragrance but no beauty, and the willow has neither. They have been compared to four types of people. The *etrog* stands for the person who has both beauty and strength of character. The palm branch represents one who has beauty but no strength of character. The myrtle—"

"Stands for strength of character but no beauty," interrupted Simon.

"And the willow for the one who has neither," chanted Ruthie.

"They are also compared to four kinds of Jews," went on their grandfather, who was enjoying himself thoroughly. "The *etrog* stands for the Jew who is educated in the Torah and does kind deeds. The *lulav* is the symbol of the Jew who knows Torah but does not practice acts of kindness."

"The myrtle," Simon took up the story, "I suppose, stands for the Jew who is ignorant of the Torah but does kind deeds."

"And the poor willow," Ruthie chanted again, "is both ignorant and unkind. I'm beginning to feel sorry for the willow."

"Talking about the willow makes me think of the services in the synagogue this morning," Danny remarked. "The willow really did get special attention then. The whole congregation formed a procession," he explained to the others, "and we marched around the pews. The rabbi stood on the little platform in the center, holding a Scroll of the Torah. Then we all took the willow branches and beat them on the ground until the leaves came off. It was fun."

"Why did they do that, Grandfather?" asked Simon.

"Today was the seventh day of the Sukkot festival," the old man replied. "It has a special name, all its own—Hoshana Rabbah. The prayers which are chanted during this procession that Danny described begin and end with the word "*Hoshana*," which means *save us*. Every day of Sukkot, the congregation forms a procession and marches around one time, but on Hoshana Rabbah, the day of the Great Hosanna, the procession marches around seven times.

"The ceremonies have remained with us since the days of the Temple in Jerusalem, two thousand years ago," Grandfather went on. "Sukkot was celebrated with great festivities in those days. There, everyone marched around the great altar, but today we circle around the Torah in the synagogue, for the Torah is now the center of Jewish life."

"You haven't explained why they beat the willow branches on the ground, the way Danny said they did," Simon reminded him.

"That custom, too, has survived from Temple days," Grandfather explained. "It is a symbolic way of asking for a fertile crop. The willow grows on the banks of streams and in other moist places and therefore represents plentiful rain and a good soil."

For the rest of the evening, Grandfather told them more about Sukkot. Simon learned that this festival is the longest of the Jewish year. It consists of nine days. After the first two days come five half-holidays. The seven days of Sukkot are followed by Shemini Atzeret, the Eighth Day of Solemn Assembly. It is no longer really necessary to eat in the *sukkah* after the seventh day, but many people like to do so. The ninth day of the holiday is Simhat Torah, Rejoicing in the Law. On this day, the reading of the Torah, which has taken a whole year, is concluded, and then immediately begun again. A portion of the Torah is read in the synagogue every Sabbath. Simhat Torah expresses the joy of the Jewish people in their precious possession, the Torah.

The next two days which the children spent with their relatives were happy ones. Simon especially enjoyed the services in the synagogue on Simhat Torah. On this occasion, even the women and girls, who usually sit up in the gallery in the Orthodox synagogue, may come into the main hall of worship. Simon watched with interest as the Scrolls of the Torah were taken out of the ark. Each Scroll was handed to a member of the congregation. A procession was formed, the men bearing the Scrolls going first, the children following gaily after them. Some of the boys and girls carried small flags of white and blue. The group circled around the pews, chanting psalms in joyous voices. A cantor and a choir of young boys led the prayers. Many of those who were seated, reached over and kissed the velvet coverings of the Scrolls. Seven times the procession moved around the hall, carrying its precious burden. Thus Israel expressed its joy for the sacred heritage of the Torah, which the Jews have given to the world.

It was Simon's first real Simhat Torah, and he found it a very interesting experience.[7]

❧ ❧ ❧

THE HOSHANA OF RABBI EPHRAIM
DAVID EINHORN

leading modern Yiddish poet and essayist and columnist for the Jewish Daily Forward; *author of many children's stories based on folklore and legends, some of which have been translated into English*

(*age level eleven to fourteen*)

The endless Russian plains stretch as far as the eye can see. Here and there a lake dots the landscape, with lush, green grass fringing the water's edge. In olden times, scattered villages nestled in the hills and dales bordering the lakes.

Once, a Jewish village lay sprawling near just such a lake. To get to the water, one walked a short distance from the town, climbed a sloping hill, and there it was—its surface like a gleaming mirror reflecting the deep blue of heaven. The horizon was unbroken save for one old willow tree whose drooping branches swayed in eternal mourning. Occasional drops of water fell from the branches like tears and made rippling circles in the still water. To the Jews of the village the tree became known as "Ephraim's *hoshana.*"

Many years ago (said the old folks) a wealthy man lived in the village. He had an only child, a brilliant boy named Ephraim.

His schoolmates called him "the curious dreamer" because he asked so many questions and because he spent whole summer days at the lake, lost in daydreams.

Each Sukkot his father would assign a task to Ephraim, a duty which the boy considered a great honor.

In those days of primitive transportation, an *etrog* and *lulav* were very expensive. They had to be brought from far overseas, and only the wealthiest people could afford them. Those who were fortunate enough to own an *etrog* and *lulav* considered it a *mitzvah* to lend them to the poor so that they might pronounce the blessing.

Every morning, Ephraim made his rounds with the *etrog* and *lulav*. First he went to the old *yeshivah* teacher, Rabbi Isaiah, who lived with his wife in a little village. Rabbi Isaiah was too feeble to get about much, and he could always be found poring over a holy book.

Rabbi Isaiah and Ephraim had become fast friends. The old man was the only one to whom the boy could confide his innermost thoughts.

"Your son will one day be a great rabbi," the teacher often said to Ephraim's father.

Once, when Ephraim brought the *etrog* and *lulav* to Rabbi Isaiah, the old man's attention was drawn to the lad's troubled expression. "What is it, my boy?" said the rabbi.

"Nothing," said Ephraim. "But . . . I just cannot understand the meaning of the *etrog* and the *lulav*, the myrtle and the willow branches."

"My child," answered the rabbi, "you know the explanations our sages have given us."

"I know," said Ephraim, "but I'm still puzzled."

"Well, then," said the rabbi with a smile, "perhaps you will like my explanation. The *lulav* is a palm leaf. A palm tree reaches skyward and its leaves are like hands outstretched to heaven in prayer. The *etrog* has a delicate fragrance, and good deeds, say our sages, have the aroma of rare spices.

"The myrtle twigs, my child, represent beauty and modesty. The Hebrew word for myrtle is *hadassah* and that, as you know, was Queen Esther's name, for she was very beautiful. But it is also said that when Adam was driven from the Garden of Eden because he ate from the tree of knowledge, he took with him a myrtle branch. Later he planted it. It flowered beautifully, and when Adam looked at it, he dreamed that one day the whole world would be a Garden of Eden. We, too, wait and hope for the Messiah."

"And what about the willow branch . . . the *hoshana*?" asked Ephraim. "Why do we mistreat it so? At the morning service on Hoshana Rabbah, we beat the poor willow against the floor until all its leaves are gone! And didn't our ancestors hang their harps on the willows of Babylon because they were in exile? The willow has followed us everywhere."

44. Sukkot at the Western Wall, Jerusalem.

"Yes, my child," said the rabbi. "It is a sign of our sadness and our longing. When we dream of being freed from exile, we thrash the symbol of our exile."

"I like the poor willow best of all. It is sad and lonely like me." Ephraim's voice broke.

Rabbi Isaiah leaned over and said softly, "Bring three *hoshanot*— three willow branches—tomorrow. I will bless two with the *etrog* and *lulav*. The third I will bless separately, and you will plant it near your favorite spot at the lake. Then we shall see what happens."

Ephraim did as he was bidden.

Years passed. Ephraim became a renowned rabbi. Isaiah died. And the little twig that the boy had planted blossomed into a great willow with massive branches and thick leaves. Rabbi Ephraim forgot all about his talk with Rabbi Isaiah. Nor did he know how the old teacher had blessed the third *hoshana*.

Then one day Emperor Napoleon marched into Russia with his armies. Soldiers in strange uniforms appeared. They blocked the roads and ordered the inhabitants of the little village to stay indoors.

Now it happened that Ephraim had gone to a wedding in a town an hour away from his home. He had decided to return on foot. Dusk had fallen when he reached the outskirts of his village. Suddenly he heard a sharp command, and he was startled to see armed men, shouting orders in a language he did not understand, pointing rifles threateningly at him.

Panic seized Ephraim and he began to run. With the soldiers at his heels he came to the little vale. A mysterious force seemed to spin him around, and against his will he panted up the sloping hill and down toward the lake.

Then something beyond belief happened. The dense foliage of the old willow tree parted and enfolded Ephraim like two protecting arms. Dumbfounded, he saw the branches weave themselves into a sheltering screen. When the French soldiers came charging up to the lake they found no trace of a human being. The company commander snarled, "He couldn't have gotten through here. He'd need an ax to chop open a path. Probably ran to the village." And they left.

For two days and nights Ephraim remained in his hideaway. The long green willow leaves splashed raindrops into Ephraim's cupped palms, and he was refreshed. On the second day, sitting in silence in his shady shelter, Ephraim suddenly remembered his talk with

Rabbi Isaiah. A tremor passed through him. This tree was the third *hoshana* which Isaiah had blessed and which Ephraim had planted!

No sooner had he remembered than the branches parted again. Ephraim saw the open path and knew that it was safe to return home.

To be sure, the French soldiers had departed. The villagers greeted Rabbi Ephraim joyfully. They had been certain that misfortune had befallen him.

The very next Sabbath, Ephraim came to the synagogue and recited *Gomel*, the blessing recited by those who are rescued from danger. In his sermon he recounted his talk of long ago with Rabbi Isaiah and described how he had planted the third *hoshana* which had so miraculously saved him from Napoleon's troops.

And he took a vow in the presence of the whole congregation. "Some day, God willing," he said, "I will journey to the Holy Land with my family. When I go, I will take with me a shoot of this willow and plant it near Jerusalem, so that the willow will be blessed to see the arrival of the Messiah.

"Who knows," he concluded, his voice trailing into a whisper, "perhaps branches of this very willow may one day grace the holy altar of our rebuilt Temple of God."

Translated by Morris Epstein[8]

❦ ❦ ❦

TOO LATE
ABRAHAM REISIN

Yiddish poet, author of short stories, and editor of several magazines; his writings possess a folk quality revealing a deep understanding of the characters about whom he wrote (1876–1953)

(age level eleven to fourteen)

Antosh cracked his whip and urged his ancient mare along. It was almost noon and he was only on the outskirts of the town. But the poor horse just plodded along. Antosh lifted his whip again. "Please, move!" The horse whinnied, and it seemed that even *she* was laughing at Antosh. But what could he expect? Everyone else whom he passed on the road had laughed. Everyone. What could be wrong?

It had all begun when autumn came.

The days in Eastern Europe were getting shorter and the nights longer. Antosh, a peasant living in a small village, would have liked to light a lamp in the evening, but the kerosene jug was empty and he had no money. His supply of salt was also running very low, and he only had a very small piece of soap left. There was not a tea leaf in the pot, nor a pinch of snuff in the jar.

"It is bad," said Antosh talking to himself, "no salt, no tobacco, no soap, nothing."

And Antosh had no way of earning money. He had only one hope: to load his wagon with green branches that the Jews use to cover their *sukkot*, take it into town, and sell it.

Right after Rosh Hashanah, he began to pester the one Jew who lived in his village. "When will you celebrate Sukkot?" he used to ask every day. And each time the Jew would answer, "It is a long way off yet."

"But when?" Antosh would insist.

One day, the Jew, to stop Antosh's pestering answered, "One week from today."

Actually it was only five days to Sukkot, but Antosh did not know this, and planned to come to town with his merchandise when he thought it was two days before the holiday. This was, of course, the first day of Sukkot.

That day Antosh rose early, hitched up his sleepy, half-starved horse, took his ax, and drove into the forest. He began to cut branches and put them into the wagon. He chose the longer and thicker branches. "Good merchandise sells better," he thought. The load continued to grow and at last the wagon was full.

Now Antosh drove slowly, and as he drove he was thinking of the soap, tobacco, flour, and other things he would be able to buy with the money he earned from the sale of his merchandise.

When he reached the outskirts of the town and saw that the festival booths were covered, his heart skipped a beat and his head began to whirl. He steadied himself and thought, "It is the same every year. Some Jews cover their *sukkot* early and others later."

He rode on. Two women were standing in front of a house. They were pointing at him and laughing.

"Why are you laughing?" Antosh asked angrily.

"Because you brought the branches so early," they mocked.

"What do you mean, early?" Antosh asked, not understanding

why they made fun of him. He was answered by peals of laughter. Antosh spat angrily and rode on, thinking to himself, "How can it be? If I counted right, today is two days before the holiday."

He broke out in a cold sweat, because it occurred to him that he might have lost count of the days. He was too late. Certainly, too late. All the *sukkot* were covered. He would have no salt, no tobacco.

Sadly he drove on and his horse, who seemed to sense her master's misfortune, pulled the wagon with head bowed.

At last, he reached the village square. "I have green twigs and branches for your *sukkot*," he called. "Who will buy roof-coverings from Antosh?"

His voice echoed back. Except for a goat or two ambling along the road, the square was deserted. And then, suddenly, the big doors of the synagogue in the center of the square swung open and the men started pouring out. Jews in well-brushed black coats and fur-trimmed hats, little boys whose sidecurls had barely begun to grow. And they seemed to be heading toward Antosh.

Ah, here they were! Now he could sell his wares. He cried, "Here is Antosh, the woodchopper, with twigs for your booths. I have branches, I have—" Antosh stopped.

The crowd has surrounded Antosh and his wagon. "Thank you for coming," said one. "Only—you are a little late. One little day late. Can't you see that it is already Sukkot?—that today is the holiday itself?"

"Everyone's *sukkah* is already covered," said another.

But Antosh, confused by his misfortune, cried, "Buy, buy, I need salt, I need tobacco, I need soap. . . ."

The crowd around the peasant stopped laughing. Even Antosh grew silent. He lowered his head in misery and shame. No use standing there like the big oaf he was. Might as well go home and eat his twigs. The people looked at the poor, hungry peasant, saw his worried face, and felt sorry for him.

"A poor peasant; it's a pity," one of them said.

"He had high hopes, and all of a sudden—nothing," said another.

"We ought to buy his green branches," another man suggested.

"But how can we? It's a holiday today," his neighbor asked.

"No salt, no kerosene, no soap," the peasant continued to cry.

"Wait a minute," said someone. "Listen to me, everybody." The speaker jostled his way through the crowd. Clambering up on Antosh's wagon, he shouted to the townsfolk.

"Antosh has worked so hard. He meant well. It's our duty to help him now. And we can help him. We don't have to pay him. He doesn't need money. He needs merchandise—food and kerosene. We can't let him go away empty-handed. Won't you open your shops and give Antosh what he needs in return for his labors?"

Everyone was quiet for a moment. Then Jonah, the baker, said in his deep voice, "He is right. I will give Antosh six loaves of bread." And Reuben, the grocer, nodded. "I'll throw in five cans of kerosene." And David, the fishdealer, said, "I give two pickerel and seven carp."

Then they all chimed in and offered tobacco and barley and rice until Antosh's wagon was filled with all kinds of good things.

Antosh had never known such kindness in all his life. The peasant was beside himself with joy. He did not know whether to laugh or cry. Slowly he stood up in the wagon.

"Dear people," he stammered, "Antosh cannot make speeches. He can only say he is grateful. He says it now. Antosh is grateful."

He sat down.

As he was about to drive away, someone gave him a big piece of *hallah*.

"Here, take it home," he was told.

"Here's another piece," said someone else. Then everyone began to bring Antosh *hallah*. He was so confused that he could only murmur over and over—"Thank you. Thank you!"

Everyone was happy. Mordecai, a jolly Jew who spared nothing in celebrating the holidays, and who had a future son-in-law visiting him, brought out a glass of whiskey for Antosh. "Here, drink this and farewell," he said.

Antosh swallowed the whiskey in one gulp, took a bite of *hallah* and cried out, "I'll never forget it, never."

Translated by Jack Noskowitz[9]

✹ ✹ ✹

THE BEAUTIFUL WILLOW
AUTHOR UNKNOWN

(*age level eleven to fourteen*)

Of course, everyone knows that the weeping willow is so named because it also wept by the waters of Babylon.

When the Jews were taken into captivity by Nebuchadnezzar

they sat down along the river banks of Babylon and cried bitterly and longingly for the freedom which they lost and for the holiness and beauty of the Temple which was destroyed. Now, the willow trees near the rivers, moved by sympathy for the unfortunate souls sitting beneath their boughs, bent their heads in sorrow and joined the unhappy Jews in crying for the glories that were no more. Hence, "weeping" willow.

However, few people know that this noble act of the willows had its beginning many, many years before, when the willows were . . .

It happened in that strange and distant place which is inhabited by the souls and spirits of all living things. I am not too familiar with the geography of the place, never having been there (that I know of), but I do know that there is a special section there for the spirits of all trees and flowers and grasses—and a beautiful place it must be, too. Everyone knows that a soul is more beautiful than a body. Can you imagine, then, how much more beautiful are the souls of a rose or an orchid than the flowers themselves, or the souls of an evergreen or a fern than their earthly embodiments?

Why do you look at me so strangely? Because I said that grasses and flowers and trees have souls? Well, you needn't take *my* word for it; I'm just repeating what the Talmud says. It's written in the Talmud, black and white, that there isn't a single blade of grass in this world that doesn't have a spirit which tells it to grow! But I'm wandering from the story. . . .

It seems that many, many years ago there was some trouble in the spirit world of the grasses. As a matter of fact, at that time there was an air of high excitement in all parts of the spirit world. You see, word had somehow gotten around that the Almighty, King of the universe (which, of course, includes all worlds), was planning to give the Torah to the Jewish people, with certain commandments for them to perform. As each commandment became known to the different inhabitants of the spirit world, there was much excitement and joy and pride, as they each became involved in the performance of one or another of the commandments.

Sad to say, however, that there was one exception to the pride and joy which greeted each commandment. The exception happened with the Four Kinds. As you know, this commandment called for the Jews to take during the week of Sukkot, a *lulav* (palm branch), an *etrog* (citron), three *hadasim* (myrtle branches), and two *aravot* (willow branches). What the intent of the Almighty was, none of the four knew; all they had heard was that all four of them were to be combined in the fulfillment of this one commandment. And, at first, like all the others, they too were proud to have been chosen to play a part in the performance of the Lord's will on earth.

But after the first flush of pride had passed, three of the Four Kinds were not so pleased at all. The three—the palm branch, citron, and myrtle—were not so much displeased at having been chosen themselves, as they were at the willow's having been chosen —and, what's more, lumped together with them. As often happens in such cases, the three found themselves meeting each other more and more as they went strolling about the gardens of the greens' spirit world, and whenever the willow would approach them, they would casually walk off in another direction. And of course, they never said they had anything against the willow—after all, the Almighty had chosen her and He certainly knew best. All they said was that they failed to see why the Almighty should have chosen the willow. They just couldn't understand, really they couldn't!

Of course, they could very well understand why they were chosen. Any fool could see that. And as they strolled together, that's all they talked about.

"Now, take me, for instance," the *etrog* would say. "Where else could you find a fruit with a form as beautiful as mine? Not to mention my color and my delicate aroma. Why, I'm so refined that even the wood of my tree tastes exactly like me. Now that's what I call beautiful! Of course," the *etrog* would hasten to add, "I don't mean to boast or anything. I just mean to say that the glory of the Almighty would be enhanced by choosing me for one of His commandments."

The myrtle was also very understanding. "It's easy to see why I was chosen. Who has such smooth and almond-shaped leaves. And my fragrance! When the Jews will be commanded to smell pleasant things when they chant the *Havdalah* at the close of the Sabbath, I shall be one of them. And did you know that my namesake, Hadassah, is the Hebrew name of a woman destined to be famous in history for her beauty—Queen Esther! Of course, I speak only for the glory of the Almighty."

The palm seemed to be most upset of all. "I can see why the Almighty should have chosen a tall and stately tree like myself. Not only do I wear my branches like a crown, but I also give fruit and shade. Furthermore, you don't find me just anywhere, like most other trees. Frankly, I think it's a disgrace, the way the willow droops her branches and leaves. It's not fitting."

And so, the *etrog* and myrtle and palm found a new friendship among themselves, and a common cause. The willow just kept her silence and minded her own ways.

Now, the Almighty moves in mysterious ways His wonders to perform, and I can't say for certain how it all came about. Even the record of it in the Midrash only hints at the full story. But I have a feeling that this is what happened. . . .

A date palm near the village of Chamson became ill. Her trunk began to flake, her branches began to dry, and she stopped bearing fruit. The owner of the palm did what anyone else would have done in such a case—he called a doctor. He was a tree doctor and he was called Diklai. When Diklai came and examined the sick palm near Chamson, he began the usual cure. He went to another palm tree, a healthy one, cut off a branch, and then grafted it onto the sick palm tree. If the sick palm was at all still curable, this would do it. It had worked in the past and there was no reason why it shouldn't work now.

45. *Hakkafot* at Kfar Habad, Israel.

But the fact was that it didn't work now. For some reason, the sick palm would not become healthy again. Diklai was very upset about this, not only because his cure had failed, but also because it had once been a beautiful palm tree and it was saddening to see it die. However, there was nothing else he could think of, so he gave up and went home.

On his way home, Diklai stopped by a stream to get a drink when he decided to sit down and rest awhile. He saw a pleasant willow tree near the bank and lay down at its foot. A steady breeze rustled the willow's leaves as he dozed lazily on the soft ground. Suddenly, not quite sure whether he was dreaming or awake, Diklai heard whispered words in the leaves' rustling.

"Diklai, Diklai," he heard, "why do you give up so easily? Why don't you try to heal the sick palm tree?"

"What do you mean, why don't I try? I can't. I don't know how. I've done what I could."

"No, you haven't, Diklai. Do you feel sorry for the tree? Do you sympathize with the sick palm?"

"Of course," answered Diklai, a little angrily, "but what does that have to do with it?"

"If you would really feel with the palm," answered the willow softly, "you would know what ails her. Your heart would feel what her heart feels."

"Nonsense," Diklai almost shouted, "sheer nonsense. If you're so smart then you tell me what ails her!"

"I'll tell you, but you must promise me that you'll do what I say. I'm almost sick myself with sympathy for that poor tree. Promise me."

"Oh, all right," said Diklai. "What is it?"

"The sick palm tree," said the willow, "has a friend, another palm tree, near Jericho, and she is sick with longing for her. If you will go to Jericho and take a branch from that palm tree and graft it onto the palm tree here at Chamson, she will become well again."

Diklai sat up. "What! Now I'm to go to Jericho for a grafting branch! All the way to Jericho just for a sick tree! Anyway, I already tried grafting and it won't work."

The willow did not become angry. She just said, quietly, "Diklai, you promised. Besides, how can you see another suffering and not suffer yourself? If you are a man, you must go! You will see that I am right."

Diklai stood up and shook his head, perhaps with disbelief. He stood thinking for a moment—and then set out for Jericho.

As things turned out, the willow was right. With a graft from the Jericho palm, the Chamson palm soon became well again, a joy and pride to all who saw her and had pleasure from her. She herself felt very grateful for her recovery and said so to Diklai, the tree doctor.

"Oh, no, no," said Diklai, modestly but honestly, "don't thank me. Thank yonder willow by the stream. She cured you, for she was sick with you. What a beautiful soul that tree must have!"

Up in the spirit world of the greens, the *etrog*, myrtle, and palm all saw what had happened, and when they heard Diklai speak of the willow's beautiful soul, they looked at each other a little ashamed. They finally realized that there is another sort of beauty—a beauty of the soul, a goodness of the heart, a fitness of character. Then, they all smiled at each other and, without another word, went out together to welcome and greet their fourth and rightful partner in the Almighty's commandment—all partners in the beauty of holiness.[10]

֎ ֎ ֎

WHAT THE *ETROG* TOLD ME
JOSHUA MARGOLIN

founder of an institute for teachers of biology in Tel Aviv and author of Hebrew books and children's stories on nature (1877–1947); the following story is translated from his book Arbaat Minim (Four Species)

(*age level eleven to fourteen*)

The end of Adar at Gan Shmuel. The rainy season has passed. The blue skies arch like a tent over the flower-wreathed earth. The poppies blush red, the chrysanthemums twinkle their golden eyes. The citrus grove, only recently relieved of its golden fruit, is bedecked with fragrant white blossoms, harbingers of new fruit.

I stroll among the blooming trees. My feet sink in the soft, recently ploughed soil. Thousands of bees hum gaily, fragrant odors invade my nostrils, the green of the leaves and the white of the flowers dance before my eyes. Suddenly I catch sight of a row of trees whose pink-violet blossoms stand out sharply amid the white of the orange flowers. I examine the trees and find that although they resemble the orange trees in general characteristics they differ from them in the color of their flowers and the shape of their leaves. The petioles of their leaves are not spiked at the base of the petals, as are those of the orange trees. The edges of the leaves are toothed like a saw blade, whereas the orange leaves have smooth edges. Sharp hard thorns bristle from the branches, while the branch of the orange tree has no thorns whatever.

But what a marvel! Fruit glistens among the petals of the flowers! The trees bear fruit and flowers at the same time! I examine the fruit, I inhale its scent—it is the *etrog*, the *etrog* in whose fragrance my soul has been steeped since childhood days. A myriad of memories floods me. I sit in the shade of one of the trees listening to the spring song of the bulbul, the nightingale of Palestine. A soft sea breeze rustles through the leaves as an *etrog* begins to tell me a story:

"You see us here lost among the thousands of orange trees. We are all members of the citrus family, but they, the oranges, are newcomers in Palestine. Their ancestors were brought here from a strange country only a few centuries ago. But we, the *etrogim*, are ancient citizens of this country. I am going to tell you the story which has been repeated in our family from generation to generation for many centuries.

"My ancestors flourished in the gardens of the Medes and Persians, many, many years ago. The air of the gardens was heavy with the scent of spikenard and saffron and many other spices, and trees of various kinds bore beautiful edible fruits. But most fragrant of all scents and most beautiful of all fruits was the *etrog*. The sun blessed it with a golden tint, the skies gave of their brightness, the air endowed it with beautiful scents, and the earth gave of its strength and warmth, and the fruit was beautiful to behold and graced the tables of kings.

"One of your ancestors who was exiled from his own country to Persia saw this fruit, and intoxicated with its beauty and fragrance, coveted it, and swore an oath. 'If the Lord will be with me and return me in peace to the country of my birth, to my home and estate in the plain along the coast of the blue Mediterranean, I will plant this tree in my orchard, and I will offer its fruit as a thanksgiving in the House of the Lord.'

"The man died in exile, but he bequeathed his great love for his country together with the oath he had taken to his sons. One of these, Aminadav, was overwhelmed with longing for the country of his fathers, the land of Judea, and he left the land of his exile and went up to the land of his fathers, and took with him an *etrog*. When he arrived in Judea he purchased a field near Jaffa and planted orchards and groves and sowed the seed of the *etrog*. The shoots that sprouted from these seeds were delicate and tender; and because they were liable to perish if struck by cold winds, Aminadav hooded them with a shelter, and watered them, and tended them, and guarded them very carefully, so that at the end of the year the saplings were sturdy and upright. Aminadav then uprooted them, and planted them in even rows within the orchard so that the older trees would guard them against unruly winds.

"As the days passed the tender saplings grew to be strong trees, protected by sharp thorns against marauding beasts and careless men. Their leaves were leathery, and tiny follicles full of a fragrant oil were scattered on them, and the leathery protective covering and the fumes of the evaporating oil preserved the moistness of the leaves.

"In the third year after planting, clusters of flowers were seen at the ends of the branches. Aminadav plucked these flowers one by one, and discarded them, as the Jewish law forbids the fruits of the third year. In the fourth year the trees again yielded fruit, and the orchard was filled with the fragrance of the *etrogim*, and many people came to enjoy it. The fame of the fruit reached the high priest in the holy Temple and he came, with a company of many sages, to the orchard of Aminadav to behold the fruit and to inhale its scent. In the spring they came and they marveled at the tree that bore fruit and flower simultaneously. Some of the fruit had but a short while previously emerged from their flowery swaddling clothes and were almost black in color. Others, slightly older, gave forth a greenish glint from beneath a dark violet veil. Still others, full-sized, were a bright yellow and emitted a delicate odor. The high priest and his coterie enjoyed the fragrance, which surpassed in beauty that of any scent they had previously encountered.

"The high priest said to the sages: 'How splendid is this tree and how magnificent is its fruit. The Torah enjoins us, "You shall take the fruit of goodly trees." Is there, then, any tree whose fruit is more gracious than this?' One of the sages remarked, 'The heart may be likened unto the *etrog*. Just as the *etrog* is full of a beautiful fragrance, so is the heart of man full of the spirit of wisdom and knowledge.' A second sage observed, 'The Torah itself may be likened unto the *etrog*. Just as all men may inhale the *etrog*'s scent and not detract from its fragrance, so may all men draw wisdom and knowledge from the Torah and not detract from its worth.' A third sage said: 'The *etrog* is the fruit of paradise, the fruit of that tree of knowledge from which Adam and Eve partook, for the fruit is as pleasing as wisdom and a pleasure to the eyes.' Then said the sages among themselves, 'There is no fruit so magnificent, so refreshing, so illuminating, and so enlightening as is this fruit, and we are therefore commanded to bring it as an offering in the House of the Lord at the harvest festival.'

"Aminadav was overjoyed and presented *etrogim* to the high priest and to the sages and distributed them lavishly among the townspeople, saying, 'Now shall I be able to go up to the House of the Lord, and fulfill my father's oath.'

"And the *etrog* was beloved of all the dwellers of the land, and the inhabitants of the Judean Plain and the Plain of Sharon planted it in their orchards. Aminadav died at a ripe old age and his sons and sons' sons tended the grove of *etrogim*, and it flourished and was beautiful and was known as the 'Grove of Aminadav.' Its fame spread to all lands, and messengers came from distant countries to obtain the saplings for planting in their own lands.

"Once upon a time a messenger came from a distant land and told Aminadav's sons the following tale. 'The king of my country was very sick and was unable to eat. He wasted away, and the doctors could find no cure for his illness, until the court physician said, "There is a fruit in Eretz Israel called the *etrog*, which is sacred to the Jews, who bring it as an offering in the House of the Lord at the harvest festival. Its fragrance soothes the soil and its substance heals the body; its peel is cooling and its pulp is warming and increases the appetite. Only the *etrog* can cure our king." The king thereupon commanded his servants to examine the boats that touched his ports and inquire of the travelers if they had *etrogim* to sell. One day a boat came in among whose travelers was a poor Jew bearing a shabby sack. The servants asked him whether he had anything to sell, and he replied, "I am a poor man and have nothing." When they examined his sack they found that it contained several *etrogim*, and they conducted him to the presence of the king, who ate the *etrogim* and was immediately cured. He then asked the poor man,

"Where have you come from and what has brought you here?" The poor man replied, "I am come from Eretz Israel. I distributed all my money among widows and orphans, and nothing remained wherewith to support my own family. So I determined to go abroad to seek my fortune and took with me several of the *etrogim* of Aminadav so that I might be reminded in a foreign land of the House of the Lord and the fragrance of my country. I embarked on the boat, and it brought me to your shores." These words pleased the king, and he ordered the poor man's sack to be filled with gold, and he sent him home to his country and his family. And I, the messenger, have been sent by the king to you for several *etrogim* to plant in his own orchard.' "

The *etrog* continued. "Many years passed and the Roman legions invaded Judea. Aminadav's descendants fought bravely for their homeland, and many were killed, their blood watering the orchard which was so dear to them. Only one survived the wars and clave to his ancestors' estate and guarded the orchard zealously. Every year at the Feast of Sukkot he plucked the *etrogim* from the trees, his eyes streaming with tears and whispered, 'The Temple is destroyed and the people of the Lord is in exile. Go, *etrogim* to my brothers in exile, and bring them the fragrance of their homeland, so that they may long for their country and return to it and rebuild its ruins.' And he sent the fruit to all the countries of the Diaspora, and his sons after him did likewise.

"And the people wandered in exile for many, many centuries. But they never forgot their homeland"—the *etrog* concluded—"and my tree and all the *etrog* trees in this grove have been planted by your brothers, the pioneers who have returned from exile and watered our roots with the sweat of their brows and tended us to the accompaniment of their songs of hope."[11]

20

POEMS FOR CHILDREN

❧ ❧ ❧

THE *LULAV*
JESSIE E. SAMPTER

American poetess who settled in an Israeli kibbutz, where she wrote
about the life she lived (1883–1938)

We live in narrow alleys
    Where hovels stand in rows—
Our hearts are in the valleys
    Where Rose of Sharon grows.

From bartering, peddling, selling
    We seek a moment's calm—
Our hearts today are dwelling
    Where citron grows with palm.

We come from stinting, suffering,
 From streets that pennies yield;
And bring the Lord our offering,
 The produce of the field.

Unlanded, robbed, and driven,
 And happy to escape,
Our dreams today are given
 To farm and flock and grape.

In many a stone-bound city,
 Still roofed beneath the skies,
The Lord of boundless pity
 Lets little bowers arise.

And in those tabernacles—
 The wanderer's blessed relief—
He turns our heavy shackles
 To strings of fruit and leaf.

Who bring in want and sorrow
 The stranger's fruit with psalms,
Shall plant in joy tomorrow
 Their citrons and their palms.[1]

❧ ❧ ❧

MY VINEYARD
JESSIE E. SAMPTER

My vineyard, my vineyard! The vintage is full!
Come help me, my children, the clusters to pull!
I've cared for the buds, for the leaves, for the flowers,
My vineyard I've kept in the land that is ours.

I once was a tailor, I stitched for my crust,
I once was a peddler all covered with dust;
They made me the keeper of riches indeed,
But I was a beggar despised for my need.

Come help with the vintage, come share in the wine,
Whoever is hungry shall eat what is mine.
Come help me, my brothers, the clusters to pull!
Our homeland is calling! The vintage is full![2]

❧ ❧ ❧

SUKKOT

HAYYIM NAHMAN BIALIK

*recognized as the greatest of modern Hebrew poets; also wrote verse
for children (1873–1934)*

In the *sukkah* nestle darkness and peace,
Through the lattice roof the moonbeams seep;
In its silver cradle on soft fleece
Like a baby the *etrog* lies asleep.

Watching above it, the *lulav* sheaf
Of myrtle and willow leans on the wall,

46. *Hakkafot* in the Florentine Quarter, Tel Aviv.

Weary and silent, and finds relief
Slipping down, asleep in the fall.

Both of them sleep, but their hearts are caught
Each in his dream in his own moonbeam.
Oh, who can fathom the stranger's thought,
Unravel the secret of his dream?

Do they dream of lovely garden ways,
Do their hearts hold fast to homeland skies?
Are they sick of wandering all their days
That have dried their sap and dimmed their eyes?

Or their dream may seal the finished feast,
Since only sorrow unites their lot;
Their bond is torn, their fragrance ceased,
Their beauty marred by spot and rot.

None can tell—through the lattice-shed
Softly the pale, faint moonbeams glide.
In a silver box on its fleecy bed
The *etrog* sleeps by the *lulav*'s side.

> Translated by Jessie E. Sampter[3]

❧ ❧ ❧

BEATING THE WILLOW

HAYYIM NAHMAN BIALIK

A voice announces:
    Come, my knight,
Beat the willow
    With all your might!

Here is a pounding
    And here a crushing,
Pillars of dust
    And darkness rushing.

Leaves and branches
    We beat and tread,
Fly in the air and
    Fall down dead.

Crash and smash them,
    You valiant boys,
And pounce on the fallen
    With plenty of noise.

            Translated by Jessie E. Sampter[4]

❧ ❧ ❧

ELEGY ON THE *ETROG* AND THE *LULAV*

HAYYIM NAHMAN BIALIK

O my *lulav*,
    Who has stripped
Off your belt,
    Your glory ripped?

Who has damaged
    My *etrog*?
Nipped his stem,
    His navel broke?

My fruit of gold
    Is dried and done,
My *lulav* just
    A skeleton.

Their feast is past,
    Their beauty fast
Is gone with none
    To save at last.

In jam its end
    The *etrog* breathes.
The *lulav* I
    Shall weave in wreaths.

Tiny wreaths
    And braids and bands,
And even rings
    For little hands.

            Translated by Jessie E. Sampter[5]

❦ ❦ ❦

THE *SUKKAH* ON THE ROOF
SULAMITH ISH-KISHOR

*recipient of awards for some of her numerous contributions to the
literature for Jewish children*

Bring up boughs with greenest leaves,
    Bring up ripest fruits,
Make a heap of autumn flowers,
    And of strong young shoots!

Nail together sturdy planks,
    Cover them with branches.
Wrap them round with curly vines,
    And leaves in avalanches!

Make a sky of quivering green,
    Where fruit hangs down like stars;
Breezes creep to look at them
    Between the wooden bars!

Though the city's full of noise,
    In our tent we stay
And only hear our father's prayer
    That brings the holiday![6]

❦ ❦ ❦

THE *ETROG*
PHILIP M. RASKIN

*lifelong Zionist and prolific poet who created in English, Hebrew,
and Yiddish (1878–1944)*

The Day of Atonement is over;
    My father an *etrog* has bought
And never the eyes of a lover
    Did sparkle as his, when he brought

And showed us the fruit that was shining
  With sheen of a tropical star,
The fruit for which hearts are still pining
  From homeland long exiled and far.

And never was valued a jewel
  As dear as the fruit was to him—
A value the centuries cruel
  Could neither efface nor bedim.

I looked at the *etrog* the golden,
  And dreamt of the orchards of gold,
I dreamt of the ages the olden,
  That never in hearts will grow old.

I dreamt of the rills and the fountains
  That watered these gardens of yore,
The plains, and the vales, and the mountains,
  That blossomless, blossom the more. . . .

I looked at my father caressing
  The fruit that bejeweled his feast,
And mutely my heart sent a blessing
  To Zion—the Queen of the East. . . .[7]

❧ ❧ ❧

A SONG FOR SUKKOT
ELMA EHRLICH LEVINGER

author of twenty-five books for Jewish children, including stories, poems, texts, and plays (1887–1958)

The fields are gold with harvest,
  The vines in purple glow;
Thy people, blest with plenty,
  Their bounteous reaping show;
Dear God, who gave the sunshine
  And sent the summer rain,
Shed blessing on the offerings
  We render Thee again.

Of old the singing pilgrims
    With offerings sought Thy shrine;
The richest yield of field and tree
    Was consecrated Thine.
Today we Jewish children
    Our grateful harvest bear,
To lay upon Thine altar
    With this, our Sukkot prayer:

"Dear God, who gave the harvest,"
    Thy happy children pray,
"Thanks for the bounteous blessings
    We reap in joy today.
Teach us to share them gladly
    With those less blest than we,
Since all we give to others
    We render back to Thee."[8]

❧ ❧ ❧

THE TREASURE

ELMA EHRLICH LEVINGER

It was good to give thanks to the Lord
    For the sun and the rain,
For the corn and the wine He bestowed,
    For the golden-wreathed grain;
But now, as the festal week ends,
    'Neath the palms which we wave,
We cry thanks to the Giver of Good
    For the Torah He gave.

For the Law of the Lord it is good,
    And His precepts are right:
The simple of heart He makes wise,
    His commandments bring light;
More goodly His words than fine gold—
    Aye, a treasure to save;
And we thank, with rejoicing, our God,
    For the Torah He gave.

O harvesters, rich in your spoils,
    Not alone by the bread
Which we win by the sweat of our brows
    Are the sons of dust fed;
Nay, we live by the word of His mouth,
    And, 'neath palms which we wave,
We cry thanks to the Giver of Good
    For the Torah He gave.[9]

❧ ❧ ❧

SIMHAT TORAH
ABRAHAM BURSTEIN

rabbi, author, and editor who penned a book of Jewish verse for children (1893–1966)

Rejoice upon this festal day!
When should honest Jews be gay?
    Once more unroll
    The sacred Scroll,
And greet the feast with song and play!

We chant the Law through all the year,
Our minds intense, our hearts austere;
    Today we jest
    With mirthful zest,
To show we hold our Torah dear!

Come, comrades all, and merry be—
Come, raise a lilting melody;
    And let the sky
    Receive our cry,
That sounds the Torah's jubilee![10]

47. U.S. soldiers observing Sukkot. Pusan, Korea. 1953.

✻ ✻ ✻

THE BUILDING OF THE *SUKKAH*
HENRY SNOWMAN

Hebraist, Zionist, lawyer, and poet who translated much verse from Hebrew, including the original English translation of Hatikvah *(1878–1969)*

"Dwell ye in booths," thus reads the sacred page;
In booths, frail shelter 'gainst the storm and wind:
And lo, in booths we dwell through all our pilgrimage!

"And the shadow shall be more than sun's bright rays";
The shadow more than sun, soft filtering through:
Alas, the shadow more than sun on all our ways!

"But ye shall see the stars through, shining clear";
The stars, above the storm-rack and the night:
Ah, yes, we still can see the stars through; God is near![11]

❧ ❧ ❧

SEVEN TIMES ROUND
SADIE ROSE WEILERSTEIN

author dedicated to Jewish children's literature; writer of many widely disseminated books

First Time Round

Hi, for Simhat Torah night!
Isn't this a jolly sight?
Every *Sefer Torah's* out;
All the children march about;

Bessie, Leonard, Dave, and Lou,
Saul and Judith, Ann and Sue.
Every friend I have is here.
It's the best night of the year!

Second Time Round

Don't the Torahs all look fine?
Guess there must be more than nine!
Velvet mantles, red and blue,
Silver crowns and breastplates, too!

Torah bells go tinkle, tinkle!
Paper flags go crinkle, crinkle!
Step along and keep in line!
Wave your flag and I'll wave mine!

Third Time Round

Wish that baby were here too!
She would clap her hands and coo.

We could make her carriage fine
With a paper flag like mine.

Baby in her ruffled bonnet!
Paper flag with lions on it!
How the people all would smile.
When we wheeled her down the aisle!

Fourth Time Round

There! We've caught up with the men
And we're starting out again.
I see Grandma! I see Mother!
I see Uncle Harry's brother!

Look! My Daddy has a Scroll.
(That's another word for roll.)
Grandma kisses it with awe.
'Cause it holds God's holy Law.

Fifth Time Round

Now once more we wait and stand
While again the Scrolls change hand.
All the men take turns, you know.
Seven times around we go!

Wave your flag and step along!
Sisu ve-simhu! Join in song!
Sing away with all your might!
This is Simhat Torah night.

Sixth Time Round

Soon the boys will have their turn;
The *bar mitzvah* ones who learn
What the Torah bids you do
If you want to be a Jew.

My turn, too, will come some day
When I grow as big as they.
Goodness me! I'll be so proud—
To bear the Torah through the crowd!

Seventh Time Round

Take a seat and rest awhile?
Mother dear, you make me smile.

Rest with Simhat Torah here!
It comes only once a year.

Wave your flag and sing your song!
Rejoice! Be merry! Step along!
Have you read the Torah through?
Roll it back and start anew![12]

❊ ❊ ❊

SUKKOT SONG
ILO ORLEANS

*lawyer by profession and poet by avocation; prolific author of verses
which are included in anthologies, textbooks, and music books*

It's harvest time,
It's harvest time,
How rich is nature's yield
In fruit of earth
and bush and tree,
From orchard, farm, and field.

It's autumn time,
It's autumn time,
When leaves turn gold and red.
In smiling sky
And land and sea
God's glories are outspread.

It's Sukkot time,
It's Sukkot time,
This day of our thanksgiving.
We hymn the praise
Of God above
For all the joys of living.[13]

21

PROGRAMS AND ACTIVITIES

❧ Sukkah *Construction* ❧

The construction and utilization of an outdoor *sukkah* is mandatory
for the appropriate observance of the Feast of Booths. A booth can
be built by an individual family, or it may be an exciting group
project. Before drawing the plans, the traditional requirements for
a *sukkah* should be studied, and illustrations of various booths examined. The festival shelter requires at least three walls and a
temporary roof open to the sky. When one is building a booth for
the first time, consideration should be given to constructing it in
such a manner that it can be readily dismantled and stored for subsequent years.

The first consideration is the selection of an appropriate site—a lawn, a back yard, or a roof. The outside wall of a house or a garage may be used as one of the *sukkah* walls. The need to run electric wiring from an indoor outlet into the booth should be borne in mind. The size of the booth is determined by the number of people expected to use it, allowing sufficient space for all to be seated around a table. A *sukkah* 6 x 8 feet can accommodate four to six people; one 8 x 8 feet will seat eight to ten; and one 10 x 20 feet will allow for up to thirty persons.

While the walls may be made of any material, they should be sufficiently sturdy to withstand a normal wind. Lumber or piping may be used for the frame, and canvas, plywood, or other boards for the walls. Some congregations make arrangements with a local lumberyard to supply the necessary lumber fabricated to size, in order to facilitate the assembly of the booth.

The roof has distinctive characteristics as a temporary booth. It must consist primarily of vegetation from the soil—tree branches, twigs, reeds or bamboo poles supported by narrow slats laid over the walls. The roofing during the day should permit more shade than sunlight; the stars must be visible at night.

Decorations for the *sukkah* are discussed below.

❧ Sukkah *Social* ❧

A social or party in a *sukkah* can be held with songs, stories, games, and refreshments. Invitations may be in the form of a double card, with a picture of a booth on the outside and the wording inside; or it may be a single page decorated with the festival symbols. Place-cards shaped like an *etrog* or *lulav* can be prepared. A cake with symbolic decorations on the icing might serve as a centerpiece.

This affair can be designated a *Simhat Bet ha-Shoevah,* the traditional joyous celebration during the intermediate days of Sukkot. The program can be preceded by a torchlight parade terminating in the *sukkah.*

❧ *Meetings in the* Sukkah ❧

The communal *sukkah* should be used as often as possible for a variety of programs and activities. Group meetings scheduled for the festival week can be held in the booth.

❦ A Sukkah *Tour* ❦

Arrangements may be made for a walking or an automobile tour of communal and private booths during the festival. At each visit, a snack might be served and a brief program held; or the program might be conducted in the last booth on the tour. Photographs of the exterior and the interior of the booths can be taken by the visitors and an exhibit of the pictures arranged, with an award to the best photographer.

❦ *Contests* ❦

A community-wide contest for the most beautiful *sukkah* may be sponsored. During the intermediate days of Sukkot, a committee of judges can inspect the booths entered in the competition. Prizes for children in different age groups can be offered for the best miniature booths created.

❦ *Sukkot Sing* ❦

A "sing" can be held in advance of Sukkot for the purpose of teaching the festival liturgical melodies or during the holiday for the sheer enjoyment of group singing. *Mahzorim,* songbooks or song sheets should be distributed.

❦ *Discussion and Lecture Themes* ❦

To introduce and stimulate a discussion, an appropriate selection may be read to the group from the chapters in this book devoted to medieval and modern literature (chapters 4 and 8). The following themes may be used for discussions or lectures:

The Joy of Jewish Living
The Festival of Rejoicing and Gladness
The Feast of Booths in Many Lands
The Festival of Wandering and Rest
The Transience of Human Life
The Universal Character of Judaism
Sukkot and the American Thanksgiving Day: Parallels and Contrasts
Israel's Harvest Festival and That of Other Peoples

The *Sukkah* as Symbol of Jewish Life in the Diaspora
The Four Species: Symbol of Jewish Unity
The People's Festival—Simhat Torah
The Unbroken Torah Cycle
Simhat Torah in New York, Moscow, and Jerusalem
Judaism and Nature

❧ *Story-telling* ❧

A story hour devoted to Sukkot tales and legends can be held in a *sukkah*. After a story is told, a dramatization of it can be improvised or it can be used for a game played with stories. See the chapters on Talmud and Midrash and children's stories. Some of the adult stories in this book can also be adapted for children.

❧ *Exhibits* ❧

A variety of exhibits pertinent to Sukkot may be arranged; it can include photographs and illustrations relevant to the festival, adult and children's books open to Sukkot illustrations, *sukkah* decorations, *etrog* containers, Simhat Torah flags, miniature booths, and other arts and crafts work.

❧ *Games* ❧

A party in a *sukkah* can start with a game of musical chairs. Pantomimes can be enacted on such subjects as the harvest, building a *sukkah*, blessing the *lulav*, reading from the Torah, and *hakkafot*. Other popular games, using terms associated with Sukkot, can be played. Quiz programs based on the background of the festival can be prepared.

❧ *Audiovisual Materials* ❧

There are available a few films, filmstrips, and a tape which present various aspects of the Feast of Booths that can be used at different functions. See Bibliography in this volume.

❧ *Dances for Children* ❧

See next chapter on "Dances for Sukkot and Simhat Torah."

✻ *Kindergarten* Sukkah ✻

A small *sukkah* can readily be built on the kindergarten playground to accommodate several children at one time. Sheets of plywood or beaverboard can serve as the walls. The small kindergarten tables and chairs can be moved into the booth where lunch and refreshments can be served throughout the week, weather permitting. The children will be able to make paper chains and other original decorations to adorn the *sukkah*. The kindergartners may have their own *hakkafot* with miniature Torah Scrolls and flags.

✻Lulav *and* Etrog *Distribution* ✻

Facilities may be provided to encourage and enable members of the community to purchase *etrogim* and *lulavim*. A committee can be charged with the responsibility of soliciting and delivering orders for the Four Species in time for the festival.

✻ *Sukkot Pamphlets* ✻

Pamphlets expounding the Sukkot traditions can be purchased, or original brochures prepared for wide distribution to encourage observance of the festival. Such pamphlets may include the story of Sukkot, suggestions for ways to build booths, songs, recipes, and arts and crafts projects.

✻ *Workshop for Parents* ✻

A workshop to prepare parents for participation in all aspects of the Sukkot observance can include a presentation by a rabbi, a discussion on an appropriate subject, singing of traditional, modern, and children's songs, instructions for constructing and decorating a *sukkah*, arts and crafts, and cooking and baking demonstrations. Participation in the workshop may include children so as to make it a family affair. In view of the elaborate preliminary arrangements required for the festival so close to the High Holy Days, it may be desirable to conduct the workshop before Rosh Hashanah.

✻ *Visiting the Sick* ✻

Bringing holiday cheer to patients in hospitals, residents of homes for the aged, and shut-ins can be undertaken by volunteers. Visitors can bring pamphlets on Sukkot, delicacies, and the Four Species to enable the patients and the aged to recite the traditional blessings.

❧ Honoring the Simhat Torah Bridegrooms

Invitations to Simhat Torah services in the format of wedding invitations can be mailed to congregational members, to encourage their attendance and to honor the bridegrooms of the Torah and of *Bereshit* and the *baal maftir*. During the service the guests of honor may be seated on the pulpit, and at its conclusion a *kiddush* may be tendered by them or by the congregation.

❧ Consecration Service ❧

As Simhat Torah marks the completion and the renewal of the reading of the Pentateuch, some congregations conduct a consecration ceremony for new religious school pupils, either at the evening or morning services. The children, carrying miniature Scrolls, enter the sanctuary in a procession and ascend the pulpit, where they are greeted and blessed by the rabbi. Following a brief ceremony, they participate in the traditional circuits carrying flags.

❧ Demonstrations in Behalf of Soviet Jewry ❧

In recent years many congregations and communities conduct Simhat Torah demonstrations as a link of solidarity with Soviet Jewry. See "The Simhat Torah Celebration in Moscow" by Elie Wiesel (pages 204–215) and "Simhat Torah Demonstrations in America" (pages 339–340).

❧ Arts and Crafts ❧

Miniature Sukkah: A small booth can be improvised from a shoe box or, if a larger one is desired, from a cardboard or corrugated box, an egg or fruit crate, with the open side serving as the roof. A door and windows should be cut into the sides. To allow for viewing the interior, one large picture window should be provided. Windowpanes may be made of cellophane and cloth curtains hung on them. Both the interior and exterior can be painted or crayoned to resemble wood. Heavy cord, strips of wood, or corrugated paper may be placed on top to hold the roofing foliage, which may be natural or artificial. The *sukkah* may be furnished with doll furniture or hand-made chairs and table and wall decorations. The table can be set for a festive meal with paper dolls or pipe-cleaner figures seated around it. Miniature fruit made of clay, paper chains, lanterns, and strings of red cranberries and green peas can be hung from the rafters. If the booth is the size of an egg box, a string of small electric light bulbs can be installed.

Sukkah *Decorations*: Adorning the booth can be a project for the entire family. While many *sukkah* decorations can be purchased, original embellishments created by those who will use the booth will have much more significance. A variety of things can be hung from the roofing: fruits (choose ones that will stay fresh for at least several days), vegetables (red and green peppers, corn, carrots, squash, gourds), small jars of honey, olive oil and wine, strings of cranberries alternating with green peas, paper chains, and colored electric bulbs. The walls may be covered with autumn leaves and cornstalks, paintings pertinent to the festival, and friezes depicting harvest scenes, the procession of the priests in the Temple, Jerusalem the Golden, the seven species, the twelve tribes, and the seven *ushpizin*. A visualization of the *ushpizin* can be created by a series of dioramas depicting episodes of the lives of the seven guests traditionally welcomed in the *sukkah*. Jackets of Jewish books and Rosh Hashanah greeting cards

48. U.S. soldiers blessing the *lulav*. Nha Trang, Vietnam. 1966.

are also decorative adornments. Signs can be made with such legends as "Blessed are you who enter," "You shall live in booths seven days" (Leviticus 23.42), "You shall hold the Feast of Booths for seven days" (Deuteronomy 16.13), "You shall rejoice in your festival" (Deuteronomy 16.14), and "A land of wheat and barley, of vines, figs, and pomegranates, a land of olive oil and of honey" (Deuteronomy 8.8), referring to the seven species of the land of Israel. A poster with the blessings to be recited when eating in the *sukkah* can be displayed in a conspicuous place. A cornucopia over-flowing with fruits and vegetables may be placed in a corner or used as a table centerpiece. For other decoration ideas, see "Unusual Booths in Israel" by Solomon Feffer, pages 151–153, and "The Adornment of the Booth," pages 153–155.

Birds: A traditional *sukkah* decoration is the bird made with an egg. Gently pierce a raw egg at both ends and blow out the yoke and white substance. Then make two holes where wings will be inserted. Cut three 5 x 5-inch pieces of colored paper; fold them as fans; insert two of the fanlike papers for the wings and the third for the tail. Draw or paint a bird's head and attach it with transparent tape. Use tape to attach a string for hanging the dove of peace.

Etrog Boxes: Containers to hold *etrogim* may be made in various ways. Tin coffee cans and small cardboard gift boxes can be used. Cigar box wood, heavy corrugated paper, copper foil, and sheets of tin will make appropriate boxes. A lining of absorbent cotton covered by silk or some other material will protect the citron from damage. The exterior may be decorated with designs of one or more of the Four Species and a legend such as "the fruit of the goodly tree" and "Feast of Booths." Among the other media that can be utilized for citron containers are ceramics, basketry, and papier-mâché.

Lulav and Etrog: The Four Species can be artificially made with a number of craft media—plaster casting, woodcarving, and linoleum cutting.

Simhat Torah Flags: Flags for the processions on Simhat Torah can be made simply. Use white cloth, muslin, cardboard, or heavy construction paper, approximately 9 x 12 inches. Decorate the flag with wax crayons or paints, using symbols of the festival and appropriate biblical verses. A more elaborate flag can be made by embroidery or by the use of collages. If wooden flag sticks with slits are unavailable, use a ¼-inch dowel, 18 to 24 inches in length. If an apple is to top the flag, whittle one end of the stick. Staple the flag to the stick, allowing 2 inches of the whittled end to protrude above the stick. Core the apple so that when a candle is inserted it will fit snugly.

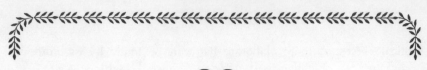

❦ 22 ❦

DANCES FOR SUKKOT AND SIMHAT TORAH

❧ ❧ ❧

PITCHER AND TORCH DANCE
(PROCESSIONAL)[1]
DVORA LAPSON

This dance is reminiscent of the Simhat Bet ha-Shoevah *(The Festivity of the Water Drawing) ceremony, which was conducted in Jerusalem during the days of the Temple. At that time, a priest would pour a water libation on the altar from a large golden pitcher to the songs of the Levites, and torch-bearers would juggle their torches as they danced far into the night.*

Formation: The pitcher-bearers are dressed in long gowns, with sashes around their waists and with flowing headdresses. Each one holds a golden pitcher on her left shoulder.

The torch-bearers wear pants and three-quarter tunics of striped material, headdresses with a zigzag crown effect, and a torch in each hand.

The pitcher-bearers are arranged at the rear of the stage. The torch-bearers (half the number of pitcher-bearers) stand ready to enter from the front wings.

Phrase 1. The pitcher-bearers take one polka step* facing to the right, one polka step facing to the left, four steps forward, and pivot in place with a right turn.

Phrase 2. One polka step toward the right, one polka step toward the left, then four steps forward.

Phrase 3. The odd person extends left foot slightly, bending knee and places pitcher on extended knee.

Even person pretends to pour water from her pitcher into odd person's pitcher.

While the pitcher-pouring is in progress, the torch-bearers appear from the wings, and leap across the stage. All end by taking their places in different parts of the stage—one torch-bearer between two pitcher-bearers.

Phrase 4. The two pitcher-bearers in each set of three change places with each other with four polka steps, ending by pivoting in place and three stamps. The same is repeated back to place on the repetition of the music.

The torch-bearers, meanwhile, pivot in place while the others are changing places, and take three polka steps forward and three stamps in place while the pitcher-bearers are pivoting. On repetition of this music, repeat same steps, except for moving backwards with three polka steps.

Phrase 5. All the groups form a long procession mixing polka steps with pivots and all proceed off stage.

* Polka step = three steps in one direction, then hop.

MI YAGUR BE-OHALEKHA?

"Lord, who shall sojourn in Thy tabernacle?....He that walketh uprightly."

Hasidic
Words: Psalms 15: 1-2

Lightly

Mi_ ya-gur be-o-ha-le-kha? Mi_ yish-kon_ be-

har_ kod-she-kha ho-lekh ta-mim u-fo-el tze-dek, ve-

1.
do-ver e-met bil-va-vo, ho-
2.
do-ver e-met bil-va-vo.

La la la la la la la la la la la la

etc.....

⚘ ⚘ ⚘

YOM TOV LANU[2]
CORINNE CHOCHEM

Commemorating the time when the ancient Hebrews lived in tents in the desert, Sukkot is a holiday of little wooden booths covered with green branches and boughs. The traditional dance of the Hasidim *circles round and round the table inside the* sukkah *in a mood of contained exhilaration.*

Formation: Dancers stand in a circle with hands joined and held shoulder high.

Steps: First four bars: Facing slightly toward the right, and starting with the right foot, take six slow walking steps. On the seventh count, dancers drop hands, and twisting the body first to the right, snap fingers of both hands to the right (1), then twisting the body to the left, snap fingers of both hands to the left (2). (Snap fingers above shoulder level, at the same time turn head toward the hands and bend the knees slightly.)

Second four bars: Join hands again and starting with the left foot, repeat the above pattern moving to the left.

Third four bars: All face in toward center of the circle. Take one step to the right, bring left foot up to the right with a slight stamp on the ball of the foot (3), bending the knees slightly on the stamp. At the same time, clap the hands to the right toward the outside of the circle. Take one step to the left, bring right foot up to the left with a light stamp on the ball of the foot and a bend of the knees, and clap the hands toward the left (4). Repeat the above pattern again to right and left.

Next two bars: All face center. Extend right foot forward pointing heel on floor. Return foot to place and rise up on toes, at the same time raising hands high above the head; snap fingers (5) while sinking back onto heels. (When snapping fingers, the head is turned upward.) Pause for the last count.

Last two bars: Bring hands down and repeat the above pattern with the left foot. On the last note, all clap hands, bending the knees at the same time and crouching slightly. Now the dancers take hands to begin the dance over again.

YOM-TOV LANU

Folk song arranged by Trudi Rittman
Hebrew words: Levin Kipnis
English words: Ben Aronin

⚘ ⚘ ⚘

SISU VE-SIMHU[3]

CORINNE CHOCHEM

Like the preceding dance, this dance for Simhat Torah reflects the restrained ecstasy of the Hasidim, as it is especially evoked in the variation. The chorus is danced with abandon.

Formation: Dancers stand in a circle with hands joined.

Steps: First four bars: 1. Step to the right; bring left foot up to right (1). Step again to right; quickly bring left foot up to right and immediately extend the right foot diagonally to the right with the heel on the floor (2). (Bend the body and look down at extended foot.) Then bring right toe close to left foot (3). (At the same time, turn the head to look over the left shoulder.) Extend the right foot diagonally to the right again with heel on the floor (4). (Bend again and look at extended foot.) Bring right foot back to place and stamp three times, right, left, right (5).

Second four bars: Repeat the above pattern starting with the left foot and extending the left heel.

Chorus: Third four bars: Step to the right and kick left foot across the right while hopping on the right foot. Step to the left and kick right foot across the left, while hopping on the left foot. Step to the right, place left foot behind the right; step again to the right and kick left foot across the right while hopping on the right. Step to the left, kick right foot across left, while hopping on the left foot. Step on right foot, kick left foot across in front of right, while hopping on the right. Dropping hands, each dancer makes a complete turn in place to the right with three small stamps.

Last four bars: Repeat the steps of the chorus.

Variation: 2. The steps are the same as in Figure 1; the only change is in the direction of the movement. Still holding hands, all turn so that right shoulders are toward the center of the circle.

First four bars: Moving sidewards toward the center of the circle, step right and bring left foot to right (1). Step again to the right, bring left foot up to right and extend the right foot with the heel on the floor (2). (Bend body and look down at extended foot). Place right toe close to left foot (3). (At the same time turn head and look over left shoulder.) Extend right foot again with heel on the floor (4). (Bend again and look at extended foot.) Bring right foot back to place and stamp three times, right, left, right (5).

Second four bars: Raising the joined hands above shoulder level, repeat the above pattern starting with the left foot and leading with the left shoulder. On the three stamps, all turn in to face the center of the circle, preparatory to dancing the chorus.

Chorus: Moving to the right in the circle, repeat the steps of the chorus as before.

3. In order to achieve a more exalted mood, now finish the dance by repeating Figure 1 without the chorus, in a somewhat slower and quieter tempo.

SISU VE-SIMHU BE-SIMHAT HAG

Arrangement: Trudi Rittman
Hebrew words: B. Caspi*
English words: Jacob S. Golub

Slow and sustained

Si - su ve-si-me-hu be - sim - hat hag___
Re-joice and be hap - py in fes - tive glee and

Ma - ha - u - ka - pa - yim! Nag - nu___ shir___ be -
gai - ly___ clap___ your___ hands. Clang brass___ cym - bals___

kol ha - zak___ U - vim - tzil - ta - yim.
loud and free and sing in___ mer - ry bands.___

Yad el___ yad ku - la - nu ke - e - had___
Yea, sing a song to___ hea - ven a - bove, The

Ko___ ba - sakh___ na - a - vo - rah,
source___ of___ joy___ and___ light___

she - vah la - El___ ki le - Yis - ra - el hai -
Who has sus - tained us___ with___ his___ love through___

tah___ sim - hah___ ve - o - rah.
Is - ra - el's___ dark - est___ night.___

*Hebrew lyrics © Copyright by B. Caspi, Israel.

❧ 23 ❧

MUSIC FOR SUKKOT AND SIMHAT TORAH

COMPILED AND EDITED BY PAUL KAVON

BLESSINGS FOR SUKKOT

Blessing recited upon entering and seating oneself in the sukkah.

Old Melody

Ba - rukh   a - tah A - do - nai   E - lo -
he - nu Me-lekh ha-o - lam____ a-sher kid' - sha - nu be-mitz-vo-
tav ve - tzi - va - nu le - shev ba - suk - kah.____

Blessing recited on taking the etrog and the lulav.

Old Melody

Ba - rukh   a - tah A - do - nai   E - lo -
he - nu Me-lekh ha-o - lam____ a-sher kid' - sha - nu be-mitz-vo-
tav ve - tzi - va - nu al ne - ti - lat lu - lav.____

Prayer of thanks to God for His having brought us unto this season.

Traditional
Arrangement: Harry Coopersmith

Ba - rukh   a - tah A - do - nai   E - lo -
he - nu Me-lekh ha-o-lam she - he - he-ya-nu ve - ki - ye-ma-nu ve -
hi - gi - ya - nu la - a - ze - man ha - zeh.

HOSHA NA

Refrain sung for the processional with the etrog and lulav in the synagogue.

Arrangement: I. & S. E. Goldfarb

Ho - sha na ho - sha na le - ma - an - kha E - lo - he - nu ho - sha — na ho - sha — na.

2. Ho-sha na, ho-sha na; le-ma-an-kha Bor-e-nu
   Ho-sha na, ho-sha na;

3. Ho-sha na, ho-sha na; le-ma-an-kha Go-a-le-nu
   Ho-sha na, ho-sha na;

4. Ho-sha na, ho-sha na; le-ma-an-kha Dor-she-nu
   Ho-sha na, ho-sha na;

HAKKAFOT-ANA ADONAI

Refrain sung for the first processional with the Torah Scrolls on Simhat Torah.

Traditional
Arrangement: Harry Coopersmith

Slowly

A - na A - do - nai ho - shi — ah na, A - na A - do - nai — hatz - li - hah na, A - na A - do - nai a - ne - nu ve - yom kar - e - nu. —

2. E-lo-hei ha-ru-ḥot ho-shi-ah na
   Bo-ḥen le-va-vot hatz-li-ḥah na
   Go-el ḥa-zak a-ne-nu ve-yom kar-e-nu.

U-SHEAVTEM MAYIM

"Joyfully shall ye draw water from the wells of salvation."
Words: Isaiah 12. 3
Music: E. Amiran (Pugatchov)

U'she-av-tem ma-yim be-sa-son mi-mai-ney ha - ye-shu-ah

mi-mai-ney ha - ye-shu-ah Ma-yim, ma-yim, ma-yim, ma-yim Hoi ma-yim

be-sa-son be-sa-son Hey, hey, hey, hey Ma-yim, ma - yim,

ma-yim, ma-yim, ma-yim ma-yim be-sa-son ma-yim, ma-yim be-sa-son.

SIMHU NA BE-SIMHAT HA-TORAH

"Rejoice in the joy of the Torah."
Yemenite Melody
English words: Jacob Sloan

Sim-hu na — sim-hu na ____ be-sim - hat — ha-To-rah.

Yis- me-ḥu ____ a - ḥu - vim — be - sim - ḥat — ha- To- rah.

2. Yis-me-ḥu be-ru-khim be-sim-ḥat ha-To-rah
   Yis-me-ḥu be-ru-khim be-sim-ḥat ha-To-rah.
   Chorus

3. Yis-me-ḥu gi-bo-rim be-sim-ḥat ha-To-rah
   Yis-me-ḥu gi-bo-rim be-sim-ḥat ha-To-rah.
   Chorus

CHORUS: Let us rejoice, let us rejoice
In the joy of the Torah.

2. Rejoice, ye blessed ones,
In the joy of the Torah.

1. Rejoice, ye beloved
Who love the Torah

3. Rejoice, ye brave men,
In the joy of the Torah.

EIN ADDIR KE-ADONAI

Israel will receive the blessing of its incomparable God.

Babylonian

Ein ad - dir___ ke - A - do nai

ein a - huv___ ke - ven Am - ram___ ein a - hu - vah___

ka - To - rah___ ein da - gul ___ ke - Yis - ra - el ___

Mi - pi El mi - pi El yit - ba - rakh___ Yis - ra - el.

SISU VE-SIMHU BE-SIMHAT TORAH

Torah is our strength and our light.

Words : Liturgy
Melody : Ḥasidic

Moderately

Si - su ve-sim-hu___ be-Sim-hat To - rah ut'-

nu___ ka - vod___ la-To-rah.___ ki tov___ sah - rah - mi -

Fine

kol se - ḥo-rah. Mi-paz u-mif-ni-nim___ ye-ka-rah.

Na - gil ve-na-sis na - gil___ ve-na-sis be-

zot___ ha-To-rah___ ha-To - rah___ ki hi la-nu oz, ki

D. S. al Fine

hi la-nu oz oz, oz ve-o - ra. Si -

AGIL VE-ESMAH

Torah is a tree of life and everyone can share its fruits.

Arrangement: A. Zitomirsky

A - gil ve - es - mah be - Sim - hat To - rah bo

ya - vo tze - mah be - Sim - hat To - rah To - rah hi

etz ha - yim le - khu - lam____ ha -

yim To - rah hi etz____ ha - yim le -

khu - lam____ ha - yim. Ki____ im - kha me -

kor____ ha - yim me - kor____ ha - yim. Av -

Allegretto

ra - ham sa - mah be - Sim - hat To - rah be -
Ya - a - kov sa - mah be - Sim - hat To - rah be -

Sim - hat be - Sim - hat To - rah____ Yitz - hak sa - mah
Sim - hat be - Sim - hat To - rah____ Mo - she sa - mah

be - Sim - hat To - rah be - Sim - hat To - rah.
be - Sim - hat To - rah be - Sim - hat To - rah.

LAMAH SUKKAH ZU?

A "riddle" song about the holiday of Sukkot.

Folk Song
English words: Jacob Sloan

Playful

La-mah suk-kah zu a - ba tov she - li?

Slightly slower

Ley-shev ba-suk-kah ya-ki-ri ley-shev ba-suk-kah ha - vi - vi

ley-shev ba-suk-kah ye-led hen— ye-led hen she-li.

Ley-shev ba-suk-kah ye-led hen— Ye-led hen she-li.

2. La-mah ley-shev bah,a-ba tov she-li?
Avo-ten-nu, ya-ki-ri,
Avo-ten-nu, ha-vi-vi;
Avo-ten-nu, af gam he-mah
Yash-vu ba-suk-kah.

3. Ma ba-kuf-sah yesh, a-ba tov she-li?
Etrog, etrog, ya-ki-ri,
Etrog, etrog, ha-vi-vi,
Etrog, etrog, ye-led hen,
Ye-led hen sheli.

1. What is this hut for, daddy dear?
This hut's to sit in, sonny dear?
This hut's to sit in, bunny dear?
This hut's to sit in, my sweet lad,
O darling lad of mine!

2. Why sit in it, daddy dear?
Because our fathers, sonny dear,
Because our fathers, bunny dear,
Because our fathers, even they,
Sat in this hut too.

3. What's in this box, daddy dear?
A citron's in it, sonny dear,
A citron's in it, bunny dear,
A citron's in it, my sweet lad,
O darling lad of mine!

KINDER, MIR HOBN SIMCHES TOYRE!

As our rabbi used to say, 'Torah is the best merchandise.'

Text and Tune:
Morris Warshavsky

Kin-der mir ho-bn Sim-ches Toy-re, Sim-ches Toy-re oyf der gan-tservelt.

Toy-re iz di bes-te s'choy-re, A-zoy hot der Re-be mit undz ge-knelt.

Chorus:

Oy, vey, oy-oy-oy, Frey-lech kin-der ot a-zoy!

Rend-lech shit-n zich fun di zek, Frey-lech__ on an ek!

2. Chotsh ich bin mir an orim Yidl,
Un es dart mir gut der moych.
Simches Toyre, zing ich a lidl,
Un mach a gute koyse oych!
Chorus

3. Ver se kon nit mayne tsores,
Zol zey nit konen, zog ich aych;
Nor take, glaych mit ale s'rores,
Bin ich im Simches Toyre raych!
Chorus

4. Dvoyre, gib mir di naye kapote,
Ich vel zi onton take atsind,
Ich vel dir zogn, altsding iz blote,
Abi men iz borech-Hashem gezint!
Chorus

5. Vu iz Berl? Vu iz Dvosye?
Ruf zey ale in shtub arayn!
Di mume Sose, dem feter Yose,
Zoln zey ale freylech zayn!
Chorus

6. Oy vey Dvoyre, vos hostu moyre?
Ch'bin abisl freylech, ch'ken nit shteyen?
Dvoyre-lebn, u,m Simches Toyre,
Ver iz nit freylech, zog aleyn!
Chorus

THE ETROG AND LULAV

We celebrate the harvest season by carrying the etrog and the lulav.

Melody based on the Geshem chant
Words: Judith K. Eisenstein

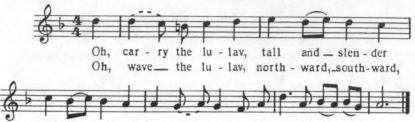

Oh, car - ry the lu - lav, tall and — slen - der
Oh, wave— the lu - lav, north - ward, south-ward,

and the— et - rog fra-grant and gold-en the et-rog and— lu - lav!
east - ward, west-ward, up - ward, down-ward the et-rog and— lu - lav!

HARVEST SONG

Let us praise the Lord as we rejoice in the harvest.

Hasidic
Arrangement and words:
Judith K. Eisenstein

Cut down the gold-en wheat, Bind — it in stur - dy—

sheaves, Oh! pluck off the jui - cy grapes, Heap them in bas - kets—

high. Build a Suk-kah cov-ered with leaves, O - pen— to the

sky, for now that our har - vest is in, Hal - le - lu - yah,—

Hal - le - lu - yah,— Hal - le - lu - yah, we cry!

❀ NOTES ❀

❀ ❀ ❀

1 SUKKOT IN THE BIBLE

1. Selections from the Pentateuch in this chapter are from *The Torah: The Five Books of Moses: A New Translation . . . according to the Masoretic Text* (Philadelphia: Jewish Publication Society of America, 1962). The selections from the other biblical books are from *The Holy Scriptures according to the Masoretic Text* (Philadelphia: Jewish Publication Society of America, 1917).

❀ ❀ ❀

2 SUKKOT IN POSTBIBLICAL WRITINGS

1. R.H. Charles, ed., *The Apocrypha and Pseudepigrapha of the Old Testament* (Oxford: Clarendon Press, 1913), 1:145, 132–33.

2. Ibid., 2:38–39.
3. Ibid., pp. 61–63.
4. F.H. Colson, trans., *Philo* (Cambridge, Mass.: Harvard University Press, 1937), 7:435–41.
5. H. St. J. Thackeray, trans., *Josephus* (Cambridge, Mass.: Harvard University Press, 1930), 4:433–37.
6. Ibid., pp. 561, 575–77.
7. Ibid., Ralph Marcus, trans. (1937), 6:387–91.
8. Ibid. (1943), 7:349–51.
9. Ibid., p. 413.
10. Ibid., H. St. J. Thackeray, trans. (1927), 2:523.
11. Yigael Yadin, *Bar-Kokhba: The Rediscovery of the Legendary Hero of the Second Jewish Revolt against Rome* (New York: Random House, 1971), p. 129.

❧ ❧ ❧

3 SUKKOT IN TALMUD AND MIDRASH

1. William G. Braude, trans., *Pesikta Rabbati: Discourses for Feasts, Fasts and Special Sabbaths* (New Haven: Yale University Press, 1968), 2: 867–68.
2. Selections from *The Babylonian Talmud* are from the translation under the editorship of Isidore Epstein (London: Soncino Press, 1935–1950).
3. Jacob Z. Lauterbach, trans., *Mekilta de-Rabbi Ishmael* (Philadelphia: Jewish Publication Society of America, 1933), 2:25.
4. Ibid., 1:108.
5. *Pesikta Rabbati*, 2:857, 859.
6. Selections from the *Midrash Rabbah* are from the translation under the editorship of H. Freedman and Maurice Simon (London: Soncino Press, 1939–1951).
7. William G. Braude, trans., *The Midrash on Psalms* (New Haven: Yale University Press, 1959), 1:209–11.
8. *Pesikta Rabbati*, 2:873–74.
9. Ibid., p. 872.
10. Ibid., p. 883.
11. *The Midrash on Psalms*, 2:203–4.

❧ ❧ ❧

4 SUKKOT IN MEDIEVAL JEWISH LITERATURE

1. Moses Maimonides, *The Guide for the Perplexed*, trans. M. Friedlaender (London: George Routledge & Sons, 1904), pp. 353–54.
2. Maurice Simon and Paul P. Levertoff, trans., *The Zohar* (London: Soncino Press, 1933), 4:384.
3. Ibid., 5:135–36.

4. Aryeh Newman, ed., *The Festivals: Pesach, Rosh Hashana, Sukkot* (Jerusalem: Department for Torah Education and Culture in the Diaspora, World Zionist Organization, 1956), p. 97.
5. Gersion Appel, "The *Mitzvah* of *Hakhel*: A Historic Assembly in Jerusalem," *Tradition: A Journal of Orthodox Jewish Thought* 20, no. 1 (Fall 1959): 129–31.

❧ ❧ ❧

5 SUKKOT AND SIMHAT TORAH IN JEWISH LAW

1. Solomon Gandz and Hyman Klein, trans., *The Code of Maimonides*, book 3, *The Book of Seasons* (New Haven: Yale University Press, 1961), pp. 380–95.
2. Ibid., pp. 396–408.

❧ ❧ ❧

6 SUKKOT AND SIMHAT TORAH LITURGY

1. David de Sola Pool, ed. and trans., *The Traditional Prayer Book for Sabbath and Festivals* (New York: Behrman House, 1960), p. 634.
2. Ibid., p. 636.
3. *The Union Prayer Book for Jewish Worship*, rev. ed. (Cincinnati: Central Conference of American Rabbis, 1941), part 1, p. 184.
4. Alice Lucas, trans., *The Jewish Year: A Collection of Devotional Poems for Sabbaths and Holidays throughout the Year* (London: Macmillan, 1898), pp. 163–64.
5. Theodor H. Gaster, *Festivals of the Jewish Year: A Modern Interpretation and Guide* (New York: William Sloane Associates, 1952), p. 85.
6. Ibid., p. 86.
7. Pool, *Traditional Prayer Book*, pp. 530–32.
8. *Jewish Quarterly Review* 11, no. 4 (1899): 301.
9. Arthur Davis and Herbert M. Adler, eds., *Service of the Synagogue: A New Edition of the Festival Prayers with an English Translation in Prose and Verse: Tabernacles* (London: George Routledge & Sons, 1907–1908), pp. 184–85.
10. Ben Zion Bokser, trans., *The Prayer Book: Weekday, Sabbath and Festival* (New York: Hebrew Publishing Co., 1957), pp. 179–81.
11. Davis and Adler, *Service of the Synagogue*, pp. 77–78.
12. *Sabbath and Festival Prayer Book, with a New Translation, Supplementary Readings and Notes* (New York: Rabbinical Assembly of America and United Synagogue of America, 1946), pp. 216–17.
13. Pool, *Traditional Prayer Book*, pp. 576–78.
14. Davis and Adler, *Service of the Synagogue*, p. 202.
15. Ibid., p. 203.

ꙮ ꙮ ꙮ

7 HASIDIC TALES AND TEACHINGS

1. Parts of this chapter are reprinted, in revised form, from Philip Goodman, *Rejoice in Thy Festival: A Treasury of Wisdom, Wit and Humor for the Sabbath and Jewish Holidays* (New York: Bloch Publishing Co., 1956), pp. 114–25, 135–36.

ꙮ ꙮ ꙮ

8 SUKKOT AND SIMHAT TORAH IN MODERN PROSE

1. Herman Wouk, *This Is My God* (New York: Doubleday & Co., 1959), pp. 79–81.
2. Samson Raphael Hirsch, *Judaism Eternal: Selected Essays* . . . , trans. Isidor Grunfeld (London: Soncino Press, 1956), 1:12–13.
3. Nahum N. Glatzer, ed., *Franz Rosenzweig: His Life and Thought* (New York: Schocken Books, 1953), pp. 323–25.
4. Joel Blau, *The Wonder of Life* (New York: Macmillan Co., 1926), pp. 189, 191–92.
5. Israel Herbert Levinthal, *A New World Is Born: Sermons and Addresses* (New York: Funk & Wagnalls Co., 1943), pp. 68–71.
6. André Neher, *Moses and the Vocation of the Jewish People*, trans. Irene Marinoff (New York: Harper Torchbooks, 1959), pp. 158–60.
7. Alexander Alan Steinbach, *Sabbath Queen* (New York: Behrman House, 1936), pp. 171–74.
8. Solomon Schechter, *Some Aspects of Rabbinic Theology* (New York: Macmillan Co., 1909), pp. 148, 150–52.
9. Hermann Cohen, "Joy in the Holy Days" (from *Die Religion der Vernunft aus den Quellen des Judentums*), *Commentary* 22, no. 6 (December 1956): 560–61.

ꙮ ꙮ ꙮ

9 SUKKOT AND SIMHAT TORAH IN ART

1. See Baruch Kanael, *Die Kunst der antiken Synagogue* (Munich, 1961).
2. Joseph Gutmann, "When the Kingdom Comes: Messianic Themes in Medieval Jewish Art," *Art Journal* 27 (1967): 169–70.
3. Mendel Metzger, "Souccoth dans l'enluminure juive," *Bulletin de nos Communautés* 16 (1960): 8–9.
4. *Monumenta Judaica*, catalog of exhibition held at Kölnisches Stadtmuseum, October–March 1964 (Cologne, 1964), p. E 596. See also pp. E 591–620.

5. Heinrich Frauberger, "Verzierte hebräische Schrift und jüdischer Buch-schmuck," *Mitteilungen der Gesellschaft zur Erforschung jüdischer Kunstdenkmäler* 5/6 (1909).
6. Louis Loeb, "Esrogdose," *Reallexikon zur deutschen Kunstgeschichte* 6 (1966): 39–42; Joseph Gutmann, *Jewish Ceremonial Art* (New York, 1968), p. 24; and Isaiah Shachar, *The Feuchtwanger Collection* (Jerusalem, 1971), pp. 178 ff.
7. Philip de Vries, *Joodse Riten en Symbolen* (Amsterdam, 1968), illustration opposite p. 97.
8. For customs described, see Dov Sadan, *Galgal ha-Moadim* (Tel Aviv, 1964), pp. 163–78, and Akiva Ben-Ezra, *Minhage Haggim* (Jerusalem, 1962), pp. 64–130. See also Mordecai Narkiss, "Omanut be-tokh ha-Sukkot," *Moed ve-Atzeret: Yalkut le-Hag ha-Sukkot*, ed. Judah P. Cohen (Jerusalem, 1944), pp. 83–88.

⚹ ⚹ ⚹

10 THE DEVELOPMENT OF THE FESTIVAL

1. Isaac N. Fabricant, *A Guide to Sukkoth* (London: Jewish Chronicle Publications, 1958), pp. 43–46.
2. *Universal Jewish Encyclopedia*, 5:465–66.
3. Julius H. Greenstone, *Jewish Feasts and Fasts* (Philadelphia, 1945), pp. 77–80.
4. *Jewish Chronicle* (London), no. 3,416 (September 28, 1934): 20, 24.

⚹ ⚹ ⚹

11 THE SUKKAH

1. Julius H. Greenstone, *Jewish Feasts and Fasts* (Philadelphia, 1945), pp. 61–64.
2. Israel Abrahams, *Festival Studies: Being Thoughts on the Jewish Year* (Philadelphia: Julius H. Greenstone, 1906), pp. 63–75.

⚹ ⚹ ⚹

12 THE FOUR SPECIES

1. *Commentary* 26, no. 4 (October 1958): 300–7.
2. Israel Abrahams, *Festival Studies: Being Thoughts on the Jewish Year* (Philadelphia: Julius H. Greenstone, 1906), pp. 13–17.
3. Ibid., pp. 111–18.
4. Julius H. Greenstone, *Jewish Feasts and Fasts* (Philadelphia, 1945), pp. 68–69.
5. A.S. Sachs, *Worlds That Passed* (Philadelphia: Jewish Publication Society of America, 1928), pp. 189–91.

❧ ❧ ❧

13 SUKKOT AND SIMHAT TORAH IN MANY LANDS

1. Hayyim Schauss, *The Jewish Festivals: From Their Beginnings to Our Own Day* (Cincinnati: Union of American Hebrew Congregations, 1938), pp. 189–99.
2. Maurice Samuel, *The World of Sholom Aleichem* (New York: Alfred A. Knopf, 1943), pp. 66–68, 72–75.
3. Wolf Zeev Rabinowitsch, *Lithuanian Hasidism*, trans. M.B. Dagut (New York: Schocken Books, 1971), pp. 83–84.
4. Meir Bar-Ilan, *Me-Volozin Ad Yerushalayim* (Tel Aviv: Committee for the Publication of the Writings of Rabbi Meir Bar-Ilan, 1971), 1:114–15.
5. Yehudah Leb Hakohen Maimon (Fishman), *Haggim u-Moadim* (Jerusalem: Mosad Harav Kook, 1944), p. 66.
6. Herman Pollack, *Jewish Folkways in Germanic Lands (1648–1806): Studies in Aspects of Daily Life* (Cambridge, Mass.: M.I.T. Press, 1971), pp. 172–75, 190–91.
7. M. Papo, "The Sephardi Community of Vienna," *The Jews of Austria: Essays on Their Life, History and Destruction*, ed. Josef Fraenkel (London: Vallentine, Mitchell, 1967), pp. 339–40.
8. M. Yechezkieli, "Joy of the Festivals in the Hassag Labor Camp," trans. Moshe Barkany, *The Jewish Observer* 6, no. 10 (October 1970): 11, 13–14.
9. Abraham I. Katsh, ed. and trans., *Scroll of Agony: The Warsaw Diary of Chaim A. Kaplan* (New York: Macmillan Co., 1965), pp. 45, 210, 214.
10. Arie L. Eliav, *Between Hammer and Sickle* (Philadelphia: Jewish Publication Society of America, 1967), pp. 70–71.
11. Elie Wiesel, *The Jews of Silence*, trans. Neal Kozodoy (New York: Holt, Rinehart and Winston, 1966), pp. 44–57, 59–64, 66.
12. *Yeda-Am* 5, nos. 1–2 (Autumn 1958): 34–37.
13. Eric Werner, "The Eduard Birnbaum Collection of Jewish Music," *Hebrew Union College Annual* 18 (1944): 414–15.
14. Benjamin Disraeli, *Tancred: or, The New Crusade* (Leipzig, 1847), 2: 152–55.
15. Jacob R. Marcus, *The Colonial American Jew, 1492–1776* (Detroit: Wayne State University Press, 1970), 1:132; 2:982.
16. A.M. Klein, *The Second Scroll* (New York: Alfred A. Knopf, 1951), pp. 7–9.
17. Oscar M. Lifshutz, "*Sukkah* in Bavaria: Courtesy U.S. Army Engineers," *Jewish Life* 26, no. 1 (October 1958): 17–19.
18. Solomon Poll, *The Hasidic Community of Williamsburg: A Study in the Sociology of Religion* (New York: Free Press of Glencoe, 1962), pp. 160–66.

19. David G. Mandelbaum, "The Jewish Way of Life in Cochin," *Jewish Social Studies* 1, no. 4 (October 1939): 456–58.
20. Ida G. Cowen, "Calcutta's Sukkot Queen of Beauty," *Reconstructionist* 35, no. 10 (October 10, 1969): 20–21, 24–25; reprinted in her *Jews in Remote Corners of the World* (Englewood Cliffs, N. J.: Prentice-Hall, 1971), pp. 183–85, 189–91.
21. Devora and Menahem Hacohen, *One People: The Story of the Eastern Jews*, trans. Israel I. Taslitt (New York: Sabra Books, 1969), pp. 52–53.
22. Ibid., pp. 144, 136.
23. Erich Brauer, "The Jews of Afghanistan: An Anthropological Report," *Jewish Social Studies* 4, no. 2 (April 1942): 136.
24. Moshe Dluznowsky, "Jewish Holidays in North Africa," *The Jews of Morocco* (New York: Zionist Youth Council, 1956), p. 52.
25. Wolf Leslau, trans., *Falasha Anthology* (New Haven: Yale University Press, 1951), p. xxxii.
26. Chaim Weizmann, *Trial and Error: The Autobiography of Chaim Weizmann* (Philadelphia: Jewish Publication Society of America, 1949), 1:229–31.
27. *Iggeret Lagolah*, no. 55 (August/September, 1955), pp. 34–36.
28. *The Gates of Zion* 22, no. 2 (Winter 1967): 2–3 (Published by Synagogue Council of Zionist Federation, London).
29. Eliezer Eliner and Hayyim Hamiel, eds., *Mayanot: Measef le-Inyane Hinukh ve-Horaah*, vol. 2, *Sukkot* (Jerusalem: Department of Torah Education and Culture in the Diaspora, World Zionist Organization, 1966), p. 168.
30. Tzvi Givone, "The Festivals," *The Religious Kibbutz Movement: The Revival of the Jewish Religious Community*, ed. Aryei Fishman (Jerusalem: Zionist Organization, 1957), pp. 84–86.
31. *Jewish Chronicle* (London), no. 4,666 (September 26, 1958): 17.

❧ ❧ ❧

1 4 SUKKOT AND SIMHAT TORAH IN POETRY

1. *Jewish Quarterly Review* 15 (1903): 275–77.
2. Joseph Friedlander, comp., *The Standard Book of Jewish Verse*, ed. George Alexander Kohut (New York: Dodd, Mead and Co., 1917), pp. 300–1.
3. Israel Zangwill, *Blind Children* (London: William Heinemann, 1903), p. 126.
4. Israel Efros, ed., *Selected Poems of Hayyim Nahman Bialik: Translated from the Hebrew*, rev. ed. (New York: Bloch Publishing Co. for Histadruth Ivrith of America, 1965), pp. 237–38.
5. Harry H. Fein, trans., *Gems of Hebrew Verse* (Boston: Bruce Humphries, Inc., 1940), p. 21.
6. Ibid., pp. 22–23.
7. A.M. Klein, *Hath Not a Jew . . .* (New York: Behrman's Jewish Book House, 1940), pp. 61–62.

8. Leo W. Schwarz, ed., *The Menorah Treasury: Harvest of Half a Century* (Philadelphia: Jewish Publication Society of America, 1964), pp. 733–34.

9. *Union Hymnal: Songs and Prayers for Jewish Worship*, 3d ed. (Central Conference of American Rabbis, 1940), p. 212.

10. *Commentary* 2, no. 2 (Autumn 1946): 136.

11. Ruth F. Brin, *Interpretations for the Weekly Torah Readings* (Minneapolis: Lerner Publications Co., 1965), p. 159.

12. Mollie R. Golomb, *How Fair My Faith and Other Poems* (Philadelphia: Dorrance & Co., 1968), p. 52.

✹ ✹ ✹

15 SUKKOT AND SIMHAT TORAH IN THE SHORT STORY

1. Leo W. Schwarz, ed., *The Feast of Leviathan: Tales of Adventure, Faith and Love from Jewish Literature* (New York: Rinehart and Co., 1956), pp. 182–88.

2. Sholom Aleichem, *The Great Fair: Scenes from My Childhood*, trans. Tamara Kahana (New York: Noonday Press, 1955), pp. 213–16.

3. Ibid., pp. 295–302.

4. Sholom Aleichem, *Old Country Tales*, trans. Curt Leviant (New York: G.P. Putnam's Sons, 1966), pp. 272–77.

5. Maurice Samuel, *Prince of the Ghetto* (New York: Alfred A. Knopf, 1948), pp. 235–39.

6. Shmuel Yosef Agnon, "The Tale of the Scribe," trans. Isaac Franck, *Midstream* 13, no. 2 (February 1967): 24–25; reprinted in Agnon's *Twenty-One Stories*, ed. Nahum N. Glatzer (New York: Schocken Books, 1970), pp. 22–24.

7. Irving Howe and Eliezer Greenberg, eds., *A Treasury of Yiddish Stories* (New York: Viking Press, 1953), pp. 280–84.

8. Lamed Shapiro, *The Jewish Government and Other Stories*, trans. Curt Leviant (New York: Twayne Publishers, 1971) pp. 173–74.

9. Jacob Picard, *The Marked One and Twelve Other Stories*, trans. Ludwig Lewisohn (Philadelphia: Jewish Publication Society of America, 1956), pp. 73–83.

10. Joseph Opatoshu, *A Day in Regensburg: Short Stories*, trans. Jacob Sloan (Philadelphia: Jewish Publication Society of America, 1968), pp. 117–23.

11. Joseph Leftwich, ed., *Yisroel: The Jewish Omnibus* (London: Heritage, 1933), pp. 107–14.

12. Yom-Tov Lewinski, ed., *Sefer ha-Moadim . . .*, vol. 4, *Sukkot* (Tel Aviv: Oneg Shabbat and Dvir, 1951), pp. 66–69.

✹ ✹ ✹

16 SUKKOT AND SIMHAT TORAH MISCELLANY

1. Simhah Asaf, "Aliyah le-Torah ve-Simhat Torah," *La-Moed: Kovetz Sif-ruti le-Hag ha-Sukkot* (Jerusalem: Mizrah, 1946), 2:15–16; Abraham Yaari, *Toldot Hag Simhat Torah* (Jerusalem: Mosad Harav Kook, 1964), pp. 20, 28.
2. Otto Schnitzler, "The Particularity of the Number Seven and the Origin of the Seven Days' Week," *Folklore Research Center Studies,* ed. Dov Noy and Issachar Ben-Ami (Jerusalem: Magnes Press, 1970), 1:73–80.
3. Abraham ben Nathan ha-Yarhi, *Sefer ha-Manhig* (Constantinople, 1519), p. 71b.
4. Sidney B. Hoenig, *The Scholarship of Dr. Bernard Revel* (New York: Yeshivah University Press, 1968), p. 19; Elkan N. Adler, ed., *Jewish Travellers: A Treasury of Travelogues from 9 Centuries* (New York: Hermon Press, 1966), pp. 226, 337.
5. Cyrus H. Gordon, *Before Columbus: Links between the Old World and Ancient America* (New York: Crown Publishers, 1971), pp. 89–90. See also idem, "The Metcalf Stone," *Manuscripts* 21, no. 3 (Summer 1969): 159–68.
6. J.J. Rivlin, "Hagra ve-Talmidav be-Yishuv Eretz-Yisrael," *Sefer Hagra,* ed. J.L. Maimon (Jerusalem: Mosad Harav Kook, 1954), part 3, p. 113.
7. Sukkah 2.3.
8. *A Thought for the Week* 1, no. 51 (October 11, 1968): 4.
9. S.D. Gotein, *A Mediterranean Society,* vol. 1, *Economic Foundations* (Berkeley: University of California Press, 1967), p. 121.
10. Yom-Tov Lewinski, *Sefer ha-Moadim . . . ,* vol. 4, *Sukkot* (Tel Aviv: Oneg Shabbat Society and Dvir, 1951), p. 95.
11. Menahot 27a.
12. "Selections from Two Letters Written by Obadja da Bertinoro," trans. A.I.K.D., *Miscellany of Hebrew Literature* (London: N. Trubner and Co., 1872), 1: 116.
13. Yaari, *Toldot,* pp. 202–3.
14. Lionel D. Barnett, trans., *El Libro de los Acuerdos: Being the Records and Accompts of the Spanish and Portuguese Synagogue of London from 1663 to 1681* (Oxford: University Press, 1931), pp. 6, 128–29.
15. "The Earliest Extant Minute Books of the Spanish and Portuguese Congregation Shearith Israel in New York, 1728–1786," *Publications of the American Jewish Historical Society* 21 (1913): 110–11.
16. Jacob R. Marcus, *American Jewry: Documents: Eighteenth Century* (Cincinnati: Hebrew Union College Press, 1959), pp. 94–95.
17. Menashe Unger, *Chassidus un Yom-Tov* (New York: Farlag Chassidus, 1958), p. 156.
18. M. Friedlander, "Simhat Torah & Chassidism," *Jewish Chronicle* (London), no. 4,562 (September 28, 1956): 13; Isidore Epstein, *The*

"Responsa" of Rabbi Solomon Ben Adreth of Barcelona (1235–1310) as
a Source of the History of Spain (New York: Hermon Press, 1968), p.
59.
19. Yaari, *Toldot,* pp. 166–79.
20. *New York Times* 121, no. 41,535 (October 11, 1971): 13; *Jewish Week
and The American Examiner* 181, no. 23 (October 14, 1971): 1.

✸ ✸ ✸

17 SUKKOT AND SIMHAT TORAH HUMOR

1. Adapted from Philip Goodman, *Rejoice in Thy Festival: A Treasury of
Wisdom, Wit and Humor for the Sabbath and Jewish Holidays* (New
York: Bloch Publishing Co., 1956), pp. 120–21, 125–38.

✸ ✸ ✸

19 CHILDREN'S STORIES FOR SUKKOT AND SIMHAT TORAH

1. Sadie Rose Weilerstein, *What the Moon Brought* (Philadelphia: Jewish
Publication Society of America, 1942), pp. 28–37.
2. Sadie Rose Weilerstein, *The Adventures of K'tonton: A Little Jewish
Tom Thumb* (New York: National Women's League of the United
Synagogue, 1935), pp. 81–85.
3. Ibid., pp. 86–89.
4. Morris Epstein, *My Holiday Story Book* (New York: Ktav Publishing
House, 1958), pp. 14–19.
5. Hermann Schwab, *Dreams of Childhood: Stories for Jewish Children*
(London: Anscombe, 1949), pp. 9–11.
6. Helen Fine, *G'dee* (New York: Union of American Hebrew Congregations, 1958), pp. 36–43.
7. Dorothy F. Zeligs, *The Story of Jewish Holidays and Customs for Young
People* (New York: Bloch Publishing Co., 1942), pp. 45–60.
8. Ezekiel Schloss and Morris Epstein, eds., *The New World Over Story
Book: An Illustrated Anthology for Jewish Youth* (New York: Bloch
Publishing Co., 1968), pp. 150–54.
9. *World Over* 19, no. 1 (November 1, 1957): 6–7.
10. Barton's Candy Corporation, New York.
11. *The Projector,* Jewish National Fund (Jerusalem, August, 1940), pp.
10–13.

✸ ✸ ✸

20 POEMS FOR CHILDREN

1. Jessie E. Sampter, *Around the Year in Rhymes for the Jewish Child* (New
York: Bloch Publishing Co., 1920), pp. 18–19.

2. Ibid., p. 20.
3. H.N. Bialik, *Far Over the Sea: Poems and Jingles for Children*, trans. Jessie E. Sampter, illus. Louis Kobrin (Cincinnati: Union of American Hebrew Congregations, 1939), pp. 56–57.
4. Ibid., p. 58.
5. Ibid., pp. 64–65.
6. *The Young Judean*, October 1924, p. 2.
7. Philip M. Raskin, *Poems for Young Israel* (New York: Behrman House, 1925), p. 71.
8. Elma Ehrlich Levinger, *Jewish Festivals in the Religious School* (Cincinnati: Union of American Hebrew Congregations, 1923), p. 48.
9. Ibid., p. 46.
10. Abraham Burstein, *A Jewish Child's Garden of Verses* (New York: Bloch Publishing Co., 1940), p. 51.
11. Nina Salaman, ed., *Apples & Honey: A Gift-Book for Jewish Boys and Girls* (New York: Bernard G. Richards Co., 1927), p. 226.
12. Sadie Rose Weilerstein, *The Singing Way: Poems for Jewish Children*, illus. Jessie B. Robinson (New York: National Women's League of the United Synagogue, 1946), pp. 15–17.
13. Ilo Orleans, *Within Thy Hand: My Poem Book of Prayers* (New York: Union of American Hebrew Congregations, 1961), p. 62.

❧ ❧ ❧

22 DANCES FOR SUKKOT AND SIMHAT TORAH

1. Dvora Lapson, *Jewish Dances the Year Round* (New York: Jewish Education Committee Press, 1957), pp. 93–94.
2. Corinne Chochem, *Jewish Holiday Dances* (New York: Behrman House, 1948), pp. 33–35.
3. Ibid., pp. 38–41.

GLOSSARY OF SUKKOT AND
❧ SIMHAT TORAH TERMS ❧

❧ ❧ ❧

ARAVAH, pl. *aravot* (willow). One of the Four Species. See ARBAAH MINIM
and LULAV.

ARBAAH MINIM (Four Species). The Four Species are the *etrog, lulav, hadas,*
and *aravah,* the plants used in the Sukkot ritual.

BAAL MAFTIR. The person called to the reading of the last portion of the day's
Torah reading, and to read the portion of the Prophets.

BOOTHS. See SUKKOT.

BRIDEGROOM OF GENESIS. See HATAN BERESHIT.

BRIDEGROOM OF THE LAW. See HATAN TORAH.

CITRON. See ETROG.

ETROG (citron). One of the Four Species; called "fruit of a goodly tree"
in the Bible. See ARBAAH MINIM.

FEAST OF BOOTHS. See SUKKOT.

FEAST OF TABERNACLES. See SUKKOT.

FOUR SPECIES. See ARBAAH MINIM.

GESHEM (rain). Prayer for rain read on Shemini Atzeret.

HADAS, pl. *hadasim* (myrtle). One of the Four Species. See ARBAAH MINIM and LULAV.

HAG HA-ASIF (Festival of Ingathering). See HAG HA-SUKKOT.

HAG HA-SUKKOT. Feast of Booths; Feast of Tabernacles. See SUKKOT.

HAKKAFAH, pl. *hakkafot* (circuit). The processional circuits in the synagogue on Simhat Torah when the participants carry the Scrolls of the Law. Similar processions with *etrog* and *lulav* are conducted on Hoshana Rabbah.

HALLEL (praise). Psalms 113–118, recited on the festivals.

HATAN BERESHIT (bridegroom of Genesis). Title of honor bestowed on the person called on Simhat Torah to the Torah reading inaugurating the yearly cycle of the weekly scriptural portions.

HATAN TORAH (bridegroom of the Law). Title of honor bestowed on the person called on Simhat Torah to the Torah reading that completes the yearly cycle of the weekly scriptural portions.

HAZKARAT NESHAMOT (remembrance of souls [of the deceased]). Memorial services for the departed recited on the last day of the festivals and on Yom Kippur.

HOL HA-MOED. The intermediate days of Sukkot, considered half-holidays, between the first two days and Shemini Atzeret.

HOSHANA, pl. *hoshanot* (please save). On Hoshana Rabbah, circuits are made with the Four Species while reciting the *Hoshana* invocations for forgiveness and redemption.

HOSHANA RABBAH (Great Hosanna). The seventh day of Sukkot, being the last of the five intermediate days of the festival, on which God's final judgment for the year is sealed; the name derives from the recitation of more *Hoshana* prayers recited on this day while making circuits with the Four Species than on any other festival.

HOSHANOT (willow twigs). Bundle of willow twigs tied together, which are used for striking at the conclusion of the circuits on Hoshana Rabbah.

KIDDUSH (sanctification). A prayer usually chanted over wine in sanctifying the Sabbath and festivals.

LULAV (branch of a palm tree). One of the Four Species. See ARBAAH MINIM. It is also a generic term for the bouquet of palm branch, the three myrtle twigs, and the two willow twigs bound together.

MAHZOR (cycle). Prayer book for the cycle of holy days and festivals throughout the year; also applied to the festival liturgy in which *piyyutim* are included.

MYRTLE. See HADAS.

PALM. See LULAV.

PITMA (protuberance). The pestlelike protuberance on the blossom end of the citron, having the appearance of a pestle set in a mortar.

PITUM. The popular name of *pitma*.

PIYYUT, pl. *piyyutim* (poem). A liturgical poem of praise recited on a festival.

SEKHAKH (overhanging boughs). Branches and twigs of trees, bamboo sticks, and other vegetation of the soil used for the *sukkah* roofing.

SHALOSH REGALIM (three pilgrimages). The three major festivals (Passover, Shavuot, and Sukkot); also known as the pilgrimage festivals.

SHEMINI ATZERET. Eighth Day of Solemn Assembly; the concluding day of Sukkot, which falls on Tishri 22; also considered a separate festival.

SIMHAT BET HA-SHOEVAH (rejoicing of the house of [water] drawing). A joyous celebration held on each night of the intermediate days of Sukkot to recall these events in the days of the Temple.

SIMHAT TORAH (Rejoicing in the Law). The Festival of Rejoicing in the Law on which the annual cycle of the Torah reading is concluded and begun anew. It occurs on Tishri 23, the day following Shemini Atzeret. In Israel it coincides with Shemini Atzeret.

SUKKAH, pl. *sukkot* (booth, tabernacle). The temporary structure erected in fulfillment of the commandment to live in booths during Sukkot; it recalls the frail booths in which the children of Israel dwelt during their wandering in the wilderness after the exodus from Egypt.

SUKKOT (booths, tabernacles). Feast of Booths or Tabernacles; Festival of Ingathering; the last of the three pilgrimage festivals, commencing on Tishri 15, which marks the harvest season and commemorates the sojourn of the Israelites in the desert after their departure from Egyptian bondage.

TABERNACLES. See SUKKOT.

TIKKUN LEL HOSHANA RABBAH. Order of service for the night of Hoshana Rabbah.

TISHRI. The seventh month of the Hebrew calendar, in which Rosh Hashanah, Yom Kippur, and Sukkot occur.

USHPIZIN (divine guests). The fancied celestial guests—Abraham, Isaac, Jacob, Joseph, Moses, Aaron, David—who, according to Jewish mysticism, appear in the *sukkah*, one on each day of the festival, and are welcomed by reciting Aramaic greetings.

YIZKOR (remember). See HAZKARAT NESHAMOT.

YOM TOV (good day). A festival.

ZEMAN SIMHATENU (Season of Our Rejoicing). The term applied to the Feast of Booths in the liturgy.

BIBLIOGRAPHY

※ ※ ※

GENERAL REFERENCES

Abrahams, Israel. *Festival Studies: Being Thoughts on the Jewish Year.* Philadelphia: Julius H. Greenstone, 1906, pp. 13–18, 56–75, 111–23.

Amorai, Y., and Ariel, Z., eds. *Moreshet Avot (Entziklopediah "Mayan").* Tel Aviv: Joseph Sreberk, n.d., pp. 75–89.

Ariel, Shlomoh Zalman. *Entziklopediah Meir Netiv.* Tel Aviv: Massadah, 1960.

Ariel, Z., ed. *Sefer ha-Hag veha-Moed.* Tel Aviv: Am Oved, 1962, pp. 77–126.

Aslikenazi, Touvia, ed. *Haggim u-Moadim: Antologiah. Vol. 1. Hag ha-Sukkot.* Pittsburgh: Hebrew Institute, 1944.

Ausubel, Nathan. *The Book of Jewish Knowledge.* New York: Crown Publishers, 1964.

Ayali, Meir, ed. *Haggim u-Zemanim: Mahzore Kriah le-Moade Yisrael.* Vol. 2. Tel Aviv: Gazit, 1955, pp. 217–376.

Bader, Gershom. *Naye Horizonten Vegen Unzere Alte Yamim-Tovim.* New York: Pardes Publishing House, 1938, pp. 43–69.

Beker, Hayyim S., ed. *Yalkut le-Moadim: Hag ha-Sukkot.* Jerusalem, 1967.

Ben-Ezra, Akiba. *Minhage Haggim.* Tel Aviv: M. Newman, 1963, pp. 64–130.

———. *Yamim Noraim ve-Sukkot.* New York: Mizrachi National Education Committee, 1949, pp. 36–56.

Berlin, Meir, ed. *La-Moed: Kovetz Sifruti le-Hag ha-Sukkot: Kovetz 5.* Jerusalem: Hamizrah, 1947.

Bial, Morrison David. *Liberal Judaism at Home: The Practice of Modern Reform Judaism.* Summit, N.J.: Temple Sinai, 1967, pp. 117–22.

Birnbaum, Philip. *A Book of Jewish Concepts.* New York: Hebrew Publishing Co., 1964.

Chomsky, William, ed. *Sukkot ve-Simhat Torah: Zeman Simhatenu.* New York: Jewish Education Committee of New York, 1960.

De Vaux, Roland. *Ancient Israel: Its Life and Institutions.* New York: McGraw-Hill Book Co., 1961, pp. 495–502.

Ehrmann, Elieser L. *Sukkot und Simchat Tora: Ein Quellenheft.* Berlin: Schocken Verlag, 1937.

Eisenstein, Ira. *What We Mean by Religion: A Modern Interpretation of the Sabbath and Festivals.* New York: Reconstructionist Press, 1958, pp. 62–98.

Eliner, Eliezer, and Hamiel, Hayyim, eds. *Mayanot: Measef le-Inyane Hinukh ve-Horaah.* Vol. 2, *Sukkot.* Jerusalem: Department of Torah Education and Culture in the Diaspora, World Zionist Organization, 1966.

Encyclopedia Judaica. 16 vols. Jerusalem: Keter Publishing House, 1971. See vol. 1, Index.

Fabricant, Isaac N. *A Guide to Succoth.* London: Jewish Chronicle Publications, 1958.

Finkelstein, Louis. *The Pharisees: The Sociological Background of Their Faith.* Vol. 1. Philadelphia: Jewish Publication Society of America, 1940, pp. 102–15.

Fishman (Maimon), Judah Leb. *Haggim u-Moadim.* 2d ed. Jerusalem: Mosad Harav Kook, 1944, pp. 55–78.

Freehof, Lillian S., and Bandman, Lottie C. *Flowers and Festivals of the Jewish Year.* New York: Hearthside Press, 1964, pp. 62–79.

Frishman, Isaiah, ed. *Hag ha-Sukkot: Homer Hadrakhah le-Morim be-Bate ha-Sefer ha-Memlakhtiim: le-Kitot 1–4.* Jerusalem: Ministry of Education and Culture, 1967.

———, ed. *Hag ha-Sukkot: Homer Hadrakhah le-Morim be-Bate ha-Sefer ha-Memlakhtiim.* Jerusalem: Tarbut ve-Hinukh, 1969.

Gaer, Joseph, and Wolf, Alfred. *Our Jewish Heritage.* New York: Henry Holt and Co., 1957, pp. 87–92.

Gaster, Theodor H. *Festivals of the Jewish Year: A Modern Interpretation and Guide.* New York: William Sloane Associates, 1953, pp. 80–104.

Goldin, Hyman E. *A Treasury of Jewish Holidays: History, Legends, Traditions.* New York: Twayne Publishers, 1952, pp. 40–51.

———. *The Jewish Woman and Her Home.* Brooklyn, N.Y.: Jewish Culture Publishing Co., 1941, pp. 139–46, 177–90.

Goldman, Alex J. *A Handbook for the Jewish Family: Understanding and Enjoying the Sabbath and Holidays.* New York: Bloch Publishing Co., 1958, pp. 49–89.

Goodman, Philip, ed. *Sukkot and Simhat Torah: Program Material for Young Adults and Adults.* New York: National Jewish Welfare Board, 1945.

Goren, Shelomoh. *Torat ha-Moadim: Mehkerim u-Maamarim Al Moade Yisrael le-Or ha-Halakhah.* Tel Aviv: Avraham Tzioni, 1964, pp. 105–49.

Greenstone, Julius H. *Jewish Feasts and Fasts.* Philadelphia, 1945, pp. 59–82.

———. *The Jewish Religion.* Philadelphia: Jewish Chautauqua Society, 1929, pp. 60–73.

Hagge Tishre: Homer Hadrakhah le-Gane ha-Yeladim ha-Memlakhtiim. Jerusalem: Ministry of Education and Culture, 1967, pp. 26–39.

Hag u-Moed: Divre Iyun, Mekorot. Tel Aviv: Ha-Kibbutz ha-Artzi, ha-Mahlakah le-Tarbut, n.d., pp. 66–76.

Hakohen, Menahem, ed. *Mahanaim: Massekhet le-Hayal le-Yamim ha-Noraim vele-Hag ha-Sukkot.* Tzava Haganah le-Yisrael, no. 40 (1960): 175–95.

———. *Mahanaim: Massekhet le-Hayile Tzahal le-Hag ha-Sukkot.* Tzava Haganah le-Yisrael, no. 50 (1961).

Hakohen, Shmuel; Shragai, Eliyahu; and Peli, Pinhas, eds. *Sukkat Shalom: Perakim le-Hag ha-Sukkot.* Tzava Haganah le-Yisrael, no. 7 (1950).

Harrelson, Walter. "The Celebration of the Feast of Booths according to Zech. XVI. 16–21." In *Religions in Antiquity: Essays in Memory of Erwin Ramsdell Goodenough,* edited by Jacob Neusner. Leiden: E.J. Brill, 1968, pp. 88–96.

Hirsch, Samson Raphael. *Be-Maagle Shanah: Sefer Rishon.* Translated by Aviezer Wolf. Bnai Brak: Netzah, 1965, pp. 125–52.

Jakobovits, Immanuel. *Journal of a Rabbi.* New York: Living Books, 1966, pp. 409–18.

The Jewish Encyclopedia. 12 vols. New York: Ktav Publishing House. See Bridegroom of the Law, Etrog, Festivals, Hakkafot, Harvest, Holy Days, Hoshana Rabbah, Lulab, Second Day of Festivals, Shemini Atzeret, Simhat Torah, Sukkah, Tabernacles, Water-Drawing.

Joseph, Morris. *Judaism as Creed and Life.* London: George Routledge and Sons, 1903, pp. 236–46.

Kaplan, Mordecai M. *The Meaning of God in Modern Jewish Religion.* New York: Jewish Reconstructionist Foundation, 1947, pp. 188–264.

Karlebach, Azriel, ed. *Simhat Torah: Yalkut.* Tel Aviv: Sifron, n.d.

Kitov, Eliyahu. *The Book of Our Heritage: The Jewish Year and Its Days of Significance.* Vol. 1, *Tishrey—Shevat.* Translated by Nathan Bulman. Jerusalem: 'A' Publishers, 1968, pp. 129–225.

———. *Sefer ha-Todaah: La-daat Huke ha-Elokim u-Mitzvotav Hagge Yisrael u-Moadav*. Jerusalem: Alef Makhon le-Hotzaat Sefarim, 1964, pp. 67–131.

Kohen, Yehudah Pinhas, ed. *Moed ve-Atzeret: Yalkut le-Hag ha-Sukkot*. Jerusalem: Youth Department, Zionist Organization, 1943.

La-Moed: Kovetz Sifruti le-Hag ha-Sukkot: Kovetz 2. Jerusalem: Mizrah, 1946.

Lavia, Eliezer Lipman, ed. *Otzar Maamarim: Shabbatot Haggim u-Zemanim ve-Yeme de-Pagra*. Jerusalem: Rubin Mass, 1962, pp. 94–115.

Lehrman, S.M. *The Jewish Festivals*. London: Shapiro, Vallentine & Co., 1938, pp. 71–88.

————. *Sukkoth*. [London:] Bachad Fellowship Publication, n.d.

Leshem, Haim. *Shabbat u-Moade Yisrael be-Halakhah, be-Aggadah, be-Historia, uve-Folklor*. Vol. 1. Tel Aviv: Niv, 1965, pp. 215–65. Vol. 3, 1969, pp. 71–81.

Levi, Shonie B., and Kaplan, Sylvia R. *Guide for the Jewish Homemaker*. New York: Schocken Books, 1964, pp. 97–104.

Lewinski, Yom-Tov. *Eleh Moade Yisrael*. Tel Aviv: Ahiasaf, 1971, pp. 79–98.

————, ed. *Sefer ha-Moadim*. Vol. 4, *Sukkot*. Tel Aviv: Oneg Shabbat and Dvir, 1951.

Markowitz, S.H. *Leading a Jewish Life in the Modern World*. Rev. ed. New York: Union of American Hebrew Congregations, 1958, pp. 180–98.

Massekhet Sukkah, Talmud Bavli. Wilna, 1895.

Mikhael B., ed. *Haggim u-Moadim le-Yisrael: Aggadot Shirim ve-Sippurim*. Tel Aviv: M. Biran, 1954, pp. 87–104.

Mindel, Nissan. *The Complete Story of Tishrei*. Brooklyn, N.Y.: Merkos L'Inyonei Chinuch, 1961, pp. 141–222, 225–26.

The Mishnah. Translated by Herbert Danby. Oxford: Clarendon Press, 1933, pp. 172–81.

Moore, George Foot. *Judaism in the First Centuries of the Christian Era: The Age of the Tannaim*. Vol. 2. New York: Schocken Books, 1971, pp. 43–51.

Neriah, [Moshe Z.], ed. *Asif le-Hag ha-Sukkot*. Jerusalem: Hapoel Hamizrachi and Bne Akivah, 1939.

Newman, Aryeh, ed. *The Festivals: Pesach, Rosh Hashanah, Sukkot (Mayanot Jewish Teacher's Companion)*. Jerusalem: Department for Torah Education and Culture in the Diaspora, World Zionist Organization, 1956, pp. 89–171.

Newman, Louis I. *The Jewish People: Faith and Life*. New York: Bloch Publishing Co., 1965, pp. 170–74.

————, and Spitz, Samuel. *The Talmudic Anthology*. New York: Behrman House, 1945, pp. 445–53.

Picker, Shlomoh. *Shabbat u-Moadim be-Aretz*. Tel Aviv: M. Newman, 1969, pp. 178–84, 238–46, 255–63, 273–75.

Pougatch, I., ed. *Souccoth: Origines, Signification, Célébration*. Paris: Editions O.P.E.J., n.d.

Press, Chaim, ed. *What Is the Reason: An Anthology of Questions and Answers on the Jewish Holidays*. Vol. 3, *Succoth*. New York: Bloch Publishing Co., 1966.

Rabinowitz, Esther, ed. *Haggim u-Moadim be-Hinukh: le-Mehankhim be-Gan uve-Kitot ha-Nemukhot*. Tel Aviv, 1954, pp. 100–20, 363–64.

Reik, Theodor. *Pagan Rites in Judaism*. New York: Noonday Press, 1964, pp. 3–26.

Rosenau, William. *Jewish Ceremonial Institutions and Customs*. New York: Bloch Publishing Co. 1925, pp. 93–97, 122–23.

Roth, Cecil, ed. *The Standard Jewish Encyclopedia*. Garden City, N.Y.: Doubleday & Co., 1959.

Schauss, Hayyim. *The Jewish Festivals: From Their Beginnings to Our Own Day*. Cincinnati: Union of American Hebrew Congregations, 1938, pp. 170–207.

Sdan, Dov. *Galgal Moadim*. Tel Aviv: Massada, 1964, pp. 163–78.

Seidman, Hillel. *The Glory of the Jewish Holidays*. Edited by Moses Zalesky. New York: Shengold Publishers, 1969, pp. 100–23.

Shalem, Matityahu, and Likvar Yosef, eds. *Sukkot: Hivui u-Moed*. Tel Aviv: Ha-Vaadah ha-Benkibbutzit, 1966.

Shecter, Tzvi, ed. *Moade Yisrael. Hoveret 2, Hagge Hodesh Tishri*. Jerusalem: Ministry of Education and Culture, Youth Department, 1966, pp. 81–105.

———. *Moade Yisrael: Pirke Kriah ve-Nigun*. Jerusalem: Ministry of Education and Culture, Youth Department, 1966, pp. 81–105.

Sidrat Moadim: Sukkot. Jerusalem: Ministry of Education and Department of Torah Culture, 1968.

Soltes, Mordecai. *The Jewish Holidays: A Guide to Their Origin, Significance and Observance*. Rev. ed. New York: National Jewish Welfare Board, 1968, pp. 7–9, 26–28.

Starkman, Moshe, and Horowitz, Israel M., eds. *Succot*. New York: Farband Labor Zionist Organization, 1969.

Stolper, Pinchas, ed. *Sukkot*. New York: National Conference of Synagogue Youth, 1960.

Straus, Hagit, with Hagi Ben-Yehoshua, eds. *Sukkot: Reshimah Bibliografit*. Jerusalem: Municipality of Jerusalem Department of Education and Culture, 1965.

Succot. New York: Union of Orthodox Jewish Congregations of America, n.d.

Sukkah. Translated by Israel W. Slotki. In *The Babylonian Talmud*, edited by Isidore Epstein. London: Soncino Press, 1938.

Thieberger, Friedrich, ed. *Jüdischer Fest: Jüdischer Brauch*. Berlin: Jüdischer Verlag, 1936, pp. 313–42.

Tishri: Textes pour Servir à la Préparation des Fêtes de Rosh Hashanah, Kippour et Soukkoth. Paris: Editions des E.I.F., 1945, pp. 147–88.

Tverski, Shimon, ed. *Moadim: Massekhet le-Yamim Noraim vele-Hag Sukkot*. Tzava Haganah le-Yisrael, no. 15 (1953), pp. 47–78.

The Universal Jewish Encyclopedia. 10 vols. New York: Ktav Publishing House, 1968. See Etrog, Hatan Bereshith, Hatan Torah, Holidays, Hoshana Rabbah, Lulab, Processions, Shemini Atzereth, Simhath Torah, Sukkah, Sukkoth.

Unterman, Isaac. *The Jewish Holidays*. 2d ed. New York: Bloch Publishing Co., 1950, pp. 81–99.

Vainstein, Yaacov. *The Cycle of the Jewish Year: A Study of the Festivals and of Selections from the Liturgy.* Jerusalem: Department for Torah Education and Culture in the Diaspora, World Zionist Organization, 1964, pp. 116–25.

Wahrmann, Nahum. *Hagge Yisrael u-Moadav: Minhagehem u-Semalehem.* Jerusalem: Ahiasaf, 1959, pp. 61–90.

———, ed. *Moadim: Pirke Halakhah, Aggadah ve-Tefillah le-Khol Moade ha-Shanah.* Jerusalem: Kiryat Sepher, 1957, pp. 48–70, 178–82, 207, 213–16, 234–35.

Werblowsky, R.J. Zevi, and Wigoder, Geoffrey, eds. *The Encyclopedia of the Jewish Religion.* New York: Holt, Rinehart and Winston, 1966.

Yaari, Abraham. *Toldot Hag Simhat-Torah: Hishtalshelut Minhagav be-Tefutzot Yisrael le-Dorotehen.* Jerusalem: Mosad Harav Kook, 1964.

Yedion le-Inyane Tarbut ve-Hasbarah (Tel Aviv), no. 9 (September 1965): 17–22; 2, no. 7 (September 1967): 19–25; 5, no. 1 (August 1969): 22–29; 6, no. 1 (September 1970): 18–32.

Zeitlin, Solomon. "The *Bet ha-Shoebah* and the Sacred Fire," *Jewish Quarterly Review,* n.s. 43, no. 3 (January 1953): 217–23.

Zobel, Moritz. *Das Jahr des Juden in Brauch und Liturgie.* Berlin: Schocken Verlag, 1936, pp. 94–131.

❧ ❧ ❧

THE FOUR SPECIES

The "Four Species" (wall chart). New York: Torah Umesorah, 1966.

Malachi, A.R. "Le-Toldot Mishar ha-Etrogim," *Perakim be-Toldot ha-Yishuv ha-Yashan.* Tel Aviv: Tel Aviv University and Hakibbutz Hameuhad, 1971, pp. 168–78.

Nahlon, Aharon. "The 'Four Varieties' in the Commune: Collective or Private Property?," *The Religious Kibbutz Movement.* Edited by Aryei Fishman. Jerusalem: Religious Section, Youth and Hehalutz Department, Zionist Organization, 1957, pp. 93–97.

Rubenstein, Shmuel Leib. *The Four Species of Succoth: A Guide to the Proper Observance of a Mitzvah.* Edited by Menachem Yehudah Nussbaum. Brooklyn, N.Y.: S. Rubenstein, 1963.

Seidman, Hillel. *Festival of Joy: Significance, Symbolism and Rules of the Four Species.* New York: Judaica Press, 1965.

Tolkowsky Samuel. *Hesperides: A History of the Culture and Use of Citrus Fruits.* London: John Bale, Sons & Carnow, 1938, especially pp. 51–65.

———. "The Meaning of *Peri Etz Hadar,*" *Journal of the Palestine Oriental Society* (Jerusalem): 8, no. 1 (1928): 17–23.

———. *Peri Etz Hadar: Toldotav be-Tarbut ha-Amim, be-Sifrut, be-Omanut uve-Folklor, me-Yeme Kedem ve-Ad Yamenu.* Jerusalem: Bialik Institute, 1966, pp. 49–68.

ᵞᵉ ᵞᵉ ᵞᵉ

SUKKOT AND SIMHAT TORAH IN JEWISH LAW

Berman, Jacob. *Halakhah la-Am: Haggim u-Zemanim, Tzomot, Teshuvah ve-Yamim Noraim.* Tel Aviv: Abraham Zioni Publishing House, 1962, pp. 219–57.

The Code of Maimonides. Book 9, *The Book of Offerings.* Translated by Herbert Danby. New Haven: Yale University Press, 1950, pp. 47–59.

The Code of Maimonides. Book 3, *The Book of Seasons.* Translated by Solomon Gandz and Hyman Klein. New Haven: Yale University Press, 1961, pp. 380–408.

Eisenstein, Judah D. *Otzar Dinim u-Minhagim.* New York: Hebrew Publishing Co., 1938, pp. 12, 32, 80, 94–96, 105, 146, 251, 285, 361, 423, 426.

Galis, Yaakov. *Minhage Eretz Yisrael.* Jerusalem: Mosad Harav Kook, 1968, pp. 188–203.

Ganzfried, Solomon. *Code of Jewish Law.* Vol. 3. Translated by Hyman E. Goldin. New York: Hebrew Publishing Co., 1927, pp. 1–23, 93–108.

Greenblatt, Efraim. "Simhat Torah," *Noam: Shanaton le-Birur Bayot be-Halakhah* (Jerusalem): 13 (1970): 222–58; 14 (1971): 205–32; 15 (1972): 101–27; additions in manuscript.

Karo, Joseph. *Shulhan Arukh, Orah Hayyim,* "Hilkhot Sukkot," "Hilkhot Lulav," 625–69.

Laws and Customs of Israel. Vol. 3. Translated by Gerald Friedlander. London: Shapiro, Vallentine and Co., 1934, pp. 333–48, 376–89.

Moses Ben Maimon. *Mishneh Torah.* Amsterdam, 1702, "Sefer Zemanim."

Sperling, Abraham Isaac. *Reasons for Jewish Customs and Traditions.* Translated by Abraham Matts. New York: Bloch Publishing Co., 1968, pp. 246–57.

———. *Sefer Taame ha-Minhagim u-Mekore ha-Dinim.* Jerusalem: Eshkol, 1961, pp. 343–63.

Zevin, Shlomoh Yosef. *Ha-Moadim be-Halakhah.* 2d ed. Tel Aviv: Betan Hasefer, 1949, pp. 90–141.

ᵞᵉ ᵞᵉ ᵞᵉ

SUKKOT AND SIMHAT TORAH LITURGY

Birnbaum, Philip, ed. and trans. *Prayer Book for the Three Festivals.* New York: Hebrew Publishing Co., 1971.

Casper, Bernard M. *Talks on Jewish Prayer.* Jerusalem: World Zionist Organization Department for Torah Education and Culture, 1963, pp. 75–81.

Davis, Arthur, and Adler, Herbert M. *Service of the Synagogue: A New Edition of the Festival Prayers with an English Translation in Prose and Verse: Tabernacles.* London: George Routledge & Sons, 1907–1908.

Freehof, Solomon B. *The Small Sanctuary: Judaism in the Prayerbook.* New York: Union of American Hebrew Congregations, 1942, pp. 144–61.

Idelsohn, A.Z. *Jewish Liturgy and Its Development.* New York: Henry Holt and Co., 1932, pp. 188–204, 332, 337–45.

Levi, Eliezer. *Yesodot ha-Tefillah.* Tel Aviv: Betan Hasefer, 1952, pp. 51–56, 213–16, 264–71.

Millgram, Abraham E. *Jewish Worship.* Philadelphia: Jewish Publication Society of America, 1971, pp. 199–224, 314–16, 467–68.

Munk, Elie. *The World of Prayer.* Vol. 2, *Commentary and Translation of the Sabbath and Festival Prayers.* Translated by Gertrude Hirschler. New York: Philipp Feldheim, 1963, pp. 270–300.

Pool, David de Sola, ed. and trans. *Prayers for the Festivals according to the Custom of the Spanish and Portuguese Jews.* New York: Union of Sephardic Congregations, 1947.

———. *The Traditional Prayer Book for Sabbath and Festivals.* New York: Behrman House, 1960.

Readings and Prayers for the Pilgrimage Festivals. Vol. 2, *Sukkot and Shemini Azeret.* New York: Reconstructionist Press, 1956.

Sabbath and Festival Prayer Book: With a New Translation, Supplementary Readings and Notes. New York: Rabbinical Assembly of America and United Synagogue of America, 1946.

Silverman, Morris, ed. *Simhat Torah Service.* Hartford: Prayer Book Press, 1941.

The Union Prayerbook for Jewish Worship. Rev. ed. Part 1. Cincinnati: Central Conference of American Rabbis, 1941.

※ ※ ※

HASIDIC TALES AND TEACHINGS

Goodman, Philip. *Rejoice in Thy Festival: A Treasury of Wisdom, Wit and Humor for the Sabbath and Jewish Holidays.* New York: Bloch Publishing Co., 1956, pp. 113–38.

Kariv, Avraham, ed. *Shabbat u-Moed be-Derush uve-Hasidut.* Tel Aviv: Oneg Shabbat and Dvir, 1966, pp. 271–329.

Lipson, M., *Mi-Dor Dor.* Vol. 3. Tel Aviv and New York: Dorot, 1938, pp. 170–80.

Newman, Louis I., and Spitz, Samuel, *The Hasidic Anthology: Tales and Teachings of the Hasidim.* New York: Bloch Publishing Co., 1944.

Unger, Menashe. *Chasidus un Yom-Tov.* New York: Farlag Chasidus, 1958, pp. 113–82.

Zevin, Shlomoh Yosef. *Sippure Hasidim . . . le-Moade ha-Shanah.* Tel Aviv: Abraham Zioni Publishing House, 1958, pp. 105–86.

ༀ ༀ ༀ

SUKKOT AND SIMHAT TORAH IN THE SHORT STORY

Antin, David. "The Remarkable Skullcap." *The Best of Ten Years in the Jewish Digest*. Houston: D.H. White & Co., 1965, pp. 333–38.

Buber, Martin. "The Day of Rejoicing." *For the Sake of Heaven*. Translated by Ludwig Lewisohn. Philadelphia: Jewish Publication Society of America, 1945, pp. 298–302.

Cohn, Emil Bernhard. "The Waters of Shiloah." *Stories and Fantasies from the Jewish Past*. Translated by Charles Reznikoff. Philadelphia: Jewish Publication Society of America, 1951, pp. 213–30.

Ibn-Sahav, Ari. "Lulavs and Etrogs." *A Gharry Driver in Jerusalem*. Translated by Sylvia Satten. Tel Aviv: Lion the Printer, 1947, pp. 49–65.

Landa, M.J. "Two Legacies." *Yisroel: The Jewish Omnibus*. Edited by Joseph Leftwich. London: James Clarke & Co., 1933, pp. 90–95.

Ogus, Aaron D. "The Essrig." Translated by Nathan Ausubel. *A Treasury of Jewish Humor*. Edited by Nathan Ausubel. Garden City, N.Y.: Doubleday & Co., 1951, pp. 426–30.

Peretz, Isaac Loeb. "Between Two Mountains." *Stories and Pictures*. Translated by Helena Frank. Philadelphia: Jewish Publication Society of America, 1906, pp. 429–46.

———. "Reb Noah and the Rabbi of Brest." *In This World and the Next: Selected Writings*. Translated by Moshe Spiegel. New York: Thomas Yoseloff, 1958, pp. 107–19.

Rabinowitz, S., see Sholom Aleichem.

Reisin, Abraham. "Late." *Yiddish Tales*. Translated by Helena Frank. Philadelphia: Jewish Publication Society of America, 1943, pp. 415–20.

Sholom Aleichem. "The Dead Citron," "The Tabernacle." *Jewish Children*. Translated by Hannah Berman. New York: Bloch Publishing Co., 1937, pp. 119–30, 106–18.

———. "The Etrog." *Some Laughter, Some Tears*. Translated by Curt Leviant. New York: Paperbook Library, 1969, pp. 23–32.

———. "The Flag." *Old Country Tales*. Translated by Curt Leviant. New York: G.P. Putnam's Sons, 1966, pp. 73–84.

———. "Hodel." *The Old Country*. Translated by Julius and Frances Butwin. New York: Crown Publishers, 1946, pp. 396–401; *Selected Stories of Sholom Aleichem*. Edited by Alfred Kazin. New York: Modern Library, 1956, pp. 383–400.

———. "The Merrymakers." *Tevye's Daughters*. Translated by Frances Butwin. New York: Crown Publishers, 1949, pp. 162–71.

———. "The Miracle of Hoshana Rabbah." Translated by Isidore Goldstick. *Sholom Aleichem Panorama*. Edited by Melech Grafstein, *Jewish Observer*, London, Ontario, 1948, pp. 158–61; *The Old Country*. Translated by Julius and Frances Butwin. New York: Crown Publishers, 1946, pp. 371–81; *Selected Stories of Sholom Aleichem*. Edited by Alfred Kazin. New York: Modern Library, 1956, pp. 372–82.

❧ ❧ ❧

CHILDREN'S STORIES AND DESCRIPTIONS OF SUKKOT AND SIMHAT TORAH

Abramson, Lillian S., "Sukkot in Colonial America," "Simhat Torah in Amsterdam." *Join Us for the Holidays*. Illustrated by Jessie B. Robinson. New York: National Women's League of the United Synagogue of America, 1958, pp. 11–12, 17–18.

Bearman, Jane. *Fun on Sukkos*. New York: Union of American Hebrew Congregations, 1946.

"The Beautiful Willow." *A Handbook for the Jewish Family: Understanding and Enjoying the Sabbath and Holidays*, by Alex J. Goldman. New York: Bloch Publishing Co., 1958, pp. 82–86.

Bronstein, Charlotte. *Tales of the Jewish Holidays as Told by the Light of the Moon*. Illustrated by Art Seiden. New York: Behrman House, 1959.

Cedarbaum, Sophia N. *Sukos and Simchas Torah*. Illustrated by Clare and John Ross. New York: Union of American Hebrew Congregations, 1961.

Cone, Molly. *Stories of Jewish Symbols*. New York: Bloch Publishing Co., 1963, pp. 54–57.

Covich, Edith S. *The Jewish Child Every Day*. Illustrated by Mary Ida Jones. New York: Union of American Hebrew Congregations, 1955, pp. 18–20.

Edelman, Lily. *The Sukkah and the Big Wind*. Illustrated by Leonard Kessler. New York: United Synagogue Commission on Jewish Education, 1956.

Edidin, Ben M. *Jewish Holidays and Festivals*. New York: Hebrew Publishing Co., 1940, pp. 69–85.

Epstein, Morris. *All about Jewish Holidays and Customs*. Rev. ed. Illustrated by Arnold Lobel. New York: Ktav Publishing House, 1970, pp. 28–33.

———. *A Pictorial Treasury of Jewish Holidays and Customs*. New York: Ktav Publishing House, 1959, pp. 36–47.

———. "The Sky for a Roof," "Parade of the Torahs." *Tell Me About God and Prayer*. Illustrated by Lawrence Dresser. New York: Ktav Publishing House, 1953, pp. 37–40, 43–46.

Farber, Walter C. *Jewish Holidays*. Detroit: Jewish Heritage Publishing House, 1967, pp. 27–33.

Fine, Helen. "Two Feasts for Sukos," "Cinnamon Grass for Simchas Torah." *G'dee*. Illustrated by Hal Just. New York: Union of American Hebrew Congregations, 1958, pp. 36–53.

Gamoran, Mamie G. "The 'Almost-Suko,'" "From Year to Year." *Hillel's Calendar*. Illustrated by Ida Libby Dengrove. New York: Union of American Hebrew Congregations, 1960, pp. 44–59.

———. *Days and Ways: The Story of Jewish Holidays and Customs*. Cincinnati: Union of American Hebrew Congregations, 1941, pp. 51–68.

————. "Hillel Gets a Letter," "The Sukko," "Leah's Consecration," "The Children Go Marching." *Hillel's Happy Holidays.* Illustrated by Temima N. Gezari. Cincinnati: Union of American Hebrew Congregations, 1939, pp. 58–86.

Garvey, Robert. *Holidays Are Nice: Around the Year with the Jewish Child.* Illustrated by Ezekiel Schloss and Arnold Lobel. New York: Ktav Publishing House, 1960, pp. 13–18.

————. "The House of Mystery," "The Noisiest Simchas Torah." *Happy Holiday!* Illustrated by Ezekiel Schloss. New York: Ktav Publishing House, 1953, pp. 16–28.

————. "Sukkot." *The First Book of Jewish Holidays.* Illustrated by Sam Weiss. New York: Ktav Publishing House, 1954.

Gersh, Harry, with Eugene B. Borowitz and Hyman Chanover. *When a Jew Celebrates.* Illustrated by Erika Weihs. New York: Behrman House, 1971, pp. 150–70.

Goldberg, David. *Holidays for American Judaism.* New York: Bookman Associates, 1954, pp. 122–31.

Golub, Rose W. "Sukos in Ancient Palestine," "Building a Suko." *Down Holiday Lane.* Illustrated by Louis Kabrin. Cincinnati: Union of American Hebrew Congregations, 1947, pp. 18–42.

Halpern, Salomon Alter. "The Price of an Etrog," "Safe Shelter." *Tales of Faith.* Jerusalem: Boys Town, 1968, pp. 154–62, 177–82.

Isaacs, Abram S. "Before Dawn." *Under the Sabbath Lamp: Stories of Our Time for Old and Young.* Philadelphia: Jewish Publication Society of America, 1919, pp. 53–70.

————. *School Days in Home Town.* Philadelphia: Jewish Publication Society of America, 1928, pp. 44–52.

Ish Kishor, Sulamith. "The Succoth Bough." *Heaven on the Sea and Other Stories.* New York: Bloch Publishing Co., 1924, pp. 179–91.

————. *Pathways through the Jewish Holidays.* Edited by Benjamin Efron. New York: Ktav Publishing House, 1967, pp. 25–36.

Jaffe, Leonard. "The Best Sukkah," "Round and Round." *The Pitzel Holiday Book.* Illustrated by Bill Giacalone. New York: Ktav Publishing House, 1962, pp. 67–80.

Kipnis, Levin. "A Roof for the Succah," "The House and the Succah." *My Holidays: Holiday Stories for Children.* Translated by Israel M. Goodelman. Illustrated by Isa. Tel Aviv: N. Tversky, 1961, pp. 23–35.

Kripke, Dorothy K. "Debbie's Moon Dream," " 'Round and 'Round and On and On." *Debbie in Dreamland: Her Holiday Adventures.* Illustrated by Bill Giacalone. New York: National Women's League of the United Synagogue, 1960, pp. 19–26.

————. *Let's Talk about the Jewish Holidays.* New York: Jonathan David, 1970, pp. 11–18.

Learsi, Rufus. "How Yokel Leaped to Fame and Fortune." *Kasriel the Watchman and Other Stories.* Philadelphia: Jewish Publication Society of America, 1936, pp. 158–73.

Levinger, Elma Ehrlich. "His Own Succah," "The Coward." *Jewish Holyday Stories: Modern Tales of the American Jewish Youth.* New York: Bloch Publishing Co., 1918, pp. 55–78.

———. "In the Tents of Israel." *Playmates in Egypt and Other Stories.* Philadelphia: Jewish Publication Society of America, 1920, pp. 22–32.

———. "Max—and Herschel—and a *Sukkah*," "The Torah in No Man's Land." *Tales Old and New.* New York: Bloch Publishing Co., 1926, pp. 40–45, 48–53.

———. "The Tent of Israel," "Simchath Torah," "The Flag of My People." *In Many Lands.* New York: Bloch Publishing Co., 1923, pp. 38–44, 49–54.

Margolis, Isidor, and Markowitz, Sidney L. *Jewish Holidays and Festivals.* Illustrated by John Teppich. New York: Citadel Press, 1962, pp. 43–52.

Max, Mosheh. *The Way of God.* New York: Feldheim Publishers, 1968, pp. 225–51.

Mindel, Nissan. "An Ethrog from the Garden of Eden," "The Reward," "*Hakkafoth* under Fire." *The Complete Story of Tishrei.* Brooklyn, N.Y.: Merkos L'Inyonei Chinuch, 1961, pp. 154–59, 159–60, 201–7.

Posy, Arnold. "The Miracle of the *Etrogim.*" *Israeli Tales and Legends.* New York: Jonathan David, 1966, pp. 193–208.

Rosenzweig, Marion Jordon, and Rosenzweig, Efraim Michael. *Now We Begin: A Manual of Stories and Instructions for Home and School.* Cincinnati: Union of American Hebrew Congregations, 1937, pp. 1–27.

Schwab, Hermann. "The Big and the Little Etrog," "Poor Lulab," "Simchat Torah." *Dreams of Childhood: Stories for Jewish Children.* Translated by Joseph Leftwich. London: Anscombe, 1949, pp. 9–17.

Sholom Aleichem. "The Simchas Torah Flag." *Yiddish Stories for Young People.* Edited by Itche Goldberg. Illustrated by Herb Kruckman. New York: Kinderbuch Publications, 1966, pp. 78–85.

Silverman, Althea O. "Yow Makes Sure to Be in the Sukkah for Kiddush." *Habibi and Yow: A Little Boy and His Dog.* Illustrated by Jessie B. Robinson. New York: Bloch Publishing Co. 1946, pp. 33–38.

Simon, Norma. *Our First Sukkah.* Illustrated by Ayala Gordon. New York: United Synagogue Commission on Jewish Education, 1959.

———. *Simhat Torah.* Illustrated by Ayala Gordon. New York: United Synagogue Commission on Jewish Education, 1960.

Simon, Shirley. "The Sukkah and the New Friends," "A Pretty Flag," in *Once Upon a Jewish Holiday*, by Bea Stadtler. Illustrated by Bill Giacalone. New York: Ktav Publishing House, 1965, pp. 22–32.

Smith, Harold P. *A Treasure Hunt in Judaism.* New York: Hebrew Publishing Co., 1950, pp. 67–79.

Sokolow, Helena. "Feast of Tabernacles." *Bible Rhapsodies.* Translated by E.W. Shanahan. Tel Aviv: Massada, 1956, pp. 37–42.

Spiro, Saul S., and Spiro, Rena M. *The Joy of Jewish Living.* Cleveland: Bureau of Jewish Education, 1965, pp. 75–91, 192–93.

Super, Arthur Saul, and Halpern, Joseph. "The *Esrog* and the Lamb." *Story-*

time: A Jewish Children's Story Book. London: Edward Goldston, 1946, pp. 152–59.

Taylor, Sydney. "Succos." *All-of-a-kind Family*. Illustrated by Helen John. Chicago: Wilcox and Follett, 1951, pp. 166–75.

Trager, Hannah. "The Feast of Tabernacles, or the Making of the Succah," "Simchas Torah." *Festival Stories of Child Life in a Jewish Colony in Palestine*. New York: E.P. Dutton & Co., 1920, pp. 125–38, 141–46.

Weilerstein, Sadie Rose. "How Danny Was a Carpenter for Real," "The Story of Danny's *Esrog*," "How Danny Marched on Simchas Torah." *What Danny Did: Stories for the Wee Jewish Child*. Illustrated by Jessie Berkowitz Robinson. New York: Bloch Publishing Co., 1944, pp. 34–50.

———. "How K'tonton Went to Synagogue and Swung on a Lulav," "How K'tonton Prayed for Rain," "How K'tonton Rejoiced and Was Merry on Simhat Torah," "How K'tonton Entertained Holy Guests in His Succah." *The Adventures of K'tonton: A Little Jewish Tom Thumb*. Illustrated by Jeannette Berkovitz. New York: National Women's League of the United Synagogue, 1935, pp. 24–26, 81–85, 86–89, 90–95.

———. "A Little Piece of Succoth," "The Story of a Sefer Torah." *Little New Angel*. Illustrated by Mathilda Keller. Philadelphia: Jewish Publication Society of America, 1947, pp. 39–46, 47–62.

———. "A Streetful of Friends," "Seven Times Round." *What the Moon Brought*. Illustrated by Mathilda Keller. Philadelphia: Jewish Publication Society of America, 1942, pp. 28–46.

Weitz, Joseph. "Great-Great-Grandfather's *Sukkah* Collapses," "Grandpa's Hut Collapses Too," "The *Ethrog*, the Citron, from Corfu." *The Abandoned Swing*. Translated by Shoshana Perla. Illustrated by Zvi Geyra. Ramat Gan: Massada Press, 1969, pp. 19–49.

Zeligs, Dorothy F. *The Story of Jewish Holidays and Customs for Young People*. Illustrated by Emery I. Gondor. New York: Bloch Publishing Co., 1942, pp. 45–66.

❧ ❧ ❧

COLLECTIONS WITH SUKKOT AND SIMHAT TORAH MUSIC

Bar-Zimra, S., ed. *Dor Dor ve-Niguno: le-Yamim ha-Noraim vele-Hag ha-Sukkot*. [Jerusalem]: Ministry of Education and Culture, 1967, pp. 11–15.

Binder, A.W. *The Jewish Year in Song*. New York: G. Schirmer, 1928, pp. 9–11.

Bugatch, Samuel, ed. *Doros Zingen*. New York: Farband Book Publishing Association, 1951, pp. 198–203.

Coopersmith, Harry, ed. *More of the Songs We Sing*. New York: United Synagogue Commission on Jewish Education, 1971, pp. 32–38.

———. *The New Jewish Song Book*. New York: Behrman House, 1965, pp. 12–20.

————. *The Songs We Sing.* New York: United Synagogue Commission on Jewish Education, 1950, pp. 95–107.

Eisenstein, Judith Kaplan. *Festival Songs.* New York: Bloch Publishing Co., 1943, pp. 6–15.

————. *The Gateway to Jewish Song.* New York: Behrman House, 1939, pp. 71–78.

————, and Prensky, Frieda, eds. *Songs of Childhood.* New York: United Synagogue Commission on Jewish Education, 1955, pp. 201–27.

Ephros, Gershon, ed. *Cantorial Anthology.* Vol. 3, *Sholosh R'golim.* New York: Bloch Publishing Co., 1948.

Goldfarb, Israel, and Goldfarb, Samuel E., eds. *The Jewish Songster: Music for Voice and Piano.* Part 1. Brooklyn, N.Y., 1925, pp. 134–49.

Idelsohn, Abraham Zevi. *The Jewish Song Book for Synagogue, School and Home.* Music edited by Baruch Joseph Cohon. Cincinnati: Publications for Judaism, 1951, pp. 131–64, 168–85, 419–28.

Levy, Sara C., and Deutsch, Beatrice L. *So We Sing: Holiday and Bible Songs for Young Jewish Children.* New York: Bloch Publishing Co., 1950, pp. 18–23.

Nisimov, N., ed. *Le-Rosh Hashanah vele-Sukkot: Pirke Zimrah.* Tel Aviv: Hamercaz Letarbut, 1949, pp. 11–18.

Pasternak, Velvel, ed. *Songs of the Chassidim II.* New York: Bloch Publishing Co., 1971, pp. 89–114.

Rubin, Ruth, ed. *A Treasury of Jewish Folksong.* New York: Schocken Books, 1950, pp. 146–51.

Shiray Yeladim: Songs for Children. Music by Samuel H. Adler. Words by Margie Lipman, Raymond Israel, and Ilo Orleans. New York: Union of American Hebrew Congregations, 1970, pp. 19–21.

Sukkot and Simchat Torah Songster. New York: Board of Jewish Education, 1941. Words only.

Union Hymnal: Songs and Prayers for Jewish Worship. 3d ed. New York: Central Conference of American Rabbis. Part 1 (1940), pp. 197–214, 224–29, 499–509. Part 2 (1936), pp. 353, 358–59.

Union Songster: Songs and Prayers for Jewish Youth. New York: Central Conference of American Rabbis, 1960, pp. 163–75, 193–202.

❦ ❦ ❦

PROGRAM AND AUDIOVISUAL MATERIALS

Films

Count Your Blessings. New York: Jewish Chautauqua Society. 16 mm, black and white, sound, 13½ minutes. The meaning of the Sukkot festival in a modern home against the background of Thanksgiving.

In the Beginning. By Joseph Mindel. New York: National Academy for Adult Jewish Studies, United Synagogue of America. 16 mm, black and white, sound, 28 minutes. A teacher trapped in the Warsaw ghetto celebrates Simhat Torah.

Succot. New York: United Israel Appeal. 16 mm, color, sound, 14 minutes. Scenes of *sukkah*-building in Israel, the *etrog* and *lulav* market in Tel Aviv, and harvesting.

Succoth. Produced by Yehoshua Brandstatter. New York: Israel Information Services. 16 mm, color, sound, 14½ minutes. The celebration of the festival in Israel.

Filmstrips

Gil Is Building a Succah. Edited by Moshe Singer. Tel Aviv: Or & Kol Israel Corporation for Educational Materials, 40 Ibn-Gabirol St. 35 frames, color, Hebrew captions.

The Sacred Festival of Sukkoth: The Four Species of the Lulav. Edited by Yaakov Reshef and Nogah Hareuveni. Produced by Neot Kedumim. New York: America-Israel Cultural Foundation. 45 frames, color, narration. The symbolism of the Four Species and their association with Sukkot.

A Story of an Etrog That Was Proud. Based on a story by Levin Kipnis. Tel Aviv: Or & Kol Israel Corporation for Educational Materials, 40 Ibn-Gabirol St. 33 frames, color, Hebrew captions.

The Story of Succot and Simchas Torah. By Samuel J. Citron. New York: Board of Jewish Education. 60 frames, black and white, narration. A family celebration of the festival at home and in the synagogue.

The Succah That Wept. By Yeshoshua Padon. Tel Aviv: Or & Kol Israel Corporation for Educational Materials, 40 Ibn-Gabirol St. 35 frames, color, Hebrew captions.

Sukkos and Simchas Torah—Festival of Harvest and Joy. By Mel Alpern. Produced by Samuel Grand. New York: Union of American Hebrew Congregations. 42 frames, color, narration and teacher's guide. Festival preparations and observance in a Reform Jewish school.

Sukot and Simhat Torah. New York: Jewish Agency Department of Education and Culture. 53 frames, color, narration and teacher's guide. Observance of the festivals in the Diaspora and in Israel.

Tape

The Timeless Tabernacle. Narrated by Modzitzer Chorale Ensemble, Geula Gill, Free Synagogue Choir and Av Bondarin. New York: Commission on Interfaith Activities for the Union of American Hebrew Congregations. No. 61. 7-inch reel, 30 minutes. The music of the festival and a reading of Sholom Aleichem's "The Dead Citron."

Recordings

Baal Shem Suite (includes "Simhat Torah"). By Ernest Bloch. Columbia ML 2122.

High Holidays and Autumn Festivals Album. Performed by Maurice Goldman and choir. Bureau of Jewish Education of the Los Angeles Jewish Community Council.

Sholosh R'golim; Modzitzer Melodies. Neginah Records, NRI202.

Sholosh Regolim Service. Sung by Abraham Davis. M NO-10.

Songs for Sukkot and Simhat Torah. Directed by Harry Coppersmith. New York: Board of Jewish Education. 1002.

Succot and Simhat Torah. Narrated by Eve Lippman. Sung by Gladys Gewirtz. House of Menorah, H-6.

Dances

Lapson, Dvora. *Folk Dances for Jewish Festivals.* New York: Jewish Education Press, 1961, pp. 126–39.

———. *Jewish Dances the Year Round.* New York: Jewish Education Press, 1957, pp. 90–95.

Arts and Crafts

Comins, Harry L., and Leaf, Reuben. *Arts-Crafts for the Jewish Club.* Cincinnati: Union of American Hebrew Congregations, 1934, pp. 51–55, 180–83, 246.

Gezari, Temima N. *Jewish Festival Crafts.* New York: National Jewish Welfare Board, 1968, pp. 10–13.

How to Build a Sukkah. New York: National Conference of Synagogue Youth, 1967. 15 pp.

Kra, Tzvi, ed. *Yifat: Hatzaot le-Bitu Omanuti Shel Nosim Yehudiim.* Vol. 5, *Sukkot.* Jerusalem: Ministry of Education and Culture Department of Torah Culture, 1963, pp. 1–40.

Ness, Jack. *Arts and Crafts for Jewish Youth.* New York: Yeshiva University Community Service Division, n.d., pp. 11–17.

Robinson, Jessie B. *Holidays are Fun.* New York: Bloch Publishing Co., 1950, pp. 15–25.

Sharon, Ruth. *Arts and Crafts the Year Round.* Vol. 1. New York: United Synagogue Commission on Jewish Education, 1965, pp. 85–125.

Activity and Related Materials

Abramson, Lillian S., and Leiderman, Lillian T. *Jewish Holiday Party Book: A Practical Guide to Parties Planned for Children Ages 5 to 12.* New York: Bloch Publishing Co., 1966, pp. 15–28.

Aunt Fanny. *Junior Jewish Cook Book.* Illustrated by Cyla London. New York: Ktav Publishing House, 1956, pp. 28–33.

Brody, Roxane, ed. *Planning for Sukkot: United Synagogue Program Notebook.* New York: United Synagogue of America, 1957, pp. 1–12.

Campeas, Hyman. *Workbook: All About Jewish Holidays and Customs.* New York: Ktav Publishing House, 1959, pp. 23–28.

Eisenberg, Azriel, and Robinson, Jessie B. *My Jewish Holidays.* New York:

United Synagogue Commission on Jewish Education, 1958, pp. 38–61.

Engle, Fannie. *The Jewish Holidays and Their Favorite Foods: With Easy Recipes for Mother and Daughter*. Illustrated by Dorothy M. Weiss. New York: Behrman House, 1958.

Fine, Helen. *G'dee's Book of Holiday Fun*. Illustrated by Hal Just. New York: Union of American Hebrew Congregations, 1961, pp. 9–14.

Fischman, Joyce. *Holiday Work and Play*. New York: Union of American Hebrew Congregations, 1961, pp. 9–19.

Goodman, Hannah Grad. *Pupils' Activity Book for Days and Ways*. New York: Union of American Hebrew Congregations, 1964, pp. 31–35.

Levinger, Elma Ehrlich. *Jewish Festivals in the Religious School: A Handbook for Entertainments*. Cincinnati: Union of American Hebrew Congregations, 1923, pp. 19–50.

Lister, Rebecca. *Workbook: Pathways through the Jewish Holidays*. New York: Ktav Publishing House, 1967, pp. 18–32.

Pessin, Deborah, and Gezari, Temima. *The Jewish Kindergarten: A Manual for Teachers*. Cincinnati: Union of American Hebrew Congregations, 1944, pp. 77–96.

Purdy, Susan Gold. *Jewish Holidays: Facts, Activities, and Crafts*. Philadelphia: J.B. Lippincott Co., 1969, pp. 25–30.

Stadtler, Bea, and Simon, Shirley. *Workbook: Once Upon a Jewish Holiday*. Jingles by Gay Campbell. New York: Ktav Publishing House, 1966, pp. 23–30.

Sukos Unit for the Flannelboard. By Judith Oren. New York: Union of American Hebrew Congregations.

Sussman, Samuel, and Segal, Abraham. *50 Assembly Programs for the Jewish School*. New York: United Synagogue Commission on Jewish Education, 1948, pp. 159–61.